Imperial Culture in Germany, 1871–1918

EUROPEAN STUDIES SERIES

General Editors: Colin Jones and Richard Overy, Joe Bergin, John Breuilly and Patricia Clavin

Published

Robert Aldrich	Greater France: A Short History of French Overseas Expansion
Nigel Aston	Religion and Revolution in France, 1780–1804
Yves-Marie Bercé	The Birth of Absolutism: A History of France, 1598–1661
Janine Garrisson	A History of Sixteenth-Century France, 1483–1589
Gregory Hanlon	Early Modern Italy, 1550–1800
Michael Hughes	Early Modern Germany, 1477–1806
Matthew Jefferies	Imperial Culture in Germany, 1871–1918
Dieter Langewiesche	Liberalism in Germany
Martyn Lyons	Napoleon Bonaparte and the Legacy of the French Revolution
Hugh McLeod	The Secularisation of Western Europe, 1848–1914
Robin Okey	The Habsburg Monarchy, c. 1765–1918
Pamela M. Pilbeam	Republicanism in Nineteenth-Century France, 1814–1871
Helen Rawlings	Church, Religion and Society in Early Modern Spain
Tom Scott	Society and Economy in Germany, 1300–1600
Wolfram Siemann	The German Revolution of 1848–49
Richard Vinen	France, 1934–70

Imperial Culture in Germany, 1871–1918

MATTHEW JEFFERIES

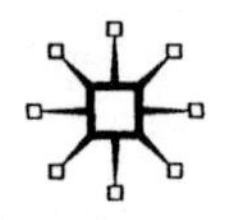

First published 2003 by
PALGRAVE MACMILLAN
Houndmills, Basingstoke, Hampshire RG21 6XS and
175 Fifth Avenue, New York, N.Y. 10010
Companies and representatives throughout the world

PALGRAVE MACMILLAN is the global academic imprint of the Palgrave Macmillan division of St. Martin's Press, LLC and of Palgrave Macmillan Ltd. Macmillan® is a registered trademark in the United States, United Kingdom and other countries. Palgrave is a registered trademark in the European Union and other countries.

ISBN 1–4039–0420–0 hardback
ISBN 1–4039–0421–9 paperback

This book is printed on paper suitable for recycling and made from fully managed and sustained forest sources.

A catalogue record for this book is available from the British Library.

Library of Congress Cataloging-in-Publication Data
Jefferies, Matthew.
Imperial culture in Germany, 1871–1918 / Matthew Jefferies.
p. cm. – (European studies series)
Includes bibliographical references and index.
ISBN 1–4039–0420–0 (alk. paper)
ISBN 1–4039–0421–9 (pbk. : alk. paper)
1. Germany—Intellectual life—19th century. 2. Art and state—Germany—History—19th century. 3. Art and society—Germany—History—19th century. 4. Germany—Social life and customs—19th century. I. Title. II. European studies series (Palgrave Macmillan (Firm))

DD67.J44 2003
943.08'3—dc21 2003040478

10 9 8 7 6 5 4 3 2 1
12 11 10 09 08 07 06 05 04 03

Printed in China

Contents

List of Illustrations

Acknowledgements

I would like to thank the following institutions for their support in making this book a reality: the Alexander von Humboldt-Stiftung (Bonn), for granting me a year's fellowship at the University of Hamburg; the Stiftung F.V.S. (Hamburg), for its ongoing generosity; the British Academy, for a Small Research Grant; and the University of Manchester's Small Grants Fund, for its helpful contribution towards the cost of illustrations.

I am also indebted to the following individuals at universities in Germany and Britain: Hermann Hipp (Hamburg), John Röhl (Sussex), Hartmut Pogge von Strandmann (Oxford), Robin Lenman (Warwick), John Breuilly (Birmingham), Mary Fulbrook (London) and Alastair Thompson (Durham). My colleagues in the German and History Departments at the University of Manchester deserve special mention for their continued support and encouragement: Martin Durrell, Steve Parker, Matthew Philpotts, Hannah Barker and Maiken Umbach all made valuable comments on earlier drafts; while Liz Nolan, Wendy Howat and Maxine Powell contributed expert secretarial assistance. In Germany I owe a particular debt of gratitude to Hans Dieter Giersch and his family for twenty years of hospitality; also to Anja Seddig, Frauke Dünnhaupt, Margarete Jarchow, Conny Mucha, Paul and Caroline Probert, and to Jörg Damm of the Internationale FKK-Bibliothek, Baunatal. I must also thank Michelle Kane, Gordon Midwood, Dan Stead and Kathryn Townend for making my year in Hamburg so hugely enjoyable: the next round is on me!

Above all, this book would not have been possible without my students at the University of Manchester. Since 1991 it has been my pleasure to teach some of the brightest, most inquisitive and enthusiastic students one is ever likely to come across. This book is dedicated to them.

The author and publisher wish to thank the following for permission to use copyright material:

AKG London, for use of the following images: *The Proclamation of the German Empire*, 'Palace' Version (1877) by Anton von Werner. Reproduced courtesy of AKG London, and Archiv für Kunst and Geschichte, Berlin; *The Proclamation of the German Empire*, 'Friedrichsruh' Version (1885) by Anton von Werner. Reproduced courtesy of AKG London and Bismarck-Museum.

Bildarchiv Preussischer Kulturbesitz, for use of the following images: *Isle of the Dead* (1883) by Arnold Böcklin. Reproduced courtesy of Staatliche Museen zu Berlin – Preussischer Kulturbesitz Nationalgalerie; © Bildarchiv Preussischer Kulturbesitz, Berlin, 2003. Photograph by Jörg P. Anders, Berlin; *The Iron Rolling Mill* (*Modern Cyclops*) (1872–3) by Adolph von Menzel. Reproduced courtesy of Staatliche Museen zu Berlin – Preussischer Kulturbesitz Nationalgalerie; © Bildarchiv Preussischer Kulturbesitz, Berlin, 2003. Photograph by Klaus Göken, 1992; *Goosepluckers* (1871/72) by Max Liebermann. Reproduced courtesy of Staatliche Museen zu Berlin – Preussischer Kulturbesitz Nationalgalerie; © Bildarchiv Preussischer Kulturbesitz, Berlin, 2003; *Apocalyptic Landscape* (1912–13) by Ludwig Meidner. Reproduced courtesy of Staatliche Museen zu Berlin – Preussischer Kulturbesitz Nationalgalerie and the Ludwig Meidner-Archive at the Jewish Museum, Frankfurt.

Deutsches Historisches Museum photo archive for use of the images *High Watch* (better known as *Prayer to Light*, 1894) by Fidus, and *Winter in Wartime* (1917) by Hans Baluschek. Photograph: Arne Psille; © Deutsches Historisches Museum, Berlin.

Fagus-Grecon Greten GmbH & Co. KG, for the photograph of the Fagus factory, Alfeld an der Leine (1911–14). Architect: Walter Gropius. Reproduced courtesy of Fagus-Grecon Greten GmbH & Co. KG.

Ludwig Meidner-Archive at the Jewish Museum, Frankfurt, for use of the image *Apocalyptic Landscape* (1912–13) by Ludwig Meidner; © for the works of Ludwig Meidner by the Ludwig Meidner-Archive at the Jewish Museum, Frankfurt. Reproduced courtesy of the Ludwig Meidner-Archive and Staattiche Museen zu Berlin – Preussischer Kulturbesitz Nationalgalerie.

Städtische Galerie im Lenbachhaus, Munich, for use of Wassily Kandinsky's final study for the cover of *The Blaue Reiter Almanac* (1911). Reproduced by permission of Städtische Galerie im Lenbachhaus; © ADAGP, Paris and DACS, London 2003. Photograph © Städtische Galerie im Lenbachhaus, Munich.

Tate Enterprises, for use of the painting *Bathers at Moritzburg* (1909, reworked 1926) by Ernst-Ludwig Kirchner; © Tate, London 2003, and Dr Wolfgang and Ingeborg Henze-Ketterer, Wichtrach/Bern, Switzerland. Reproduced courtesy of Tate Enterprises and Galerie Henze & Ketterer.

V+K Publishing, Blaricum, Netherlands, for the prizewinning design for the Reichstag Building, Berlin, by Paul Wallot (1882). Reproduced courtesy of V+K Publishing.

The following photographs were taken by, and supplied courtesy of, the author: Hermann monument, Detmold (1838–75), Architect: Ernst von Bandel; Kaiser Wilhelm I monument, Koblenz (1895–7), Architect: Bruno Schmitz; Deutsche Werkstätten Furniture Factory, Hellerau (1909), Architect: Richard Riemerschmid; Völkerschlacht monument, Leipzig (1900–13), Architect: Bruno Schmitz.

Every effort has been made to trace the copyright holders but if any have been inadvertently overlooked the publisher will be pleased to make the necessary arrangement at the first opportunity.

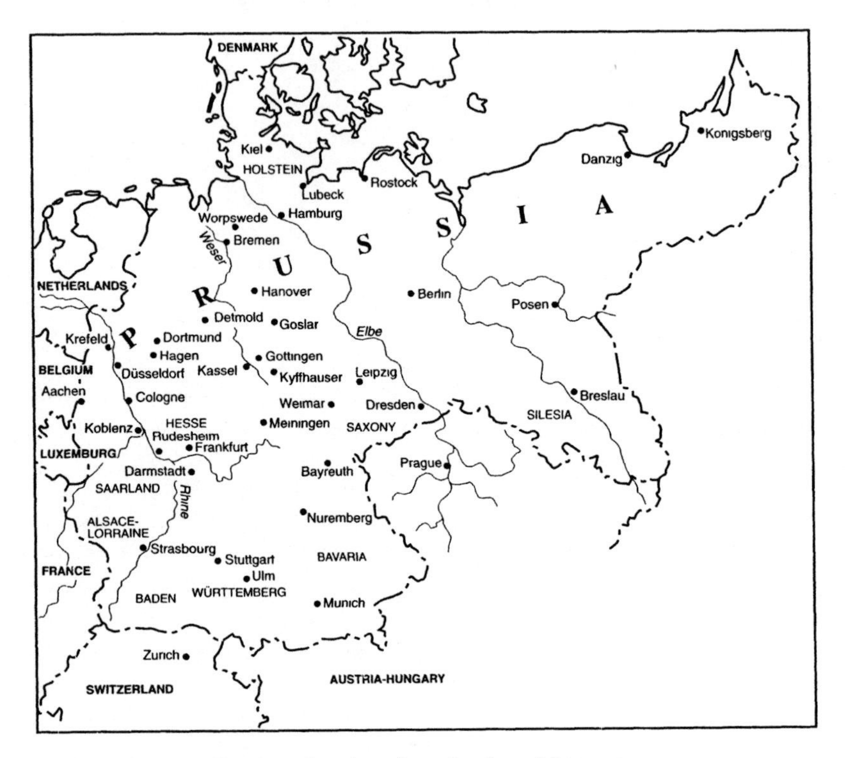

Map of German Empire, showing sites of cultural interest

(adapted from J. Heskett, *Design in Germany, 1870–1918* (London: Trefoil Books, 1986) p. 6)

Introduction

This book has grown out of a popular undergraduate course at the University of Manchester, 'Culture and Society in Germany, 1871–1918'. The premise of the course, and of the book, is that Germany's 'Imperial Culture' was every bit as fascinating, revealing and at times troubling, as the far more celebrated 'Weimar Culture' that evolved from it after 1918. The higher profile enjoyed by 'Weimar Culture' owes much to a cluster of contextual studies written in the 1970s by Peter Gay, Walter Laqueur and John Willett,[1] but synthetic works in this vein are conspicuously absent from the historiography of the imperial era. The very phrase 'Imperial Culture' looks unusual with capital letters, and has little of the comforting familiarity of its Weimar equivalent (or, indeed, the discomforting familiarity of 'Nazi Culture'). Even the basic narrative of cultural developments between 1871 and 1918 can be difficult to reconstruct without reference to several shelves of secondary literature. Of course, some names from the period – Nietzsche, Wagner, Mann – are anything but underexposed, yet their prominence as individuals has tended to obscure our view of the wider culture in which they worked.

The first aim of this book is therefore to offer an accessible introduction to German high culture between 1871 and 1918, in the context of imperial society and politics. By balancing description, discussion and interpretation, it seeks to provide a map of the cultural landscape, to be used as a guide through the dense undergrowth of the specialist literature from a number of disciplines, including German Studies, art history and architectural history. The cultural products and producers examined in this book, however, have not been selected simply on the basis of their aesthetic quality or artistic significance, but also for what they tell us about the German Empire. The context, in other words, is just as important as the 'texts' themselves. Some of the latter do have considerable intrinsic value, and merit a wider audience too, but that is not our motivation here. Rather, the book's second objective is to complement the wide range of new perspectives cast on the social and political history of the Second Empire since the Fischer Controversy and the historiographical upheavals of the 1960s.[2] Whilst research into the imperial era has undoubtedly flourished since the first publication of Hans-Ulrich Wehler's *Das deutsche Kaiserreich 1871–1918* in 1973,[3] neither the Wehler-led 'new orthodoxy' of the Bielefeld school, nor the cohort of British historians whose subsequent critiques of Wehler's model were to prove so influential,[4] have shown much interest in high culture.[5] With some honourable exceptions – Thomas Nipperdey, Wolfgang J. Mommsen, Gordon Craig – the major players in Wilhelmine historiography have largely left the field of high culture free for less prominent researchers. Perhaps it should come as no surprise then that today's students of the imperial era are likely to know more about the content of Hamburg pub conversations, or Kaiser Wilhelm II's sexuality, than the first German to win the Nobel Prize for Literature (it was Paul Heyse in 1910).

So, now that we have entered what Geoff Eley has referred to as 'an important moment of historiographical transition',[6] why should students of German history devote precious time to what might seem like an esoteric or peripheral field? There are many reasons, but four will suffice at this juncture. Firstly, high culture was far from peripheral in the minds of nineteenth-century Germans: it was an essential component of middle-class identity, part of 'a set of skills and values designed to produce the best possible human being', as Charles McClelland puts it.[7] This legacy of late eighteenth- and early nineteenth-century neo-humanist idealism, and more particularly of the education reforms inspired by it, may have been waning by the 1870s, but its influence was still strongly felt, with many educated Germans unshakeable in the conviction that their duty as cultivated men was to guard the cultural heritage of Goethe and Schiller, Fichte and Kant. Moreover, as Dieter Langewiesche points out, the German bourgeoisie 'had always justified its claim to social pre-eminence . . . with its cultural status.'[8]

In an age of growing secularization, culture was regarded with quasi-religious respect, and the shared etymological root of the words *Kultur* (culture) and *Kultus* (the cultic or religious), was reflected in the design of its temples: the theatres, art galleries and museums which became such a feature of the nineteenth-century townscape.[9] At the same time, the demand for culture was growing from those who felt unable to pass through such hallowed portals. Industrial workers may have been hampered by their social and economic status – and by the restricted access to supposedly 'public' institutions[10] – but they were sufficiently convinced of culture's importance to dedicate a full session at the Social Democratic Party conference to the value of Naturalist drama.[11]

Secondly, it is well known that artists, writers and thinkers had been prominent in developing the very idea of 'Germany' in the late eighteenth and early nineteenth centuries. It was principally through culture that the national movement had articulated conceptions of Germany in the decades before unification, and it was central to the fledgling Empire's state-building efforts after 1871. Yet the development of this culture, so important in establishing the legitimacy of the new political order and in the process of 'making Germans',[12] still barely merits a mention in some of the most respected accounts of the imperial era. Chapter 2 of this book is designed to fill at least part of that gap.

In comparison, the cultural critics, radicals and reformers of the late nineteenth and early twentieth centuries regularly feature in German history courses, but they are usually approached through the works of historians searching for the cultural and intellectual roots of National Socialism. While this is a perfectly valid and worthwhile undertaking, it can lead to a partial and even distorted view of the imperial period itself.[13] The only 'continuities' considered worthy of pursuit are those of a regressive, anti-modernist or 'crypto-fascist' kind,[14] while other aspects of Imperial Culture are either conveniently ignored, or are deemed to belong to an autonomous aesthetic realm, somehow unconnected to social and political reality. This long-standing practice has had the effect of obscuring the extent of support for cultural renewal and innovation that existed within the Empire, and not just on the fringes of society. The third reason for reading this book is therefore to acquire a more rounded and balanced view of an era that threw up more than one interesting line of continuity to later periods of German history.

Finally, most historians today would agree that, despite the absence of major constitutional change, the German Empire was fundamentally transformed in the five decades between 1871 and

1918. This was not, I would argue, simply the result of industrialization, urbanization and the forward march of the 'masses'. Cultural change had a direct impact on German society too. It may be harder to quantify, but such were the social and political energies expended in the realm of aesthetic culture during the imperial era that no analysis of the *Kaiserreich* can be truly complete without it. Primarily, these energies were expended by, and for, members of the middle classes (*Bürgertum*): that much-maligned section of German society whose failings have been castigated by generations of historians, and which features so prominently in arguments about the *Sonderweg* (the notion that Germany deviated from the western world's recommended route to modernity, and pursued its own fateful 'special path' that ultimately led to the gates of Auschwitz).[15] While there are signs that the *Sonderweg* debate may now have run its course, much scholarly interest still focuses on the *Bürgertum* and on what some see as a comparative lack of bourgeois virtue in German society, the so-called *Defizit an Bürgerlichkeit.*[16]

Of course, culture is one area in which all historians have been willing to concede bourgeois hegemony in the Empire, but this has often only been granted on the grounds that German artists and writers shunned social and political engagement, preferring instead to retreat into a cosseted state of 'inwardness' (*Innerlichkeit*). This is a view which owes much to the great novelist Thomas Mann who, in a number of essays and lectures during and immediately after World War One, argued that inwardness was the finest characteristic of the typical German, and that the literary form which best embodied this trait – the introspective novel of personal cultivation and development, the *Bildungsroman* – was the distinctively German alternative to the social novel of France and Britain.[17] This was not entirely without foundation, for the 'unpolitical German' certainly existed,[18] but Mann's thesis was a pointed generalization, and an anachronistic one at that. Whatever its merits with regard to the German novel, it should not be applied uncritically to the products of Imperial Culture as a whole. Strangely, however, it continues to set the tone in many of the best-known treatments of the subject. We read in Gordon Craig's *Germany 1866–1945*, for instance, that 'before 1914 it was only on rare occasions that German artists were interested, let alone stirred, by political and social events and issues';[19] and from Wolfgang J. Mommsen that 'those social groups that underpinned developments in literature, scholarship and the arts . . . stood at a clear remove from the ruling political elites'.[20]

This book takes a rather different view. Whether one focuses on the painters, poets and architects who helped to create an official imperial identity after 1871 (Chapter 2), the cultural critics and reformers of the later nineteenth century (Chapter 4), or the new generation of cultural producers which emerged in the years around 1900 (Chapters 5–6), the cultural, social and political were never far apart. While the idealist notion of an autonomous aesthetic realm may have remained influential – and it was, of course, a perfectly legitimate place for a poet or painter to dwell – nothing could stop social and political concerns from impinging on cultural production, and with increasing regularity. This is a dimension of imperial German culture that is all too often overlooked, yet it should not require a great leap of faith to accept that significant political energies were invested in painting, writing, designing or composing. After all, it has long been recognized that a significant part of the Empire's political life took place beyond the conventional structures of parties and parliaments: in economic or nationalist pressure groups; in the youth and women's movements; and in the social and cultural reform leagues of the 1900s.[21]

This book, however, should be regarded as a work of synthesis rather than as an attempt to advance a bold new thesis. Unlike Peter Gay's aforementioned classic study of Weimar Culture, it posits no grand interpretative framework, but seeks to bring together the findings of many specialist studies on specific aspects of German art and literature; architecture and design; music and drama; cultural criticism and reform, that have appeared in recent years. These works, together with a growing number of essay collections,[22] can seem daunting to the general reader, especially to those without a knowledge of the German language. The few attempts at synthesis currently available in English, such as the chapters on culture in textbooks by Gordon Craig, Volker Berghahn or Rob Burns,[23] are too short to offer more than a rapid survey. Moreover, like the translated essays of Wolfgang J. Mommsen,[24] they remain disappointingly reliant on well-worn stereotypes, such as the aforementioned retreat into inwardness, the 'cultural pessimism' of the educated middle class, or the 'feudalized' bourgeoisie's penchant for aping the aristocracy. As Karin Friedrich notes, even the *Sonderweg* continues to cast its shadow over much of this work: 'Although this paradigm has been persuasively challenged in many areas of German social, economic and political history during the last decade, it still pervades many works on German cultural and intellectual history.'[25]

Before we go any further the book's structure requires some explanation. The initial chapter seeks to establish the historical context, highlighting some of the most important divisions in imperial society and sketching the major socio-cultural milieus. Inevitably, this is done with a broad brush, but it aims to give readers unfamiliar with Imperial Germany sufficient grounding to appreciate the more detailed material that follows. The second chapter consists of a series of case studies drawn from the Empire's official culture as it developed between 1871 and around 1900. Further aspects of official culture, particularly where it came into contact with the artistic avant-garde, are dealt with in the subsequent chapters, which are organized around broad themes and proceed chronologically. This chronological framework is partly to capture the sense of movement and change that characterized the period, but also to provide a coherent narrative thrust: thus Chapter 3 focuses on the 1870s; Chapter 4 on the 1880s and 1890s; and Chapters 5 and 6 on the years after 1900.

Of course, by attempting to mould a complex mass of frequently contradictory developments into a single narrative, one risks distorting what Jay Winter has referred to as the period's 'messiness, its non-linearity, its vigorous and stubbornly visible incompatibilities'.[26] Nevertheless, a broadly chronological structure allows for connections to be made more easily than in a volume divided into separate chapters on each area of cultural activity, such as Eva Kolinsky and Wilfried van der Will's recent *Cambridge Companion to Modern German Culture*.[27] For all the undoubted expertise of that volume's contributors, its division into separate chapters on painting, poetry, drama, architecture, philosophy and so on, can only hamper the search for connections and intersections. Making such connections is surely vital, for without them one may as well leave paintings to the art historian, novels to the literary historian, and buildings to historians of architecture.[28]

Some consideration must also be given here to the 'c'-word, and the way it is used in this book. 'Culture' has been described as 'one of the two or three most complicated words in the English language',[29] with more than 200 rival definitions, and several quite different meanings in everyday use.[30] One of these is more or less synonymous with the arts, and is often divided into sub-categories such as 'high' and 'popular' culture, which are problematic in themselves. Another usage indicates a whole way of life, including values, practices and 'representations', for a particular group of people. In recent years the definition of culture by the anthropologist Clifford Geertz has proved particularly influential: 'an historically transmitted pattern of meanings embodied in symbols, a system of inherited conceptions expressed in symbolic forms by means of which men communicate, perpetuate, and develop their knowledge about and attitudes towards life.'[31] It is this wider anthropological view of culture that has underpinned the development of interdisciplinary Cultural Studies on college campuses around the world: '[c]ulture is not artifice and manners, the preserve of Sunday best, rainy afternoons and concert halls. It is the very material of our daily lives, the bricks and mortar of our most commonplace understandings, feelings and responses', as Paul Willis memorably put it.[32]

However, if Cultural Studies highlights the 'ordinariness' of culture, the German word *Kultur* tends to privilege its 'special' qualities. *Kultur*, which shares the same semantic roots as its English equivalent and came into general use around 1780, was until recently used predominantly to signify an activity of an intellectual, spiritual or artistic nature, or as the Brockhaus Encyclopaedia defined it: 'the ennoblement of the individual through the cultivation of his moral, artistic and spiritual powers; and the products of the actions of such cultivated people'.[33] The well-known distinction often made in German intellectual discourse during the imperial era between *Kultur* and *Zivilisation* is one indication of this. This is not to say that the meaning of *Kultur* is clear-cut: the German writer Herder (1744–1803) once claimed that 'nothing is more indeterminate than this word'.[34] It does, however, help us to explain the working definition of culture used in this book. For the most part, the focus here is on *Kultur* as it would have been understood by imperial Germans, rather than the broader notion of culture favoured in contemporary Cultural Studies. Thus, although brief references are made to working-class culture, popular culture and the beginnings of the 'culture industry', the book's principal concern is with high culture. Care has been taken, however, to consider not only the dominant orthodoxies of the age, and the avant-garde revolts that would lay the foundations of future orthodoxies, but also to probe some of the era's shadier nooks and crannies: to highlight movements and individuals who may not have been responsible for canonical works, but who nevertheless contributed in significant ways to the Empire's cultural life.

Needless to say, even within this comparatively narrow conception of culture, generalizations, simplifications and omissions are inevitable. One omission in particular is regrettable: very little is yet known about the reception of the various cultural products under discussion. Both 'reception theory' and 'reception history' (*Rezeptionsgeschichte*) – which argue that readers, as well as authors, make meaning – have been fashionable in Germany for several decades,[35] but comparatively little empirical research has been undertaken on the way in which particular cultural products were 'read', and hence shaped, by imperial Germans.[36] This reflects the limitations of the sources rather than the willingness of researchers, as I found in my own research work on the industrial architecture of Imperial Germany.[37] As with much cultural history, writing on the reception of particular buildings, books or paintings can often seem haphazard and anecdotal, lacking in historical specificity and scientific rigour. To some extent it is possible to sidestep these dangers by emphasizing those aspects of culture which are quantifiable – such as the numbers attending particular art exhibitions, or the frequency with which certain book titles were borrowed from libraries – but by avoiding direct engagement with actual 'texts', the historian surely risks missing out on a rich seam of valuable raw materials. As Peter Paret has eloquently stated: 'Art and literature are among society's most determined efforts to understand itself, and through their insights, errors, and obfuscations we hear the clear voice of the past'.[38] It is that voice which this book seeks to amplify.

1 *The Historical Context*

Introduction

The German Empire, established in 1871 on the twin foundations of Prussian military strength and economic dynamism, described itself as an 'Eternal League of Princes and Free Cities': a phrase which, like the terms *Kaiser* (emperor) and *Kaiserreich* (empire), evoked the medieval past rather than a contemporary world of railways and steamships. Assembled by Otto von Bismarck's skilful statecraft, the League consisted of four kingdoms (Prussia, Bavaria, Saxony and Württemberg), six grand-duchies, five duchies, seven pocket-sized principalities, and three free cities (Hamburg, Bremen and Lübeck).[1] Under the international treaties that formed the legal framework of the *Reichsgründung* ('founding of the Empire'), sovereignty remained with the individual states and rulers, who agreed to cede certain powers to the Empire, whilst retaining many key areas of competence (such as direct taxation) and their own governmental institutions. These included not only royal courts and parliaments but also, in some cases, diplomats and nominally independent armies too. As David Blackbourn therefore notes, 'the federal Empire resembled more closely the present-day European Union than it did contemporary federal (but republican) states such as the USA or Switzerland'.[2]

The Empire's federalism was unbalanced by the fact that just one of the twenty-five states, Prussia, accounted for about 60 per cent of the population and territory, permanently provided the emperor, and possessed an effective veto on all constitutional change. As Prussia was a bastion of monarchical conservatism, this was to be a major obstacle to reform. The imperial constitution of 16 April 1871, originally drawn up by Bismarck for the North German Confederation of 1867, envisaged an idiosyncratic mix of absolute monarchy, parliamentary representation and plebiscitary democracy. It was to remain fundamentally unaltered until the last days of the Empire (although there were significant 'informal' changes), and produced a polycratic form of government variously described as 'pseudo-constitutional', 'sham-parliamentary', 'semi-autocratic', or less snappily, 'semi-constitutional, with supplementary party-political features'. Whatever epithet one chooses, however, it is clear that this 'system of skirted decisions' was increasingly ill-suited to the running of a complex modern state, especially after Bismarck's enforced departure in 1890 upset their delicate equilibrium. The finances of the Empire, in particular, proved a permanent headache for Germany's leaders, as imperial spending increasingly outstripped its limited revenue-raising powers.

The constitution sought to balance federal and imperial interests. The former were safeguarded by the *Bundesrat* (Federal Council), made up of delegates appointed by the twenty-five state governments; and the latter by a parliamentary assembly, the *Reichstag*, whose 397 members were elected directly by universal male suffrage. Legislation had to be passed by both institutions. Parliamentarians therefore had some ability to control the executive by amending or blocking legislation – including the annual budget – but they could not determine the composition of the government. Bismarck was determined to limit the powers of elected politicians and their parties, particularly over military and foreign affairs, and resisted efforts to establish ministerial responsibility or parliamentary government. Thus it was the emperor who hired and fired the chancellor and other imperial officials (called 'secretaries of state' rather than ministers), and who also summoned and closed parliamentary sessions.

The constitution was a comparatively short document of just seventy-five articles. One further aspect merits brief mention here: under article four, responsibility for the 'classical' areas of culture, namely the arts, education and religion, remained with the individual states rather than the Empire.[3] This element of autonomy was jealously guarded, especially by the smaller states which viewed cultural policy as an important counterweight to Prussian political and military hegemony, and all attempts to increase the imperial role met with fierce opposition.

The real distribution of power within Imperial Germany's governmental system (as opposed to the theoretical structures of its constitution), its shifts and fluctuations, and the extent to which it provided scope for reform, have all been the subject of heated historiographical debate.[4] Even so, the apparent discrepancy or disjunction between the Empire's increasingly dynamic industrial economy, and the 'backward' or 'authoritarian' nature of its core political structures, lies at the heart of most standard works on Imperial Germany. It is this 'deficient' or 'incomplete' modernization that is said to have allowed 'pre-industrial' elites to retain a disproportionate hold on power, with serious consequences for Germany's long-term development. Responsibility for this state of affairs is usually placed on the German bourgeoisie and, in particular, the failings of its liberal political representatives.

In recent years, however, this 'new orthodox' view has been subject to a number of revisions. It has been pointed out, for instance, that relatively weak parliaments and politically privileged aristocrats were far from unusual in Europe at this time; that 'asynchronic' development is normal rather than exceptional; and, more controversially, that an authoritarian state was not necessarily incompatible with bourgeois interests and values.[5] Geoff Eley, in particular, has stressed the need to 'free ourselves from the binary distinction between "modernizing" liberalism and "backward" authoritarianism'.[6] This particular debate – which is sometimes reduced to the deceptively simple question of 'how bourgeois' or 'how modern' the *Kaiserreich* was[7] – is likely to remain unresolved, given the quantity of ammunition available to both sides. It is clear, however, that while Imperial Germany developed an increasingly sophisticated political culture, with well-functioning elections, rising turnouts (from 52 per cent in 1871 to more than 84 per cent in the 1912 General Election), and lively parliamentary debates, party politics was by no means the only channel for political energies. After 1890, in particular, the parties had to compete with a host of interest groups, leagues and associations, representing every conceivable faction in what was a highly segmented and pluralistic society.[8]

In fact, while the founding of the Empire is referred to in English as the 'unification' of Germany, 'unified' Germany was deeply divided from the start. Not only did some 2.4 million Prussian Poles have scant cause to rejoice at their inclusion in the Empire, but other internal minorities such as the Danes of North Schleswig, Alsatians, Masurians and Sorbs also felt little affinity with the new 'superstate'. Such minorities, numbering over 4 million by 1914, were predictably perceived as a latent threat to imperial unity, but even amongst the ethnic German population there were many who viewed its foundation with deep misgivings. It is important to remember that the dramatic events of 1866–71 had represented a partition of the German lands as well as their unification, with more than 9 million ethnic Germans left beyond the Empire's borders in Austria, Bohemia, Moravia and throughout eastern Europe. Small wonder then that the *Reichsgründung* is often viewed as the beginning of German unification, rather than its climax.

Germans continued to be divided by history, religion and custom long after 1871, and although these differences diminished in time, other divisions became increasingly apparent. The result was a heterogeneous, fractious society, which often seemed close to meltdown, but which nevertheless possessed sufficient cohesion to survive – and in some respects flourish – until the trauma of imminent defeat in 1918. Despite the assertions of later historians that the Empire was virtually ungovernable, and in a state of 'permanent' or 'latent' crisis, it should not be forgotten that its legacy of national legitimacy successfully withstood two world wars and 40 years of division. Even so, it was clearly unfortunate for Germany that at the very moment it gained what Rudy Koshar calls 'the institutional framework for "making Germans", for constructing a notionally stable national identity, its political culture produced an array of multiple identities' that would make that process very much more difficult.[9] This chapter begins by taking a brief look at four major 'fault-lines' that ran through imperial society – the regional divide; the confessional divide; the gender divide; and the urban–rural divide – before proceeding to introduce some of the Empire's most important social milieus.

The regional divide

Just as Germans today are said to be divided by a mental barrier which separates the 'new' from the 'old' (i.e. pre-1990) federal states, so imperial Germans regarded the *Mainlinie* – the course of the River Main which runs through central Germany and separated the territory of the North German Confederation from the four south German states – as a significant cultural divide. It is important to remember, however, that such divisions come and go: regional identities are formed by people, and change in time. One must be careful therefore not to exaggerate the height or permanence of this barrier. In the states of central and southern Germany defeated by Prussia in the war of 1866, anti-Prussian sentiment was understandably strong. Nevertheless, as Blackbourn points out: 'No sectional division within Germany could be compared to the north–south divide that undermined the unity of Italy.'[10] That said, there can be no doubt that particularism – loyalty to, or identification with, a particular locality, dynasty or historical tradition – remained a significant factor in the life of the Empire long after 1871.[11] French-style centralization was not an option. The Germans were, in Celia Applegate's words, 'a nation of provincials'.[12] Local studies, like Applegate's work on the Rhenish Palatinate or Alon Confino's case study of Württemberg,[13] following on from Mack Walker's pioneering book on German 'home towns',[14] have highlighted the difficulties nineteenth-century Germans faced in reconciling their particularist and national identities.

In the case of the Palatinate there were many who supported the idea of a Prussian-led solution to the national question as a means of transcending an unloved attachment to an intermediate state. The Palatinate had belonged to the Kingdom of Bavaria since 1816, but was geographically isolated from Munich, and perceived to be out on a limb in economic, political and confessional terms too. Enthusiasm for unification was often strongest in such areas. However, while the Empire was warmly embraced there after 1871, a new form of popular local patriotism also emerged, which no longer possessed an anti-Bavarian thrust, and was in fact actively encouraged by state officials. These two strands of identity were complementary, and came together under the umbrella of *Heimat* – a flexible and elusive concept of rootedness, evoking much more than the English equivalents 'home' or 'homeland'. Through a 'gradual re-imagining of the German locality', the notion of *Heimat* was able to 'link the intimate ties of the locality with the abstract solidarity of a modern nation', and the German people were able to 'catch up' mentally with the nation-state sprung on them in 1871.[15] Confino sees a similar pattern emerge in Württemberg, where the grassroots celebration of local diversity, embedded in a broader national feeling of 'home', was far more effective at 'making Germans' than anything imposed from above.

We will return to the notion of *Heimat* in Chapter 5, but it is important to stress that it was not only in small-town Germany that powerful local and regional identities could be found. It has long been recognized that the industrial Ruhr, with its disparate migrant population, also had a strong and vital regional identity through the imperial era and beyond.[16] It too was a *Heimat*, albeit a less picturesque one. Elsewhere, in Bavaria, Württemberg and Hanover, particularist or dynastic parties achieved considerable success in the first decades of the Empire. These tended to decline around the turn of the century, undermined not only by the tangible reality of the *Reich*, but by the revolution in transport and communications, and by the evolution of a single economic market. Even so, those nineteenth-century progressives who denounced particularism as 'reactionary' and 'bankrupt' were probably guilty of underestimating the enduring power of such emotional ties. As contemporary debates on European integration indicate, particularism is still a force to be reckoned with in the era of globalization.

The confessional divide

Nominally at least, the population of the German Empire was overwhelmingly Christian in religious affiliation. Some 62 per cent identified with the Evangelical (Protestant) churches, and 36 per cent with Roman Catholicism.[17] These figures remained remarkably constant throughout our period. Judaism accounted for around 1 per cent of the population, while atheists, agnostics and freethinkers made up an even smaller minority, albeit a growing one. The Catholic population could be found in significant concentrations in the south (Bavaria), west (Rhineland) and east (Silesia) of the Empire. The Pope had fewer followers in the north, but there were still twice as many Catholics in Prussia than in Bavaria.[18] Examples of mixed marriages and interdenominational friendships can easily be found, but on the whole Germany's Protestants and Catholics regarded each other with mutual suspicion, and often outright hostility. In most people's minds it was still a case of Wittenberg versus Rome.

Both of the principal Christian confessions were divided internally too. Each had what could be termed 'orthodox/conservative' and 'reformist/liberal' factions. The degree of pluralism within German Protestantism was, however, much greater than within Catholicism, which for all its shades of opinion had a clear chain of command leading ultimately to Rome. In contrast, Protestantism remained organized on a state-by-state basis – the *Reichsgründung* did not produce an Empire-wide 'Church of Germany' – and some theological and liturgical differences existed between the various state churches. These tended to diminish after 1871: 'The Empire and the Empire of God moved closer together,' as Thomas Nipperdey put it.[19] In each case, however, the dynastic ruler remained head of the Protestant state church, and the ties between the two – the 'alliance of throne and altar' – were slow to loosen. In Prussia, where the Lutheran and Calvinist traditions had been united from the throne in 1817, Protestant pastors continued to spend much of their time preaching a conservative message of obedience to authority and political quietism. Johann Gottfried von Herder, speaking from personal experience, had once dubbed them 'civil servants in vestments', and in terms of education, salary and outlook this picture still held true.

Both major confessions had to contend with a decline in the number of regular worshippers during the imperial era.[20] This decline was more marked amongst Protestants than Catholics; in towns than the countryside; and amongst men than women. Despite ambitious church building programmes, neither confession was able to keep pace with the migration of Germans to the cities. Even so, religion remained a central normative force in German life, and secularization was neither a predictable nor linear process. So, although the controversial Protestant scholar David Friedrich Strauss (1808–74) caused a great stir in 1872 with a book entitled *The Old and the New Faith* – which posed the question 'Are we still Christians?' and answered it in the negative – we should not assume this gives a full picture. Religious faith did not just disappear with Charles Darwin and the railways.

In fact, the language and iconography of Christianity was ever-present in Imperial German culture; in the sphere of morality Christian values predominated; and every eighth book published in 1871 was a work of theology.[21] Births, deaths and – to a lesser extent – marriages continued to be associated with church-based rituals, as did key dates in the agricultural year. The churches and their charitable foundations still played a vital role in providing elementary education, health and social welfare. As the large-scale celebrations to mark Martin Luther's 400th birthday in 1883 illustrated, Prussia's official culture was as vigorously Protestant as ever. Even amongst those who quit mainstream Protestantism in search of new forms of piety – be it monism, theosophy, spiritualism, or a 'Germanic' Christianity – a strong sense of religiosity was invariably apparent.

On the other side of the confessional divide, Catholicism also seemed in surprisingly good health in the late nineteenth century, with increasing numbers partaking in pilgrimages; a thriving cult of the Virgin Mary; increasing sales of devotional kitsch; and even the establishment of a 'German Lourdes' at Marpingen in the Saarland.[22] Ironically, these expressions of a popular, grassroots Catholic revival, whose energies the church authorities struggled to control, were at least in part the product of persecution and despair. It was the infamous confrontation between the Prussian state and the Catholic church of the 1870s, which the scientist and left liberal parliamentarian Rudolf Virchow (1821–1902) memorably dubbed the *Kulturkampf* (variously translated as the 'cultural conflict', 'struggle for culture', or 'struggle between cultures'), which provided the spark.[23]

No account of the confessional divide in Imperial Germany can bypass this key episode in the early life of the Empire. Conflicts between church and state were, of course, far from unusual in nineteenth-century Europe, and liberals were strongly anti-clerical in most parts of the continent. They regarded Catholicism as obscurantist and hidebound: the religion of the 'uneducated', and an impediment to social and economic progress. Even so, the conflict became more politicized in Prussia than elsewhere in Europe, and its legacy of bitterness lingered longer. The decade of German unification had coincided with a steady worsening of relations between the conservative Pope Pius IX and Europe's secular states, as a result of the Syllabus of Errors (1864), and the Vatican Council's confirmation of the doctrine of Papal Infallibility six years later. These pronouncements, which seemed to slam the door on the modern world, horrified liberals everywhere, and most German Catholics were deeply troubled. For a time it seemed as though the Catholic church in Germany would split in two, but most anti-infallibilist bishops were finally brought into line, and only a small 'Old Catholic' faction under Ignaz Döllinger (1799–1890) and Franz Xaver Kraus (1840–1901) broke from Rome. Nevertheless, the new Empire's Catholic population was divided and dispirited – Prussia's victory over Austria in 1866 had been a crushing blow – and it would take the heavy-handed intervention of the Bismarckian state to restore a sense of solidarity in adversity.

The Prussian government's response to the 'infallibility' crisis was to close down the Catholic section of the Ministry for Spiritual, Educational and Medical Affairs (*Kultusministerium*) in July 1871 and, in the following year, to appoint a liberal and anti-clerical minister Adalbert Falk (1827–1900). Falk oversaw a raft of new legislation, including the introduction of state supervision for church schools (Prussian law of 1872); obligatory civil marriage ceremonies (Prussian law of 1874; imperial law of 1875); and a total ban on the Jesuit Order (imperial law of 1872). While Catholics might have come to accept some or all of these measures, the Prussian 'May Laws' of 1873 – with a second punitive instalment in 1874 – were a different matter entirely, since they allowed the state to intervene in what were seen as purely ecclesiastical affairs: the appointment of priests and the education of the clergy. The Catholic population felt besieged, and with some justification, for Bismarck and the liberals had deliberately escalated the conflict into a war against political Catholicism.

In a recent study, Ronald Ross concludes: 'Bismarck's legislation proved far less injurious to the Roman church than Catholics feared or its advocates confidently anticipated.'[24] Even so, though the image of overworked policemen desperately pasting up 'wanted' notices for dissident bishops may seem vaguely comic, the seriousness of the conflict should not be underestimated: some 1800 priests were imprisoned or exiled, and 16 million Reichsmarks (RM) worth of church property seized.[25] Displaying a newfound sense of solidarity, the Catholic community responded to the legislation with a policy of passive resistance and symbolic gestures, such as flying the papal flag, or wearing the Pope's colours of yellow and white. The electoral beneficiary was the Centre Party, which had originally been founded in 1870 to defend the religious rights and values of both confessions, but quickly became a bastion for German Catholics and other minorities. The Centre advanced from 58 Reichstag seats in 1871 to 91 in 1874, winning over 80 per cent of the Catholic vote. Despite its socially disparate electorate, which ranged from Westphalian aristocrats to Polish peasants; and from Rhineland artisans to Ruhr coalminers, it was to remain a significant force in German politics until 1933, achieving a remarkable consistency in its share of Reichstag seats, if not in its political direction.[26]

While the *Kulturkampf* is often portrayed as an example of Bismarck's tactic of attempting to unite the Protestant majority by identifying and isolating enemies within (which he referred to as *Reichsfeinde* or 'enemies of the Empire'), this probably was not his primary motivation: he was genuinely worried about the loyalty of the 'ultramontanes', and he saw a confrontation with Rome as a more painless way of satisfying liberal demands than the introduction of constitutional reform. It was not a success, for it united the Catholics and failed to quell liberal ambition. Eventually Bismarck realized that the conflict was proving counter-productive, and the death of the unbending Pope Pius IX in 1878 paved the way to an end in hostilities.[27] Later, after the Iron Chancellor's fundamental political realignment of the late 1870s, Centre votes would help to pass many of the imperial era's best-known Reichstag bills. However, despite the gradual 'nationalization' of the Catholic masses, the social and economic status of Germany's Catholic community would lag behind that of the Protestants for many years to come.

The gender divide

Even by nineteenth-century standards, Imperial Germany was a highly patriarchal society. Women's inferior status was not just a matter of popular prejudice or convention, but was cemented in legislation. Under the Empire's long-awaited Civil Legal Code (*Bürgerliches Gesetzbuch*), which came into force on 1 January 1900, married women had no say over their children's education, and all money or property brought into a marriage became the husband's responsibility. As the Code bluntly stated: 'the husband takes the decisions in all matters affecting married life'.[28] Meanwhile, under the Empire's Criminal Code, abortion was illegal (even in the case of rape), and those found guilty of performing or assisting in such operations faced up to five years' imprisonment. As Richard Evans notes, this was typical of the era's double standard in questions of sexual morality: 'according to which women were responsible for the consequences of sexual intercourse but men were not.'[29] Similarly, women merely suspected of prostitution were forced to undergo a compulsory medical examination at the hands of the dreaded 'Morals Police' (*Sittenpolizei*), whereas their male clients faced no such humiliation. This double standard coloured much of the Civil Code; not least the section on divorce, which was only to be granted in very limited circumstances.[30]

For a graphic illustration of how all this could impact on individuals, one could do worse than to turn to Theodor Fontane (1819–98), whose novels – particularly *L'Adultera* ('The Adulteress', 1879); *Irrungen Wirrungen* ('Trials and Tribulations', 1888); and *Effi Briest* (1895) – frequently explored the situation of women in contemporary Germany society.[31] The latter novel recounted the tragic tale of young Effi, who was made a permanent social outcast because of a minor act of adultery committed some six years previously; while her husband was accepted back into society within a matter of weeks, despite having killed his rival in a duel. Although this might sound the very stuff of Victorian melodrama, Fontane's story was in fact all too real: it was based on an actual case from the mid-1880s and only the names had been changed.

It is clear from these and other literary works that women's inferior status in Imperial Germany was not just a product of legislation, but of a social consensus which ascribed fundamentally different character traits to the sexes, with separate standards of sexual morality and contrasting roles in society: 'Nature had created two distinct creatures and endowed each with immutable intellectual and emotional traits and corresponding "proper" spheres of activity', as Jean Quataert puts it.[32] With their nurturing instincts, emotional sensitivity and natural submissiveness, women were suited to the domestic realm rather than the public sphere. The natural boundaries for women were therefore drawn around the three 'K's – *Kinder, Küche, Kirche* (children, kitchen and church) – and the female population was all but barred from public life. There were strong institutional pressures from the churches, the army and others, to keep things this way. It was only in 1908 that women gained the right to join political parties, or even to attend public meetings, in all states of the Empire.[33] The right to vote in Reichstag elections was not secured until 1918.[34]

All women were confronted with such discrimination, yet the nature of the female experience in Imperial Germany was nevertheless dependent on wealth and social status. For the economically secure, the 'deadening boredom' of domesticity had its compensations, and it was certainly not impossible for bourgeois women to develop a sense of self-worth. With the time and space for reading and reflection, writing and music-making; the chance to attend concerts or theatrical productions; to give dinner parties or even host salons, there were more opportunities for self-fulfilment than might seem apparent today. To give one example, although relatively few women feature in literary histories of Imperial Germany, it has been estimated that around 6000 female writers were active in Germany during the second half of the nineteenth century, and some were extremely successful.[35] The highest sales figures belonged to Eugenie Marlitt (actually Eugenie John, 1825–87), an author of sentimental romances, but other women were able to tackle more challenging themes. Hedwig Dohm (1833–1919), Gabriele Reuter (1859–1941) and Helene Böhlau (1859–1940), for instance, all explored what was becoming known in the 1890s as the 'women's question' (*Frauenfrage*). This term, which was first included in the Brockhaus Encyclopedia of 1898, originally referred to a perceived surplus of unmarried middle-class women, and the need to provide them with employment in the years between leaving school and their eventual marriage.[36] Later, however, the *Frauenfrage* became synonymous with the question of women's rights in general.

Another phrase which began to appear in print around 1900 was 'the sex war' or 'war between the sexes'.[37] In the front line of this conflict were organizations such as the 'League for the Prevention of the Emancipation of Women' (1912) and, on the other side of the barricades, the German women's movement. Until the 1970s, this aspect of the Empire's history had been shamefully neglected. Since then, however, many historians have published work on aspects of early German feminism, revealing a complex and contradictory picture.[38] The German women's movement was weakened by its division into two entirely separate and antagonistic factions – bourgeois and proletarian – that perceived each other as 'enemy sisters'. The latter faction, led by Clara Zetkin, argued that the emancipation of women could only come after the overthrow of the existing political and economic order; a view famously espoused in August Bebel's immensely popular *Die Frau und der Sozialismus* ('Woman and Socialism', 1879).[39]

The bourgeois women's movement, meanwhile, preferred to agitate on a broad range of social and cultural issues – education and employment rights, sexuality, prostitution, the rights of mothers and the protection of illegitimate children – rather than focus on the suffrage question. 'Votes for Women' was a cause pursued with much less vigour in Germany than in Britain or the United States. With this in mind, the bourgeois women's movement in Imperial Germany – from the General German Women's Association (*Allgemeine Deutsche Frauenverein*, ADF) founded by Louise Otto-Peters in 1865; to the League of German Women's Associations (*Bund Deutscher Frauenverbände*, BDF), a loose federation established in 1894 which claimed 500,000 members by 1914[40] – has often been portrayed as a 'tepid movement ... based on notions of distinct male and female values, contributions, and proper roles'.[41]

However, in recent years historians such as Ann Taylor Allen and

Jean Quataert have challenged this view. Allen has highlighted significant ways in which she suggests the German bourgeois women's movement was more radical than its Anglo-Saxon counterparts.[42] Whether one accepts this view or not depends largely on one's view of the 'equality versus difference' debate in contemporary feminist discourse. Whilst Anglo-American feminists pursued a liberal individualist 'equal rights' approach, the early German women's movement sought to create a distinctively female form of citizenship based on 'organized motherhood'. Emancipation, it was argued, should not be confused with conformity to male standards: 'motherly' policies were required to humanize the family and society at large.

This maternalist approach, which emphasized the collective over the individual, was by no means unique to Germany in turn-of-the-century Europe, and was endorsed by some socialist as well as bourgeois feminists. Even so, it is portrayed by the likes of Richard Evans and Claudia Koonz as fundamentally conservative, and Koonz goes as far as to suggest a line of continuity between the ideals of early German feminism and National Socialism.[43] As Allen points out, however, a number of contemporary feminists have recently moved away from narrow 'equal rights' agendas to reassert the value of 'maternal thinking'.[44] Two things are undisputed: the radicalism of at least some early German feminists was undoubtedly down-played by the conservative women who wrote the first histories of the movement in the 1920s; and secondly, the BDF did adopt a distinctly more cautious line in the years before World War One. Ironically, as Evans has shown, it was an important emancipatory reform – the new Imperial Law of Association of 1908 – that was largely responsible for the latter change.[45] Many moderate women, who had previously shied away from political campaigning, joined women's associations in the aftermath of 1908, and succeeded in outvoting the radicals. Evans emphasizes, however, that the BDF 'was still committed to the reform of the social and political institutions of Wilhelmine Germany. It did not accept the status quo'.[46]

It is important to remember, of course, that avowedly feminist organizations actually accounted for only a small proportion of women's associational life in late nineteenth- and early twentieth-century Germany, but it is the very breadth of this organizational activity which has led Ute Frevert to conclude that: the 'widely-held notion that everyday life for middle-class women centred exclusively on the triad of kitchen, children and church has to be revised'.[47] Education and employment opportunities for women certainly expanded during the imperial era. With regard to the former, provision was still woefully inadequate, but there was a substantial improvement in the decade either side of 1900. One by one, the German states began to establish girls' grammar schools, and the prospect of a university education for young women at last loomed over the horizon, some twenty years after England (1878) and forty years after France (1861). At first, females were only accepted in lecture halls as 'auditors', but after 1900 the German states belatedly began to award degrees to women: Baden took the lead by allowing female students to matriculate in 1901; Württemberg followed in 1903; and Prussia's universities brought up the rear in 1908. As for women's employment, it is important to note that by the late nineteenth century one-third of the German workforce was already female, and not only in 'traditional' areas of female work – domestic service, agriculture, textiles – but in retailing, nursing, teaching, and the rapidly-growing 'white blouse' occupations too.[48]

Work outside the home provided women with new contacts and experiences, and could bring a degree of economic independence, if not yet financial equality. Women's employment was, however, a double-edged sword, for the prevailing code of morality suggested that 'respectable' women did not work for money, but rather devoted their energies to their homes and families. The maintenance of family life, a key expression of bourgeois values, was also regarded as an important civic duty.[49] Those who threatened the status quo in the home were seen to challenge the very foundations of a stable society. Yet many women had no option but to find a job, and for them employment was less an opportunity than a curse. Weighed down by the formidable triple burden of full-time work, child-rearing and household management, such women had little time for social activism, and were left to seek fleeting moments of leisure and pleasure in a life of general drudgery.

The urban–rural divide

The Empire covered vast swathes of central Europe, stretching from the vineyards of Alsace-Lorraine in the west, to the forests of the Russian Baltic provinces in the east, and had a population of nearly 41 million in 1871. Despite the continuing emigration of Germans to the New World the population was to rise dramatically; passing 56 million at the turn of the century, and reaching 67 million by 1913, as a result of high birth rates and declining mortality. In the first decade of the Empire, average life expectancy from birth was under 36 years for men, and little more than 38 years for women; these figures had improved to 45 and 48 respectively by the 1900s.[50] Just before World War One, only 5 per cent of the German population was aged over 65; more that 34 per cent was aged 15 or less.[51] Despite this youthful and dynamic demographic profile, however, large areas of the Empire remained sparsely inhabited, such as the agricultural lands of East Prussia or Pomerania, which existed uneasily alongside industrial regions like Saxony, Upper Silesia and the Ruhr.

At the time of the *Reichsgründung* some 64 per cent of Imperial Germans lived in communities with 2000 or fewer inhabitants. Although there were eight cities with a population in excess of 100,000, these accounted for less than 5 per cent of the total population.[52] Germany was essentially an empire of small towns. By 1910, however, 60 per cent lived in larger towns or cities; 48 of which had populations of more than 100,000, and one (Berlin) had more than 2 million inhabitants. This meant that Imperial Germany possessed almost as many cities as the rest of continental Europe put together, and some of them were growing at a phenomenal rate.[53] There were also a number of major urban conurbations which may have lacked metropolitan status or character, but which nevertheless accommodated large and growing populations, as industrialization forged together dozens of small villages and towns into sprawling agglomerations of buildings and people.

Although the urban–rural separation was never as clear-cut as one might think – city-dwellers often kept farm animals; many countryfolk worked seasonally in towns – the speed and scale of German urbanization was startling. By the 1900s only about a half of the Empire's population still lived in the place where they were born. Urbanization was not, however, simply the product of migration from the country to the town: there was considerable movement in both directions, even if the net inflow was greater than the outflow. Nor was the change merely quantitative. The term 'urbanization' implies a qualitative change too: a spreading familiarity with urban goods, practices and values across the Empire as a whole. In effect, the very centre of gravity in German society was moving, with profound implications for the Empire's politics and culture.

As we shall see in Chapter 4, this was a cause of alarm for many German writers and thinkers, who made the city a scapegoat for all the ills of the modern world; and who exaggerated both the harmonious nature of village life and the stability of its population. Their fears were not ungrounded. The pace of urbanization produced a profound sense of dislocation and disorientation, and the already considerable differences between the Empire's western and eastern territories were exacerbated. At the same time, however, there were others who saw Germany's new urbanity as a cause for celebration: as a product of communal achievement, as a dynamo of emancipation or as an aesthetic spectacle.[54]

For the thousands of people, mostly young and single, who were seduced by the city, substantial mental adjustments were required. Not the least of these was to accept the rule of the clock. In the countryside, work followed the natural rhythm of the day. It began early, but generally ended when dusk fell. In the artificially illuminated cities there were no such limitations. If this represented a triumph for man over nature, however, his ability to house the new urban masses was much less impressive. As cities expanded outwards, dismantling their historic defensive walls, and swallowing up surrounding villages, residential areas became increasingly segregated along class lines.[55] In working-class districts, tenement blocks were hastily erected by speculative developers, with poor heating, little natural light and primitive sanitation. These 'rental barracks' (*Mietskasernen*) were cramped, squalid and unhealthy: many families in one- or two-room apartments even had to share their beds with lodgers (*Schlafgänger*). Despite municipal measures to improve hygiene, such as the laying of sewers and clean water pipes, outbreaks of cholera and typhus continued to plague German cities right up until the end of the nineteenth century.[56]

It would be wrong, however, to imagine that in the rush to reach the cities, the Germany countryside was left barren and deserted. In fact, rural labourers and smallholders comprised the Empire's largest social group until the 1890s, and agriculture remained a cornerstone of the German economy well into the twentieth century. More than one-third of the workforce was still employed in the primary sector on the eve of World War One (compared to nearly one-half in 1880).[57] This figure might even have been higher had German farmers not achieved some notable productivity gains, through the use of things like artificial fertilizers and modern agricultural machinery. Therefore, while the contemporary debates on the relative merits of Germany as a predominantly agrarian or industrial state (*Agrarstaat* versus *Industriestaat*),[58] may have ended in a *de facto* victory for the latter, the Empire retained a much larger and stronger agricultural base than many of its competitors. On the other hand, structural problems and a very competitive world market meant that talk of a crisis was never far away. As farm workers voted with their feet and headed for the towns, German landowners became increasingly reliant on temporary foreign labour. By 1914 there were around 500,000 of these seasonal migrants: mostly Russian Poles in the east, and Italians in the south.

Social change and the formation of cultural milieus

It was not only migration and urbanization that made the German Empire a society in 'restless movement'.[59] The belated but rapid industrialization from around 1850, which was such an important precursor to unification, also set in motion a new social mobility.[60] The latter was, admittedly, much more apparent around the middle of the social scale than at its top or bottom, but modest changes were occurring there too. The growing complexity of the industrial economy, with its new technologies and structures, required a better-educated and more flexible population. Traditional privileges and status counted for less; money and merit for more. Those who owed their wealth or position to an accident of birth were forced to adapt to changing circumstances. Careers, and fortunes, were there to be made and lost. Germany was evolving from a corporate or estates-based society (*ständische Gesellschaft*) to one based on relations of class.

It was becoming a society of vast inequalities in health, wealth, education and housing; a society of segregated cities and demarcated spaces, in which forms of group consciousness were understandably quick to develop. Class, however, was by no means the only form of social stratification. Confession, ethnicity, gender and generation could all cut across class lines, while the class divisions themselves were more complex and fluid than theory might suggest. For this reason, historians of the imperial era often prefer to employ the concept of the 'milieu' – formed by a combination of class, religion, region and culture – rather than class alone.[61] Wolfgang Mommsen, for instance, identifies four such milieus, and although it would not be difficult to suggest further examples, his schema will be followed here.[62]

Courtly and aristocratic culture

With its four monarchs and 18 other princely rulers, the German Empire had no shortage of royal courts. Indeed, as John Röhl has noted, just as Germany 'approached the apogee of its industrialisation, there simultaneously occurred a "monstrous" blossoming of a court culture of a kind not seen before in the whole of its history'.[63] The cost was huge. Röhl has calculated that on the eve of World War One, the annual Crown Endowment in Prussia alone was around twice the size of the British monarchy's civil list. Judged on these terms, the Bavarian royal court was ranked eighth in the world (one place behind Japan), with the Kingdom of Saxony ninth. Altogether German taxpayers had to find some 42 million RM per annum to support their kings, princes and court followers; four times as much as it cost to maintain a British monarchy not noted for its frugality.[64] This was certainly the Empire's most expensive, as well as most exclusive, milieu.

In view of the scale and political importance of these German courts, it is perhaps surprising that they have not attracted more scholarly attention: their rituals and ceremonies are arguably less well documented than those of Ruhr coalminers. That cannot be rectified here, however, so a few general observations must suffice. It was standard practice for royal courts in Germany, as elsewhere, to organize a formal 'season'. Those who wished – and were entitled – to attend at court, applied in writing ahead of the season's first event, a 'promenade', in which guests were presented to their ruler in rank order. Nowhere was this ranking more complicated than in Prussia, which listed sixty-two separate ranks in its 'Court Precedence Regulation' (*Hof-Rang-Reglement*) of 1878, compared to just three in Bavaria, and only five in Habsburg Austria. The Prussian ranking system produced numerous absurdities: at official court banquets just before World War One, for instance, the Imperial Chancellor Bethmann Hollweg was relegated to the bottom end of the table, because his military rank was only that of a major (a lowly 54th in the court hierarchy). Court balls, the mainstay of the season, could attract several thousand guests, and invitations were highly prized. This was particularly the case with balls in the candle-lit Berlin palace: glittering, colourful affairs, memorably captured on canvas by the Prussian painter Adolph Menzel (1815–1905).

Of course, the contribution of Germany's sovereign rulers to the Empire's cultural life did not begin and end in the mysterious and claustrophobic world of court ceremonial. They could exert a direct influence on cultural affairs through their power of appointment (to run royal opera houses, theatres and galleries, for instance); or through the award of honours and prizes; as well as through more direct forms of patronage.[65] Some of the minor German courts, in particular, had long and honourable traditions in this regard: not only Goethe and Schiller's Weimar, but also in Coburg and Munich, where a full-scale 'Writer's Circle' was supported by King Maximilian II in the 1850s and 1860s. As we shall see, the Grand Duke of Saxe-Weimar, the Grand Duke of Hesse-Darmstadt and the Duke of Saxe-Meiningen all pursued serious and sometimes innovative policies in the cultural sphere during the imperial era.

In addition to its royal courts, the Empire possessed more than a hundred 'mediatized' noble families from the old Holy Roman Empire, who were recognized as being of equal birth to the offspring of Europe's ruling houses, and so provided an invaluable pool of potential marriage partners. There was also a far greater number of lesser aristocrats: perhaps 15,000–17,000 families in total.[66] Each was listed in the directory of German nobility known colloquially as 'the Gotha', which had been appearing since the mid-eighteenth century, and was divided into five colour-coded volumes: red for the royal court; dark green for counts; violet for barons; light blue for the ancient aristocracy (*Uradel*); and light green for the more recently ennobled (*Briefadel*).[67] Whilst this may seem relatively straightforward, the full intricacies of the noble hierarchy were understood by only a select few, as were its unwritten codes of behaviour and 'honour', which acted as a bond for insiders and as a barrier for outsiders.

When people think of the German aristocracy today it is generally the Prussian *Junker* who come to mind. In fact, by no means all noblemen who owned large country estates east of the River Elbe were *Junker* – the word simply means 'young lord'[68] – nor was every *Junker* 'a rude, domineering, arrogant type of man, without cultivation or culture, aggressive, conceited, ruthless, narrow-minded and given to a petty profit-seeking'.[69] Of course, there were many who did conform to this stereotype, which owed much to the work of nineteenth-century bourgeois novelists like Friedrich Spielhagen,[70] but it should not be forgotten that Prussia had its version of the enlightened 'Whig' aristocrat too.[71] Theodor Fontane, a critical friend of the nobility whose novels included a fair few as characters (most notably Dubslav von Stechlin in *Der Stechlin*) commented in a letter of 1881: 'All in all, they are better than their reputation, these much-maligned "Junkers" – different and better'.[72] We should not assume, therefore, that every *Junker* was a dull, provincial philistine, who only tolerated art if it had an equestrian theme, and whose reading was limited to the arch-conservative *Kreuzzeitung* newspaper. In fact, too little is known about their lifestyle and culture to make any very confident assertions in this regard, although it does appear that patronage of the arts, or a love of literature, was not common in their milieu. Perhaps predictably, riding and other country pursuits seem to have accounted for the largest proportion of their leisure time.

It should not be forgotten that most of Germany's aristocrats, and particularly the *Junker*, lived in geographic and social isolation, and were forced by harsh economic reality to treat agriculture (and its derivatives, such as sugar and distilled alcohol) as a serious business. Indeed, rising indebtedness meant that many had to sell up: as early as 1868, of the 10,123 estates in the six eastern provinces of Prussia, only 5595 were still in noble hands.[73] Not surprisingly, those who were able to retain their holdings placed much emphasis on the historical ties and obligations that bound them. A strong streak of Prussian particularism remained an important part of their identity, long after their initial hostility to the creation of the German Empire had subsided.

The homes of the East Elbian *Junker* were often surprisingly spartan, and offered few of the creature comforts to be found in suburban villas at this time. The same could not be said, however, for the palaces of the Upper Silesian aristocracy.[74] It is surely significant, however, that many of these Silesian noblemen owed their vast wealth principally to coal mining, industry and banking. For, in the second half of the nineteenth century it was 'new money' which increasingly set the tone, as profits from industry and commerce outstripped those from agriculture. The declining influence of the landed aristocracy was more rapid in the socio-economic sphere than in politics and administration, where the constitutional structure of both Prussia and the Empire ensured that they continued to wield a disproportionate influence. This was based on their stranglehold on the Upper House of the Prussian parliament, and a weighty presence in both the Prussian and imperial executive, rather than strength in the Reichstag. Here their principal mouthpiece was the German Conservative Party (DKP), founded in 1876. The DKP's electoral strongholds lay in rural districts east of the River Elbe –

urban conservatives voted for the pro-governmental 'Free Conservatives' (*Reichspartei*) or supported right-wing National Liberals – and only ever held a modest number of seats (a peak of 80 in 1887, but only 40 in 1912).[75]

Other bastions of aristocratic privilege remained too – the diplomatic service; the higher echelons of the Prussian civil service; and the officer corps (particularly in the better regiments of the Prussian army) – although these were gradually becoming less exclusive. Some historians, such as Hans-Ulrich Wehler, have argued that such remnants from a pre-industrial or 'feudal' past not only highlighted the remarkable persistence of the old order, and a concomitant deficit in bourgeois values, but also a fatal flaw in Germany's historical development; the notorious 'special path' (*Sonderweg*).[76] This view was contested, however, by a succession of publications in the 1980s and 1990s,[77] and the notion that wealthy middle-class Germans underwent a process of 'feudalization' has certainly fallen out of favour, even with the likes of Wehler. While it is true that some of the upwardly mobile sought to ape the culture and lifestyle of the aristocracy (as they did elsewhere in Europe) their motives were mixed, and many others steadfastly refused to be 'corrupted' by country estates, duels and decorations.[78]

Bourgeois culture

After years of neglect, historiographical interest in the German middle classes was revived with a vengeance in the last two decades of the twentieth century, leading to a reassessment of many long-standing assumptions about the role of the *Bürgertum* in modern German history.[79] The aforementioned 'feudalization' thesis was an early casualty; though the counter-argument, that Germany underwent a 'silent' bourgeois revolution, has remained contentious too.[80] As well as highlighting the problematic nature of the terminology – the words 'bourgeoisie', *Bürgertum* and 'middle class' are not in fact synonymous [81]– this important body of scholarship has emphasized the great diversity of interests and viewpoints which existed around the middle of the social scale in the late nineteenth and early twentieth centuries. Thus the established German practice of differentiating between the *Wirtschafts-* or *Besitzbürgertum* (the commercial or propertied bourgeoisie, which accounted for about 3–5 per cent of Imperial Germans), and the *Bildungsbürgertum* (the educated or professional elite who made up no more than 1 per cent of the population),[82] now appears to be just one of a host of subdivisions within this most heterogeneous of social groupings.

Significantly, however, there seems little desire to ditch the concept of the middle classes altogether. As the preface to one collection of essays put it: 'it is both useful and legitimate to regard such groups as bankers, merchants, industrialists, higher civil servants, doctors, lawyers, professors and other professionals as constituting a social stratum bound by common values, a shared culture and a degree of prosperity'.[83] These 'common values' included a deep respect for laws and rules; a belief in self-help, the sanctity of property and the family; and a faith in science and progress.[84] There was also a strong sense of being different, even morally superior, to the 'unproductive' nobility above and to the 'dangerous' masses below. Defining oneself *vis-à-vis* others has, of course, always been an important part of class identity.[85]

It was the *Bürgertum* that took the lead in the emergence of civil society in the century before 1871, as bureaucratic expansion, educational reform, professionalization and a growth in commerce all enlarged the 'public sphere'. Reading rooms and newspapers were important in this process, but arguably the most significant new institution was the voluntary association. Such associations (*Vereine*) emphasized their independence from old corporate institutions like the church and the guilds, and were comparatively open and democratic in their structure (although often closed to women). Developing at a time when political rights were extremely limited, they became a vital safety valve for what would become known as public opinion. The first associations – whether for gymnastics, choral singing, rifle shooting or self-improvement – were dominated by the *Bürgertum*. Later, however, the form was adopted throughout the social spectrum. Indeed, it became something of a defining characteristic of German society as a whole, and by the start of the twentieth century the pejorative term *Vereinsmeierei* (meaning an over-zealous clubbishness) was already in everyday use.

It is, however, the 'shared culture' which principally concerns us here, since it is culture as conceived by the bourgeoisie – culture with a capital 'C' – which forms the focus of the following chapters. Culture and education were central to German middle-class identity. As Thomas Mann, author of the German language's most important literary study of nineteenth-century bourgeois life (*Buddenbrooks*, 1901), wrote in his 'Reflections of a Non-Political Man'

(*Betrachtungen eines Unpolitischen*, 1918): 'Yes, I am a *Bürger*, and in Germany that is a term whose meaning has as much to do with thought and art, as it has with dignity, solidity and contentment'.[86] The idea of *Kultur* was something common to the entire *Bürgertum*: to all its factions and subdivisions, to the 'makers' as well as the 'thinkers', to the provincials as well as the metropolitans. Of course, this does not mean that every German *Bürger* regularly attended concerts or galleries – the middle classes were, after all, home to the philistine *Spiesser* as well: people known for their narrow minds and limited horizons – but the very fact that such people were singled out for ridicule indicates the lofty perch on which the values of culture and education were placed in nineteenth-century Germany.

Such values were largely a product of the *Gymnasien*, the selective grammar schools founded as part of Wilhelm von Humboldt's Prussian educational reforms of 1810, and derived from classical humanism and German idealism. Humboldt's pedagogic philosophy was focused on the individual, and viewed learning as a quest for knowledge involving all the human faculties. It entailed more than just the acquisition of specific facts or subject skills: it was geared to the process of character formation or cultivation known in German as *Bildung*.[87] This was a concept of vital importance to middle-class Germans throughout the nineteenth century, even if its emancipatory thrust diminished as the century wore on. Count Harry Kessler (1868–1937), who was educated in both Britain and Germany, recalled that on his arrival in Hamburg he found the all-pervasive cult of *Bildung* to be something of a mystery. For a middle-class German to be considered *ungebildet*, he noted, was the equivalent of being labelled 'ungentlemanly' in Britain.[88]

Only a small minority of Germans could actually attend a grammar school – some 238,000 in 1885, out of a total school population of around 8 million[89] – but its influence was greater than such figures might suggest. It offered a nine-year curriculum with a strong emphasis on the Classics: not only were the Greek and Latin languages taught, but the aesthetic values of ancient Greece and Rome, with their stress on symmetry, harmony and balance, were studied too. An idealized vision of Greek antiquity as an earthly paradise, based on works like J. J. Winckelmann's *History of Ancient Art* (1764), subsequently shaped the outlook of generations of grammar-school boys (the 'Tyranny of Greece over Germany', as E. M. Butler put it).[90] It encouraged young middle-class Germans to view the realm of culture and ideas as autonomous; and to see the world in aesthetic terms. Combined with another legacy of the German Enlightenment – the tendency to separate *Geist* (mind or spirit) and *Macht* (power): to allow intellectual freedom, but to demand obedience to secular authority – it could act as a 'social sedative',[91] and lead to an other-worldly introspection or inwardness.

For this reason the *Gymnasium*, and the distinctive outlook it promoted, often feature in debates on the alleged German *Sonderweg*. Even historians who are generally wary of the *Sonderweg* paradigm have accepted that a 'vulgar idealism' became an important feature of bourgeois life and culture in Imperial Germany. We read, for instance, that: 'in the world of the arts, talents that might have been employed for constructive social criticism were used timidly, if at all, and the majority of writers and artists either tacitly accepted the system or professed a spiritless and ineffective alienation';[92] and, from another leading historian: 'little attention was paid in the visual and performing arts to the political dimension of culture, either in a favourable or a hostile sense'.[93] Certainly, it is not difficult to find examples of 'unpolitical' German intellectuals and aesthetes who shunned the low and dirty world of politics and 'civilization'. They represent, however, only part of the picture. As the following chapters indicate, political and social concerns were never far from the surface of Imperial Germany's increasingly varied cultural life.

A second important reason why culture was so central to the educated middle class in Germany was its association with the national movement. The identification of culture and nation can be traced back to the late eighteenth-century period of *Sturm und Drang* ('Storm and Stress'), and particularly to the works of Herder, who argued that each people (*Volk*) – identified by its language – had its own unique character (*Volksgeist*). This view was taken on by the poets, painters and thinkers of the Romantic generation, whose search for a distinctively German vocabulary took place against the backdrop of the Napoleonic wars. Not surprisingly, it was in opposition to France that the newly emerging German culture was conceived and defined, though it would be wrong to think of these romantic 'awakeners to Germanness' (*Erwecker zur Deutschheit*) as nationalists in the modern sense. Few, if any, believed 'Germany' as a cultural entity could or should be synonymous with a single nation-state. In the course of the nineteenth century, however, the nascent national movement came to derive much of its self-justification from the existence of a distinctive German culture; and, after 1871, it was nationalism that connected the sphere of culture with the state.[94]

Indeed, although the cultural consensus built up by middle-class Germans during the course of the nineteenth century became increasingly contested towards the century's end, it was this national dimension – the conviction that Germany had a particular cultural identity, even mission – which continued to unite nearly all the Empire's cultural producers; traditionalist and avant-garde alike.

Nationalism was also very apparent in the sphere of party politics, where the Protestant bourgeois milieu was the most congested and volatile battleground of all, lacking the 'affirming solidarities' enjoyed by other milieus.[95] This state of affairs, which would pertain until 1933, was in part Bismarck's responsibility. The *Kulturkampf* effectively killed off any prospect of an interdenominational bourgeois party emerging in Imperial Germany, whilst his earlier handling of the Prussian constitutional conflict of the early- to mid-1860s (together with his great foreign policy successes) had split German liberalism in two. A broadly pro-Bismarck grouping, the National Liberal Party (NLP), was founded in 1867 and thereafter competed with a more oppositional faction, usually referred to as left liberals, who were themselves subject to frequent splits and secessions.

Other liberal handicaps could be characterized as self-inflicted: a reluctance to enter into dialogue with the working class; a pronounced anti-Catholicism; a deep-seated suspicion of organization; and a failure to establish an associational sub-culture, which all made the transition from a politics dominated by local elites (*Honoratiorenpolitik*) to the new age of mass politics particularly difficult. The aforementioned inability to engage with the growing socialist movement was also reflected in the German language, where the adjective *bürgerlich* became not just a reference to social class or citizenship, but to party politics as well. Non-socialist parties – conservative as well as liberal – are known in German as 'bourgeois' parties, regardless of their social origins.[96]

In the first Reichstag elections, the combined liberal parties won more than half the seats, but their share was to decline steadily in subsequent polls: less than one-third of the seats in 1890; and less than one-quarter in 1912. This electoral decline – which was more pronounced for the NLP than for the left-liberal parties – coupled with a loss of influence on government after Bismarck's shift to the right in the late 1870s, and an inability (or unwillingness) to secure a Westminster-style parliamentary system, add up to a frequently-painted picture of liberal 'failure' in the Empire. Unlike the socialists, Catholics or Conservatives, the liberals did not possess a broadly homogenous social or geographic constituency: their supporters came from both town and country; industry and handicraft; the professions and farming. It became ever more difficult for the liberal parties to speak with one voice: the disparate and conflicting economic interests they represented could only be held together by waffle and fudge. It was hardly surprising then that bourgeois politicians sought solace in nationalist slogans and anti-socialist rhetoric. That these could be effective was demonstrated in the General Elections of 1887 and 1907, but the 'bourgeois' coalitions that secured modest triumphs on each occasion proved unsustainable, and the long-term consequences were damaging.[97]

It should be noted, however, that historians have generally become more sensitive to the particular problems faced by German liberals – not least the unusually generous franchise, which led to the rise of mass political parties much earlier than elsewhere in Europe – and their 'failure' has to some extent been relativized.[98] It has been argued, for instance, that their Reichstag election performance resembled a series of peaks and troughs, rather than a steady decline; and that it only tells half the story, since their real strongholds lay in municipal and state government (where they were beneficiaries of more restricted franchises). The liberals were also to some extent victims of their own success, as Dieter Langewiesche reminds us: 'It may be one of the great ironies of German history that the liberal parties had to pay for the surprisingly rapid consolidation of the national state with the loss of their own political hegemony'. Their success as a national movement, he argues, 'was reflected in their weakness as political parties'.[99]

The political, social and economic dislocations experienced by the German middle classes in the decades either side of 1900, and the pluralization of culture that occurred at around the same time, have been linked by many historians. For some, such as Wolfgang Mommsen, the breakthrough of a multifaceted avant-garde was symptomatic of the 'crisis' in bourgeois society; marking the 'decomposition' of an already heterogeneous class into a host of competing economic and social interest groups.[100] Dieter Langewiesche believes that the rise of cultural modernism, along with new discoveries in the natural sciences, 'undermined the cultural monopoly of the educated elites'. 'Culture', he argues, 'was their most important form of capital, the ground on which their social status rested. And now this capital had been reduced to nothing.'[101] For Thomas Nipperdey on the other hand, the bourgeoisie's 'discovery' of aesthetic modernism was one of its greatest achievements: a notable success for a much-maligned class. Modernism, he argued, established itself in Germany not in spite of the middle classes, but because of them.[102]

These views are actually less far apart than they might first appear. Clearly, the support and patronage of middle-class Germans was vital in the breakthrough of the artistic avant-garde; a fact that was long neglected by historians preoccupied with the *Sonderweg* and the roots of National Socialism. By the same token, however, it is evident that such people cannot be viewed as typical of an entire social stratum, especially one as complex as the German bourgeoisie. If one could talk of a single, coherent 'bourgeois culture' at the beginning of the imperial era, it is certainly no longer the case at the end.

The Catholic cultural milieu

Germany's bourgeois culture was predominantly Protestant, but it should not be forgotten that there was a growing Catholic middle class too. It played a leading role in the creation of a broad and multifaceted socio-cultural milieu, which by the end of the nineteenth century boasted some of Germany's largest mass organizations; an impressive network of local and regional newspapers;[103] and even its own musical, artistic and literary heroes. Middle-class Catholics did read Goethe, but they were more likely to reach for the works of Franz Trautmann, Franz von Seeburg and the prolific 'Konrad von Bolanden', nicknamed the *Preussenfresser* ('Devourer of Prussians'), but actually a priest called Joseph Bischoff. The contents of his books were often betrayed by their titles: *Canossa* (1872–3); *Die Reichsfeinde* ('The Enemies of the Empire', 1872–3); and the trilogy *Urdeutsch* ('Totally German', 1875). Towards the end of the century, Bischoff's polemical approach lost ground to the more anodyne piety of Joseph Spillmann (1842–1905), whose sentimental stories with religious settings enjoyed huge popularity.

Although the formation of a Catholic cultural milieu owed much to the *Kulturkampf*, some elements of it were in place well before the Catholic population became an embattled minority in the new Empire. For instance, the Borromeo Association (which ran Catholic lending libraries), the Boniface Association and the Cecilia Association (for the promotion of Catholic music), all predated the *Reichsgründung*, as did the General Assembly of Catholic

Associations, which first met in 1856. The clubs and lodging houses for Catholic journeymen devised by Adolf Kolping (1813–65) dated as far back as the religious revival of the 1840s. These were the forerunners of the Catholic workers' clubs and trade unions of Imperial Germany, which by 1912 boasted around 500,000 and 350,000 members respectively.[104] It was in the last decades of the nineteenth century, however, that the majority of Imperial Germany's Catholic lay clubs and associations were founded. David Blackbourn, whose works have done so much to shed light on the Empire's Catholic milieu, writes: 'As the century went on, almost no Catholic subgroup lacked its own organization . . . they institutionalized the comforts of the faith and nurtured allegiance to the church.'[105] Amongst the more important were: the Augustine Association for the Promotion of the Catholic Press; the charitable Vincentians and the Elisabeth Association; the Brotherhoods of St Michael (for support of the Vatican) and St Barbara (for miners); the Catholic German Women's League; and the scholarly Görres Society. Many of these associations were originally founded by the Church, but quickly developed independent identities of their own, and their relationship with the clerical hierarchy was often uneasy.

The largest of all the lay societies was the People's Association for Catholic Germany ('Volksverein für das katholische Deutschland'), founded in 1890, which had 805,000 members by 1914. It employed 173 full-time staff at its headquarters in Mönchengladbach, and many Centre politicians had good reason to be grateful for its training courses and publicity machine.[106] The People's Association attempted to protect the electoral constituency of the Centre Party from the lure of socialism, and to ensure a Catholic perspective was always available on the moral and social issues of the day. In this it was certainly more effective than its Protestant counterpart, the Evangelical League, but then, as Walter Laqueur once noted, in Imperial Germany '[t]o be a Protestant meant so much less in daily life than to be a Catholic.'[107]

Despite such impressive feats of organization, the inward-looking and defensive posture of the Catholic milieu was all too apparent. Increasingly, progressive Catholics grew concerned at the 'ghettoization' of Germany's Catholic community, and in a famous essay of 1906, the Centre politician Julius Bachem (1845–1918) urged Catholics to leave their embattled 'tower' and engage constructively with the rest of German society. Much the same message, but in the cultural field, came from the young journalist Carl Muth

(1867–1944), who bemoaned the lack of 'crossover' appeal in the works of Catholic novelists like Joseph Spillmann. Muth particularly objected to the milieu's kneejerk hostility to any artistic or literary endeavour that appeared to break with established tradition ('the malformed products of an age of licence', as one Catholic politician labelled them).[108] In an effort to promote fresh thinking, Muth founded the lively cultural journal *Hochland* in 1903.

As Muth, Bachem and other educated Catholics knew only too well, their confession was still numerically under-represented in higher education, in the bureaucracies of the German states, in the law and in business. This was in part a product of discrimination, and in part a consequence of geography: Catholics tended to live in 'backward' rural and small-town Germany, rather than the major urban centres. It was also, however, a self-inflicted wound, stemming from the Catholic milieu's ghetto mentality, and from the Church's long-standing hostility to the modern world. Indeed, as the sociologist Max Weber argued in his famous 1904 treatise on *The Protestant Ethic and the Spirit of Capitalism*, Catholics and Protestants had long displayed fundamentally different attitudes towards education, enterprise, and personal advancement. The acrimonious reception given to Bachem's and Muth's arguments would seem to indicate that many in the Catholic community still felt the need for thick protective walls, long after the *Kulturkampf* had ended.

Working-class culture

As we have seen, the Catholic milieu embraced many industrial workers. It is important to stress, therefore, that the terms 'working-class culture' and 'labour movement culture' are not synonymous, even if contemporary socialists were prone to using the terms interchangeably.[109] Three-quarters of the German working class remained outside the socialist labour movement, and as Lynn Abrams bluntly puts it: 'The alternative culture of a future utopian society envisaged by leading Social Democrats only made sense to a few educated workers. Saving, adult education, cultural edification: such concepts did not enter the vocabulary of the majority of the working class before the First World War.'[110] Not only did Catholic and ethnic minority workers have their own diverse and often highly localized milieus; there was also a host of working-class associations which had little time for politics or religion of any sort: rabbit breeders, pigeon fanciers, allotment gardeners and so on. Moreover, a popular proletarian culture existed beyond the cosy world of associational life, as the frequent socialist attacks on the *Lumpenproletariat* indicated.[111]

In recent years, much more has been discovered about this wider working-class culture than ever seemed likely, due in large part to the growth in Germany of *Alltagsgeschichte*, the history of everyday life. Such historians have focused in particular on the home, the workplace and the pub, as the key locations of working-class life.[112] Innovative work has also been done on crime, prostitution and sport. It was a culture which retained elements of pre-industrial folk culture (*Volkskultur*) – such as the celebration of saints' days and parish fairs; itinerant street entertainers and wandering minstrels – but had few points of contact with the products of high culture featured elsewhere in this book. There were certainly exceptions, but 'literature' for most working-class Germans meant pulp fiction; and 'art' meant cheap reproduction prints of sentimental or devotional motifs. For reasons of time, money and psychology, galleries and museums were largely out of bounds, while poor and cramped housing left little room for aesthetic considerations. In most respects, however, there appears to have been little fundamental difference between working-class taste and the stylistic choices of the bourgeoisie. Indeed, it seems that most sought to emulate it, as far as their modest means would allow.[113]

Most historiographical attention has focused on the 'alternative culture' of the socialist labour movement, which accompanied working-class Germans from cradle to grave.[114] This multitude of clubs and co-operatives, with evocative names like 'Forwards', 'Freedom' and 'Unity', began to develop during the years of the Anti-Socialist law (*Sozialistengesetz*), first introduced by Bismarck as part of the governmental shift to the right of the late 1870s. The Iron Chancellor regarded socialists as 'fellows without a fatherland' because of their failure to support the Franco-Prussian war and their expressions of sympathy for the doomed Paris Commune of 1871. Taking two failed attempts to assassinate Kaiser Wilhelm as his flimsy pretext, Bismarck introduced a law – which passed at the second attempt in 1878 – to prohibit all social democratic, socialist or communist parties, assemblies and publications, although not the participation of individual socialists in elections. The principal target was the Socialist Workers' Party of Germany (SAPD), which had been formed three years earlier by a merger of Ferdinand Lassalle's

General German Workers' Party and the Social Democratic Workers' Party, led by Wilhelm Liebknecht (1826–1900) and August Bebel (1840–1913). The SAPD – renamed the Social Democratic Party of Germany (SPD) in 1890 – had won almost 10 per cent of the vote in the 1877 Reichstag elections, but was forced underground by the new law. However, despite imprisoning some 1500 socialists in the twelve years of its operation, the law failed to halt the rise of the party.[115] Just as the *Kulturkampf* strengthened political Catholicism, so the Anti-Socialist law forged a new solidarity amongst working-class Germans; many of whom joined ostensibly non-political societies or clubs as a way of identifying with their banned party.

Long after the demise of the Anti-Socialist law, many of these clubs retained their formal independence from the SPD and the free (i.e. socialist) trade unions. Even so, as Vernon Lidtke states: 'To enroll in a club known to have labor movement connections . . . was tantamount to taking a political stand because it implied a set of preferences – political, ideological, social – that were unacceptable to most other segments of German society'.[116] There were umbrella organizations for socialist gymnasts (187,000 members in 1914), hikers, cyclists (150,000 members) and other sportsmen, singers (nearly 3000 choirs in total, with some 200,000 members in 1914) and amateur dramatics. There were educational associations, lending libraries (1100 branches by 1914), youth clubs and funeral societies. There was also a well-developed festival calendar, in which 1 May, 18 March and 31 August were annual highlights.[117]

This alternative culture has been variously portrayed as a tightly-knit 'sub-culture', distinct and isolated from the dominant culture of Imperial Germany (even if it shared many of its characteristics),[118] or as a less cohesive 'social-cultural milieu' just about held together by a number of interacting elements. These included: 'occupational identification, class awareness, secular rituals, symbolisms, the hostility of non-socialist German society, a broad and diffuse sense of ideology'.[119] Leaving aside the prolonged historical debates on whether or not it had the effect of 'negatively integrating' workers into German society, and whether or not it represented a genuine threat to the status quo, it is now widely accepted that there was no 'simple polarity between an essentially coherent "dominant culture" on the one side and an excluded Social Democratic "subculture" on the other'.[120] Neither the socialist nor the Catholic milieu was hermetically sealed.

This is very apparent when one looks at the SPD's attitude towards art and culture. The party considered itself a 'cultural movement' (*Kulturbewegung*) and attempted to explain its stance in the following terms: 'every rising class finds its artistic models in the apex of earlier development. . . . The art of socialism . . . will be an extension of the grand, classical, bourgeois art'.[121] In other words, workers should learn to appreciate the best of bourgeois culture, from Schiller to Beethoven, because it would form the foundation of the 'free and authentic human culture' that would follow from the collapse of capitalism. Although this did not necessarily imply an 'embourgeoisement' of the workers – cultural products can be interpreted in very different ways, depending on the standpoint of the viewer or listener – it is clear that little effort was made to develop a distinctive or coherent socialist cultural theory. The SPD's Central Educational Committee, which was founded in 1906 and entrusted with just such a task, never succeeded in doing so, probably because any formulation would have proved highly divisive. Certainly, for all the talk of *Arbeiterkultur*, it would not have taken much from workers' own existing culture: 'Socialists glorified the proletariat unceasingly, but in practice they did not recommend that a future socialist culture should take over the mores, customs, behavior, and cultural values as they existed in the way of life of contemporary workers'.[122]

In the years before World War One, Labour movement ideologues like Franz Mehring (1846–1919) and Karl Liebknecht (1871–1919) maintained their hostility towards the artistic avant-garde, and greeted the emerging commercial culture, with its 'penny dreadfuls' and its cinematic cheap thrills, with fear and loathing. Their concern was not misplaced, for it would be the leisure and entertainment culture of the twentieth century – the cinema, the dancehall and professional sport – which would eventually undermine their vast network of clubs and associations, although not before they had enjoyed a final flourish in the *Arbeiterkulturbewegung* (workers' culture movement) of the Weimar era.

As for the artists and writers who emerged from Imperial Germany's working-class culture, few gained lasting reputations. The visual artists associated with the milieu were committed but slightly detached observers. The cartoonist and photographer Heinrich Zille (1858–1929), whose works documented everyday life in the tenements and bars of north Berlin, had genuine working-class roots but lived in one of the imperial capital's more comfortable neighbourhoods. The artist Käthe Kollwitz (1867–1945), who lived in the deprived Berlin district of Prenzlauer Berg, originally came from a middle-class background in Königsberg. Kollwitz first made an impact on Wilhelmine society with her cycles of historical engravings, 'The Weavers' Uprising' (1893–7) and 'The Peasants' War' (1903–8), but it was her images of contemporary suffering, drawn from her experience as a socialist doctor's wife, which established her as a chronicler of working-class life. The harrowing 'Pictures of Misery' series for the bourgeois journal *Simplicissimus* (1908–11) still retains a power to shock, some ninety years later. Even so, her work did not fit the SPD's conception of art. One party critic summed up the problem: 'her work expresses a strongly and deeply felt sense of indignation, but it does not evidence a conviction of the certainty of the eventual victory of socialism'.[123] Of all the many divisions in Imperial Germany, the one separating the SPD from the bourgeois parties – and vice-versa – was certainly the most formidable.

2 *Official Culture*

Introduction

In view of the divisions outlined in Chapter 1, it is clear that the German Empire and its leaders faced a formidable task in 1871. Like all new states, the Empire had to secure the allegiance of its disparate populations, to establish its historical and political legitimacy, and to gain the recognition of the international community. It had to do so in the face of considerable opposition, yet – since sovereignty remained with the individual states and rulers – without many of the standard trappings of modern statehood: the Empire had no national anthem of its own,[1] no crown[2] and, until 1892, no official flag.[3] More seriously, with its weak executive (there was no imperial cabinet), small bureaucracy (imperial legislation was often drafted in the Prussian ministries) and modest institutional presence, this 'unfinished nation state'[4] provided its people with few points of contact, and the uninspiring legalese of its constitution was unlikely to win hearts or minds either.

In theory, of course, much of what the Empire lacked could be supplied by its largest and most powerful member state. In reality, however, a combination of initial Prussian scepticism towards the Empire – embodied in the first Emperor himself – and widespread anti-Prussian sentiment elsewhere, meant that the Hohenzollern state was unlikely to be able to perform an integrative role, outside of wartime at least. If a new imperial identity was to be created, it would have to be formed around the idea of 'Germany', and that meant from the sphere of culture. However, here too there were problems. None of the integrative myths and symbols which had been claimed for Germany during the course of the previous century could be adopted by the Empire without reservation, since all were to a greater or lesser degree contaminated by previous usage; either in the oppositional discourse of liberal nationalism, or in the name of a 'greater Germany' led by Austria. In any case, federal sensitivities ruled out all too explicit efforts to 'make Germans' out of Saxons, Württembergians or Bavarians.[5]

Yet the Empire succeeded in its task: by 1914 there was a generation of 30- and 40-year olds who had known nothing but the Empire, and for them it was synonymous with 'Germany'. Contrary to many expectations, and arguably in the face of reality, it had become accepted as a nation-state. How had this come about? To some extent, it was a consequence of 'classic' state-building measures, such as the introduction of a new national currency, the codes of criminal and civil law, or the new commercial code. Certainly, it acquired a 'creeping legitimacy' through its institutions, not least the Reichstag, with its ever-improving electoral turnouts.[6] But the emergence of a distinctive imperial culture, which gradually pervaded most areas of German life, was vitally important too. It was generated in part by the imperial government, the Reichstag and, especially under Wilhelm II, by the office of Emperor itself, but also by other new institutions such as the Imperial Post Office, and by popular forces first unleashed during the 1870–71 war. At the same time it derived much from pre-existing traditions, not only of the Prussian monarchy, army and church, but of the nationally minded middle classes as well. In this way the 'sovereignty of the individual states in cultural matters was qualified by the inescapable will of the nation to have a say'.[7]

This chapter begins with a look at one of the best-known expressions of the new imperial culture: Anton von Werner's paintings of the Empire's proclamation. It then proceeds to examine a variety of other ways in which the Empire manifested itself: not only in painting, but through architecture, monument and ritual as well. Of course, these examples cannot represent the Empire's official culture in its entirety, but they do illustrate typical trends and characteristics. Above all they show the extent to which the creation of an imperial culture depended on the initiative of individual artists, architects and officials, whose instincts and values were those of the national-liberal *Bürgertum* rather than those of the Prussian establishment. The undoubted prominence of the Hohenzollern monarchy in the iconography of the Empire should therefore not be misunderstood. The creation and transmission of this culture was very much a two-way process, which reflected middle-class aspirations every bit as much as those of the Kaiser and the 'traditional elites'.

Anton von Werner and *The Proclamation of the German Empire*

The 27-year old painter Anton von Werner (1843–1915) spent the morning of 15 January 1871 on the frozen water-meadows of the Schiesswiese in Karlsruhe, ice-skating with his fiancée Malvina Schroedter. The couple had first met nearly nine years earlier, when Werner had come from Berlin to study with her father, a successful painter of historical and genre scenes. The Schroedter household was a focal point of cultural life in the Grand Duchy of Baden, frequented by the writer Joseph Victor Scheffel and occasionally the art-loving Grand Duke himself. Even so, the arrival of a somewhat mysterious telegram that morning from the Prussian Lord Chamberlain, Count Eulenburg, on behalf of Crown Prince Friedrich Wilhelm, caused quite a stir. It was addressed to 'Historical Painter v. Werner, Karlsruhe' and, upon the young couple's return, its contents were duly revealed. It promised that if Werner could reach Versailles before 18 January, 'he would experience something worthy of his paintbrush'.[8]

Although Werner had spent a month or so at Versailles in October–November 1870, working on a commission from the Schleswig-Holstein Art Association, he had not expected to return to France in the near future. He assumed that the telegram could only refer to an attack on the French capital, which had been under siege for several months. Werner had arrived too late in October to experience the crucial battles of the Franco-Prussian War, and he had seen little of the siege, hearing only the distant thunder of artillery. He had, however, been given the opportunity to meet many of the key figures of the war, including General Moltke and Crown Prince Friedrich Wilhelm – the future Kaiser Friedrich III – through his acquaintance with the Grand Duke. Although he had not been aware of it at the time, these contacts were to prove crucial for the young artist. It is highly unlikely he would have received the 15 January telegram without them, for in 1871 Werner was a little known painter, from a much more modest background than his surname might suggest.[9]

With some excitement, Werner took up the challenge of the

telegram, and set off almost immediately for Versailles, across the snowy, battle-scarred landscape of eastern France. He did not arrive until four o'clock on the morning of the 18th, and only managed a few hours sleep before calling on Eulenburg. He was somewhat taken aback to be asked whether he had brought a tailcoat with him, and to be given an invitation to a 'festivity' in the Palace later that morning. Had he travelled all that way, in the hope of seeing some real action, only to end up at another high-society function? Well, of course, the answer was yes and no, for the young painter had been given an invitation to the most significant high-society function of the nineteenth century: the proclamation of the German Empire.

Although Werner no doubt looked smart in the tail-coat he had hurriedly purchased from a local tailor, he must have felt out of place as he entered the famous Hall of Mirrors, and found himself amongst some '600 to 800 officers'[10] in a glittering array of military uniforms, all facing a stepped podium, on which a host of flag bearers had assembled. If he had felt like a gatecrasher at someone else's party as he arrived, his status was confirmed as he tried to make his way towards the front of the long, narrow Hall. As Werner passed the imposing figure of Count Perponcher he heard him mutter under his breath: 'what's that civilian doing here?'[11] It is a testament to the young artist's talent and composure that despite his lack of sleep and the intimidating atmosphere, he was able to see through the reflected blur of uniforms, medals, swords and banners to produce a number of quick but accurate sketches and notes. Such was his concentration, however, that he had little idea what was going on around him.[12] Bismarck's speech passed him by, and it was only when the Grand Duke of Baden called out three cheers for 'Kaiser' Wilhelm that he finally realized what he had witnessed. Afterwards, the Grand Duke's words were to become the matter of some dispute: no one could quite agree on the actual phrase he had used. Werner was sure the Grand Duke had said 'Long live His Majesty, Emperor Wilhelm the Victorious'; Theodor Toeche-Mittler, who was also present and later wrote a booklet about the event, recalled 'Long live His Majesty, the German Emperor'; and the Crown Prince recorded in his diary 'Long live His Imperial Majesty, the Emperor Wilhelm'.[13]

The confusion may appear surprising given the contemporary significance of the wording,[14] but it was in keeping with the rather ad hoc nature of this impromptu ceremony that, after all, took place in wartime on foreign soil. As Werner and other witnesses later recalled, the proceedings were remarkably short, characterized less by pomp and circumstance than a rather grim sobriety. A visibly irritated Bismarck read his address in a 'wooden' monotone; Wilhelm left the podium without so much as a glance towards Bismarck. No photographers or reporters were present.[15] Thus it fell to Anton von Werner to interpret and represent the Versailles proclamation, not just to the general public, but also to the participants themselves. The three 'Proclamation' paintings Werner completed over the next decade and a half did not just chronicle the event, they helped to construct it. They assumed iconical status with almost immediate effect, and they continue to shape the way we see the proclamation of the German Empire today.

It is hardly surprising then that historians have long been fascinated with these paintings: a case of *History in Pictures* – the title of a 1993 exhibition of Werner's work[16] – or *Art as History*, the title of a 1988 book by Peter Paret, which includes a chapter on the proclamation.[17] The issue which has most exercised the likes of Paret, Dominik Bartmann and Thomas Gaehtgens, author of a monograph solely on the 'Proclamation' paintings,[18] is the extent to which the three versions differ, and why. As we shall see, the changes are explained principally in terms of the evolving nature of the Prusso-German state. It is often forgotten, however, that before Werner completed any of the famous paintings, he had already made two attempts to depict the events of January 1871.

The first was a painted banner for the main victory parade in Berlin, which took place on 16 June 1871. Unter den Linden was turned into a *Via triumphalis*: flowers rained down from top-floor windows; captured French cannons were set up under the famous lime trees; and the façade of the Academy of Arts was decorated with huge portraits of the German generals. As the parade made its way down the avenue, it passed under a series of painted banners, each around 20 by 18 feet in size. Five artists had worked night and day for two weeks to complete the banners, which each had a prearranged theme. Werner's contribution was entitled *War and Victory* and relied largely on allegory. It depicted the Prussian eagle snatching a crown from the French cockerel, as Germania's chariot crushed Napoleon III beneath its wheels. The banner quickly became something of a *cause célèbre*, for a day or two at least. Kaiser Wilhelm had objected to the degrading portrayal of Napoleon III, but the young artist refused to paint over the image. For a time, the offending bottom right hand corner was covered up by a blank sheet of canvas. This, however, just made onlookers more curious, and prompted crowds to gather around the banner, waiting for a gust of wind to lift the sheet. Berlin children even made up a new rhyme: 'Who's crawling round on his tum-tum-tum? / That must be Napolium.' After Werner raised the matter with the Crown Prince the blank sheet was removed, but it would not be the last time the artist had a difference of opinion with the Kaiser.

This controversy not withstanding, Werner was also commissioned to design a mosaic frieze for the Victory Column in Berlin. The history of the 223-foot high Victory Column, which was unveiled on the third anniversary of the Battle of Sedan in 1873, reflected the turbulent events of the late 1860s. It had been designed in 1865 by the architect Heinrich Strack (1805–80) as a Prussian memorial to the war against Denmark, but building work had stopped in 1866 due to the outbreak of war with Austria. After a revision of the plans, building began once more in 1869, only to stop almost immediately because of the war with France.[19] Werner's frieze was finished as a cartoon in 1873, but not attached to the column in mosaic form until two years later. It was an uncomfortable mixture of allegory, mythology and realism, largely because of numerous personal interventions by the Kaiser himself. On the one hand, Wilhelm – who strongly favoured a sober, realistic approach to painting – insisted on place being found for recognizable portraits of individual generals or princes; yet on the other, he objected to being portrayed personally in the frieze, and requested an allegorical female figure instead. As Werner wryly noted in his memoirs, the dilemma was which female symbol to choose: 'whether for the House Hohenzollern, Prussia, the North German Confederation or the German Empire'?[20]

Partly as a result of the time taken to complete the Victory Column frieze, the first of Werner's 'Proclamation' paintings (usually known as the 'palace' version) had a long and difficult gestation. At a dinner on 28 January 1871 it had been agreed between the Crown Prince and a number of German rulers, including the Grand Duke of Baden, that the Kaiser should be presented with a painting of the proclamation for his Berlin palace. However, difficulties surrounding the financing of the picture then emerged, and a contract was not signed until June 1872. The picture was now to be paid for by the Grand Duke of Baden alone, and was finally presented to Wilhelm I on 22 March 1877, as a surprise eightieth birthday gift from the German rulers and free cities.

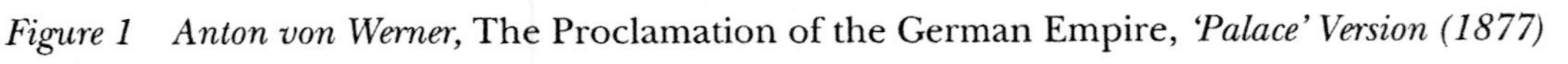

Figure 1 *Anton von Werner,* The Proclamation of the German Empire, *'Palace' Version (1877)*

The painting was widely praised at the time of its unveiling, although subsequently it was criticized by some as lacking drama and pathos.[21] It presented what appeared to be a faithful reproduction of the event, in a photo-realist style that allowed viewers to believe that this was precisely how things happened. As if to confirm this impression, the artist reminds us of his own eyewitness status by including himself in the bottom right hand corner of the painting; one of 128 recognizable individuals portrayed on the canvas. Of course, the fact that our view of the stage is much better than the artist's already suggests that an element of artifice is present in the painting, and the likes of Gaehtgens and Bartmann confirm that this was a carefully-composed construction, rather than a snapshot of historical reality. Indeed, the artist's own memoirs reveal that it was by no means easy to produce a satisfactory composition, even with the assistance of some of the great French historical paintings on hand in the palace of Versailles.

Werner's first version of the 'Proclamation' placed the crowd in the foreground: Bismarck was barely noticeable, and Wilhelm was only 'first among equals' with the other German rulers. The military tone of the proceedings was clear for all to see, but the colourful variety of uniforms – carefully arranged by the artist to ensure that no state was neglected – emphasized that the war against France was a collaborative effort; the north and south German states as comrades-in-arms. Moreover, as Peter Paret points out, the work was not particularly charged with chauvinistic feeling: 'A vindictive interpreter could have made much more of the humiliating aspect of the choice of Versailles for the announcement of German unification'.[22] In short, Werner's first attempt to portray the proclamation on canvas could be said to represent a 'national' and 'liberal' view of proceedings. This reflected Werner's own political position: as a young man, he had been a supporter of the German Progressive Party; later his views were more national liberal in character, but his nationalism was generally moderate in tone.[23] It was also, however, very much in tune with the painter's principal backers – the Grand Duke of Baden and the Crown Prince Friedrich Wilhelm – who were more enthusiastic about unification than the first Emperor himself.

The second, or 'Zeughaus', version of the proclamation was commissioned in the spring of 1880 for the late seventeenth-century Berlin arsenal (*Zeughaus*), which was being converted into a Prussian 'Hall of Fame'. In this version, which was also destroyed in World War Two, the viewer was brought much closer to the action and a number of individuals gained in prominence; notably Wilhelm, Bismarck – in a white dress-coat, rather than the blue uniform he had actually worn – and General von Moltke. The uniforms of the Prussian army now dominated the scene, and their sabres and helmets were waved with more gusto than before. When, on a visit to the Hall of Fame in November 1882, Wilhelm queried the new prominence of his Chancellor, Werner justified the change by pointing out that all the other cuirassiers present had worn white, and Bismarck would have done so, had he brought his white dress-coat with him. Wilhelm, a stickler for military correctness, accepted this explanation.[24] In his memoirs, however, Werner cites aesthetic reasons for depicting Bismarck in white: the mass of dark blue uniforms in this part of the painting needed lightening in some way.

Even more artistic licence was allowed in the third, or 'Friedrichsruh', version of the proclamation, commissioned by the Prussian royal family in February 1885 as a 70th birthday present for Bismarck. As Bismarck's birthday fell on 1 April, Werner had insufficient time to start a completely new painting. Instead, he painted

Figure 2 *Anton von Werner,* The Proclamation of the German Empire, *'Friedrichsruh' Version (1885)*

over one of his preparatory sketches for the Zeughaus version, making sure to add Bismarck's late friend the War Minister Roon, who had been absent from the actual event (and the other versions of the painting) due to illness. He also ensured that Bismarck was portrayed wearing the prestigious order *Pour le mérite*, which he had only been awarded in 1884. Curiously, all the major participants were portrayed as they looked in the 1880s, rather than in 1871, since Werner had recently completed a new set of portrait-sittings. This version of the proclamation – the smallest of the three, and the only one still in existence – came in a highly ornamented frame, topped by an impression of the imperial crown.

A little-known fourth version of the proclamation was painted by Werner in 1913, as a mural for a school hall in his birthplace of Frankfurt an der Oder. Only a fragment of a preliminary sketch survives, but this suggests it was little different from the Friedrichsruh version. As Bartmann notes, this would seem to imply that Bismarck's birthday present came to be seen as 'the only valid version, despite all of its historical untruths'.[25] Whether this was the case or not, all the later versions differ from the original in two important ways: first, the event is portrayed as a predominantly Prussian rather than national affair; and secondly, its legitimacy as an act 'from above' is emphasized by the exclusion of the popular mass, in favour of a select group of powerful individuals around the Prussian crown. It is understandable, therefore, that historians tend to view the changing nature of Werner's 'Proclamation' pictures in overtly political-historical terms: 'the later versions express how Prussia's claim for leadership of the German Empire had become a political reality', as Gaehtgens puts it. [26]

This may well be so, but it is important to stress two other reasons why Werner's view of the proclamation appeared to change over time. First, under the terms of the contract for the first 'palace' version, Werner agreed to make no further copies of the painting, and this may be a perfectly good explanation as to why the other versions turned out so differently. The second reason is perhaps more compelling. We know from the victory parade banner and the Victory Column mosaic that Werner played with many different approaches to the proclamation, allegorical as well as realistic. In the final analysis, however, he was always dependent on the wishes of his clients. Each of Werner's Proclamation paintings was commissioned for a specific purpose and location, and fulfilled a different function. As we have seen, the first version, with its evocation of a German nation united as comrades-in-arms, met with the full approval of the men who commissioned it: the Grand Duke of Baden and the liberal Crown Prince Friedrich Wilhelm. It was only to be expected that a commission for the Prussian Hall of Fame, in the former arsenal, would produce a stronger emphasis on things Prussian and military. Similarly, it was hardly surprising that a painting commissioned as a birthday present for Bismarck should place the recipient centre-stage, surrounded by his friends.

Anton von Werner's desire to give his clients what they wanted reflected his own understanding of the artist's role.[27] It was a rather traditional view, even in the 1870s, but it was made easier by the fact that 'his was an observing not a questioning eye'.[28] If Werner ever had regrets about the compromises such an approach entailed, he could always console himself with the rewards it brought: money and titles, but also the opportunity to observe events in Imperial Germany from the very top. Without ever receiving a formal title, Werner became, in effect, the Empire's official chronicler: the Congress of Berlin (1878); the foundation-stone laying of the Reichstag (1884); the deaths of Wilhelm I and Friedrich III (1888), were all recorded by his sharp eye and steady hand. Admittedly, none of these works gained the same level of recognition as the Proclamation, and none would be remembered today for their aesthetic qualities alone. It is Werner's dubious fate to be remembered in history books, rather than in works of art history.

One other Werner project merits brief mention. As the heroic roll-call of Germany's 1870 victories – Gravelotte, Wörth, Vionville, Sedan – became a patriotic mantra, attempts were made to recreate the 'Sedan experience' for those who had not been present in those muddy French fields at lunchtime on 1 September 1870. The medium chosen was the panorama: a large-scale circular painting with a central viewing point.[29] The 115-metre long Sedan Panorama in Berlin was a commercial undertaking by a Belgian company, and so was rather different from the other paintings discussed in this chapter. Nevertheless, when it was opened on 1 September 1883 it was Wilhelm I who did the honours, in the presence of Moltke and other 'war heroes'. It was not the Empire's first panoramic portrayal of Sedan; nor was it the first war panorama in Berlin; but it was certainly the largest. Painted by a ten-strong team under Werner's leadership, it was housed on the top-floor of a purpose-built structure near Alexanderplatz railway station. Visitors observed the main battlefield scene from a central platform, the outer ring of which rotated at slow speed.[30] This gave people a sense of being in the middle of the action; an illusion heightened by the use of lighting and props. Grass, rocks, weapons and other objects were arranged between the viewer and the canvas to create a three-dimensional effect.

Over the next two years Werner added three supplementary dioramas for the middle floor of the building. These depicted the main events following the Battle itself and were lit from above, while the viewers stood in darkness. Werner went to great lengths to create what he considered was an 'objective' view of the battle. Not only did he visit the site and speak to participants on both sides, but he also carried out detailed research to ensure the uniforms, weaponry and formations were historically accurate. The Kaiser, who had a notoriously sharp eye for military detail, spent an hour and a half studying the panorama and was impressed by its accuracy. For a decade or more it did good business, until the advent of film spelt the end for panoramas and dioramas everywhere.[31]

The restoration of the Imperial Palace in Goslar

Anton von Werner was not the only artist to receive an official commission to paint a representation of the Versailles proclamation. In 1877 the Düsseldorf painter Hermann Wislicenus (1825–99) won a competition to provide a large number of murals for the eleventh-century Imperial Palace in Goslar, which was to include the proclamation as its centrepiece. Before we look at Wislicenus's work, however, it is worth mentioning the project to restore the Imperial Palace itself, which can be seen as one of the earliest expressions of the new imperial culture, even if the restoration was not paid for out of imperial funds.[32] Most of the Palace dated from the mid-eleventh century. It had flourished for around two centuries, hosting numerous Imperial Diets, before a fire in 1289 badly damaged the building. Thereafter it had fallen into disrepair. The collapse of a wall in 1865 appeared to be the final straw, since the town council of Goslar, which owned the building, could not afford to pay for its restoration.

The architectural significance of the former palace, which was the oldest secular building in Germany and the largest Romanesque palace anywhere in Europe, was recognized by art historians, and under public pressure a deal was secured with the Kingdom of Hanover, which gained possession of the building. However, no sooner had the building been sold, than Hanover was annexed by Prussia. The building, which continued to decay, thereby changed hands once more. Then, in the midst of the Franco-Prussian War, the people of Goslar seized the initiative. A petition, pointing out the building's importance and signed by hundreds of the town's citizens, was sent to Prussia's King Wilhelm in Versailles. For the first time, not only the architectural significance of the building was stressed, but also its symbolic value to the nation, as a unique document of German greatness from an earlier era.

With the proclamation of the German Empire in 1871, this symbolic value was increased still further, as a second petition from Goslar town council to the Reichstag in May 1871 made clear: 'A great age has given birth to great events; the German Empire has been re-established . . . once again a German Reichstag is sitting, as in the very best days of German history'.[33] No doubt the town council's enthusiasm for unification was genuine, but to play on these historical links represented sound tactical thinking too. Although the Reichstag was unable to provide assistance – the building was Prussian property – a large majority of members expressed the wish that the Prussian government should act to save it. Subsequently, both Wilhelm I and the Prussian government supported the idea of restoration, and work began in early 1873. The architects entrusted with the project were criticized in some quarters for their comparatively sober and sensitive designs, but after six years hard work they could at least point to a building that was no longer in danger of collapse.

The restoration was paid for by Prussian taxpayers and by contributions from the private funds of Wilhelm I, who visited the site in 1875 accompanied by Prince Karl and Crown Prince Friedrich Wilhelm. It was the Crown Prince who was later widely credited with the idea of 'decorating' the main hall, although this had been suggested by the local authorities some months before.[34] Between December 1876 and August 1877 the Prussian *Kultusministerium* staged a competition to find an artist capable of providing sufficient murals for the 48-metre hall. The competition guidelines had little to say on the content of the paintings, except that the proclamation of 1871 should be depicted, as should subjects from the period 1050 to 1253, when the Imperial Palace was at its zenith.

Wislicenus was a controversial but deserving winner, not least because he alone attempted to resolve the difficulty of having to portray recent events and historic tales on the same walls, whilst bringing both into harmony with the Romanesque setting. He was convinced that a realistic depiction of the Versailles proclamation or the Battle of Sedan would not sit easily alongside medieval scenes, so he resolved to use the same idealistic and allegorical approach for all the murals. In this, Wislicenus differed from all but one of the other entrants, who followed Anton von Werner in depicting the events of 18 January 1871 in a realistic style. Wislicenus's proposals were also more ambitious than those of other competitors, involving paintings of various sizes and on three different narrative levels: saga (the Barbarossa legend); fairy tale (Sleeping Beauty) and history (medieval and modern), with the scenes from medieval history framed by an additional prologue (Charlemagne) and epilogue (Luther). It was, in short, an original pictorial programme of some thought and complexity.

Of course, Wislicenus's iconography may now appear anything but original, since the image of Wilhelm I as 'Barbablanca', a latter-day incarnation of the Hohenstaufen Emperor Friedrich Barbarossa, became something of a cliché in the Second Empire,[35] and the metaphor of the German nation as Sleeping Beauty does not seem overly subtle either. It would appear, however, that at least some contemporaries found Wislicenus's cycle difficult to follow. When the competition entries went on display in the Berlin National Gallery in 1877, the critic of the semi-official *Norddeutsche Allgemeine* newspaper commented: 'The choice of his subjects is arbitrary and lacks not only a main theme, but also fails to penetrate deep into the spirit of history',[36] and the correspondent of the *Reichsanzeiger* made much the same complaint. The principal reason for their difficulty would appear to have been the artist's choice of historical scenes, which did not show the medieval Emperors in a uniformly positive light. Even so, neither the Prussian government nor the Kaiser objected to the jury's decision, and on 8 March 1878 Wislicenus received the request to proceed with the first of fifty-three murals, to be painted directly onto plaster. In fact, it is likely that the authorities were delighted with Wislicenus's proposed picture-cycle. Clearly, the Prussian government wanted the murals to make the connection between the 'first' and 'second' German Empires: to emphasize a line of continuity between emperors medieval and modern. Wislicenus's designs did that, but they also offered something else. Not only did they help to legitimize the 1871 Empire and its ruler, but they also suggested reasons why the first Empire had failed, and in this sense they fulfilled a pedagogic function too.

It should be noted that at the time of the *Reichsgründung*, the instrumentalization of the Holy Roman Empire in the service of Imperial Germany was highly contentious, and its acceptance was by no means inevitable. For many who supported a Prussian-led 'little German' solution to the national question, including the so-called Prussian or 'Borussian' School of historians, the Holy Roman Empire had always been an object of contempt or pity. Not only had it been weak and divided, but it had for centuries placed German national interests behind those of the Church of Rome. This was a view shared by many close to the Prussian throne, who regarded the 'Kaiser' title with considerable ambivalence. Before 1871, those sympathetic to the medieval Empire tended to be Catholics, or supporters of a 'greater Germany' under Habsburg leadership. It took a considerable re-writing of history to reclaim even part of the Holy Roman Empire's past for the new Empire, which had, after all, completely different borders, was ruled by a different dynasty, and had a very different relationship with the Roman Church. However, there were some, such as the historian Johann Gustav Droysen (1808–86), who were prepared to try. Droysen, whose fourteen-volume history of Prussia had established the Borussian school in the 1850s, highlighted a particularly dim and distant chapter of the medieval Empire's history, the Hohenstaufen era, when the emperors had been in frequent conflict with Rome, but which was nevertheless 'in a certain way . . . the pinnacle of our history'.[37]

For some Borussian historians, such as Heinrich von Sybel (1817–95), these conflicts had been a tragic waste of German effort; an example of the medieval emperors' preoccupation with their Italian rather than German territories. For Droysen and others, however, it was just about possible to portray the Hohenstaufen emperors as spiritual forefathers of Luther and Bismarck, challenging Papal supremacy in the name of the German people. This particular historical view – a strand of Borussian historiography sometimes known as 'Ghibellinism' – was reflected in many expressions of Imperial Germany's officially sanctioned culture, including the Goslar murals. Even if, as Monika Arndt suggests, Wislicenus himself was closer to the Sybel view, his picture cycle would have been unimaginable without the work of 'Ghibelline' historians.[38]

It took nearly twenty years for Wislicenus to complete the murals, partly because he remained a full-time professor at the Düsseldorf Academy of Art until 1882, but also because the municipal authorities in Goslar were anxious not to damage the nascent tourist trade.

While Wislicenus painted, the Palace remained open, and parties of visitors trooped by with disturbing regularity. The picture cycle was finally finished in 1897 and unveiled with remarkably little ceremony on the artist's 72nd birthday. In the eyes of contemporaries it was the picture cycle that was largely responsible for converting the historic building into a national monument, although it is interesting to note how quickly this function faded in the absence of regular ceremonies or rituals, which as we shall see were the life-blood of such structures. Even so, the picture cycle was a considerable personal achievement for Wislicenus, who died less than two years later, and an influential one as well. By the time the full cycle was complete, few citizens would have had difficulties in understanding its imagery or historical framework.

Multi-purpose monuments: Cologne Cathedral and the Hermann Monument

The completion of Cologne Cathedral in 1880 – some 580 years behind schedule – still came too soon to mark the definitive end of the *Kulturkampf.* Nevertheless, despite serious misgivings on both sides, hostilities between the Prussian state and organized Catholicism had lessened sufficiently for both monarch and at least some clergy to participate in a grandiose state ceremony. In time, the cathedral would become a monument to the reconciliation of Catholic Church and Prussian state. This was, however, just one strand in a complex web of symbolic meanings which became attached to the cathedral, and which made it a truly multi-purpose monument.[39] The ceremony was held on 15 October 1880; the birthday of the late King Friedrich Wilhelm IV, who had done much to further the project.

While still Crown Prince, the romantically inclined Friedrich Wilhelm had made his first visit to the cathedral (1814) and enthusiastically taken up a cause championed by the likes of Goethe, Humboldt, Schlegel, Görres and Arndt. The ramshackle, half-finished cathedral, which had been used as a military store during the years of French occupation, had provided writers and poets with an all-too-obvious metaphor for the state of the German nation, especially since its long-ridiculed Gothic style of architecture was identified – erroneously as it happens – as quintessentially German.[40] Patriotic fervour at the victory over Napoleon in the Battle of Leipzig

(1813) prompted calls for the cathedral to be completed as a national monument, and Sulpiz Boisserée (1783–1854) began to put together a fine collection of drawings and copperplate prints, including views of how a finished cathedral might look. In the repressive political climate that followed the Congress of Vienna little more was heard. Even so, without the interest of such individuals, it is quite conceivable that Cologne's cathedral could have gone the same way as those in Goslar and Hamburg, and been demolished in the early nineteenth century. In the 1820s and 1830s, the rump cathedral was restored, but nothing more: there certainly appeared to be little support in the wider population for the notion of re-starting the half-finished building.

This began to change around 1840, for a wide variety of reasons: an upsurge in popular Catholicism, particularly in the Rhineland; a wave of patriotism stimulated by renewed fears of French invasion; the Gothic revival in architecture throughout Europe, which also produced the Houses of Parliament at Westminster; and the onset of industrialization in the Cologne area, which produced an increasingly wealthy and self-confident bourgeoisie in the city. Most important of all, however, was the accession of Friedrich Wilhelm IV to the Prussian throne. It was Friedrich Wilhelm who in 1842 gave the order to recommence building, even if the precise details of what was to be built remained unclear. The project was to be funded jointly by the Prussian crown and by private donations, which were to be raised by the Cathedral Building Association, founded in Cologne in 1840 and with some 10,000 members by 1845.

Around 1842 the cathedral project was a genuinely popular cause, supported by a bizarre coalition that stretched from Karl Marx's newspaper (the *Rheinische Zeitung*) and the dissident poet Heinrich Heine, to the Hohenzollern monarchy and the Catholic Church. Thomas Nipperdey memorably termed this the 'omnibus function' of the cathedral-building movement.[41] Marx and Heine soon disembarked – Heine's scepticism is already obvious in *Germany: A Winter's Tale* (1844) – but the project retained the backing of large sections of the population. It was the breadth of this coalition that kept the project on course, even when money was in short supply. It was the fact that the building was simultaneously a national monument, an architectural monument and a religious monument that ensured its completion. It also meant, however, that Catholics faced a constant struggle to uphold the religious significance of the cathedral, against an increasingly dominant national-political discourse.

This was reflected in the largely secular character of the 15 October 1880 ceremony, and in the following day's carnival-style procession around the streets of Cologne, funded by local businesses and wealthy individuals to the tune of 140,000 RM.[42] The floats, a series of *tableaux-vivants*, featuring scenes from Rhineland and German history, were designed by artists from the Düsseldorf Academy, and thousands of participants appeared in historical costume.[43] As the last section of the procession passed the cathedral, a bell made from captured French cannons and donated by Wilhelm I tolled in celebration. Religious contemplation was in short supply. Not that the predominantly Catholic population of Cologne seemed to mind: the long-awaited completion of their cathedral was a great excuse for a party. Moreover, despite a long-standing hostility to all things Prussian – which had as much to do with the post-Napoleonic settlement as with the *Kulturkampf* – even the Kaiser was warmly welcomed. Wilhelm himself was pleasantly surprised: 'Not one discordant note was heard, and even the famously tactless Cologne public was respectable in its enthusiasm, in a way that I have never seen before'.[44]

The nineteenth-century building project that had most in common with the completion of Cologne Cathedral was arguably the construction of a monument to Hermann or Arminius, the legendary Germanic leader who defeated the Romans in the Battle of the Teutoburg forest in 9AD. Just like the cathedral, this project was a dream of the Romantic movement; stimulated by a revival of interest in Germany's distant past, and by the victory over Napoleon in 1813; paid for in large part by voluntary donations from ordinary citizens; subject to the shifting fortunes of four turbulent decades for the German national movement, and ultimately unveiled by a triumphant Kaiser Wilhelm I. Of course, the Hermann Monument is a less substantial work of art than Cologne Cathedral, but its political symbolism is every bit as interesting and complex.[45]

The monument, which was built on the Grotenburg near Detmold in the tiny principality of Lippe between 1838 and 1875, was the life's work of one man: the sculptor Ernst von Bandel (1800–76). Like many Romantics, Bandel saw Hermann – rather fancifully, it must be said – as the first man to have a vision of a united Germany. His intention was to erect a genuinely national monument, funded by donations from ordinary Germans and without reliance on the dynastic rulers of the individual states.[46] Voluntary associations in all the German states, including Austria, raised some impressive sums,

Figure 3 *Hermann monument, Detmold (1838–75). Architect: Ernst von Bandel*

and further contributions came from more unexpected quarters.[47] It was slow going, however, and on several occasions building stopped altogether. Like the national movement itself, the monument was given fresh impetus by Prussians in the 1860s, and in particular by Wilhelm I, who visited the site for the first time in June 1869 and then essentially took the project over.[48] By the time the copper-plated Hermann was unveiled by the Kaiser in August 1875, in a ceremony watched by some 30,000 people, he had become a symbol of the new 'little' German Empire and its rulers. Indeed, Andreas Dörner has described the Hermann Myth as the 'central founding-myth of the Empire'.[49]

Hermann's outstretched (and Krupp-sponsored) sword, with its inscription 'German unity is my strength / My strength is Germany's power', had initially symbolized a 'humanity united in freedom'. Now it was seen to be warding off Germany's enemies, whether across the border in France, or over the Alps in Rome, from where Hermann's original foes had come. At the height of the *Kulturkampf* such historical parallels were inescapable, even though many Catholics had contributed to the building of the monument in the first place. The following section will attempt to demonstrate, however, that if the Hermann Monument was essentially a popular project hijacked by the Prussian state and the Hohenzollern monarchy, there were many other monuments that were conceived by the Hohenzollern monarchy and, at least in part, reclaimed by the people.

National monuments in Imperial Germany

Both the Imperial Palace in Goslar and Cologne Cathedral were frequently referred to as 'national monuments' during the imperial era, even though neither building had originally been conceived with this function in mind. It was only in the nineteenth century that they became thought of in these terms. The timing was no coincidence, because the years spanning the French Revolution to World War One were a golden age for monuments, whether national or dynastic, old or new.[50] In German speaking Europe, for instance, so-called national monuments were built for the 'nations' of Prussia, Austria and Bavaria, as well as for a variety of 'Germanies'. They were commissioned by different groups of people for different purposes, and reflect different conceptions of nationhood.

Such monuments were seen as an important tool in the construction of identities, serving to anchor myths and symbols in the consciousness of the people, and providing a focal point for ceremonies and festivals. They were particularly common in newly created, expanded or restored states, where rulers were particularly eager to establish their legitimacy, and where symbols of unity were in great demand. The proliferation of monuments in the nineteenth century can also be explained in terms of the need for symbols of permanence in a rapidly changing society. It was no coincidence that the monument mania coincided with the great age of archaeology. The survival of ancient pyramids and temples seemed to demonstrate that monumental architecture could guarantee, if not eternity, then at least some kind of permanence. The purpose-built monuments were erected in three main waves during the imperial era: monuments to commemorate the wars of 1864–71 and the creation of the Second Empire; Kaiser Wilhelm monuments to mark the centenary of his birth in 1897; and Bismarck monuments, mostly built after the Iron Chancellor's death in 1898 (see Chapter 3).

The vast majority of monuments in the first wave were simple local war memorials, although these often commemorated the creation of the Empire too, by including a symbol such as the imperial eagle, or a portrait of the first emperor. Apart from the Victory Column in Berlin, the most important monument to be commissioned and erected during the reign of Wilhelm I was undoubtedly the Niederwald Monument, built on a hillside above the Rhine between 1877 and 1883.[51] Although the project was first mooted in the victory year of 1871, it was made clear from the beginning that it to be a 'national' rather than a 'victory' monument, and vulgar triumphalism was generally avoided in both its design and in speeches at the opening ceremony.[52] Thus the ten-metre bronze figure of Germania, the focal point of the monument, did not seek confrontation with France – her gaze is directed towards her own land – and the sword in her left hand is not brandished as aggressively as Hermann's in the Teutoburg forest.

The design, by Johannes Schilling (1828–1910), was only accepted after a wearisome process. Two committees had been established to oversee the project, but the monument was to be paid for by the general public, through voluntary donations and the fund-raising activities of veterans' associations, gymnastics societies, choirs and the like. The target was 750,000 RM, but by 1877 only two-thirds of that figure had been scraped together. Competitions to find an appropriate design had been held in 1872 and 1873, but none of the favoured entries could be built with the limited funds available. Schilling, who had entered both competitions, was eventually commissioned to produce a more modest design, which won general approval. Ironically, the final cost reached some 1.2 million RM, and the shortfall had to be made up by money from imperial government funds.[53]

The monument, which was completed in 1883, portrays Germania holding the new imperial crown aloft in her right hand, as if she is about to place it on her head. She stands on a plinth decorated with depictions of the unification process, including 190 lifesize portraits of German rulers and generals who had met at Versailles. The whole ensemble is dedicated to the 'courageous and victorious uprising of the German people' in 1870–1, rather than the actions of monarchs and generals. This was one reason why the monument was so disliked by Bismarck, who pointedly stayed away from the unveiling ceremony. The choice of Germania as the central figure also met with his disapproval for, as Lothar Gall has shown, this was a young woman with a contrary character, who had displayed oppositional tendencies in the past.[54]

Whilst 'Germania' had a long tradition as a literary or geographical term, its use as an iconographical symbol for the German empire or nation only emerged in the eighteenth century. In the aftermath of the French revolution, and the discovery – or invention – of the nation as a political, as well as a linguistic or cultural concept, Germania took on some of the character traits of her French sister Marianne. In the first half of the nineteenth century, a number of paintings and unbuilt monuments employed Germania as an anti-dynastic symbol, representing the 'eternal' German nation, above and beyond the existing political order. As such, Germania could be a symbol of popular sovereignty, and also a symbol for supporters of a 'greater Germany'; neither of which rested easily with Bismarck's view of the Second Empire, or indeed its constitutional realities.

On the other hand, Germania was a vague and malleable icon, which could be used in very different ways. This was apparent even at the opening ceremony for the Niederwald Monument, when the Prussian government's representative in Wiesbaden, Botho Eulenburg, made a speech that 're-interpreted' Johannes Schilling's design in a manner acceptable to the Hohenzollern monarchy.[55] Thereafter, Germania featured frequently in the official iconography of the Empire: not only in other monuments of the 1870s and 1880s, but also in a large bronze sculpture on the roof of the Reichstag building, on a set of stamps first issued in 1900,[56] and on a 100 RM banknote, where she is portrayed sitting under an oak tree, as battleships from the imperial navy steam past in convoy. Perhaps most famously of all, she is depicted guiding the peoples of Europe to salvation from the 'Yellow Peril' in the widely-reproduced 1895 drawing by Hermann Knackfuss, 'Peoples of Europe, protect your holiest goods', which was based on a sketch by Kaiser Wilhelm II himself.

Wilhelm II was, of course, a skilled self-publicist, who delighted in monuments, festivals and processions. His role in the cultural life of the Empire will be looked at in more detail in Chapter 5, but it is important to note at this point his contribution to the second wave of national monument building in the German Empire. The pretext was the centenary of Wilhelm I's birth in 1897, which led to some 400 new monuments being built during the 1890s dedicated specifically to the first Emperor. In this way, Wilhelm II hoped to elevate his grandfather to the posthumous status of 'Wilhelm the Great'. In part, this was another instalment in the ongoing effort to legitimize the Hohenzollern dynasty by linking the Second Empire to that of Charlemagne (known in German as Karl the Great), but it was also an expression of Wilhelm's personal desire 'to rule, as well as to reign'. Although 'Wilhelm the Great' was indeed inscribed on most of the monuments, the term did not gain widespread usage and ultimately did Wilhelm II (who gained the nickname 'Wilhelm the Other') more harm than good. Kaiser Wilhelm monuments were built throughout the Empire, but the distribution was far from even. Particular concentrations were to be found in Prussia's conservative eastern provinces, and in its western provinces of the Rhineland and Westphalia, which it had only gained in 1815. By way of contrast, there were less than 40 Kaiser Wilhelm monuments in the whole of southern Germany, and just a handful in Bavaria. The best-known monuments in this category are probably those at the Deutsches Eck in Koblenz, Hohensyburg and Porta Westfalica in Westphalia, and the Kyffhäuser Monument in north western Thuringia.

Many of these were landscape monuments: that is to say, like the aforementioned Hermann and Niederwald Monuments, they were built in the open country rather than in urban locations, even if most were within easy reach of major urban centres. They were usually built on hills, often with historical, mythical or literary associations, and were visible for many miles. Landscape monuments, which had their origins in the enclosed world of the cemetery, had progressed to the private realm of the landscape garden in the seventeenth and eighteenth centuries, before reaching the open countryside around the start of the nineteenth century. That progression was more marked in Germany than elsewhere in Europe.

It is tempting to contrast the proliferation of landscape monuments in Germany with the more metropolitan settings of national monuments in other European states, and to find an explanation not only in the absence of an undisputed capital city, but also in a peculiarly German bond with nature. In this vein, George Mosse characterizes the monuments as churches, for what he terms the 'secular religion' of nationalism; 'sacred spaces' where the nation could worship itself.[57] It is certainly true that many of the best-known monuments were sited at what might be termed 'sacred spaces'. Not only were places like the Teutoburg forest, the Rhine gorge and the Kyffhäuser hills, full of historical and mythical associations, but the actual monument sites were cheek by jowl with important archaeological remains. The Hermann Monument was built just a few hundred metres from a prehistoric circle; the Niederwald Monument is surrounded by ruined castles and towers; and few sites have richer historical associations than the Kyffhäuser: it was reputed to be a sacred hill in pre-Christian times, it became a centre for Christian pilgrimage in the early Middle Ages, and then the site of an important fortress, the Reichsburg. Above all, of course, it became associated with the myth of Barbarossa, the medieval Emperor whose legend was used in the monument to convey historical legitimacy on Kaiser Wilhelm and the Hohenzollern dynasty.

Many of the German monuments were first conceived in the Romantic era, and some of their promoters, such as Ernst von Bandel, were indeed prone to mythologize the German landscape in pseudo-religious terms. Clearly, by placing a monument in an 'unspoilt' natural landscape, the intention was to establish some sort of link with the past and to establish lines of continuity to the present. However, nineteenth-century monument builders played fast and loose with both history and nature. Leaving aside the fact that there was little historical evidence to suggest that the Battle of the Teutoburg forest had actually taken place there, the promoters of the Hermann Monument decided to plant oak trees around the monument, even though there was no record of oaks ever standing on the site. They did so only because the oak tree was an important national symbol, and featured prominently in literary and artistic accounts of Hermann's escapades. Even more crassly, when the

Kyffhäuser Monument was built, the ruins of the medieval Reichsburg were all but destroyed in the process, wiping out centuries of history in the space of a few months. This act of historical vandalism made a mockery of the pious tones adopted by the monument's promoters, and casts doubt on the site's 'sacred' status. In fact, as we shall see, the atmosphere at these monuments was generally far from sacred.

The Reichsburg was sacrificed because of the mammoth proportions of the Kyffhäuser Monument, and size was of course a key feature of all these monuments. As part of a garden or a cemetery, landscape monuments had generally been modest in scale, but in the open countryside there were no constraints. Only the sky was the limit, and Imperial Germany's national monuments were amongst the largest in the world; a fact which unsettled sensitive aesthetes at the turn of the century. Maximilian Harden's journal *Die Zukunft* attacked the 'hollow pathos' of Wilhelmine monuments; and terms like 'monument plague', 'monument mania' and 'monument madness' become commonplace around 1900.[58]

It was not that monument architects were oblivious to the surrounding environment. Bruno Schmitz (1858–1916), who was responsible for many of the national monuments of Imperial Germany, designed each one for a particular topographical situation and demonstrated an evolving appreciation of how large-scale monuments work.[59] Rather, it was the wide variety of roles the monuments were expected to perform, which forced them to adopt such gargantuan proportions. First, there was the political role. Wilhelm II made no secret of his belief that these monuments should serve a didactic purpose, and his officials followed suit. Their role as political weapons was widely and explicitly acknowledged. An 1891 discussion paper issued by the Rhineland provincial government on their planned monument to Wilhelm I described it as a 'counterweight against the efforts of the Socialists'.[60] The Kaiser-Wilhelm-Monument on the Hohensyburg outside Dortmund, which was largely funded by Ruhr industrialists, was described as a place where the industrial worker could forget the burdens of the working day, and realize once more 'that there is no greater pleasure for him on earth than to be a German'.[61]

Meanwhile, the Kyffhäuser Monument was the brainchild of Alfred Westphal, one of the leaders of the 'Deutsche Kriegerbund', an increasingly anti-socialist and anti-semitic veterans' association. In his speech at the foundation stone laying ceremony the local prince,

Günther von Schwarzburg-Rudolstadt, said the monument should be 'a warning to future generations, that they should remain true to Kaiser and Empire, to patriotism and to the institutions of the monarchical state'.[62] For their part, the Social Democrats were the only party to vote in the Reichstag against the expenditure of 4 million RM on the Kaiser-Wilhelm-Monument in Berlin, attacking the 'patriotic masquerade' of this 'monument nonsense'.[63] In effect, such monuments were expected to occupy the commanding heights of the German countryside on behalf of certain ideological positions, and to do so effectively, they had to be visible for miles around. In the words of the architect Wilhelm Kreis, they had to become 'architectural mountains'.[64]

The extent to which monuments succeeded in creating 'political landscapes' is best illustrated by reference to a monument which ironically is not on a hill: the Kaiser-Wilhelm-Monument at the Deutsches Eck ('German Corner') in Koblenz. Of course, the confluence of two major rivers – in this case the Rhine and Mosel – is an unusual and visually arresting natural feature, but it was in fact the monument which was responsible for creating the now-familiar landscape. Prints and early photographs show that until the late nineteenth century, the point at which the two rivers merged was a genuine 'corner', almost a right angle. At that time, it had no historical or literary significance. The name 'Deutsches Eck', although centuries old, had no political meaning but merely referred to a nearby hospital established by the Germanic Order in medieval times. The characteristic 'ship's bow' feature we know today only came with the building of the monument in 1895–7, which moved the mouth of the Mosel River some 200 metres north, and also involved the construction of a 350-metre promenade.

The monument's own dimensions were equally eye-catching. In total it was some 36 metres in height, and the equestrian statue of Wilhelm I alone had a height of 14 metres, making it the tallest in the world at the time of construction. The portrayal of rulers on horseback – holding the reins of state – has a very long tradition, but an interesting feature of the Koblenz design was the apparent recognition that a simple equestrian statue was no longer sufficient in an age of mass movements, iron and blood. Thus the statue, by Emil Hundrieser (1846–1911), was placed in a vast architectural setting, with a rustic columned hall and an 88-metre pergola by Bruno Schmitz.[65] At this point Schmitz was still searching for a distinctively Germanic architectural language, which would reach its apogee in

Figure 4 *Kaiser Wilhelm I monument, Koblenz (1895–7). Architect: Bruno Schmitz*

his design for the Völkerschlacht Monument in Leipzig (see Chapter 6). After the completion of the Koblenz monument, with its inscription 'The Empire will never be destroyed, if you are united and loyal', the term 'Deutsches Eck' gained a national-political connotation that had not been present before.

Rituals of authority were played out at the unveiling ceremonies of each of these monuments. Invariably, Wilhelm II was present, along with local princes, dignatories, maids-of-honour and a variety of martial and musical accompaniments. The date was usually chosen to coincide more or less with a significant historical event, and the day's programme was mapped out and rehearsed for weeks in advance. The opening ceremony for the Kyffhäuser monument, for instance, took place on 18 June 1896, which was in the anniversary week of both the Battle of Waterloo and the entry of Wilhelm I into Berlin after the victory of 1871. On this occasion there was a 101-gun salute and a military march past, reflecting the fact that the monument was the pet project of a veterans' association. At other monument openings, local volunteers or sharpshooter societies generally provided the firepower.

These were events on a very large scale. At the unveiling of the Kaiser-Wilhelm-Monument at Porta Westfalica, for example, there was a band of 1300 trombonists, while some 43,000 gymnasts participated in the opening of the Völkerschlacht Monument. Even so, things did not always go to plan. The unveiling ceremony for the Koblenz monument, on the morning of 31 August 1897, was struck by a thunderstorm and torrential downpour and had to be postponed until later that afternoon.[66] With a nod towards the Nuremberg rallies, George Mosse makes much of these rituals. Certainly, national monuments need to be seen as more than the sum of their material parts. To bring such a stone colossus alive, active participation and imagination is required: without this participation, monuments quickly lose their intended meaning. However, although Mosse refers frequently to the national festivals and ceremonies that were intended to take place at monument sites, it would appear that in practice the opening ceremonies were not followed up by regular patriotic or political events.

In fact, with most of these monuments, the desire to place an ideological marker on the landscape was only one part of a complicated mix of motives. Towns and districts competed for monuments in Imperial Germany in much the same way that today they compete for the right to host major sporting events. Brochures and leaflets would be published; politicians and officials lobbied; rival bids rubbished in the local press. Often the final decision was taken by a vote in a provincial or state parliament. Behind the patriotic rhetoric, there generally lay much more pragmatic calculations. When Koblenz won the race for the Rhine province's official monument to Wilhelm I, it did so despite fierce competition from larger cities such as Cologne, and with widespread local support. More than 80,000 RM was raised in this predominantly Catholic town in 1888 alone. A large donation even came from the Catholic Reading Circle, which had been banned during the *Kulturkampf* in 1874. This reflected not only the improved relationship between Catholics and the state in Wilhelmine Germany, but also recognition in the leading circles of the town that such a monument would be good for business. Indeed, almost all the post-1871 monuments were built with a commercial function in mind.

A good example is the aforementioned Niederwald Monument. The initial instigator of this project was not a nationalist association, the government or the Kaiser, but Ferdinand Heyl, an author of tourist guidebooks and sometime spa director in Wiesbaden, and who saw a new monument as a way of attracting more paying visitors to the region.[67] The idea was picked up by a couple of local officials, including the prefect of Rüdesheim, a small winemaking town, which was eager to stimulate trade. The monument was built at a point that offered the best view of the Rhine, as it entered the dramatic valley landscape of cliffs, castles and vineyards, 225 metres below. The civic authorities, eager to ensure that visitors to the monument should first walk through the narrow streets of their town, encouraged the building of a rack and pinion railway to carry visitors from the centre of Rüdesheim to the monument. The railway opened in 1884, by which time the town's shops and winebars were already doing a roaring trade. In the space of a few years, Rüdesheim was transformed from a nondescript working town into the archetypal Rhineland tourist trap.[68]

Similarly, although the Kyffhäuser hills were never likely to be able to match the Rhineland in terms of tourism, the building of a monument there was also seen as good for business. In 1889 an architectural journal, the *Deutsche Bauzeitung*, wrote: 'Even if neither the location, nor probably the monument itself, is likely to be able to compete with the Niederwald and its Germania, it is certainly not to be doubted that upon completion, the Kyffhäuser will be able to exert a strong pull on the stream of pleasure-seeking travellers'.[69]

Thus when the plans for the monument were drawn up, a large restaurant and public house were included as a matter of course by the architect Bruno Schmitz. In other words, the leisure and tourism function was not a later development, but an integral feature of the original conception: observation platforms, coin-in-slot telescopes, refreshment and souvenir stands were there from the start. Contemporary guides to the Kyffhäuser explicitly praised not only the monument, but the beautiful view from the restaurant windows, and the quality of the catering.

The restaurant building also features prominently in many of the 250 different postcards of the monument in circulation in the 1900s. Other postcards on sale at monuments were less site-specific. In 1878, for example, a grammar school headmaster wrote a letter of complaint, after his teenage son bought a photograph of a scantily clad woman at the Hermann Monument. There is no record of such items being removed from sale. Meanwhile, at the Deutsches Eck, photographers touted for business on the monument's steps, offering tourists a personal memento of their visit. So lucrative was the trade that acrimonious turf-wars broke out between rival photographers. The authorities responded by employing a permanent, uniformed monument-keeper, who had his own hut from 1899, and by introducing a licence fee for approved photographers. Thousands of individuals and groups were photographed here: some were tourists, others were professional or political groups. The latter were by no means only of a nationalist or right-wing character.

The commercial development of monument sites went on unabated in the later imperial era. The village of Porta Westfalica, for instance, gained an improbably large railway station and numerous guesthouses in the 1900s, to cope with the upturn in tourist trade which had followed the opening of their Kaiser-Wilhelm-Monument (also designed by the ubiquitous Bruno Schmitz). For day-trippers from the Ruhr or Hanover, Porta Westfalica represented a good day out, and much the same could be said of the chain of Bismarck towers built across the Empire after 1898. These towers were erected as 'mighty granite beacons' to Bismarck's memory, but it was the splendid views that accounted for their popularity with walkers and hikers.

Perhaps the most blatant example of a monument landscape developed for commercial gain comes from the town of Edenkoben in the Palatinate.[70] Ferdinand Kuby, a local notable whose family owned both a vineyard and the town's leading hotel, was eager to develop Edenkoben as a spa, and to boost its profile against the neighbouring towns of Landau and Neustadt. To this end, Kuby was the driving force behind the 'Edenkoben and District Beautification Association', whose first attempt to put Edenkoben on the tourist map was to build a road to a nearby hill, which had been renamed the Werderberg in 1871. A small monument, the Strassburg Stone, was erected on the hill in the 1870s, but when this failed to attract much interest, a much more substantial monument was planned: the so-called Victory and Peace Monument was started in 1895 and completed in 1899. Further monuments were added in 1898 (a Bismarck Stone), 1902 (a Moltke Stone), and at regular intervals thereafter: all of which were proudly depicted on panoramic postcards of the day. It appears that Kuby's efforts to stimulate local tourism were successful, because in 1898 he was able to open the Waldhaus, a new hotel within walking distance of the monuments, and thereafter the family wine business went from strength to strength.

In the end, it was not the rituals of authority that brought the national monuments of Imperial Germany to life, but the growth of leisure and tourism, as income levels rose and the railway network expanded. The result was a 'national communion' of a very different kind: one that included workers and women, Catholics and Jews. This does not mean, however, that one can afford to disregard the resonance of the monuments' political messages.[71] On the contrary, the very fact that the monuments were popular destinations, associated with leisure and relaxation, helped to anchor their myths and symbols in the consciousness of a much larger proportion of the German people. As the example of Catholic pilgrimage sites in late nineteenth-century Europe shows, the two roles of nationalist shrine and tourist attraction were not mutually exclusive. Mass tourism, blatant commercialism and devout faith could co-exist in some sort of harmony. Moreover, as the use of these national monuments in the political discourse of the 1920s and 1930s demonstrates, no amount of tourism could erase their political message. Indeed, many of them retain sufficient political charge to cause controversy today.[72]

Imperial ceremonial and festival culture

One reason why the restoration of Koblenz's Kaiser-Wilhelm-Monument in the 1990s proved so controversial was the date chosen to lift the new bronze statue from a Rhine barge on to its historic plinth. Whether intentional or not, the organizers' choice of 2 September 1993 touched a raw nerve, because this day had been used to unveil monuments before: in 1873, for example, when the Victory Column in Berlin had been opened, or in 1894 and 1896, when Kaiser-Wilhelm-Monuments had been unveiled in Königsberg and Breslau. This date was namely the anniversary of the key Prussian victory over the French at Sedan in 1870, and subsequently of a major annual festival in the German Empire.

The genesis of 'Sedan Day', as the festival became known, has been researched by a number of historians, but it is worth sketching again here.[73] National festivals, which like national monuments had their modern origins in late eighteenth-century France, became one of the German bourgeoisie's favoured methods of self-expression in the nineteenth century. The festivals at the Wartburg in 1817, at Hambach in 1832, and throughout the German states in Friedrich Schiller's centenary year of 1859, are most frequently cited, but the pan-German gatherings of gymnasts, choirs and shooting societies which all began on an annual basis in the 1860s, were important too.[74] The state-orchestrated Sedan Day festivals of the later Wilhelmine era were, in contrast, highly regimented occasions with a strong streak of authoritarianism. Even so, it should not be forgotten that Sedan Day also had bourgeois roots, and was not imposed from above.

In 1871 several separate groups – all of a Protestant, national-liberal character – began lobbying for an annual national festival to celebrate the *Reichsgründung*. One such group was Bluntschli and von Holtzendorff's 'Protestant Association', which argued: 'No law and no parliamentary debate is capable of doing as much damage to the radicals and socialists, to the Jesuits and the ultramontanes, as an annual public festival to serve as a reminder of just who were the founders of the German Empire in 1870, and who were its enemies'.[75] Another group was led by the vicar and charity worker Friedrich von Bodelschwingh, who had been pressing for a 'festival of peace' with a strong religious content since the 1860s. It was one of Bodelschwingh's colleagues who first suggested 2 September as an ideal day for such an event, which should proceed along the lines of the 'German Festival' drawn up by Ernst Moritz Arndt during the Napoleonic wars. Despite an early and unexpected reverse for campaigners in April 1871, when Wilhelm I declined to back legislation for the introduction of a Sedan Day holiday, a number of unofficial Sedan festivals took place on a local basis in 1871 and 1872.[76] These early festivals, organized by the Lutheran church and national-liberal circles, had a strong religious character, with thanksgiving services, prayers for peace, bell-ringing, bonfires and patriotic songs.

Wilhelm's decision did not mean the idea of a national festival lacked official support, but reflected the fact that under the 1871 constitution, public holidays and festivals were the responsibility of the individual states. As early as August 1871 the Prussian government made it clear that officials and schoolchildren should be allowed to participate in Sedan Day celebrations. The day began to take on a more official character in Prussia from 1873 onwards. That year's Sedan Day witnessed the opening ceremony of the Victory Column in Berlin, complete with parades of soldiers and veterans. Parades were repeated in the following years, but outside of Berlin and a few garrison towns the organization of Sedan Day events remained in the hands of committees of bourgeois notables. Sedan Day in the industrial town of Harburg can be taken as typical. The celebrations always began with a mid-day peal of bells from the town's churches, followed an hour later by a salute of cannon-fire from the Schwarzenberg, a hill to the west of the town. In the late afternoon a procession of veterans, schoolchildren, gymnasts and patriotic associations would make its way from the town centre to the Schwarzenberg. The evening's festivities were concentrated here, with a bonfire and a large marquee. Inside the marquee the pattern of proceedings changed little over the decades, with music, *tableaux-vivants*, toasts and a patriotic speech, invariably given by the headmaster of the local grammar school.[77]

In 1889 and in many subsequent years, 2 September coincided with the Prussian army's annual autumn manouevres, and this together with the predilections of the new Kaiser opened up new opportunities for military spectacle. The manouevres were a key date in the social, as well as the military calendar, and Wilhelm II used the numerous gala dinners and receptions to give some of his most outspoken speeches. Sedan Day celebrations reached their zenith in 1895, when the twenty-fifth anniversary of the battle was commemorated with the opening of the Kaiser-Wilhelm-Memorial Church in Berlin.

Opposition to Sedan Day developed quickly amongst socialist and Catholic groups. The internationalist Eisenach faction of the labour movement had been opposed from the beginning, while in the early 1870s the Lassallean faction celebrated their own deceased leader as an explicit alternative to the 'Sedan festival-fuddle', with a similar mixture of ritual, rhetoric and songs.[78] A socialist counter-demonstration to 'St Sedan's Day' was held in Brunswick as early as 1872. Catholic opposition was first articulated by Bishop Ketteler of Mainz, who in 1874 banned priests in his diocese from participating in Sedan Day events. He claimed, with some justification, that it was not a national festival, but a purely national-liberal and Protestant celebration, although not all Catholics supported his action. There was one point, however, on which the Catholic Ketteler and the Protestant Bodelschwingh were in complete agreement: after 1873 the festival was no longer a day for sombre reflection and Christian prayer. This was not only the consequence of its increasingly military tone, but also of the drinking and dancing that quickly became a feature of every 2 September. This was precisely the sort of behaviour that Bodelschwingh had wanted to avoid, but there was little he – or the Catholic priests who referred to it as 'Satan Day' – could do.

One proposal to combat this 'misuse' of Sedan Day was the idea, first muted in 1895, of staging a Germanic equivalent of the Olympic Games, which were of course revived in 1896. The idea of a games festival, to be held in the first week of September every five years, was promoted by a new National Festival Society, in conjunction with the Central Committee for the Promotion of Popular and Youth Games. The festival was to be staged at or near the site of a national monument, and seven sites competed to host the first event in 1900: Rüdesheim, Leipzig, Kassel, Mainz, Goslar, Porta Westfalica and the Kyffhäuser. The Goslar bid included a games village designed by Anton von Behr, and a 12,000 capacity festival hall. The Kyffhäuser bid included a vast arena for up to 400,000 participants and spectators. In 1898 three sites were shortlisted, with Rüdesheim eventually selected to stage the festival. However, the planned arena was never built and the festival never staged. Despite the establishment of a nationwide fund-raising committee, insufficient donations were received for the festival to proceed.

Sedan Day itself declined in importance after the turn of the century – not least after Germany and France had co-operated in the military 'task force' to China in 1900 – and neither the imperial nor the Prussian governments took action to revive it. Outside of Prussia, it had always been celebrated inconsistently. Only ten of the twenty-five imperial states recognized it as an official holiday: few, if any, events took place in Upper Bavaria, and little interest was registered in Silesia either. In Baden it was too close to an important dynastic celebration to be celebrated as a major state occasion. In Hamburg the parade was switched from 2 September to the nearest Sunday in the hope of attracting bigger crowds, but with little success. By 1915 only six states were still commemorating 2 September, and the last major Sedan Day ceremonies were held in 1917, when they provided the backdrop to the founding of the ultra-nationalist German Fatherland Party. In 1919 the new republican government formally brought Sedan Day festivities to an end.

Apart from Sedan Day, the ceremonial calendar of the German Empire was dominated by royal birthdays, weddings and funerals in the individual states. Although Prussian royal occasions now became imperial affairs – the birthdays of Wilhelm I (22 March) and Wilhelm II (27 January) were marked throughout the Empire during their respective reigns, even if only fifteen states declared them as official holidays – little else changed.[79] Indeed, Wilhelm I specifically asked that his birthday should continue to be celebrated in the pre-1871 fashion. In Prussia this meant prayers in church for the monarch on the Sunday before his birthday, as well as on the day itself; parades of the guards' regiments in Berlin; an extra portion of meat for prison inmates; special assemblies in schools, with speeches, prayers and patriotic songs; then banquets, with music, drinking and dancing in the evening. The Prussian *Kultusministerium* stated the purpose of such birthday celebrations was 'to arouse and to nurture love of the Fatherland, reverence for the hereditary ruling family, patriotic feeling, and the loyalty of subjects'.[80] A similar pattern was followed for the Kings of Bavaria, Saxony and Württemberg, and in all the other dynastically ruled states of the Empire.

With the accession of Wilhelm II, imperial birthday celebrations became more elaborate and took on an air of ancestor worship. The new Emperor ensured that the recurring theme of the day was to pay homage to former Hohenzollern rulers, and particularly his grandfather Wilhelm I. The academic Wilhelm Oncken was commissioned to write a hagiography of the first Emperor that gained widespread distribution in schools and ministries. The 1897 centenary of Wilhelm I's birth, which as we have seen was marked by a host of new monuments, also witnessed a special three-day festival planned by Wilhelm II. Every effort was made for the celebrations to appear spontaneous and popular – Prussian state employees were given paid leave to participate – but the reality was very different. In fact, imperial birthday celebrations became ever more orchestrated. This was particularly the case in 1909, when Wilhelm II's 50th birthday fell during the '*Daily Telegraph* Crisis', prompting a series of events staged for the benefit of the international press corps.

Building the Empire: imperial architecture from post office to parliament

The federal structure of the Empire meant that most public buildings remained the responsibility of the individual states or municipal authorities. Post office buildings were one of the few ways in which the Empire became present in every German city and town, outside of Bavaria and Württemberg at least.[81] Indeed, one could argue that it was through the post office that the new Empire became a reality for ordinary Germans. Before 1871, the majority of post offices in the German states were either located in coaching inns or in small, often temporary, buildings. Many of those that had been established by the private Thurn-und-Taxis post office were in a state of decay, and some of the state buildings were little better. They also tended to be located in the wrong place, since they had developed along old coaching routes, and were no longer able to meet the needs of an increasingly urban society, whose principal transport artery was the railway. The *Reichsgründung* led to a unification of German postal services – minus Bavaria and Württemberg – firstly under the name of the General Post Office, and then from 1880 as the Imperial Post Office. The General Post Office began, however, with just 233 of its own post offices, with another 4408 sub-post offices in rented premises. A major building programme was clearly necessary.

Between 1871 and 1875 some half dozen new main post offices were built. The design of the buildings at this time was the responsibility of the general building or public works departments of the individual states. In 1875, however, a new Imperial Building Department was established. It was funded out of the imperial budget and was initially intended to provide a service for all sections of the imperial administration, although in practice almost all its work was for the Post Office. Under its first head, August Kind (1824–1904), the Empire was divided into thirteen districts, and each was allocated an architectural official, whose principal job was to ensure that a predetermined set of building guidelines was followed.[82] When it came to the design of major post offices or other important public buildings, these officials were often overlooked in favour of more prominent men in private practice.

The practice of 'going outside' the imperial administration for the design of prestige projects proved controversial, and was frequently attacked in Reichstag budget debates as a waste of public money. It was strongly defended, however, by the Postmaster-General Heinrich von Stephan (1831–97), who was first appointed in 1870 and who became known as the 'Bismarck of the Post Office'. The architecture of the Imperial Post Office is nowadays more closely associated with the name of Stephan than any architect or designer. This is largely justified, since Stephan insisted on vetting all building plans personally, and was not afraid to reject work either. Proposals for the facade of the main post office in Strasbourg, for instance, had to be revised three times before they met with his approval. Stephan was also responsible for the guidelines that all post office architects had to follow. Between 1875 and Stephan's death in 1897 around 300 new post offices were built, and if one counts the sub-post offices which were designed by the Post Office and built by the private sector, the figure would rise to several thousand.

Stephan insisted that architects working for the Post Office should always build in harmony with the local surroundings and traditions; use high-quality materials; and meet the latest health and safety requirements, with regard to access, heating, ventilation and lighting. For the facades unnecessary ornamentation was to be avoided, though a wide variety of historical styles were employed. Amidst their stylistic diversity there were a number of features common to nearly all Stephan's post offices: the imperial coat of arms, a clock and a lively roofscape, often involving towers and domes. Following the amalgamation of postal and telegraph services in 1876, such roof structures were considered necessary to house the growing web of telegraph wires.

The new post offices had a mixed reception. Although many admired their architecture, others complained about the 'extravagant' use of public money. The term 'postal palaces' (*Postpaläste*) was used widely, and with derogatory intent. Largely in response to such criticisms, it was decided in 1880 that all major postal building projects should be audited by the Prussian Ministry of Public Works. This practice continued for a decade, until Heinrich von Stephan was able to convince the imperial government that it was unnecessary. In this he was aided by the new Emperor, Wilhelm II, a great admirer of Stephan's post office architecture. Thereafter, the Kaiser effectively assumed the role of the Prussian Ministry of Public Works himself. It is difficult to ascertain the true extent of his role, but sixty-one of the Post Office plans displayed in the Post Office Museum in Berlin in 1904 featured comments and alterations in Wilhelm II's hand.[83]

Stephan's critics also highlighted the fact that many of the main post office buildings were decorated with expensive sculptures. Vast sums were indeed expended, but Stephan always justified the expense by arguing that cheaply-constructed buildings cost more to maintain, and were therefore more expensive in the long run. Moreover, it was pointed out by Stephan that the post office was the public's most common point of contact with the state, and therefore had to be worthy. Ultimately, he argued, the buildings of the Imperial Post Office were 'monuments to unification' and had to reflect this in their appearance.[84] In this way Stephan, who rose from a modest background to become a hereditary peer, had a major influence on the urban landscape of Imperial Germany.

Apart from post offices, imperial buildings were conspicuous only by their absence in the early years of the Empire. The buildings for the major imperial institutions, such as the Imperial Bank in Berlin or the Imperial High Court in Leipzig, took decades to get off the ground. The latter was awarded to Leipzig in 1877, but the land was not purchased until 1883 and the building was not finally completed until 1895. A large number of legal buildings were also erected by the individual states around the same time, culminating in Friedrich Thiersch's massive 330-room Munich courthouse of 1890–8, which also accommodated the Bavarian Ministry of Justice.[85] Such structures really were 'palaces of justice', in which the full weight of the law was brought to bear on the hapless individual, expressed through an architecture of monumental Baroque staircases, towering entrance halls and cold marble floors.[86]

The expansion of the imperial administration, resulting from legislation like Bismarck's social welfare bills, also produced a number of new buildings in the 1880s and 1890s, and most of these, such as the Imperial Insurance Office's headquarters, were to be found in Berlin. Even so, the city with the most imperial German architecture was arguably not the Prussian metropolis, but Strasbourg, the capital of annexed Alsace-Lorraine, which more than doubled in size under the terms of an 1875 contract between the city and the Empire. In addition to the aforementioned post office, a new railway station, hospital, law courts, university, library, government buildings and an Imperial Palace, were all built in the city before the end of the century.[87] Although shell damage from the 1870 war made a certain amount of rebuilding unavoidable, these politically-motivated prestige projects were masterminded from the Imperial Chancellor's Office in Berlin, in the manner of a colonial administration. The impression of a colonial capital was strengthened by the manner in which most of these monumental pale sandstone buildings were grouped together around a *forum imperiale*, the Kaiserplatz, at the centre of the spacious new town, some distance from the narrow medieval streets of the old city.

The expansion of the city served two functions: to accommodate the expected population influx from the other side of the Rhine (the word 'Germanization' was used frequently and shamelessly); and to impress on the local population that the German presence would be permanent. With symbolic intent, the redevelopment of Strasbourg began with the Imperial Palace, requested by Wilhelm I in 1873 and built between 1883 and 1889. The eclectic and highly ornamented facade of the Palace, however, failed to impress either German or French architectural critics, and the Kaiser (who likened it to a railway station) was disappointed too. The Palais du Rhin, as it is known today, occupied one side of Kaiserplatz. It was soon joined by government buildings and the university library in monumental Italian Renaissance style.

Facing the Imperial Palace, at the other end of a 500-metre axis, stood the main building of the new university, designed after an 1878 competition and opened in 1884. The Kaiser-Wilhelm-University was financed from imperial funds and had its professors appointed by the Emperor himself. It had first been proposed in May 1871 by the liberal Reichstag deputies Thomas and Köchly, and opened in temporary premises just one year later. The stated intention was to demonstrate to Alsatians the superiority of German intellect over French mannerism, and amongst its innovations was the very first university Chair in Modern German Literature (1872).[88] However, the majority of the local population stayed away, both from the German department and the university as a whole, preferring to send their children to French universities instead.

Other cultural institutions to receive some imperial funding included the privately established Germanic National Museum in Nuremberg (1852), and the Romano-Germanic Museum in Mainz. In later years the imperial budget also expanded to include limited funds for the support of German exhibitions abroad; for the purchase of paintings and sculptures for public buildings; for monuments; and for a number of archaeological and scientific research institutions. Even so, this expenditure represented only a small fraction of the annual education and culture budget of states like Prussia or Bavaria,[89] and all attempts to expand the imperial role further met with concerted opposition.

Initiatives like Heinrich and Julius Hart's open letter to Bismarck therefore fell on deaf ears. Their 1882 letter had reasoned: 'Should Germany's culture ever reach the height which is due to its best sons, and which it has to reach in order to maintain its position within the council of nations, it is necessary to create a special office of the Empire for literature, theatre, science, and the arts'.[90] Such efforts failed partly for constitutional reasons, reflecting the states' reluctance to cede any more sovereignty: 'If, in the course of our political development, we have had to relinquish certain political privileges, we nevertheless do not want to let ourselves be supplanted in the domain of art', as the Bavarian minister Krafft von Crailsheim put it in 1890.[91] It was also, however, a consequence of the genuine diversity of German cultural traditions and of the desire of ruling houses to maintain their own long-standing programmes of cultural promotion.

Thus it was that a national art gallery for the German Empire was never built. Admittedly, a so-called National Gallery had been established in Berlin in 1861, but it was purely a Prussian affair, based on a bequest from the businessman Johann Heinrich Wagener. Wagener left his collection of 262 oil paintings to the Prussian state on condition that the collection would not be dispersed, and would be open to the public. Wagener's collection was international in character, with French, Belgian, Dutch and British, as well as German painters represented. To expand the collection the Prussian government established a committee of artists and experts, the *Landeskunstkommission*, with a modest budget.[92] Construction of the Berlin National Gallery building began in 1866 but it did not open until a decade later. The National Gallery then took its place alongside the other institutions – the Old Museum (1824–30); New Museum (1843–55) and Kaiser-Friedrich Museum (1897–1904) – on Berlin's 'Museums Island', which had been set aside by King Friedrich Wilhelm IV as a 'sanctuary of art and learning'. All of these institutions benefited greatly from the city's elevation to imperial capital.[93]

The Berlin building project that received the most national and international press coverage, however, was undoubtedly the Reichstag. For the first two decades of the German Empire, its parliament met in temporary accommodation.[94] Its initial location was in the Leipziger Strasse, the home of the lower house of the Prussian parliament since 1849. The chamber was small and drafty, however, and members began to press for a new building almost immediately. The preference of the majority of parliamentarians was a purpose-built detached building, with a 'dignified' and 'worthy' monumental form. Bismarck and others in the government were less enthusiastic. They believed the conversion of an existing building in the Prussian government district would suffice. A joint commission was established to investigate the options, and reached the conclusion that with conditions in the Leipziger Strasse intolerable, a different short-term venue would have to be used until a permanent location was found. Thus it was agreed that the Reichstag should meet in the inner courtyard of the Royal Porcelain Factory, also in the Leipziger Strasse, which was covered and converted into a stage-set parliament, almost entirely of wood, roofing felt and glass.

The first sitting in the new chamber took place in October 1871. Although it was admired as a 'miracle' of craftsmanship, many faults soon became apparent. The tendency of glass ceiling-panels to fall into the chamber at irregular intervals was a particular worry. Even so, the Reichstag was to remain at this 'temporary' location for some twenty-three years. The commission's preferred site for a permanent Reichstag building was that of the Palais Raczynski, on the eastern side of Königsplatz, where the Victory Column was also in the process of construction. In retrospect this seems an unlikely and unfortunate choice. Not only was the site some distance from the government district, but it proved extremely difficult to gain possession of the land from the aged Count Raczynski, who had built a large villa there, and had no desire to move. However, even without possession of the land an international architectural competition was held in 1872, which attracted 101 entries, including 30 from abroad. The competition jury was divided between those who favoured a Gothic solution, such as the Catholic politician and publicist August Reichensperger (1808–95), and those who wanted a building in the Prussian Classical tradition, built by a Berlin architect. The jury's deliberations were never made public, but in the third round of voting a design by the Gotha architect Ludwig Bohnstedt (1822–85) won by a single vote.

It very quickly became apparent, however, that there was little likelihood of it being built. The issue of the land remained unresolved, and the commission reported back to the Reichstag that none of the prizewinning entries could be built without substantial alterations. For much of the next decade, attempts to gain ownership of the preferred site continued. However, so did the search for alternative locations. Critics pointed out that if the building were erected on the Raczynski site, it would almost certainly face the Square, and thus away from the political heart of Berlin: politicians and officials would enter via a back door, while the front entrance remained unused. Despite such drawbacks, the death of Count Raczynski increased the likelihood of progress, and in late 1881 a majority of the Reichstag voted to purchase the Raczynski site. To the disgust of Bohnstedt, it was decided to stage a second design competition, even though the Gotha architect had offered to make any necessary alterations to his earlier winning entry. Bohnstedt's supporters suspected a conspiracy against the non-Prussian architect, orchestrated by the *Deutsche Bauzeitung* journal on behalf of the Berlin architectural establishment. The 1882 competition was limited to German-speaking architects, but nevertheless attracted around 190 entries. The jury awarded joint first prizes to Paul Wallot (1841–1912) from Frankfurt, and Friedrich Thiersch from Munich, with the former winning the commission.[95]

Wallot became a famous name almost overnight. South German architects were delighted with his victory, since few 'outsiders' had ever been invited to build in the Prussian capital. However, winning the competition was just the start of the hard work for Wallot. It would be more than a decade before the Reichstag was finished, and in the meantime, the architect would have to revise his plans on more than one occasion. Superficially, the most problematic aspect of the building was the dome – whether it should be sited over the parliamentary chamber, or the foyer; how big it should be; and whether it was necessary at all – but the underlying problem was more fundamental. The Reichstag building was meant to represent the German people, but despite a vigorous debate no consensus could be reached about which architectural style did this best.[96]

This debate, which had been around since the late eighteenth century and would continue well into the twentieth century, went further than the official buildings of the new Empire, but it was thrown into particularly sharp relief by the Reichstag competitions. Almost every conceivable style had its supporters, but also its drawbacks. Classicism was too closely associated with Berlin and the Prussian monarchy for a national parliamentary building; academic Gothic was seen to be too Catholic; North German Brick Gothic was too Protestant; the German Renaissance too bourgeois; the Baroque too aristocratic.[97] The absence of a consensus on the national style was something Wallot himself bemoaned. He wrote in a letter of 1890: 'The one thing that I always regret, is that we are erecting a national building, without possessing a national style'.[98] Wallot's Reichstag design contained elements of the Renaissance and of the

Figure 5 *Prizewinning design for the Reichstag building, Berlin, by Paul Wallot (1882)*

Baroque, but after the building was nearly complete, he confessed in a private letter to second thoughts. The nearest thing to a German national style he now believed was the Romanesque, which – unlike the Gothic – was also sufficiently 'monumental'.[99] Wallot's dissatisfaction with the building was exacerbated by the numerous alterations requested by a succession of civil servants, parliamentary commissions and emperors. The latter, in particular, caused Wallot no end of problems.

The foundation stone of the new Reichstag was laid on 9 June 1884; a date chosen for Kaiser Wilhelm I's convenience. Around eighty people were invited to perform the ritual of hitting the foundation stone three times: the Emperor, Empress, Crown Prince, Crown Princess, the other princes and princesses, the Chancellor, the General Field Marshalls, members of the Bundesrat, members of the Prussian Ministry of State, and the heads of the imperial administration all had their go before the President of the Reichstag's turn came. As Michael Cullen puts it: 'a conscious ridiculing of parliament and the principle of popular sovereignty is a central thread running through the whole history of the building'.[100]

The ceremony to mark the completion of the Reichstag building, held on 5 December 1894, was also a predominantly royal ceremony, and was overshadowed by a growing tension between the Emperor and the architect. At the time, the building received a mixed reception. It gained praise from some unexpected quarters – the SPD politician August Bebel; progressive cultural figures like Alfred Lichtwark and Bruno Taut – and a scale model of the building won a medal at the 1893 Chicago World's Fair. On the other hand, the Berlin city architect Ludwig Hoffmann felt 'everything' about the building was wrong; he termed it a 'first-class hearse'. Hoffmann's view was famously shared by Wilhelm II. On a trip to Italy in 1893 he described the Reichstag building – or the 'imperial apehouse', as he later dubbed it – as the 'pinnacle of tastelessness'.[101]

It is not clear whether Wilhelm II's objections were principally aesthetic, political or personal, although all of these played a part. Certainly Wilhelm II took a personal dislike to Wallot, although the architect was never sure why. It may have been the result of an unintended slight, given during a royal visit to the building site in 1889. After Wallot had explained his plans to Wilhelm, the young Emperor had laid his hand on the architect's shoulder and said 'My son, we'll do it like this', before preparing to sketch some alterations. The horrified Wallot had blurted out 'Majesty, that's not possible!' which was not the sort of thing Wilhelm liked to hear.[102] Other possible reasons why Wilhelm may have turned against Wallot were the machinations of the sculptor Reinhold Begas (a royal favourite) or the fact that the Reichstag's glass dome challenged the royal palace's dominant position on the Berlin skyline. Ultimately, given that the building housed a democratically elected assembly, any design would probably have met with Wilhelm's disapproval. He paid the finished building just one single visit, in 1906, and never used the purpose-built *Kaisersalon.*

During the protracted process of building a new home for the Reichstag, all three emperors of Imperial Germany attempted to exert a personal influence on its design. Wilhelm I, who received a report of Wallot's plans in January 1883, made extensive notes in the margins: 'That the architecture is to be executed with a sense of noble and dignified simplicity is completely in agreement with my own view',[103] he commented. On the other hand his son, the future Friedrich III, was far from happy with the jury's decision. Both the anglophile Friedrich and his British wife Vicky favoured a neo-Gothic Reichstag, which would take Westminster as its model in more ways than one. As we have seen throughout this chapter, the emperors of Imperial Germany expressed views on artistic and cultural matters as a matter of course, and took many decisions that influenced the direction of cultural policy. This was inevitable given their constitutional responsibilities, even if these were essentially Prussian rather than imperial in character. As King of Prussia, the Kaiser was not only responsible for the selection and appointment of the Prussian *Kultusminister,* but also the directors of museums and galleries, such as the Berlin National Gallery, which remained an essentially Prussian institution. The King of Prussia could also veto the jury selection of medal winners at the exhibitions of the Prussian Academy of Arts.[104] However, the extent to which the different emperors attempted to make use of their influence varied considerably.

Wilhelm I was not known for his love of the arts. In the early 1830s, however, he had possessed sufficient confidence in his drawing ability to send the famous Prussian architect Schinkel his own ideas for a new palace on Unter den Linden. The palace, where Wilhelm was to live for the next half-century, was eventually built in a much scaled-down form. The cost-conscious Prince Wilhelm's frugal nature was later to cause headaches for other architects and artists. Anton von Werner, for instance, had to use all his powers of persuasion to convince the first Emperor that the mosaic frieze on the

Victory Column should be executed in Italian marble, rather than a cheaper material. Wilhelm I paid particularly close attention to the development of the Prussian Hall of Fame and the Berlin National Gallery, where he intervened to change a dedication on the building's pediment. He was also involved in the design of a number of statues and monuments in Berlin, but as a matter of principle he did not attend the unveiling of statues of civilians, such as the monument to Goethe in the Berlin Tiergarten (1880).

During his 99-day reign Friedrich III had little opportunity to exert an influence on the cultural or political life of the Empire, but as Crown Prince he had demonstrated a keen interest in art and archaeology, and at his father's instigation had overseen the expansion of Berlin's museums. His enthusiasms were shared by his wife, whose preference for artistic over courtly company was well known. Sculptors, artists and architects were frequently invited to social events at the Crown Prince's palace. The royal couple also entertained every autumn in Potsdam, inviting a small group of artists and intellectuals for a simple meal on Thursday evenings, which led Georg Malkowsky to go as far as to invoke the memory of the Medicis.[105] Before he became Kaiser, Friedrich paid regular visits to the studios of artists and sculptors with his wife. On occasions, the couple's eldest sons, Wilhelm and Heinrich, would come too, accompanied by their tutor Hinzpeter. Indeed, it was probably at this time that Wilhelm developed his own personal interest in art and architecture, which would eventually lead him to him take drawing lessons from Anton von Werner.

In essence, Wilhelm II's views on art were not so very different from his more liberal father; indeed Wilhelm saw himself as the 'heir and executor' of his parents' aesthetic vision.[106] As we shall see in Chapter 5, however, the 'young emperor' had both the desire and the opportunity to exert his influence on a much wider scale than Friedrich ever envisaged. By the time Wilhelm II came to the throne, an official imperial culture was already at least part-formed. As this chapter has indicated, its creation was a hit-and-miss affair, shaped by a disparate group of comparatively little-known individuals – Werner, Wislicenus, Schmitz, Stephan and Wallot, amongst others – who through a combination of chance, initiative and ability each found themselves in a position to interpret and express the new Empire in symbolic form.

The five named men all came from middle-class backgrounds, two were based in southern Germany, and – as far as it is possible to judge – all could be characterized as national liberal in outlook. Although they did not enjoy complete freedom of manouevre, it is also clear that their individual aesthetic solutions were arrived at independently, and with little official co-ordination. Of course, the subsequent transmission of this culture through schools and universities, the army and navy, the press and public ritual, was often highly orchestrated, but even then the outcome was seldom predictable, as the examples of Sedan Day and the national monuments illustrate. Analysis of the birth of Imperial Germany's official culture can, therefore, offer a useful corrective to histories that focus predominantly on the role of Prussia's traditional elites in the establishment and consolidation of the Empire after 1871.

3 *The* Gründerzeit

Introduction

Strictly speaking, the *Gründerzeit* or the 'age of the founders', lasted just three years, from 1871 to 1873. The term originally referred to the short-lived economic boom inspired by the creation of the German Empire, when hundreds of new businesses, banks and railways were founded and promoted on a liberalized stock-market; a period of speculative mania boosted by the influx of French reparations money, but brought to an abrupt halt by the crash of 1873, in which four German railway companies, sixty-one banks and 116 industrial concerns met their demise. In everyday usage, however, the term has increasingly come to denote the founding decades of the Empire in general:[1] a period of profound social and cultural, as well as economic and political change. Nevertheless, it is as an age of entrepreneurs and inventors, statesmen and charlatans, rather than artists or writers, that the period is usually remembered.

For German writers and critics of the late nineteenth century, the terms *Gründer* and *Gründerzeit* were used pejoratively, and the cultural products of the period have long suffered from their association with an age of ostentatious materialism and nationalistic triumphalism. The cultural historian Egon Friedell (1878–1938) suggested that stockmarket fraud was not the only *Gründerzeit* 'swindle': 'whitewashed tin masquerades as marble, papier maché as rosewood, plaster as shimmering alabaster, glass as exquisite onyx. The exotic palm tree in the bay window is waterproofed or made of paper, the tasty arrangement of fruit in the table-centrepiece is made of wax or soap'.[2] Such attitudes proved remarkably persistent, despite the subsequent dramatic upheavals in German history. An encyclopaedia from 1956, for instance, defined the word *Gründerzeit* as 'a lack of cultural style, tasteless showing off, especially in buildings and furniture'; and a 1971 *A to Z of Kitsch* ridiculed the era's 'excessive need for representation and pomp' that was the opposite of 'good taste and a sense of style'.[3] As far as furniture is concerned, a revival of public interest only set in during the 1970s,[4] and exhibitions of *Gründerzeit* painting were rare until the 1980s. In general, the art and literature of the period continue to be undervalued, even if few would now dismiss them outright as the 'surrogate' culture of a 'parvenu' generation.

While general studies of *Gründerzeit* culture remain few and far between,[5] recent works of literary-, art-, and architectural-history have gone some way to revise the scholarly view of the period. The Fritz-Thyssen-Foundation's interdisciplinary project on 'Art, Culture and Politics in the German Empire' (*Kunst, Kultur und Politik im Deutschen Kaiserreich*) has been particularly productive, with a series of valuable essay collections and monographs.[6] As these and other works have highlighted, one of the striking characteristics of age was the sheer quantity of art and literature produced, displaying more diversity than one might imagine. Certainly there was more to the *Gründerzeit* than one can cover in a single chapter, but the following pages focus on three of the key themes which dominated German cultural discourse in these years: the search for a national style; the preoccupation with history; and the cult of the hero. The many critics of *Gründerzeit* culture are then discussed in Chapter 4, along with the avant-garde and secessionist movements, whose breakthrough brought the era to a close.

The search for a national style

When, in the midst of revolution in 1848, the artists of Düsseldorf petitioned the Frankfurt Parliament to make art a 'national issue' and to create a national gallery of German art, few eyebrows were raised, since artists and writers had been closely involved with German nationalism since the start of the century. Although the 1848 petition achieved little, cultural events of all sorts – art exhibitions, music festivals, literary anniversaries and academic conferences – once more became an important platform for nationalist sentiment in the restrictive political climate of the 1850s. This could be seen clearly in an 1857 statement issued at the second annual conference of the General German Artists' Guild (*Allgemeine Deutsche Kunstgenossenschaft*) in Stuttgart: 'The unity, which our Fatherland cannot yet offer us, can at least be established in German art. We want a national art, and in it, national unity'.[7] Similar sentiments were often expressed at gatherings of physicians and natural scientists too. In a speech 'On the national development and meaning of the natural sciences' in 1865, the scientist and left liberal politician Rudolf Virchow regretted that 'we are still not in a position to cover the walls of our conference halls with German names', before going on to propose a new research project: a national history of science, with Luther as its founding father.[8] It is not surprising then, that many cultural producers greeted the events of 1871 with unbridled joy. The long sought-after national institutions, the galleries, museums and academies, appeared within easy reach; and some even prophesized a 'golden age'. However, though the existence of a distinctive, original and vital German culture had been asserted often enough, it remained to be seen whether the transformation from the humanist-idealist concept of a national community based on shared cultural values (*Kulturnation*) to the political nation-state (*Staatsnation*) would cause that culture to flourish or wither.

Initially, the founding of the Empire sparked off a display of patriotic pyrotechnics, in word, picture and object. Emanuel Geibel (1815–84), wrote a paean of praise to the soldiers of Sedan; Ernst von Wildenbruch (1845–1909) celebrated another battle in *Vionville*; Richard Wagner (1813–83) wrote a farce ridiculing the French resistance (*A Capitulation*, November 1870), a poem *To the Germany Army, Paris* (1871), and followed them up by composing an *Emperor-March* (1871); monuments were erected, processions paraded, and Heinrich von Sybel wrote to his fellow historian Hermann Baumgarten: 'How have we earned the grace of God to experience such great and mighty things? And how will we live afterwards?'[9]

In 1900 it was still just about possible for a respected literary historian to claim with a straight face that the Empire's first decade had been 'the most glorious, the richest in substance, that Germany has had in this century'.[10] However, very few literary or artistic treatments of these tumultuous days have really stood the test of time. Just as Anton von Werner's paintings are now more likely to feature in books on German history than the history of art, so writers like Geibel and Wildenbruch are dismissed as literary epigones and reactionary bogeymen, and are seldom read today. Certainly, much of their work was derivative: Geibel's sentimental lyricism revolved around stock 'poetic' subjects like the seasons, nature, history, friendship and romantic love, and placed formal precision above authentic expression; Wildenbruch's plays invariably re-worked classical themes in historic settings. Even so, it should not be forgotten that contemporaries placed Geibel's lyricism on a par with Goethe, and for a time Wildenbruch was championed as the future of German theatre. In any case, the works of Geibel and Wildenbruch, like those of Anton von Werner, remain valuable as historical documents, regardless of their aesthetic quality. They illustrate very clearly the hopes and expectations aroused by the wars of 1864–71, in educated 'little German' nationalist circles at least.

Geibel, who was dubbed the 'Herald of the Empire' as a result of pathos-laden poems like *Am Jahresschlusse* ('At the End of the Year', 1866) and *An König Wilhelm* ('To King William', 1868), was at his most swashbuckling in *Kriegslied* ('Song of War', 1870) and triumphalist in the 1871 collection *Heroldsrufe* ('Herald's Calls'). The belief that the union of German culture and Prussian power was a marriage made in heaven reverberates through all of these poems, and particularly his most infamous couplet: *Und es mag am deutschen Wesen / Einmal noch die Welt genesen* ('And the German character may / yet restore the world one day'), which Wilhelm II later made his own.[11] Not to be outdone, Wildenbruch also found a rhyme that captured a cultural trend of the *Gründerzeit* with brutal simplicity: *Deutschland ist nicht mehr in Wien, Deutschland ist in Berlin* ('Germany is no longer in Vienna, Germany is in Berlin').

For, after 1871, the meaning of the term 'German culture' underwent a remarkably rapid change. Writers and artists had long maintained that German culture could be found wherever the German language was spoken, even in Vienna. Now it was to be identified with the territory of the Empire alone. Not surprisingly, the search for appropriate imperial forms henceforth became a common theme of *Gründerzeit* discourse, lending new relevance and immediacy to the previously rather dry academic debate on the concept of style (particularly 'national style') in which German writers and thinkers had figured. It was, moreover, a search that went well beyond the narrow realm of art or architecture, affecting the law, economics and even the natural sciences.[12]

A national language?

When the German Empire was founded, both a national literary canon and a standard national language appeared to be fixtures in the cultural firmament. In fact, the former was a very recent development,[13] while the latter was far from complete. The canon of German classics, whose precise composition was contested but which was generally accepted to include the works of Lessing, Wieland, Goethe and Schiller, had received a decisive boost just four years earlier, in the so-called 'year of the classics' (1867), when 'timeless' copyright ended and cheap editions began to appear for the first time.[14] It should not be forgotten that this canon was made up mostly of works written within the previous hundred years: Schiller's place in the pantheon had only been cemented in his centenary year of 1859; while Kleist's posthumous reputation had only started to improve in the 1860s. Recent though it may have been, this body of literary classics was crucial in the formation of a 'standard' written and spoken German language, which was in essence another product of the nineteenth century.

It was only around 1800 that the educated middle-classes of the German states began to cultivate their own linguistic and literary heritage, and even then there was little interest beyond this narrow section of society. Indeed, throughout the first half of the nineteenth century, this was one way in which the educated middle class was able to distinguish itself from both the aristocracy and the masses, for increasingly, *Bildungsbürger* did not just use the German literary classics as the model for their written language, but also for the way they spoke.[15] In the course of the nineteenth century this 'standard' form of German succeeded in marginalizing competing forms of German, and other languages, to become the undisputed object of social prestige. It did not happen overnight. Aristocrats, who often continued to speak in regional dialect and to use French for representational purposes, only gradually adopted the standard language, whilst many older peasants and workers were still speaking in mutually incomprehensible dialects at the end of the century.

The *Reichsgründung* accelerated and exacerbated such long-term changes. It did so in three key ways. The standard language developed by the educated middle classes in the first half of the century was now imposed with much more vigour in schools all over the Empire, at the expense both of Low German dialects and the many languages of minority populations: Polish, Danish, French,

Masurian, Sorbian and so on.[16] To the chagrin of many southern Germans, the preferred form of the standard language was essentially that of northern and central Germany, rather than the Upper German-Austrian variant which was henceforth regarded as deviant. This led to understandable accusations of a 'Prussification' of the German language.[17] As Martin Durrell puts it: 'For the first time, the "German language" is identified exclusively with the standard *Hochsprache* which is the national language of the new state'.[18]

Secondly, orthographical rules were imposed more vigorously too. Where a wide degree of variation had previously been tolerated, after 1871, and particularly after the strict new 'Rules for the correct writing of German' of 1902, spelling was harmonized and modernized throughout the Empire. And thirdly, concerted efforts were undertaken to rid the German language of 'foreign' words. The goal of cleansing the German language of 'all unnecessary foreign elements', thereby restoring its 'pure spirit' and 'unique and essential characteristics' was pursued with the greatest zeal by the General German Language Association ('Allgemeine Deutscher Sprachverein', ADSV) founded in 1885 by a museum director from Brunswick, Hermann Riegel.[19] Although it was not the only organization of its type, the ADSV expanded to ninety local branches and a membership of 7000 in its first year; by the turn of the century it comprised about 200 local groups and 20,000 members, and on the eve of World War One it had grown to 318 chapters and 34,280 members. Although the majority of these members resided within the German Empire, the network of ADSV branches extended well beyond the frontiers of the state. As Roger Chickering notes, the membership of the ADSV was dominated by *Bildungsbürger*: a survey of 1876 men who held local office in the association between 1895 and 1914 reveals that more than a quarter possessed university doctorates, and that three-quarters were publicly employed.[20] Amongst these campaigners against 'pimples' on 'faces that are dear to us' were many of the leading professors of German philology, including Otto Behaghel and Friedrich Kluge.

The ADSV's efforts to cleanse the German language of foreign words were pre-empted by the Post Office's Heinrich von Stephan, who was made an honorary member of the association in 1887. With his decree of 31 December 1874, Stephan became the first civil servant to ensure that his administration used German words wherever possible, and his directory issued in June 1875 contained some 650 foreign words to be avoided.[21] Stephan did not try to invent

German terms for words like 'post' and 'telegraph' that were already well established. Even so, he was mocked in the press and by the general public for his efforts, as were those who suggested *Rauchrolle* instead of 'Zigarre' or *Rasenballspiel* instead of 'Tennis'. Nevertheless, the army and a number of railway companies soon followed the Post Office's example, which indicates the extent to which the German language, in one specific standardization, had come to be recognized as an official symbol of the Empire.

Another consequence of the *Reichsgründung* was that a particular view of the history of the German language assumed a dominance that would not be challenged for many decades. Just as Borussian historians sought to justify the new 'little Germany' through history, so the leading philologists of the *Gründerzeit* attempted to legitimize through language. This was perhaps not surprising, given the prominent role played by the first academic Germanists in the formative years of German nationalism. The efforts of Jacob Grimm (1785–1863) and Karl Lachmann (1793–1851) in the first half of the century were continued after 1871 by the likes of Wilhelm Scherer and Otto Behaghel. At the heart of their work was the notion that a written form of High German had been in existence since the Middle Ages – the Middle High German of the Hohenstaufen era – and had developed throughout the German lands rather than in one particular region, forming the linguistic basis of all other dialects. It was a view that relied on the projection of post-1871 certainties back through time, regardless of all the empirical evidence to the contrary. It portrayed the German language as timeless and unique, as a sacred birthright of the German people, reflecting their essential character. In fact, as Durrell makes clear, 'even in writing there is no secure evidential basis for the assumption of a supraregional language or even tendencies towards standardization in any modern sense' during the *Stauferzeit*.[22]

A national architecture?

The question of which architectural style could best represent the new German Empire was hotly debated throughout the *Gründerzeit*, and for many years thereafter. It was a complex debate in which the aesthetic and historical arguments were clouded by politics. Almost all the major styles in European architecture had some historical connection to the territories of the Empire, but it was clear that none was purely German. In the first decades of the *Kaiserreich* the running was made by the styles of the Renaissance. These had long been at the heart of the curriculum at the École des Beaux-Arts in Paris, which exerted a considerable influence on architectural trends in the German lands. Neo-Renaissance idioms, such as columns, pilasters, cornices, balustrades, decorative friezes, medallions, statues and caryatids had been employed well before 1871 by some of the leading German architects of the day, including Semper in Dresden, Neureuther in Munich and the Viennese architect Theophil Hansen.[23] It was also viewed as an extremely flexible 'language', embracing the 'dialects' of Greek and Roman Classicism, fifteenth- and sixteenth-century Italy and Germany, and for some even the Baroque and the Rococo.

As we have seen, neo-Renaissance forms of Italian provenance were often chosen for the Empire's important public buildings, since they were deemed to be suitably 'dignified' and 'monumental'. No one could claim, however, that such buildings were particularly German. On the contrary, their style belonged to the common heritage of the western world. It was perhaps not surprising, therefore, that during the *Gründerzeit* the more 'picturesque' and asymmetrical architecture of the German Renaissance – all towers, gables and bays – enjoyed particular favour, as a distinctively Germanic product of the fifteenth and sixteenth centuries. Nowhere was it more apparent than in the facades and interiors of the many new villas and apartment buildings constructed for the middle classes in fashionable districts of the Empire's growing cities.

The popularity of the German Renaissance was due in large part to the scholarly works of Wilhelm Lübke (1826–93),[24] and the more populist proselytizing of writers like Jakob von Falke and Georg Hirth (1841–1916).[25] Both Falke and Hirth believed that the key to domestic interior design was 'atmosphere' or *Stimmung*: each room should have a different mood, created partly by the style of furniture but also by different levels of light. Staircases were to be brightly lit; but in living and drawing rooms, heavy curtains and coloured, leaded window glass were deemed necessary to subdue the light and to create the desired atmosphere of cosy 'homeliness'. Modern windows were condemned as too large, and artificial lighting was to be used only with caution. All surfaces, including ceilings, had to be coloured and ornamented, while walls were to be wood-panelled in late Medieval or Renaissance fashion. The danger of what Falke referred to as the *horror vacui* was also to be averted by the use of paintings and prints.[26] With wooden parquet flooring popular too, the dominant tone was an autumnal reddish-brown, which Georg Hirth suggested was particularly suited to the German character.

As a consequence of all this, houses and apartments in the *Gründerzeit* became self-enclosed worlds, cut off from external reality. Some have suggested this represented a middle-class withdrawal from public life into a phoney 'ideal world', in the wake of successive political disappointments for the German *Bürgertum*. There was no doubt a desire to shut out a world of noise, pollution and conflict, but as Wolfgang Brönner argues: 'It would be wrong to define the whole movement in terms of a 'retreat'. The *Bürgertum* was certainly powerful and self-confident enough to expand its own culture throughout the whole environment. Rather the home must be regarded as the inner core, the smallest unit, in which the cultural values were formed.'[27] As such, it reflected an age in which theatricality, pomp and aesthetic pleasure were highly valued: and where taste and fashion were becoming internationalized. Similar trends in interior design could be found throughout Western Europe and the United States at this time. Indeed, the urban historian Lewis Mumford titled his famous book on the art and design of late nineteenth century America *The Brown Decades*.

Georg Hirth's publications combined practical tips on interior design with loftier thoughts on culture and politics. He was attracted to the 'age of Dürer' not only by its image as a time in which 'art, religion and fatherland' had been united, but also as an era of civic responsibility, in which towns like Nuremberg and Lübeck had maintained a proud record of self-government. As an active National Liberal, he suggested that middle classes of the *Gründerzeit* could identify with the Renaissance, because it had been an age in which bourgeois families had risen to great wealth and status. Furthermore, as he pointed out, the Renaissance had not only produced the Fuggers and the Medicis, but the likes of Leonardo, Raphael and Michelangelo too. By turning to the past for inspiration, Renaissance man had ushered in a glorious new age: could not *Gründerzeit* man follow suit?[28]

Such views were widely shared. The philosopher Wilhelm Dilthey (1833–1911), for instance, wrote: 'the forms of the Italian and German Renaissance seem very familiar to us, since the cultural conditions of the fifteenth and sixteenth centuries are analogous to our own age: the spirit of the bourgeoisie; the joy of life's pleasures; life's secular splendour, which speak out from the most beautiful works of that time, is our own'.[29] This also seemed to be the message of Richard Wagner's most accessible opera, *The Mastersingers of Nuremberg* (1867), which centred on the Nuremberg musicians' and poets' guild in the time of Hans Sachs (1494–1576). It was particularly appropriate, given the frequently asserted parallels between the bourgeois achievements of the Renaissance and the nineteenth century, that the main theme of the *Mastersingers* overture was conceived by Wagner as he made the long train journey from Vienna to Biebrich.[30]

The Renaissance style was also celebrated during the *Kulturkampf* by Heinrich von Treitschke as a patriotic Protestant alternative to the 'Catholic style' of the Gothic.[31] As Treitschke did not tire of pointing out, the best-known champion of the pointed arch and buttress was the Catholic politician and publicist August Reichensperger, who preached his credo that 'art must learn to pray again' in publications such as *Art is Everyone's Business* (1865).[32] It would be wrong, however, to view the neo-Gothic solely as a Catholic affair. Although Reichensperger was undoubtedly its most vocal supporter the style had Protestant backers too. Significantly, it had continued to be used for churches of both confessions in the 1870s, and was seen by some as a way of healing the rifts in German society caused by the industrial revolution and the *Kulturkampf*, since it symbolized an era predating the Church's great schism. The Gothic, it was suggested, represented an age of faith, brotherhood and social harmony, and could help to restore such values in the contemporary world. Few writers continued to argue that the origins of the Gothic style lay in Germany rather than France. One who did was Leopold Trzeschtik, who claimed that this 'German style' with its 'noble masculinity' was truly worthy of the nation, whereas the Renaissance, 'the style of individualism and luxury', was appropriate only 'for an age full of self-importance [and] arrogance'.[33]

By 1880, however, the Gothic revival was in retreat. Apart from its religious connotations, it appeared too strict and too ascetic a style for an age in which theatricality and extravagance were so warmly embraced. Of course, the Gothic could also be exuberant, but the German neo-Gothicists were more strait-laced than their British or Belgian equivalents, and the formulaic municipal gothic that could be found in every German town in the 1870s was not the stuff of architectural fantasy.

In the late 1880s and 1890s the round-arched Romanesque style, which had been important in the German lands in the Middle Ages, also enjoyed something of a revival beyond its Rhineland stronghold. It was frequently chosen for churches in the Empire, including the garrison church in Stuttgart (1875–9) and, most notably, the Kaiser-Wilhelm-Memorial church in Berlin (1891–5). The design of the latter, by Wilhelm Schwechten, was based on the medieval Marienkirche at Gelnhausen. It was sponsored by Wilhelm II, whose enthusiasm for the Romanesque had been fuelled by a series of research trips in the winter and spring of 1890, when he had collected a large number of drawings and photographs of historic buildings. Wilhelm was also the instigator of Schwechten's neo-Romanesque Imperial Palace in Posen (1905–10). Both buildings self-consciously sought to make the now familiar connection between the Hohenstaufen and Hohenzollern emperors. The Wilhelmine Romanesque revival was also reflected in the provincial government buildings at Koblenz (1902–6) and Trier (1903–5), the Prussian Health Ministry building in Berlin, and a number of major post offices.

Ultimately, however, no single style achieved dominance. This was partly because each had a foothold in the establishments where German architects were trained, and partly because of the sheer volume of building in Germany at this time. It was also, of course, a consequence of the wider aesthetic climate. With an unprecedented mastery over the gamut of architectural styles, from all ages and cultures; and unprecedented freedom in their usage, *Gründerzeit* architects and their clients were simply spoilt for choice. In such a climate, the notion that there could be one national style was always destined to fail.

A preoccupation with history

A house in the Hamburg district of St Georg has the following proud inscription carved above its front door: 'Built in the year 1874 AD, and the fourth year of the newly arisen German Empire'. The inscription not only testifies to the impact of the *Reichsgründung* on those who lived through it, but reveals something of the era's more general preoccupation with history. So does the oft-quoted comment by the nineteenth-century painter Wilhelm von Kaulbach: 'It is history we must paint. History is the religion of our age; only history is in keeping with the times'.[34] Certainly, by the *Gründerzeit*, history was regarded in German universities as the most important of the humanities, exerting a methodological and thematic influence on a host of other subjects that belied its relative youth as a scientific discipline. As Peter Paret puts it: 'The great cultural authority that history had achieved by mid-century can scarcely be exemplified in more convincing fashion than by its relentless expansion, beyond philosophy and religion, into all areas of art and literature'.[35] The proliferation of historical novels, plays and paintings; the popularity of historical essays, lectures and associations; and the prominent public role of professional historians, all contributed to what Wolfgang Hardtwig refers to as the *Geschichtskultur* ('historical culture') of mid- to late-nineteenth-century Germany.[36]

The nineteenth century's preoccupation with history, which was felt throughout the western world, was a consequence of the process of 'temporalization' or historicization that started in the eighteenth century and flourished in the 'age of revolutions'. The French revolution, the Napoleonic wars and the industrial revolution all highlighted the impermanence of political, social and economic structures. The rapid changes ushered in by these upheavals showed the extent to which life was historically determined, and prompted an upsurge of interest in the past, on the basis that 'the discovery of one's own historicity is after all the premise for an interest in the past'.[37] Two important intellectual responses followed. One was the philosopher G. W. F. Hegel's attempt to apply an historical approach to knowledge, from which he was able to speculate on the meaning and direction of history. The other, which came almost simultaneously, involved the historian turning to primary sources; to immerse himself in the specific and the particular, and to interpret these documents critically but sympathetically, with the aim of gaining an understanding of the epoch in question. This empirical-scientific approach, generally associated with the name of Leopold von Ranke (1795–1886), had its critics, but in the course of the nineteenth century it came to dominate the writing of history, and a host of other disciplines.

As history became more scientific, however, it also increased its impact on the literate public, becoming a key element of grammar school and university education. Knowledge of history became regarded as a necessary part of the individual's character formation. Only through an awareness of the past, it was suggested, could wise actions be taken in the present. Historians wrote, therefore, not only for specialists but also for a general lay public. As the example of the Borussian school shows, professional historians often focused on periods or aspects of history that were seen to have contemporary relevance, and were fully prepared to comment on current affairs, even to participate in political life. In the 1850s and 1860s Droysen, Sybel, Baumgarten and Treitschke had helped to keep the national dream of the educated middle classes alive, and after 1871 their efforts were rewarded. As Hardtwig notes, when Treitschke was invited to join the parliamentary commission planning Berlin's Kaiser Wilhelm Monument, it amounted to 'official recognition' for the Borussian approach to history.[38] This was not in itself peculiar to Germany. In the new nation-states of the nineteenth century historians were often involved in the creation of official national histories and myths, and the pattern was repeated after 1990 in Eastern Europe and the Balkans. As Eric Hobsbawm once memorably put it: 'historians are to nationalism what poppy-growers in Pakistan are to heroin addicts; we supply the essential raw material for the market'.[39]

Nevertheless, the extent to which history appeared to pervade every area of German culture and society in the second half of the nineteenth century was unusual. It became manifest, for instance, in an unprecedented obsession with anniversaries, which filled the weekly *Fest-Kalender* of popular journals like the *Illustrirte Zeitung*. No jubilee, it seemed, was too small to celebrate. Births, deaths or seemingly any minor event connected with a hero of the past – Gutenberg, Dürer, Luther, Beethoven, Schiller, Goethe – were celebrated in grand style, usually involving a procession in historic costume or the unveiling of a monument.[40] It was also expressed in the remarkable proliferation of museums: historical museums of every description; museums of archaeology, applied art and natural history; ethnographical and colonial museums all flourished in the Empire, and only in part as a consequence of German polycentrism. Of course, a sense of living through historically important times was understandably strong in those who had experienced the events of the 1860s and 1870s, but the preoccupation with history had other reasons too. In common with its counterparts elsewhere in Europe, the German *Bildungsbürgertum* saw itself as the legitimate heir of centuries of history, and attempted to express this optimistic faith in 'progress' by demonstrating a proprietorial control over the past. It was exaggerated, however, by the particular dominance in German intellectual life of what became known as *Historismus* or 'historicism'.[41]

This term, which first appeared in the works of Schlegel and Novalis around 1800 but was little used before 1850, referred to the tendency to see and explain everything historically; to believe that history alone could lead to a true understanding of human affairs. It was a tendency that was apparent not only in history itself, but in political science (Marxism) and philology; botany and geology; and numerous other disciplines too. For its defenders, the great strength of the historicist approach was that it freed historical thought from normative concepts: 'it sought to grasp historical reality in its living individuality without forcing it into the strait-jacket of concepts'.[42] By the last years of the century, however, it had become identified with a doomed search to secure an ever more detailed but ultimately meaningless knowledge of the past, 'studying each institution, and each idea or ideal as a one-time event linked to a specific historical and cultural setting',[43] with the result that one knew more and more, about less and less. Anton von Werner's Sedan Panorama, for instance, may have portrayed the battle 'as it really was', but did it ultimately contribute to a better understanding of the Franco-Prussian War?

For critics of historicism, this fruitless searching of the past was at the cost of the present. Friedrich Nietzsche's famous attack on *Gründerzeit* historicism 'On the uses and disadvantages of history for life' (1873) [44] contended that such efforts did not create a beneficial historical awareness, but merely led to a superficial retention of irrelevant information. Worse still, the 'malignant historical fever' threatened to paralyse the vital energies of the creative individual. As we shall see, such criticisms would produce a 'crisis of historicism' at the end of the nineteenth century, though the historicist tradition was to remain a powerful force in Germany for many years to come.

Historicism in architecture and design

In the early years of the twentieth century historicism was defined in a wide variety of ways (although seldom positively) and entered the discourse of a wide range of disciplines. One of the last to adopt the term, in the 1920s, was the History of Art, where it developed a specific meaning of its own. Historicism in architecture and design, refers to the deliberate and scholarly employment of historic styles in the years around 1840–1910, especially the practice of combining styles in an eclectic manner to form an historical hybrid, or a synthesis between old and new. Such solutions were often required for buildings or objects with no historical prototype – railway stations or telephones, for example – and led to the later critical charge that historicism treated history as a stockyard of motifs and idioms, to be plundered at will.

The rapid expansion of art history as an academic subject in the nineteenth century ensured that by the 1850s at the latest, all the major European styles and epochs had been documented in word and picture. For architects, master-builders, draughtsmen and craftsmen this provided an unprecedented wealth of structural and decorative solutions. Combined with the new materials and manufacturing processes offered by technological progress, the possibilities seemed endless. For many people this first became apparent not in architecture, but in product design, at the Great Exhibition in London (1851). It was here at the Crystal Palace that the notion of a 'world market' for industrial and household goods first became a tangible reality. Amongst the many expressions of awe and wonder at mankind's ingenuity, however, there were also voices which questioned the aesthetic value of much that was on display, and expressed concern that industrialization appeared to be advancing at the expense of culture and taste.

The manufacturer's reliance on the draughtsman's 'pattern-book'[45] to attract the consumer's attention, and the indiscriminate way in which 'historic' ornament was applied to mass-produced objects, became ever more apparent at the world fairs which followed. The atmosphere at these events changed after 1851, as the liberal rhetoric of the Great Exhibition gave way to a competitive and sometimes bitter international rivalry in the 1860s.[46] Since products were generally exhibited in national pavilions, it was inevitable that critics and consumers should make comparisons, and reflect on the question of national styles. In both regards, the German states were deemed to be unimpressive. Forced to exhibit their wares individually, or at best under the banner of the *Zollverein* (Customs Union), their modest pavilions did not stand out, and there was little coherence in aesthetic terms either. For those German exporters who expected to benefit from the *Reichsgründung* with a more impressive presence at international fairs, the events at Vienna (1873) and Philadelphia (1876) brought only crushing disappointment. Admittedly, individual manufacturers enjoyed some success, but the overall impression remained poor. The 'Imperial Commissar' at Philadelphia, Franz Reuleaux (1829–1905) was damning in his judgement. In the first of a series of 'Letters from Philadelphia' he made the famous comment: 'The fundamental principle of Germany's industry is "cheap and nasty"'.[47] The Empire's products, he argued, were technically backward, aesthetically poor and economically of little value.

Such trenchant criticism could not pass by unnoticed, even if the federal structure of the Empire meant that the response of the individual states was uncoordinated. The lesson learnt in Britain from the 1851 exhibition – that aesthetic training lagged behind the manufacturing capabilities of modern industry – had led to the establishment of the South Kensington Museum (1857) and the National Art Training School under Gottfried Semper, a German. It was ironic then, that it was not until the 1870s that the German states followed suit, with the first museums and schools of applied art (*Kunstgewerbe*).[48] This combination of museum and teaching establishment was no coincidence. The firm belief of the 'applied art movement' was that the quality and distinctiveness of German manufactured goods could only improve by returning to the practices of the past.

The industrial draughtsman – the job of 'designer' had yet to be invented – was to be re-acquainted with the work of his craftsman forefathers through a careful, almost Rankean, study of material sources. A major exhibition held in Munich's own Crystal Palace in 1876, the 'German Art and Art Industry Exhibition', reinforced this message. Visitors had to pass through a display of three thousand pieces of historic German furniture and *objets d'art* under the banner of 'Our Fathers' Works', before they could reach the contemporary exhibits, most of which were in neo-Renaissance style. Indeed, this was the first show in which something like a coherent national style appeared to be developing, coming as it did at the highpoint of enthusiasm for the German Renaissance in both architecture and design. However, the apparent uniformity of the exhibits in Munich was an illusion, reflecting the outlook of the exhibition organizers but not the reality of an increasingly competitive domestic and international market, in which manufacturers continued to offer their products in a range of historical styles. The establishment of the museums and schools of applied art may have marked the beginning of an improvement in the quality of German goods, but it did not lead in the direction of a national style. On the contrary, a training based on the mastery of all past styles was likely to produce more, rather than less, stylistic diversity.

In architecture, the simultaneous co-existence of a variety of historical styles gradually became accepted by all but the most dogmatic of writers. In practice, each style was perceived to represent certain values, and was tolerated within an appropriate area of architectural activity: the Gothic and Romanesque for churches; Italian Renaissance, Classical and Baroque for monumental state buildings; the German Renaissance for civic buildings and so on. Of course, the reality was somewhat more complicated, but as a rule of thumb this was not seriously challenged until the last years of the century. Problems arose, however, in the area of domestic architecture and with new building types, which the nineteenth century threw up in unprecedented numbers. As Wilhelm Lübke noted in 1886, whereas the architecture of previous centuries had been characterized by churches or palaces: 'it is no longer the privileged circles who build, but the whole people. They demand their . . . schools, museums, concert halls; their hospitals, town halls, railway stations, stock exchanges'.[49] It was the design of such buildings that later brought nineteenth-century architecture into disrepute (by no means only in Germany) for they were constructed in each and every historical style, and often in an eclectic combination of styles. Far from demonstrating an awareness for history, it would be argued, historicist architecture debased and de-historified the past, leaving only empty shells, devoid of any meaning.

The historical novel

Novels on historical themes had been popular in the German states even before the days of Sir Walter Scott and his numerous German imitators; the historical plays of Friedrich Schiller continued to exert a strong influence on German writers and artists, and the Romantics placed much of their work in a historical setting too. By the second half of the nineteenth century, historical novels had become the dominant literary form.[50] For many authors, however, an historical setting alone was no longer enough: it had to be historically accurate as well. The scholarly approach to historical fiction was perhaps best demonstrated by Joseph Victor Scheffel (1826–86). Although he is little studied now, Scheffel was one of nineteenth-century Germany's most successful writers. On his fiftieth birthday, for example, he was ennobled with a hereditary title; received the freedom of the city of Karlsruhe; and a congratulatory telegram from Bismarck, who was a great admirer of Scheffel's collection of student drinking songs *Gaudeamus*, despite the author's liberal and anti-Prussian views.

Scheffel's most successful novel was *Ekkehard* (1855), which reached its 200th reprint in 1904. Despite being a simple romantic tale of two ill-matched lovers in tenth-century Swabia, it nevertheless came with 285 footnotes (some in medieval Latin!) to lend the text an air of historical accuracy. Scheffel was a keen amateur historian, who argued that historical fiction could become 'the equal brother of history' if based on serious research.[51] *Ekkehard* can be seen as a precursor to what became known as the *Professorenroman*: novels by academics with historical settings. Examples of this genre include Georg Ebers's *Eine ägyptische Königstochter* ('An Egyptian Pharoah's Daughter', 1864), whose 314 footnotes made up approximately one third of the complete text, or *Ein Kampf um Rom* ('A Struggle for Rome', 1876), by a professor of legal history, Felix Dahn (1834–1912), which had its thirtieth reprint in 1900. The Munich professor Wilhelm Heinrich Riehl (1823–97) was another who wrote poetry and prose fiction as well as pioneering works of academic sociology and history. Predictably, 'professorial novels' often had a didactic tone, and their determination to convey historical knowledge as well as tell a story could make them difficult to digest.

As the title of Dahn's bestseller implied, a frequent theme of the professorial novel was the relationship between Germany and Rome, or between church and state. Indeed, many of the novels written at the height of the *Kulturkampf* were little more than polemical anti-Catholic tracts. Many were set at the time of the Reformation, and relied heavily on the historical myth that Martin Luther was first and foremost a German patriot. The historical novels of the Swiss-German writer Conrad Ferdinand Meyer (1825–98), which enjoyed great popularity in *Gründerzeit* Germany, reflected this aggressively Protestant tendency: *Huttens letzte Tage* ('Hutten's Last Days', 1871) and *Jürg Jenatsch* (1876) being the best-known examples. Meyer's novels were highly theatrical works, with numerous battle scenes and colourful tableaux in a costume-drama style.

Arguably the most popular work of historical fiction in the *Gründerzeit*, however, was *Die Ahnen* ('The Ancestors', 1872–81), a series of six novels by Gustav Freytag, which traced the history of two German families through the centuries up to 1848. Freytag, who had earlier written the popular novel *Soll und Haben* ('Debit and Credit', 1855) and a five-volume social history *Bilder aus der deutschen Vergangenheit* ('Pictures from the German Past', 1859–67), had given up the prospect of an academic career in favour of politics and journalism. He served as a National Liberal member of the North German Reichstag and co-edited the journal *Die Grenzboten*, but continued to produce works of both popular history and fiction. In *The*

Ancestors the 'historical' content was purely decorative and the characterization was tainted by contemporary prejudice, but this did not stop the novels becoming immensely popular, not least as a confirmation gift for generations of middle-class children. Ultimately, however, Theodor Fontane's pithy critique was perhaps more memorable. Although the books were 'sometimes dramatic, sometimes romantic and sometimes historical', he wrote, this did not make them dramatic, romantic or historical novels.[52]

Theodor Fontane's own historical novels were much more palatable, and vastly superior in terms of literary quality. He was another who wrote 'straight' history books as well as works of fiction, but he combined the two better than anyone else. Fontane did not have his first novel published until he was nearly 60 (*Before the Storm* in 1878), but he was writing all his life: poetry, novellas, journalism (as a correspondent for the conservative *Kreuzzeitung* newspaper, and as a theatre critic for the liberal *Vossische Zeitung*), and his famous *Wanderings through the Mark Brandenburg*. The latter in fact began as an historical novel, but ended up as much more: a synthesis of history, literature, and travelogue. Fontane also wrote three long histories of the wars of unification, which took him twelve years to complete. They were ambitious works which did not enjoy great popular success, and it was probably this disappointment which fuelled his determination to begin writing fiction: works like the short 1882 novel *Schach von Wuthenow*, which was set in the Prussia of Friedrich Wilhelm III and which Peter Paret feels was his 'supreme achievement'.[53] *Schach von Wuthenow* was at the same time a critique of aspects of the German Empire, and it is in this role – as an astute commentator of his own age – that Fontane is now best remembered.

The historical theatre

Along with light comedies, historical dramas formed the backbone of German theatre schedules throughout the *Gründerzeit*. In addition to the classic history plays of Shakespeare and Schiller, there was a seemingly incessant stream of new dramas with historical settings. Indeed, from ancient Greece and Rome to the Franco-Prussian war, there was hardly an historical period to escape the blank verse of German playwrights, although the variety of settings was not matched by a similar inventiveness in plot structure or characterization. Essentially the same five-act format was used time and again;

with the political narrative often subsumed under the individual tragedy or the obligatory love story. Later, modernist critics took great pleasure in ridiculing the conventions of what were mockingly known as *Oberlehrertragödien* ('schoolmaster tragedies'), and the imitative nature of *Gründerzeit* drama can hardly be disputed. Even so, it is worth remembering that theatre underwent something of a boom in Imperial Germany: in terms of the numbers of theatres operating (despite the almost total absence of state subsidies), the size of audiences, and the quantity of work produced.[54]

Although dramas set in classical Greece and Rome remained popular – Adolf Wilbrandt (1837–1911) had a massive hit with *Arria und Messalina* in 1874 and no fewer than seven *Gründerzeit* playwrights tackled the tragedy of Emperor Nero[55] – the real growth area in the 1870s and 1880s was for plays with historic German settings. The Hohenstaufen era and the Reformation were particularly favoured, since both could be contrived to seem topical: a consequence, of course, of the Empire's 're-birth' and renewed conflict with the church of Rome. Plays which attempted to make historical allusions in this way, and thus to make a contribution to the 'national integration' of the new Empire, included: *Der Graf von Hammerstein* ('The Count of Hammerstein', 1870) by Adolf Wilbrandt; Rudolf Gottschall's *Herzog Bernhard von Weimar* ('Duke Bernhard of Weimar', 1871); Arthur Fitger's *Adalbert von Bremen* (1874); Ernst von Wildenbruch's *Die Karolinger* ('The Carolingians', 1882) and a host of plays by the tireless Felix Dahn. None of the latter, however, enjoyed the popular success of his *A Struggle for Rome.*

The *Gründerzeit* preoccupation with history was also manifest in the two most notable theatrical phenomena of the 1870s: the touring productions of the Meiningen court players and Richard Wagner's music dramas, which gained a permanent home at Bayreuth in 1876. Arguably, these centres of artistic excellence had little else in common, but curiously, given their association with historical themes and costumes, both also provided important pointers for the future of theatre and music. It was perhaps no coincidence that each depended on the determination of aggressively assertive individuals with very personal artistic visions. Wagner's importance to the Bayreuth enterprise is, of course, well-known and will be addressed later, but Duke Georg II of Saxe-Meiningen (1826–1914) was no less vital to the success of his court theatre.

The Duke, who was married to the actress Ellen Franz, not only subsidized his theatre financially, but was also the driving artistic force. He was a talented draughtsman, who designed sets and costumes and, with the help of his close associate Ludwig Chronegk, was also personally involved in the direction of productions. The Meiningen theatre, which first went on tour in 1874 and quickly gained a fine reputation in Germany and abroad,[56] specialized in faithful renderings of the classics, such as Shakespeare's *Julius Caesar* or Schiller's *Maid of Orleans*.[57] For a decade or so, their productions were the talk of the artistic community, even in Berlin, and were later cited as an influence by the likes of Stanislavsky and Antoine.

The Duke was a firm believer in 'realism', which he sought to attain in the historical accuracy of costumes and settings. Indeed such emphasis was placed on finely detailed backdrops and full period costume that Meiningen productions came to resemble historical paintings. Particular care was taken to stage convincing battle and crowd scenes, which were rehearsed to perfection and became the highlight of productions like Kleist's *Hermannsschlacht*, which was performed over 100 times by the Meininger. Of course, critics of the Meiningen productions argued that the preoccupation with spectacle detracted from the content, and few would nowadays regard such an approach to theatre as productive. However, where the Meiningen court theatre did break new ground was in the uniformity of its acting style and the consistency of its approach. While other German theatres at this time were actor-driven – guest stars would perform as they saw fit, sometimes in their own costumes, and often to the detriment of the play – the Meiningen productions used actors from the ensemble interchangeably, and even stars like Josef Kainz and Amanda Lindner were allowed no special privileges. When the Deutsches Theater was founded in Berlin in 1883, under the leadership of Adolph L'Arronge, it took Meiningen as its model, and the concept of the director-driven ensemble of equals remains powerful in the theatre today, especially in Germany.

The Meiningen approach to stage and costume design was in essence adopted by Richard Wagner too, even if his artistic goals were very different. For the Bayreuth premiere of the 'Ring', for instance, Wagner's costume designer Carl Döpler toured the museums of Germany and Denmark to discover what ancient Teutons might really have worn. His research was so thorough that he made some 500 preparatory sketches of weapons and jewellery alone.[58] In the end, the first Siegfried closely resembled Ernst von Bandel's Hermann in the Teutoburg forest, with a winged helmet, short skirt, cloak and sandals. For the sets, Wagner turned to a painter, the Viennese landscape artist Josef Hoffmann, whose designs were transferred on to huge billowing backdrops. Inevitably, however, Wagner's efforts to recreate the world of the Nibelungs in a literal, 'historically accurate' fashion were limited by the primitive stagecraft and technology of the *Gründerzeit*.

This proved a tremendous frustration for Wagner, who was bitterly disappointed that the 1876 'Ring' did not live up to his high expectations. Elementary gas lighting, painted backdrops and papier-maché props could not match the power of the artist's imagination, and at least one member of the Bayreuth audience, the painter Anton von Werner, found the 'cardboard cliffs', the wobbly rainbow and above all the 'clumsy, unspeakably funny dragon' simply comic.[59] At the time, however, such views were far from common, and though subsequent generations of writers have often contrasted the radical modernity of Wagner's music with the conservatism of his staging, most contemporaries were impressed: Tchaikovsky hailed the sets as 'truly marvellous'.[60]

The historical pageant

Pageants and parades on historical themes were a frequent occurrence in the Empire. Wolfgang Hartmann gives details of no fewer than 231 historical processions between 1871 and 1914, and this probably represents only the tip of the iceberg.[61] Some of these were annual events, such as the Cologne carnival (first staged in 1823) or the Munich *Oktoberfest* (since 1810), and others were to mark particular anniversaries, such as the 600th anniversary of the Pied Piper of Hamelin in 1884, for which a large proportion of the town's inhabitants donned thirteenth century outfits. Civic, dynastic and varsity jubilees all regularly prompted processions, as did gatherings of shooting, choral and gymnastics associations.

Although much was made by contemporaries of the 'democratic' nature of the processions – anyone could watch and many could participate[62] – numerous subtle hierarchies were nevertheless apparent. It was expected, for instance, that historical figures would be portrayed wherever possible by their descendants: members of the Luther family were to the fore in the 1883 Wittenberg procession; in Ulm, the sixteenth-century mayor von Besserer was played by a nineteenth-century namesake; and in the Cologne Cathedral procession of 1880, the city's historic patrician families were represented by the 'modern patricians of trade and industry'. Such literalism was characteristic of the age of historicism, as was a strict attention to detail in the design of costumes and props. To achieve the required degree of accuracy, historians and archivists were often invited to serve on the committees that planned the processions, although in small towns, the historical expertise was often provided by the local headmaster.

Until the eighteenth century, processions had been largely the preserve of the church and the court, with the public as passive spectators. Thereafter, however, the urban middle classes took the lead. Although courtly trappings – knights, heralds, fanfares and the like – remained a common feature, the organization, planning and design now all lay in the hands of the bourgeoisie.[63] This was even the case with processions to mark dynastic anniversaries, which were viewed by royalty as an acceptable way for the people to pay their respects. The most famous and influential procession of this sort took place in Vienna in 1879, on the occasion of Emperor Franz Joseph's silver wedding. The procession, which was watched by over 300,000 people as it made its way around the recently completed Ringstrasse, is largely remembered for the Renaissance costumes of the celebrated *Gründerzeit* painter Hans Makart, who choreographed the artists' contribution as 'an apotheosis of the *Bürgertum*'. Indeed, artists were vital to this pageant culture; not only designing costumes and *tableaux-vivants*, but often taking the lead in organizational terms as well. This was in large measure due to the experience gained in mounting the art academies' annual costume- and masked balls, which frequently took historical themes. Inspired by Venetian and Florentine practices, these had been staged in cities like Munich, Berlin and Düsseldorf since the 1830s, and had quickly become a highpoint of the social calendar.

Ostensibly examples of historicism in architecture and design, the 'fairy tale' castles of Bavaria's King Ludwig II can also be viewed as an expression of the nineteenth century taste for historical pageantry. Ludwig II reigned from 1864 to his mysterious death in 1886, and inherited a vigorous tradition of royal patronage on a grand scale. As John Osborne notes, however, he surpassed both his forbears 'in enthusiasm, extravagance, naivety, and eccentricity'.[64] Ludwig II built his first castle at Neuschwanstein (1869–86) close to his father's palace at Hohenschwangau.[65] It was inspired by a visit to the recently restored Wartburg near Eisenach in 1867, and recalled in theatrical fashion the castles of the Middle Ages. It was no coincidence that the three architects who worked on the building were assisted by a stage designer Christoph Jank, who supplied the King with imaginative and colourful depictions of their plans. Ludwig's love of myths and legends, especially *Tannhäuser* and *Lohengrin*, predated Wagner's operas on the same themes, but many of the interiors came straight from the Wagnerian stage. At the time of Ludwig's premature death, Neuschwanstein was still a building site, and construction work was never completed. Although it was opened to the public as early as 1886, the castle was destined to remain unfinished.

Ludwig's two other major palace projects had French models: Linderhof reflected the Rococo taste of Louis XV and Herrenchiemsee recreated Louis XIV's Palace of Versailles, complete with a Hall of Mirrors.[66] Linderhof, which was finished in 1877, was surrounded by magnificent gardens, both landscape and formal. One of its principal attractions was a 'Venus Grotto' taken straight from *Tannhäuser*, complete with concrete stalactites, a shell-shaped boat, a waterfall and a sophisticated five-colour light show. The illusion was only possible due to the use of modern technology: the special effects were powered by a Siemens electric dynamo. Herrenchiemsee, which was started in 1878, was intended as a monument to absolute monarchy (Ludwig always referred to it as 'Tmeicos Ettal', an anagram of Louis XIV's dictum, *L'état c'est moi*). Like Ludwig's other palaces, Herrenchiemsee served no real function. Its appearance in the landscape was all that counted. The decadent extravagance of these grand follies – which left Ludwig with debts of over 14 million RM at his death, despite generous annual payments from Bismarck[67] – was emphasized by Ludwig's wish for them to be blown up on his death. Though it did not come to that, the palaces began to decay almost as soon as they were finished. As the art historian Wilhelm Lübke put it in 1886: 'One can hardly believe one is still in Europe when confronted with these things, but rather that one is looking at the effusive product of an Asian despotism'.[68]

The historical painting

Historical painting – that is to say, depictions of historical themes, rather than painting in an 'historic', old-masterly style, though that was also a feature of the *Gründerzeit* – was long regarded as the pinnacle of artistic endeavour.[69] In the hierarchy of academic art it looked down with lofty disdain upon portraiture, genre and landscape painting. The close historic relationship between academies of art and royal courts – Louis XIV's model was imitated right across the continent – meant that academic historical paintings were expected to fulfil a political function: to educate and enlighten; to uplift and inspire; above all, to convey something of the magnificence and permanence of the state.[70] They were no aesthetic luxury, but a didactic weapon.

As the official commissions for Anton von Werner indicate, the view that historical paintings could perform an important educational and political role remained strong right up to the end of the nineteenth century. Werner's photo-realist style, however, was not typical of all historical painting. One of the longest running controversies in nineteenth-century German art was the debate surrounding the question: 'accuracy or allegory'? Should the painter strive for historical accuracy, or could allegorical images be employed? In this debate Werner's paintings represented one extreme. They provided a level of realism that threatened to swamp the main actors in superfluous detail, and on occasions broke a cardinal rule of historical painting: that the main plot should be easily readable without prior knowledge. In both regards, they reflected the 'scientific' trend in historical scholarship: aspiring towards an 'objective' viewpoint; making careful use of sources; and assembling details assiduously, but at the risk of losing the 'big picture'.

The contribution that paintings could make to an understanding of history had been stressed by a succession of nineteenth-century art theorists. Gustav Adolph Scholl, for instance, had written in 1835: 'The science of History is incomplete; it lacks a medium to make its truths immediately vivid and perceptible'.[71] It was here, he suggested, that historical art could help. As Franz Kugler put it a few years later, 'what research has explored must be brought to life by art'; the task of historical painting lies in 'revealing and making present to us true historical events'.[72] Karl von Piloty (1824–86), Germany's leading historical painter for many years and Director of the Munich Academy of Art from 1874, had been one of the first to tread this path. Indeed, he took so much care over the superficial accuracy of his paintings that the Naturalist critic Otto Brahm was prompted to remark that he depicted genuine clothes, but fake people.

At the other end of the scale were men like Cornelius, Genelli and Preller, who continued to paint centaurs and giants rather than rifles and uniforms. The use of allegory in historical paintings remained particularly popular in Germany, where the legacy of idealism was strong, and where the grammar schools taught a Classics-dominated curriculum. Admittedly, by the second half of the century, most of the leading historians and critics had come down against the use of allegory, but its much-predicted death was a long time coming. Classical and mythological settings remained a staple of the art academies, and despite fundamental changes in the art market,[73] large-scale historical painting survived in Germany until the 1900s, not least due to a large number of commissions for new public buildings. Even the mythological allegory enjoyed a new lease of life in the 1890s and 1900s, only now it was electricity or consumer goods, rather than truth or beauty, which was being sold.

The cult of heroes

It is no coincidence that the first decades of the Empire became known as the *Gründer*-zeit rather than the *Gründungs*-zeit,[74] for the word reflected the era's characteristic preoccupation with the heroic individual. Whether in the world of business, politics or the arts, the focus was on the 'great men' upon whom, it was believed, history relied. Heinrich von Treitschke put it bluntly when he wrote: 'Unlike the natural scientist, the historian is not permitted to derive later developments simply from what came earlier. Men make history.'[75] Accordingly, biography became the favoured format for historians, literary- and art-historians alike; and even non-biographies, like Treitschke's own *Deutsche Geschichte im 19. Jahrhundert* ('German History in the 19th Century'), were structured around individual historical figures. In his five-volume pictorial history *Das 19. Jahrhundert in Bildnissen* ('The Nineteenth Century in Portraits', 1898–1901), Carl Werkmeister wrote: 'The character of the century is reflected in the physiognomies of its great men. . . . Their portraits should be as familiar to us as our best friends.'[76] Julius Langbehn used the seventeenth-century painter Rembrandt to embody his programme of aesthetic and political reform (*Rembrandt als Erzieher*, 1890), while Nietzsche personified a whole philosophy in one individual, Zarathustra (*Also sprach Zarathustra*, 1883–85).

Similar thoughts had earlier prompted Bavaria's King Ludwig I to build a 'Walhalla' near Regensburg: a neo-Classical temple to accommodate busts of German heroes and heroines.[77] The 'marble skull-shed' as Heine dubbed it, added steadily to its collection throughout the century. Of course, the idea that 'great men make history' was by no means unique to Germany, or indeed, to the *Gründerzeit*. It was a belief widely-held throughout the Western world in the nineteenth century, and its prominence in Germany had much to do with the popularity of translated works like Thomas Carlyle's six lectures 'On heroes, hero-worship and the heroic in history' from 1840, which contains the famous formulation 'Universal History, the history of what man has accomplished in this world, is at bottom the History of the Great Men who have worked here'.[78] Even so, the preoccupation with 'great men' was an acknowledged feature of German historicism: only foreign policy stood above the actions of heroic individuals in the historicist hierarchy. Moreover, in his widely read treatise *Händler und Helden* ('Merchants and Heroes') of 1915, the sociologist Werner Sombart would identify the 'heroic spirit' as an essential part of the German national character, in contrast to the 'shopkeeper mentality' of the British. As the following section shows, the *Gründerzeit* produced more than its fair share of new heroes. They came in many guises, but all shared an awareness of history, and their place in it, which testified to the impact of historicism on German society.

The hero as painter

That the heroes of the *Gründerzeit* included a number of painters comes as no surprise. The heavy demand for reproductions; the success of 'art associations' (*Kunstvereine*)[79] and the founding of new art journals; the popularity of art history as an academic discipline;[80] and the high attendance figures at exhibitions, all testify to a great hunger for art in the German Empire. Indeed, historians such as Thomas Nipperdey have made much of art's role as a surrogate religion in a society that was loosing its moorings as it underwent rapid industrialization and secularization.[81] Museums and galleries not only took on the architectural characteristics of temples, but some of the codes of behaviour; and a number of artists seemed to attract disciples rather than pupils. The British painter John Lavery (1856–1941), who made frequent visits to Germany in the late nineteenth century, used a different analogy: 'the status of a painter was equal to that of a General in the army; he was covered with decorations at public functions and saluted as a person of distinction'.[82] Of course, not all painters could be commercially and critically successful, but heroic status could be attained by the 'tortured' or 'misunderstood' artist too, especially if they were prepared to wait for posthumous recognition. Accordingly, there was no lack of self-confidence amongst *Gründerzeit* artists, as their assertive self-portraits readily testify. Apart from Anton von Werner, the painter most frequently mentioned outside the specialist art historical literature is Franz Lenbach (1836–1904).[83]

Lenbach was a talented portraitist, who saw himself as a latterday Titian: as a painter of princes and a prince amongst painters. He presented his subjects in stern statuesque poses, and often employed Rembrandtesque contrasts of dark and light. He made considerable use of the camera and modern photographic techniques, but also developed an artificial patina to make his paintings appear old-masterly. Lenbach's fame today, however, owes less to the quality of his painting than to the quality of his sitters – Wilhelm I, Crown Prince Friedrich, General von Moltke, Liszt, Wagner and Bismarck, the latter about 80 times over – and to the speed of his rise up the social ladder, which is often cited as characteristic of an age that worshipped the 'self-made man'.[84]

Despite a humble background, the ambitious and single-minded Lenbach was remarkably successful in cultivating social contacts after completing his education in Karl von Piloty's *atelier*. This occurred first through the collector Count Adolf von Schack (1815–94), for whom Lenbach copied the work of the old masters; and secondly, through Lenbach's friendship with Richard Wagner, which gave him access to the higher echelons of Bavarian, and indeed German society. Lenbach was ennobled in 1882; married into the Moltke family in 1887; and, after that ended in divorce, wed another aristocrat in 1896. His prominence in the cultural and social life of Bavaria required him to entertain on a grand scale, and led to the construction of a large villa complex in Munich, designed in Italian Renaissance style by his friend Gabriel von Seidl, and built between 1887 and 1891. The property originally consisted of two main buildings. One contained Lenbach's studio and family living quarters, while the other was primarily for the purposes of representation and entertainment, and was sufficiently grand to accommodate Bismarck and other prominent guests.

The frequently-photographed studio, with its wood-panelled ceilings, old masterly portraits and Renaissance furniture was, however, not simply a workplace either, as Georg Blochmann makes clear:

'Lenbach's *atelier* first and foremost had the character of a *salon*, a meeting place for high-society, where the creation of a picture became an event, and the artist himself became a sensation'.[85] It was an effect that was apparently intended to last beyond the grave. In the view of Wilhelm Wyl, a contemporary of the artist, Lenbach built his villa not simply for the representative requirements of 1890s society, but as a museum or monument to his own memory.[86] The artist's funeral, in 1904, was attended by each and every minister in the Bavarian government, and barriers had to be erected around the cemetery to restrict the crowds.

Like Lenbach, the Salzburg-born painter Hans Makart (1840–84) began in the Munich *atelier* of Karl von Piloty, and first made a name for himself as an historical painter, with subjects from the Thirty Years War, the Italian Renaissance and ancient Rome. He executed these large paintings with great technical skill, if little originality. In the late 1860s his approach became more sensationalist, especially in its treatment of sexuality, with works like *The Plague in Florence*, which caused a scandal when exhibited at the Munich art association in 1868.[87] As his fame spread Makart was enticed back to his homeland. In 1869 he was granted a house and studio in Vienna by Konstantin von Hohenlohe-Schillingsfürst, on behalf of the emperor himself. Here Makart painted his most famous works: vast, shimmering and theatrical paintings with echoes of Veronese, which led Nietzsche to describe Makart as the 'Wagner of painting'.

The artist's numerous admirers in *Gründerzeit* Germany, who had little hope of acquiring one of these paintings, made do with 'Makart hats' or 'Makart bouquets', styled on the women in his paintings. His popularity was also stimulated by his involvement in costumed art balls, pageants, such as the aforementioned Habsburg silver wedding procession that thrilled Vienna in 1879, and by his interior design work. The latter included a large first floor room for the villa of the wealthy businessman Nikolaus Edler von Dumba (1871–73) on Vienna's Ringstrasse; a street that was itself later described as having 'a Makart-procession of architectural styles'. Makart's *atelier* in Vienna became as famous as any of his paintings, and its influence on *Gründerzeit* interior design was considerable. The studio, which was open to the public between three o'clock and five o'clock every afternoon, was packed to the rafters with historical furniture, vases, busts, oriental rugs, medieval weapons and armour, skeletons, mummies, musical instruments, dried and artificial flowers, all arranged as an 'artistic' ensemble.[88] When his painting *The Entry of*

Karl V. into Antwerp went on show there in 1878, some 35,000 paying visitors were recorded, although many of these were probably attracted by the rumour that some of Vienna's high society daughters had posed as nude models. Most of Makart's sitters were, however, actresses: people such as Charlotte Wolter, whom he painted as Cleopatra.

All of this led Makart to become the target of satire and modernist contempt at the turn of the century, and his critical reputation has since undergone no substantial revision. It is worth remembering, however, that the mass mourning prompted by his tragically early death in 1884 was genuine,[89] and that his work only appears 'unoriginal' if viewed from a modernist standpoint. By emulating the old masters, Makart and Lenbach were only doing what was traditionally expected of painters, and what was demanded by their wealthy customers. To the successful middle classes of the *Gründerzeit*, contemporary themes in painting appeared insufficiently 'heroic', and contemporary dress insufficiently 'picturesque'. Even so, there can be little doubt that it was their own wealth and status they were celebrating.

If Lenbach and Makart were the archetypal 'princely-painters' (*Malerfürsten*), living highly public lives and seldom out of the society columns, the apparent counterpoint is provided by the largely unrecognized Hans von Marées (1837–87), a former close friend of Lenbach who spent the last twenty years of his life in Italy; refused to sell a single painting; and took no part in exhibitions after 1864. Marées lived from the financial backing provided by the Dresden industrialist and art historian Konrad Fiedler (1841–95), who for twenty years received nothing in return, but nevertheless penned a glowing tribute to the artist after his death. In the 1900s Marées was 'rediscovered' and his work was acclaimed by the likes of Julius Meier-Graefe and Karl Scheffler for its proto-modern preoccupation with form. Some even called him the German Cézanne. In his lifetime, however, Marées was regarded along with Feuerbach and Böcklin as a *Deutschrömer*: belonging, in other words, to that long-line of German artists who looked to the light, lifestyle and classical heritage of the Italian peninsula for inspiration.

The *Deutschrömer* did not enjoy the social privileges of Lenbach, Makart or Werner, but in general they did not suffer for their art either. Anselm Feuerbach (1829–80), for instance, whose best-known themes were taken from the Greek classics (*Medea*, 1870; *Iphigenie*, 1871) received numerous lucrative job offers from German art schools, but declined them all in favour of southern skies.[90] Feuerbach hated the decorative Makart style, and indeed all contemporary historical paintings which neglected 'timeless' themes for the sake of the banal and everyday. Like other painters of his time he thought historically, and was much preoccupied with his place in history. As he once put it in a letter: 'Often I see myself in one hundred years time, as I wander through old galleries and see my own pictures hanging on the walls in silent seriousness. . . . I will always suffer, but my works will live forever'.[91]

In 1880 Feuerbach died a suitably aesthetic death in Venice, just as Wagner would three years later. A further parallel with the Master of Bayreuth, and indeed with Nietzsche too, was provided by the way in which Feuerbach's posthumous reputation was subsequently shaped by a possessive relative – his stepmother Henriette Feuerbach – who took every opportunity to present her deceased son as a misunderstood genius, unrecognized by his own people. Georg Blochmann has likened her tireless efforts to a modern public-relations campaign,[92] deliberately focusing attention on Feuerbach's handsome features and tortured soul, rather than his fine, but unexciting, paintings of monumental sculptural figures. Two years after the artist's death, she edited his *Vermächtnis* ('Bequest'), a book that was largely responsible for creating the later public image of Feuerbach.[93] In fact, although the artist did endure periods of insecurity and depression, his 'exile' was of his own choosing, and the pathos of his letters reflected dandyish theatricality rather than true despair.

Few artists divided opinions in Imperial Germany more than Arnold Böcklin (1827–1901).[94] The idiosyncratic Swiss-born painter, who spent his last years at the Villa Bellagio near Florence,[95] was championed as a 'Germanic' answer to French Impressionism by Heinrich Wölfflin, and was hailed a 'modern hero' by the young Emil Heilbut.[96] His 70th birthday was celebrated by a specially written play by Rudolf Wackernagel, while his death was marked by a similar drama, *The Death of Titian,* from the pen of Hugo von Hofmannsthal, and a series of 'Böcklin Songs' composed by Karl Henckell. However his work found just as many detractors, such as Julius Meier-Graefe, whose 1905 book *Der Fall Böcklin* ('The Case of Böcklin') echoed Nietzsche's famous attack on Richard Wagner (*Der Fall Wagner*). Meier-Graefe's title was well-chosen, since Böcklin's pathos-laden paintings were often set in a Wagnerian late-romantic world of myth, legend and nature. It was possible to see in this a

Germanic depth and idealism, but others viewed it as decadent and unhealthy. Certainly, his pictures often explored erotic themes and this aspect of his art spawned countless imitators around the turn of the century: his *Isle of the Dead* (1880–6), of which he painted five different versions, was particularly influential.

For all of their stylistic differences, each of these *Gründerzeit* artists sought to produce 'timeless' work and to secure their place in history. Significantly, they did not belong to movements or work collaboratively; each viewed the 'competition' with a suspicion bordering on paranoia. Eventually, all of them achieved some sort of 'heroic' status, but their success was sometimes posthumous and invariably shortlived. No *Gründerzeit* painter today features prominently in general histories of nineteenth-century art, although a major Lenbach retrospective in 1987, the aforementioned Werner exhibition, and two 1988 Munich exhibitions celebrating the *Deutschrömer*, suggest that critical interest is stirring once more.

The hero as archaeologist

'From often humble beginnings, and often with a childhood fascination for antiquity, the archaeologist leaves familiar surroundings to undergo exacting professional training under a series of mentors and when armed, at last, with the intellectual weapons of the profession, sets off for unfamiliar or exotic realms, braving opposition and danger to solve an ancient mystery'.[97] This narrative scenario, so familiar to us from film and fiction, was first formed by real-life archaeologists like Austen Henry Layard, Howard Carter, and particularly, by one of Imperial Germany's great heroes, Heinrich Schliemann (1822–90). Schliemann, who has gone down in history as the man who discovered the city of Troy at Hisarlik (Turkey) in the early 1870s, was in many ways the archetypal *Gründerzeit* hero.

Born into the modest circumstances of a Mecklenburg vicar's family but blessed with an iron will, he triumphed over tragedy and adversity – conflagrations and sinking ships, tropical fever, robbers and murderers – to reach the top in a succession of careers. Before becoming the most famous archaeologist in the world, Schliemann had been an indigo merchant in St Petersburg; a banker in the California goldrush; a millionaire profiteer from the Crimean War; a travel-writer and linguist, fluent in nineteen languages; a student of the Sorbonne and academic author of ten books. He was also,

Figure 6 *Arnold Böcklin,* Isle of the Dead *(1883)*

however, 'a pathological liar',[98] whose achievements have since become the subject of bitter controversy.[99]

Although the details need not concern us here, it has been long established that Schliemann's autobiographical writings contain numerous inconsistencies: some have even questioned the authenticity of his most spectacular archaeological coups, 'Priam's Treasure' (1873)[100] and the so-called 'Mask of Agamemnon' (1876). There is little solid evidence to support the claim that the archaeologist, in desperate need of publicity-grabbing 'finds', commissioned contemporary craftsmen to forge the articles, but the circumstances of their discovery remain shrouded in doubt. The fact that both 'treasures' were discovered by Schliemann alone, at the very end of long digs and out of the gaze of the dozens of helpers, does not help to dispel suspicions, although his desire to smuggle the bounty out of Turkey and Greece may offer a partial explanation.

Schliemann was undoubtedly a conceited self-publicist, with a tendency to exaggeration and fabrication. On the other hand, it is undeniable that he pursued his hunches with regard to the location of Troy and of the tombs of the Mycenaean kings (1876–78), with more vigour and rigour than any other archaeologist of his day. Despite his 'outsider' status – the German establishment had initially placed its faith in the work of the more conventional classicist Ernst Curtius (1814–96), who believed the site of Troy was at Bunabarschi, and whose digs were supported by the Prussian general staff – Schliemann's spectacular finds captured the imagination of countless contemporaries, including Bismarck, Moltke and Crown Prince Friedrich. Though his motives were not always 'pure', and his methods were sometimes crude, Schliemann helped to make classical archaeology one of the imperial era's enduring obsessions.

In his later excavations Schliemann was assisted not only by Rudolf Virchow, but also by the architect Wilhelm Dörpfeld (1853–1940), who was director of the imperial archaeological institute in Athens,[101] and subsequently made a number of important Trojan discoveries in his own right. Although Dörpfeld revised a number of Schliemann's assumptions about the Hisarlik site, he ensured that the archaeologist's posthumous reputation did not suffer as a result. Schliemann, like other heroes of the *Gründerzeit*, was obsessed with his 'legacy' and had taken great care to ensure that his name would be cherished beyond the grave. The mythologizing memoirs; the theatrically staged funeral; and the painstaking arrangements for the display of his treasures in Berlin, all testified to Schliemann's talents for self-promotion. He had already ensured that the new building for Dörpfeld's institute would be erected in the grounds of his own Athens palace, which was itself more a museum than a family home. A German neo-Classical architect, Ernst Ziller, was responsible for both buildings, as well as Schliemann's marble mausoleum on a hill overlooking Athens. The latter had the simple dedication 'To Schliemann the Hero' inscribed on its architrave. It was truly a temple fit for a Greek god. It is difficult to exaggerate Schliemann's level of fame, which extended well beyond the borders of the German Empire. In addition to numerous books and articles, several plays and even an opera were written about him; Sigmund Freud admitted to envying Schliemann more than any other man; and an Oxford University student wrote to Schliemann in 1886: 'There is no book outside of the Bible which has exercised so good an influence on my life as your own autobiography.'[102]

The hero as composer

One of the few cultural events to claim more column inches in the 1870s than the discovery of Troy was the première of Richard Wagner's complete 'Ring' cycle at Bayreuth in 1876. This quartet of music dramas – *The Rhinegold* (1852–4), *The Valkyries* (1852–6), *Siegfried* (1856–7; 1869–71) and *Twilight of the Gods* (1869–74) – was, like the 1862 *Nibelungen* trilogy by the dramatist Friedrich Hebbel (1813–63) or Wilhelm Jordan's *Der Nieblunge* (1867–74), inspired by the twelfth-century epic poem the *Nibelungenlied.* These works would in turn generate a vast critical literature of their own. More importantly, Wagner would become viewed as one of the key figures of his century, exerting an influence far beyond the borders of the German Empire or the world of music. As the industrialist and writer Walther Rathenau recalled in 1918: 'It is scarcely possible to exaggerate how deeply the last generation was spellbound by the influence of Richard Wagner, not so decisively by his music as by the gestures of his characters, by his ideas'.[103]

In 1876 the three Bayreuth performances of the tetralogy were attended by a glittering array of *Gründerzeit* celebrities, including the painters Werner, Makart, Lenbach and Menzel; the composers Bruckner, Grieg, Tchaikovsky, Saint-Saens and Liszt; as well as the Kaiser and the world's press.[104] 'In nature and degree, this Wagnermania was unprecedented, quite unlike the devotion inspired by any other composer, or indeed by any other artistic creator in any field. It was almost religious in its fanaticism and self-sacrificing dedication.'[105] It was precisely this aspect which some found off-putting. The painter Anton von Werner, who went to Bayreuth as an admirer of Wagner's earlier operas, wrote: 'The audience, which had made its pilgrimage to Bayreuth, was so obliging, enthusiastic and willing to make sacrifices, that no author could wish for more, but the Master's household and his supporters appeared to demand more than just respect and admiration . . . worship; idolization; and that's not everyone's cup of tea'.[106] In the words of Frederic Spotts: 'One had gone to Bayreuth to attend an opera and had found a cult'.[107]

Richard Wagner and his works had always provoked strong reactions, but from the mid-1860s onwards he began to attract a new kind of devotee: young men like the philosopher Friedrich Nietzsche and the 18-year old King Ludwig II, who saw in him more than just a composer. Between 1864 and 1883 Wagner received the huge sums of 521,000 RM in subsidies and 41,851 RM in gifts from the unstable Bavarian monarch.[108] It was largely thanks to Ludwig that Wagner was able to fulfil his long-standing dream of building his own theatre. In an 1852 letter Wagner had declared that his proposed cycle of music dramas based on the Nibelung legends could not be performed in a metropolitan setting, but should take place in a 'beautiful quiet place' far from 'the smoke and disgusting industrial smell of our urban civilization'.[109] The specific choice of Bayreuth as its location came later, and was more or less arbitrary, although as a provincial town in Ludwig's Bavaria it clearly met Wagner's principal criteria.

In view of the proliferation of royal opera houses and municipal theatres in the German states, Wagner's desire for a new building all of his own merely confirmed to his critics that the monumental Wagner ego knew no bounds. Never before had a writer or composer been able to build a theatre for his works alone. Since his essay *Opera and Drama* (1851), however, Wagner had been developing a clear vision of a revolutionary kind of stage work, which would combine musical, dramatic and visual elements in a 'total work of art'. This *Gesamtkunstwerk* would require a very different kind of building, a 'festival playhouse', which would dispose of the boxes and galleries of the traditional opera house, and return to the model of the classical amphitheatre to ensure that the audience, who would not be charged for admission, all enjoyed an unhindered view of the stage. Moreover, it would only be in use at certain times of the year and would not stage the usual repertory productions. Wagner's choice of the word 'festival' to describe this vision was significant, since there were many parallels between his 'sacred space' and the sort of national festivals and monuments discussed in Chapter 2. Indeed, the goal of the festivals would be nothing less than the renewal and regeneration of German culture itself.

Wagner's background as a political radical – he had participated in the revolutions of 1848–49 in Dresden – and as a nationalist, meant that his initial vision eschewed the help of dynastic or state authorities. The festival playhouse was to be funded by a 'community' of followers, who would buy patron's certificates at 900 RM each. In reality, of course, things worked out rather differently. Less than half of the certificates sold, and Wagner had to find other ways of raising funds. Admission charges would be unavoidable, but first the building had to be finished. Hoping to cash in on the events of 1871 which he had greeted with such zeal, Wagner turned to Bismarck and Wilhelm I for assistance, but found little encouragement from either quarter. Though his ardour had cooled, Ludwig II was once again Wagner's saviour.[110] Despite financial and political difficulties of his own, the Bavarian monarch eventually acceded to Wagner's request for a loan. Even so, the theatre was erected as economically as possible, using a timber frame construction with brick infill, in the manner of a warehouse or factory. The Paris opera house, which was built at around the same time, cost some 70 times more.[111] Cheap and functional though it was, the festival playhouse ensured that Wagner's ideas gained a lasting focus. Frederic Spotts emphasizes the importance of this: 'Wagner without Bayreuth would have been like a country without a capital, a religion without a Church.'[112]

This was already apparent in 1882 when the Bayreuth stage was 'consecrated' with the première of his last work, *Parsifal*, which Wagner believed could be performed nowhere else. More a religious rite than an opera, *Parsifal* was an initiation ceremony for a theatre that was fast becoming a temple. Wagner's death in Venice followed less than twelve months later, and the composer was laid to rest in a grand mausoleum at his Bayreuth villa Wahnfried. His second wife Cosima (1837–1930) then 'lost no time in laying the foundations of a Wagner cult that became the mania for the rest of her life'.[113] With Cosima's support, Bayreuth became a rallying point for *völkisch* nationalists, virulent anti-semites and cranks of every description.

The so-called 'Bayreuth Circle' cherished 'the Master' not only as an artist, but also as a political theorist and cultural critic, and it is this Wagner who will reappear in Chapter 4.

It is all too easy to forget, however, that Richard Wagner also left a much more positive legacy. As a composer, his oeuvre linked Romanticism with the early twentieth century's experiments in atonality, influencing Debussy, Mahler, Schönberg and countless others. His mature works abandoned the traditional operatic structures, like arias and choruses, in favour of a continuous flowing form, which was far more innovative than the Germanic mythology of his librettos might suggest. In particular, his use of the *leitmotiv* – individual fragments of melody or harmony which acted as musical 'calling cards', to be repeated whenever a character, object or theme was evoked in the drama – was ground-breaking.[114] Wagner was also cited as an influence by several generations of architects, painters, poets and even politicians. The former were especially attracted by the concept of the *Gesamtkunstwerk*, re-interpreting the term to suit their aesthetic requirements.[115]

The hero as statesman

The Bismarck cult started much earlier than one might imagine.[116] The first ship to bear his name was launched in 1867, the first naval vessel a decade later. A hill was named after him in 1869. In the same year a 'Bismarck tower' was built on a country estate south of Breslau, and a succession of other small-scale monuments sprang up in the following years. Guido Schmidt's famous painting of Bismarck as the blacksmith of German unity dates from 1870. Three years later a town in the United States (today the capital of North Dakota) was named after him, as was the steel-works town of Bismarckhütte, Upper Silesia. Even the term 'Bismarck-Cult' is itself of late nineteenth-century provenance. Bismarck's birthday was first celebrated on a large scale in 1890,[117] and thereafter 1 April was always marked by public events. Nearly half a million pre-printed cards were sent to him on his eightieth birthday in 1895, and his last home, the Friedrichsruh estate near Hamburg, became a popular pilgrimage destination for thousands of Germans, even before his death in 1898.

There was a Bismarck Archipelago in New Guinea; Bismarck oaks and 'Bismarckia' palm trees; the colour 'Bismarck brown'; Bismarck hotels and coal mines; Bismarck streets, squares and bridges; Bismarck hats, shirts, soap, springs, cakes, strawberries, tobacco and herrings. The production of Bismarck kitsch became a significant industry in its own right, and considerable sums of money were made from exploiting the Iron Chancellor's name.[118] Few manufacturers, however, were as blatant as Bismarck's former barber, who secretly collected his master's locks for many years and later sold the hairs three-at-a-time, encased in a gold brooch with a certificate of authenticity.

The best-known and most tangible symbols of the Bismarck cult are the countless monuments to his memory, which remain such a familiar feature of the German skyline and townscape. Some seventy Bismarck monuments were built before his death, and hundreds more followed around the turn of the century. Some, like the Reinhold Begas (1831–1911) bronze monument in front of the Reichstag (1901),[119] were expressions of official policy and paid for by the state, but many others were the work of local committees and relied on grassroots fund-raising. In view of the fact that up to 700 Bismarck monuments and towers were built, one can argue that they were more 'popular' – in both senses of the word – than the Kaiser Wilhelm monuments discussed in Chapter 2.[120] The direct comparison is unavoidable, since many who backed the Bismarck monument schemes did so out of concern for the direction of the Empire under Wilhelm II's leadership. A large proportion of the Bismarck monuments were inspired by German student societies, one of which had issued a call in December 1898 to erect simple but 'mighty granite beacons' to Bismarck's memory, forming a widely visible chain across the Empire.[121] Of 150 Bismarck monuments planned by German student associations, ninety-one had already been built by 1902, mostly based on a rustic and rather brutal design by the architect Wilhelm Kreis (1873–1955).[122] Although Bismarck monuments came in all shapes and sizes, the majority opted for sober, powerful and non-historicist forms. Significantly, many of the architects associated with the birth of modernism in Germany tried their hand at Bismarck monuments, including Peter Behrens, Hans Poelzig and Mies van der Rohe.

The geographical distribution of the monuments across the Empire was uneven. Predictably, they were more plentiful in Prussia than Bavaria, but they were spread more widely than the Kaiser-Wilhelm-Monuments. There was a notable concentration in Germany's port cities and on the Empire's western and eastern borders, where they appeared to perform a sort of 'patron-saint' role, although there were also many Bismarck monuments in Germany's African and Asian colonies too. The most famous monument was built in Hamburg, where the shadow cast by the figure of the Iron Chancellor was literally out of all proportion to even his remarkable achievements.[123] It was designed in a self-consciously 'contemporary' style by the architect Emil Schaudt and the sculptor Hugo Lederer, and was built between 1902 and 1906. Like most of the Bismarck memorials it was funded by donations from business and the general public, and its unveiling was shunned by the Kaiser.

Many have attempted to explain the origins of the Bismarck cult. One of the first was Max Weber, who suggested it was a product of the desire of the middle classes for a Caesar to protect them against both the masses from below and the machinations of the ruling dynasties from above.[124] After Bismarck's departure, none of his successors could fulfil this dual role: neither 'the well meaning Caprivi, the senile Hohenlohe, the pliant Bülow and the grey bureaucrat Bethmann Hollweg';[125] nor indeed Wilhelm II himself. Thus the only way to preserve Bismarck's influence in a time of increasing tension and uncertainty was to embody him in stone, as a larger than life, semi-mythical figure. Bismarck monuments therefore not only reflect gratitude for the achievement of unity, but a desire for protection from future dangers.

Realism in *Gründerzeit* literature and art

In much the same way as the German middle classes have been accused of cowering under Bismarck's monumental shadow – of succumbing to 'feudal' temptations and hence failing in their historic mission – so German writers and painters have frequently been the subject of unfavourable comparisons with their foreign equivalents. In both Great Britain and France the mid-nineteenth century had seen the emergence of what became known as the 'Realist' approach to literature and painting: an approach closely associated with the 'rising' bourgeoisie.[126] Realists attempted to depict contemporary life in an objective rather than an idealized manner, and did not shy away from exploring social divisions and conflicts. It is often suggested, however, that because of nineteenth-century German culture's tendency to privilege the poetic over the prosaic, the aesthetic over the real, it 'failed' to produce an equivalent of writers like

Balzac, Dickens or Zola, or indeed of painters like Courbet or Millet.[127]

There are several potential responses to this line of argument. Just as Blackbourn and Eley have pointed out the dangers of adopting an idealized Anglo-American yardstick by which to measure German social and political development,[128] so one could highlight the high level of aesthetic artifice that actually characterized many classics of European literary and artistic Realism. A more constructive response, however, would be to take what Germany did have to offer more seriously, for the *Gründerzeit* was not as devoid of Realism as is sometimes suggested.[129] While the best-known Realists writing in the German language, such as Theodor Storm (1817–88) and Gottfried Keller (1819–90), did indeed feel most at home in a rural, pre-industrial setting, there *were* writers prepared to confront the social realities of the 1871 Empire. Both Karl Gutzkow (1811–79) and Friedrich Spielhagen (1829–1911), for instance, attempted to tackle the spivs and speculators of the *Gründerzeit*; most notably in Spielhagen's *Sturmflut* ('Storm Tide', 1876).

In Spielhagen's entertaining novel the *Gründerzeit* is portrayed as an uncontrollable natural force – the storm tide of the title – breaking over German society. The focal point of the story is a speculative railway project reminiscent of Bethel Strousberg's schemes.[130] The Berlin–Sundin railway was to be extended to Wissow; 'a small sandy peninsula with some twenty houses' on the Baltic coast. The undertaking collapses, of course, but not before Spielhagen had satirized almost every aspect of the *Gründerzeit*, from Wagnermania to Darwinism. The fashion for monument building also features in the novel. In an effort to provide even the little town of Posemuckel with a Victory Monument, an overworked Berlin sculptor dusts off an old statue of Homer and replaces its head with that of Germania. As a character in the book remarks, a better image of German unification could hardly be found.[131]

The late 1870s and 1880s also saw a proliferation of 'Berlin novels'. Before the *Reichsgründung* few works had been set in the Prussian capital, and specific references to the city's name or streets were rare. The novelists of the 1880s, however, made no attempt to obscure their settings. 'Real' locations became fashionable in the works of authors like Paul Lindau (1839–1919), Fritz Mauthner (1849–1923) and Max Kretzer (1854–1941). Lindau's novels – such as *Der Zug nach dem Westen* ('The Westbound Train', 1886) and *Arme Mädchen* ('Poor Girls', 1887) – confronted the superficial 'salon culture' of the early Empire, but remained predominantly positive in tone, reflecting the author's urbanity and progressive optimism. Mauthner's trilogy *Berlin W.* was set in the same bourgeois milieu of bankers, stockbrokers and civil servants. Max Kretzer focused on the other side of the city: the tenements, allotments, bars and brothels of working-class East Berlin, in novels such as *Die beiden Genossen* ('The Two Comrades', 1880), *Die Betrogenen* ('The Deceived', 1882) and *Die Verkommenen* ('The Dissolute', 1883).[132]

Then there was Theodor Fontane, whose acutely observed social novels have already been mentioned in other contexts. Although Fontane was never much concerned about literary labels, he wrote in an 1853 essay: 'Realism in art is as old as art itself; in fact, it IS art.'[133] If Realism was about being truthful and displaying human understanding, then he was happy to be called a Realist, which was certainly preferable to the 'hypocritical sentimentality' of Romanticism or to vulgar idealism. Fontane believed, however, that merely depicting the wretchedness of everyday life would never be sufficient. Since ugliness and beauty existed side by side in life, so they must both be present in a truly realistic literature, and it was the artist's responsibility to ensure this was the case. Fontane's enduring popularity has much to do with this sense of balance, but also his dry sense of humour and a fondness for irony; his good ear for dialogue, especially the slang of his own day; and the accessibility of his carefully crafted prose. These qualities have not always been recognized, and have led some to claim his work lacks real depth, but the 'Gentle Critic'[134] remains one of the few *Gründerzeit* novelists to retain their popular appeal a century later.

The crowning achievement of German Realist literature, however, did not arrive until 1901, and the publication of Thomas Mann's *Buddenbrooks.* Mann was only 25 years old when he sent his weighty manuscript to the publisher Samuel Fischer, but there was nothing youthful about his cool, detached prose or the epic scope of this study, which was subtitled the 'decline of a family' and traced the fortunes of a north German merchant family (very much like Mann's own) in the years between 1835 and 1877. Beneath its elegant and conventional surface, critics have found all manner of radical and modern literary devices – rapid changes of perspective; the author's ironic distance from his characters; his willingness to alienate the reader 'by the confusing use of different linguistic levels'[135] – but the aspect of most interest to historians is Mann's treatment of *Bürgerlichkeit*: not only the celebrated clash between the bourgeois and the artistic temperament, but also his portrayal of social change and mobility. Although the strains of industrialization, urbanization and the rise of the labour movement barely impinge on the world of the Buddenbrooks, it is clear that the family's struggle is with modernity itself. Many critics, therefore, have seen the Buddenbrooks as exemplifying the German middle class experience more generally: 'the reader should recognize that the fate of the Buddenbrook family was also that of the social class to which they belonged', as Martin Travers puts it.[136] Yet even within the confines of Mann's novel, it is clear that the Buddenbrooks represent only one side of the coin: while they are in decline, the more ambitious and entrepreneurial Hagenströms are on the rise.

Thomas Buddenbrook's apparent rejection of modernity and desire to seek refuge in an inner world of art and philosophy is frequently interpreted in the context of the cultural pessimism or 'cultural despair' that historians such as Fritz Stern have identified as a highly influential mood in late nineteenth-century Germany.[137] However, as Hugh Ridley notes, this reading tends to overlook the 'sense of liberation which Mann – and potentially his characters too – felt in leaving those bourgeois values behind'.[138] It also neglects the Hagenströms, whose materialism and 'vulgar optimism' can be viewed as equally characteristic of their age. Indeed, it may be that the real value of Mann's treatment of the German bourgeoisie lies in the way it captures the ambivalence and ambiguity of middle-class responses to economic and social modernization.

Before we leave the topic of Realist literature, it should also be noted that not all *Gründerzeit* plays were clichéd historical-mythological dramas or trivial comedies either. In fact, there was a strong public demand in the major German cities for productions that reflected contemporary life, albeit without the 'bad taste' of Flaubert's *Madame Bovary* or Zola's *Nana.* Paul Lindau, who wrote plays as well as novels, was one writer who met this need, with his satirical tales of the urban middle classes. His successes included *Maria und Magdalena* (1872), *Ein Erfolg* ('A Success', 1874) and two plays from 1880: *Verschämte Arbeit* ('Embarrassing Work'), which dealt with women's employment, and *Gräfin Lea* ('Countess Lea'), which attacked contemporary anti-semitism. Lindau, who was himself Jewish, became the subject of racist pamphlets as the result of the latter, but the play was a critical and commercial success. Admittedly, Lindau's Realism never strayed beyond the bounds of the bourgeoisie, and his satire was not particularly savage, but the popularity of such pieces nevertheless reminds us that there was more to *Gründerzeit* theatre than first meets the eye.

In painting, the German whose approach seemed closest to Courbet or Millet was Wilhelm Leibl (1844–1900). Indeed, Courbet was so impressed with the German's work that he invited him to Paris, where Leibl spent some nine months, and also met Edouard Manet. He should not, therefore, be dismissed as an insignificant genre painter. Leibl is best known for his studies of Upper Bavarian rural life like *Two Dachau Women* (1875), *The Ill-matched Couple* (1877) or *Three Women in Church* (1881). These paintings, which exude an air of quiet dignity, were certainly somewhat idealized, but were refreshingly free of *Gründerzeit* pomp. As for depictions of industry and labour, it is true that they were few and far between in German painting before the 1890s, but there were exceptions here too. The most famous of these is the *Iron Rolling Mill*, painted between 1872 and 1875 by Adolph Menzel. The painter had made his name as 'the Homer of the Hohenzollerns' thanks to his prints of Friedrich the Great and numerous other pictures on royal and historical themes, including Wilhelm I's official coronation painting (1861–5), so this powerful portrayal of modern industry caused an immediate sensation. It was not, however, Menzel's first attempt at a factory scene. A couple of years earlier he had been commissioned by a Berlin metal-working firm to paint the frontispiece for a fiftieth anniversary album (1869), which had included two realistic shopfloor scenes in a decorative architectural framework, supported by six Atlas figures and presented by a classical Fortuna.

For the 1875 painting, Menzel dropped the mythologizing framework and aimed for accuracy, making at least 150 preparatory sketches at one of Germany's most advanced foundries, the Königshütte in Upper Silesia, where railway tracks were being manufactured for the *Gründerzeit* boom. Although the artist's respect for the workers is apparent, the painting eschews pathos or crude comment on the rights or wrongs of industrial capitalism. Like his close friend Fontane, Menzel – who was ennobled in 1898 – succeeded in remaining an independent and sceptical artist, admired by cultural progressives and conservatives alike. Subsequently, as Françoise Forster-Hahn has pointed out, his work has been used by art historians in the construction of both a German national tradition of painting and an international modernist canon.[139] The critical and popular reaction to the *Iron Rolling Mill* was almost entirely

Figure 7 Adolph von Menzel, Iron Rolling Mill (Modern Cyclops) *(1872–3)*

positive, and it was much in demand at world exhibitions, appearing in Paris (1878 and 1885), Chicago (1893) and St Louis (1904).

By the time of the American shows, the *Gründerzeit* was already history. Germany had changed in significant ways. In the cultural sphere, this had much to do with the treatises of the critics and reformers who are the initial focus of Chapter 4. This did not mean, however, that the themes which we identified at the start of this chapter – the search for a national style; the preoccupation with history; and the cult of the hero – quickly disappeared from German cultural discourse. The search for a national style, in particular, was to remain a feature of German cultural life throughout the imperial era.

4 *Cultural Critics and Revolts*

Introduction

On 10 August 1897 Felix Hoffmann, a chemist working for Bayer and Co. in Elberfeld, synthesized the acetyl derivative of salicylic acid to produce a new chemical compound: acetylsalicylic acid, or ASS for short. It was registered with the Imperial Patent Office's list of tradenames in 1899 and within a few years it had become one of the world's most popular medical products, for use against headaches, fever, inflammations and rheumatism. ASS was sold first in powdered form and then as a tablet: it was marketed under the name of 'Aspirin'. The invention of Aspirin was just one of many scientific and technological achievements chalked up during the lifetime of an Empire whose nineteen universities and eleven institutes of technology attracted young researchers from around the world; whose language was unavoidable in a number of disciplines; and whose scientists enjoyed unparalleled success during the first quarter-century of Nobel prizes.[1]

In the *Kaiserreich*, as elsewhere in nineteenth-century Europe, the empirical scientific method was triumphant; the metaphysical on the decline. As the Professor of Zoology and popular science writer Ernst Haeckel (1834–1919) proclaimed: 'Progress is a natural law that no human power, neither the weapons of tyrants nor the curses of priests, can ever succeed in suppressing'.[2] Just as historicism ruled the humanities, so other positivist approaches dominated the social and natural sciences.[3] The new deity, Charles Darwin (1809–82),[4] might have been a Briton, but many German scientists and engineers were not far behind. Some literally became household names

– immortalized in the vocabulary of the twentieth century like Heinrich Hertz (1857–94), Rudolf Diesel (1858–1913) or Ernst Mach (1838–1916) – while others were celebrated for their practical application of new theoretical ideas. The inventor of the dynamo, Werner von Siemens (1816–92), developed the first electric locomotive (1879), while Carl Benz (1844–1929) and Gottlieb Daimler (1834–1900) were credited with the invention of the motorcar.

By all accounts, such advances were greeted with patriotic enthusiasm. When, in 1882, the Crystal Palace in Munich hosted Germany's first exhibition of electricity, thousands turned up to marvel at the illuminated building and its electric waterfall, which was powered from a generator over 30 miles away. Similar crowds attended the opening ceremonies for technical wonders like the *Schwebebahn* monorail, uniting the Wupper valley towns of Barmen and Elberfeld (1898–1903); or the mighty railway bridge at nearby Müngsten (1894–97); or the 60-mile long Kiel Canal (1887–95), linking the Baltic to the North Sea. On each occasion, that noted enthusiast for modern technology, Emperor Wilhelm II did the honours, befitting a monarch whose support for scientific and technological research was second to none. The research association founded in 1911 and named after him – the 'Kaiser-Wilhelm-Gesellschaft' – boasted seven separate institutes, and helped to fund the research of pioneering scientists like Max Planck (1858–1947) and Albert Einstein (1879–1955).

The establishment of the German Empire coincided not only with the era of historicism and positivism, but also with the age of liberalism. Whatever disappointments German liberals may have experienced in the political sphere, the Empire's early years witnessed a host of liberal-inspired state-building measures of which most Germans could be proud. Achievements were recorded at municipal level too: with their civic museums, theatres and other emblems of cultural progress; their trams, parks and public utilities; German cities could afford to flaunt their status in a series of imposing new town halls; more than 100 of which were erected during the lifetime of the Empire.[5] Amidst the patriotic back-slapping and self-congratulatory cheers, critical voices from the Protestant middle classes were seldom heard, but they became louder towards the end of the 1870s. The German economy took a long time to recover from the 1873 crash, and protectionist measures moved to the top of the agenda. Bismarck's fundamental political re-alignment of 1878–9, which according to some historians represented a 'second' founding of the

Empire[6] – exemplified by the introduction of new trade tariffs; a cull of liberal officials; a *rapprochement* with the Centre party; and the passing of the Anti-Socialist Law – signified that the influence of liberalism was on the wane.

In fact, liberalism, scientific positivism and historicism all came under fire at around this time. The coincidence of political unification, industrialization and urbanization meant there were sufficient targets in the 'Empire of the Rich'[7] for even the most muddle-headed and myopic snipers. Friedrich Nietzsche, who at this time was neither, talked of the 'extirpation of the German spirit in favour of the German empire' and was not alone in wondering whether the sacrifice had been worthwhile. In the first of his *Untimely Meditations* (1873), he criticized the assumption that the victory of Prussian arms had been a victory for German culture, and reminded his compatriots that 'a great victory is a great danger'.[8] At around the same time he posed the question: 'Is life to dominate knowledge and science, or is knowledge to dominate life? Which of these two forces is the higher and more decisive?' His own answer was clear: 'There can be no doubt: life is the higher'.[9]

Less stylish but more accessible critics like the columnist Otto Glagau (1834–92) launched numerous attacks on the 'swindles' of the stockmarket and the Empire's apparent willingness to sacrifice spiritual values on the altar of vulgar materialism;[10] Bismarck's banker Gerson Bleichröder, who for many critics was the *Gründerzeit* parvenu personified, came in for particularly rough treatment. The conservative sociologist Wilhelm Heinrich Riehl expressed concern about the moral corruption and growing social divisions of Germany's sprawling cities, while the historian Jacob Burckhardt questioned whether individual freedom could survive in a world of faceless uniformity. Others attacked the *Gründerzeit* tendency to elevate literary and artistic pygmies to the status of giants; or bemoaned the oppressive weight of history, which the journalist Maximilian Harden compared to a dead body on the young Empire's back. The latter was also the theme of Nietzsche's celebrated attack on historicism in the second of his *Untimely Meditations.*

As we have seen, Nietzsche's criticism was based in part on the superficiality of nineteenth-century *Geschichtskultur* and the way it detracted from the present, but there was another important aspect too. Nietzsche was one of the first to perceive the increasing relativization of values that had been bought about by historicism.

George Iggers explains: 'If the historical approach to human reality seemed at first to open a way for genuine understanding of real life, it now threatened to unveil the relativity of all knowledge and of all value. All norms that once had appeared firm seemed now to be swept away by historical and social scientific inquiry, and history began to reveal itself as a flux devoid of meaning or ethical value'.[11] Researchers had succeeded in demonstrating that even the most dominant of past cultures had not been able to escape historical change. However much the guardians of power, morality and beauty had asserted the permanence of the laws they administered, such 'permanence' had sooner or later proven temporary. The implications of this were profound. Combined with Darwin's theory of evolution, which was also predicated on the inevitability of change, it meant it was now much more difficult for anyone to uphold the inviolability of particular value systems; aesthetic or otherwise. As the art historian Richard Muther wrote in 1889: 'there is no other "eternal law" of beauty . . . than that things change'.[12] It was above all this recognition that characterized the revolt against historicism and the rise of modernism in the decades either side of 1900.

It was a recognition that also shook the very foundations of German idealist philosophy and of scientific positivism, which both presumed the existence of objective truths and norms. The intellectual challenge to positivism was led by Arthur Schopenhauer (1788–1860), whose philosophical pessimism was based on a profound disillusionment with the modern world's political, social, economic and ethical development. During his lifetime Schopenhauer had more detractors than admirers, but gained a host of posthumous converts, including Nietzsche, Wagner, and a number of lesser talents who all shared his critical and pessimistic outlook.

Cultural pessimism

At the time of the *Untimely Meditations* Nietzsche was little known outside academic circles. Having become a university professor at the age of 24, ill-health had forced him into early retirement in his mid-thirties (1879): nearly all his major works were then written in a single decade before his final mental collapse in 1889. Ironically, it was only after he had lost his sanity that his ideas gained a wider audience. In the 1890s his savage criticisms of contemporary society and culture were taken up by radicals and reformers of every kind;

progressive and reactionary alike.[13] His aphoristic style, which was unusually brutal and direct ('philosophizing with the hammer'), but unsystematic and frequently contradictory, allowed for a multiplicity of interpretations. The great 'seducer and pied piper', as Nietzsche once called himself, therefore became an influence on a disparate range of movements and individuals. This diversity is also reflected in the literature on Nietzsche, whose influence was felt far beyond Germany's borders, even if a good deal of his appeal lay in the shimmering quality of his German prose.

From the outbreak of the First World War to the aftermath of the Second, many authors sought to highlight his malign legacy, exploring his influence on twentieth-century German nationalism and militarism. He was placed in a long line of aggressive German thinkers, whose work was said to have paved the way for Hitler and the Holocaust. A more nuanced approach followed, which stressed the 'manipulation' of Nietzsche's ideas by his conservative and racist sister Elisabeth,[14] and their further 'corruption' under National Socialism. Recent authors have taken a different tack, highlighting the emancipatory impact of Nietzsche's ideas on political progressives, feminists, libertarians and cultural modernists,[15] or recreating him as the father of post-modernism, pointing out his influence on many a fashionable French theorist.[16] Certainly, his most enduring and elastic ideas – the 'Death of God', the 'Superman' and the 'Will to Power' – still retain the capacity to provoke debate and dispute more than a century later.

In this light, Kurt Tucholsky's 1929 comment '[t]ell me what you need and I will supply you with a Nietzsche citation . . . for Germany and against Germany; for peace and against peace; for literature and against literature – whatever you want',[17] appears particularly perspicacious. What has never been disputed, however, is that that artists, writers, composers, and architects were amongst Nietzsche's earliest and most devout followers. Since the philosopher viewed creative people as the vanguard of humanity – he wrote that the world was only justified as an aesthetic phenomenon and that only art could make life bearable – this mutual adoration is hardly surprising. Of course, it was not the 'princely painters' or the 'literary popes' who identified with the iconoclastic philosopher, but the young and the disaffected, the self-styled rebels, martyrs and prophets, the wannabe *Übermenschen*, who embraced Nietzsche as an ally in their revolts against the established conventions of bourgeois culture. Henceforth, any movement that sought cultural renewal and regeneration would rely on the power of his words, the strength of his convictions, and above all his sense of style.

Another inspirational figure with a problematic legacy was Nietzsche's one time friend, and later sworn enemy, Richard Wagner, whose initial enthusiasm for the *Reichsgründung* proved shortlived. As we have seen, Wagner was one of the era's most admired, but also most controversial, figures. Although many struggled with the dissonance and chromaticism of his works (and therefore sided with the more orthodox Brahms in one of the *Gründerzeit*'s great rivalries), his ability as a composer was not really in doubt. It was his status as a cultural theorist that was disputed. The latter was, however, very important to Wagner. As Frederic Spotts puts it, 'Wagner had not created an operatic and architectural revolution to recount heroic sagas against a background of beautiful music. His aim was to propound ideas'.[18]

Wagner's 'ideas' had, since the mid-nineteenth century, been dominated by his obsession with the Jews: 'In Wagner's own life, the artist in search of redemption became a modern Jesus who must rout the Jews. . . . And in Wagner's essays, Judaism becomes the absolute symbol of all that is wrong in the modern bourgeois world'.[19] Not all critics and musicologists would endorse Paul Lawrence Rose's verdict on the anti-semitic content of Wagner's operas.[20] While the character of Kundry in *Parsifal* might seem to be Jewish, the cases of Klingsor in *Parsifal*, Beckmesser in the *Mastersingers*, or Alberich in the *Ring* are far less clear. Rose's thesis, however, depends less on the 'jewishness' of individual characters than on his interpretation of Wagner's whole *Weltanschauung*, in which he argues the ideas of race and revolution were inseparably linked: '[t]he revolutionary nature of the *Ring* cycle has long been accepted. But what has not been so easily acknowledged is that, *ipso facto*, these operas are profoundly antisemitic'.[21]

Whether one accepts this view or not, it is clear that race was a central preoccupation of Wagner's theoretical writings, and not only because of his notorious essay *Judaism in Music*, first published anonymously in 1850, and then reprinted under his own name in 1869. Profoundly influenced by Schopenhauer, whom he first read in 1854, Wagner developed a version of 'Aryan Christianity' that underpinned his last music-drama *Parsifal*, and which was vigorously promoted after his death in the *Bayreuther Blätter*, founded in 1878 by Hans von Wolzogen (1848–1938) as the house journal of the 'Bayreuth Circle'.[22] Wolzogen used the journal as an ideological instrument to peddle racist and religious mysticism, with the full encouragement of Wagner's widow Cosima. Other members of the Bayreuth Circle included Karl Friedrich Glasenapp (1847–1915), author of a six-volume biography of the Master; Bernhard Förster (1843–89) husband of Elisabeth Nietzsche and author of *Parsifal Aftertones* (1883); Ludwig Schemann (1852–1938), the German translator of the French racial theorist Count de Gobineau (1816–82); and visual artists such as Franz Stassen and Hermann Hendrich. The latter's large-scale depictions of events from Nordic mythology adorned the walls of the 'Sagenhalle' in Schreiberhau (1902) and the 'Nibelungenhalle' in the Rhineland, which was built in 1913 to commemorate the centenary of Wagner's birth. The Circle considered the Wagner theatre in Bayreuth to be a 'glorious Aryan fortress' and a 'temple of art for the renewal of Aryan blood'. This line of thought was exemplified by *The Completion of the Aryan Mystery in Bayreuth* (1911), a book by the Viennese academic Leopold von Schroeder (1851–1920), which concluded: 'Through Wagner, Bayreuth has been created as the ideal focal point for all the Aryan peoples.'[23]

Another member of the Bayreuth Circle was Houston Stewart Chamberlain (1855–1927), the eccentric son of a British General, who emigrated to Germany in 1885 and married Wagner's daughter Eva in 1908. Chamberlain's *The Foundations of the Nineteenth Century* (1899), a pseudo-scientific history of the western world, explained in fashionable Social Darwinist terms, was greatly admired by Wilhelm II, who shared much of the Bayreuth Circle's racism and cultural pessimism. In general, however, the influence of the Circle in Imperial Germany was never as great as this royal approval might imply, and though the Kaiser was fond of playing the true Wagnerian – dressing up as Lohengrin; entering Hamburg on a swan boat; and playing a motif from the *Rhinegold* on his car horn – he was bemused by the composer's followers: 'What do people actually want with this Wagner? The chap is simply a bandleader (*Kapellmeister*), nothing more than a bandleader – a very ordinary bandleader!' he is said to have exclaimed.[24] Cosima's wish that he would become Bayreuth's patron and protector remained unfulfilled.

Amongst the many other cultural critics to emerge in the later nineteenth century the writings of the *völkisch* cultural pessimists Paul de Lagarde (1827–91) and Julius Langbehn (1851–1907) have attracted particular attention from historians. The former was a biblical scholar and linguist, whose real name was Bötticher, and whose main essays were written in the 1870s. The latter was a failed academic, who became famous on the back of a single book, *Rembrandt als Erzieher* ('Rembrandt as Educator'), published anonymously in 1890. Their work was first highlighted by a series of studies in the early 1960s by historians such as Fritz Stern and George Mosse, who argued that their writings typified a distinctive 'German ideology', which was hostile to most aspects of the modern world, and which offered in its place a rag-bag of neo-Romantic, irrational and radical nationalist impulses, possessing a revolutionary dynamic every bit as hostile to orthodox conservative thinking as it was to liberalism and socialism.[25] This ideology, it was suggested, exerted a lasting and damaging influence on German society, and in particular on the educated middle class.

Although the cultural pessimists certainly had more readers than disaffected intellectuals on the fringes of academia might normally expect, the extent and nature of their influence has been subject to much debate. The degree to which cultural pessimism was peculiar to Germany has been questioned too. The rapidity of the Empire's industrialization and urbanization may have given the German discourse an unusual sharpness and intensity, but it is not difficult to locate similar patterns of thought in mid-nineteenth-century Britain or *fin-de-siècle* France. As James Sheehan notes, 'self-criticism seems to be a persistent and pervasive part of bourgeois culture'.[26] Moreover, cultural pessimism in Germany developed alongside a similarly extreme strand of 'vulgar' or 'shallow' optimism, which was arguably just as typical of the bourgeois mindset. It was not a question of one replacing the other, David Blackbourn suggests, but rather 'a complex juxtaposition of the two'.[27]

The full complexities of this 'juxtaposition' cannot be entered into here, but two general observations need to be made. First, it is extremely difficult to assess the influence of any particular writer or thinker in a given society. Even where it is possible to use quantifiable data there are important caveats. Stern, for example, emphasized the large number of reprints Lagarde and Langbehn's works enjoyed – forty-nine between 1890 and 1909 in the case of *Rembrandt as Educator*[28] – as evidence of their wide readership, but sceptics can point to the fact that each of these print runs were rather small, producing more modest sales than Stern implied. The use of sales figures raises other questions too: how many people read each copy? How much do they agree with what they have read? How much have they even understood? After all, few would argue that the huge sales of Stephen Hawking's *A Brief History of Time* offer a reliable indicator of the reading public's understanding of theoretical physics today.

Secondly, it is well known that intellectuals tend to exaggerate the importance of other intellectuals. Stern's thesis propounds a rather triumphalist view of the history of ideas within society, and as one critic was quick to point out, a preoccupation with 'the political impact of a few maverick thinkers' can distract attention from those organizations in Imperial German society that had genuine 'proto-fascist' credentials.[29] No one is suggesting, however, that the influence of cultural pessimism in Germany can be dismissed altogether. Thomas Nipperdey is surely right to emphasize that one of the most important aspects of the phenomenon was the way it became possible, for the first time, to be both conservative and modern.[30] Long before the 'reactionary modernism' and 'conservative revolution' of Weimar Germany,[31] Lagarde and Langbehn's calls for cultural and spiritual renewal helped to liberate new creative energies, a fact commented on favourably by such respectable contemporaries as Thomas Mann, Wilhelm Bode and Georg Simmel. Indeed, while Lagarde and Langbehn were undoubtedly hostile to many aspects of modernity, the label 'anti-modern' seems a rather inadequate description of their work.

Langbehn's *Rembrandt as Educator*, in particular, struck a chord with forward-thinking artists, writers and other cultural producers seeking a fresh start, away from formalist conventions. It celebrated the eponymous seventeenth century Dutch (or *Niederdeutsch*) painter as the spiritual father of a new Reformation, which would place art above politics, religion or science. This would not be an academic art, based on the pattern-books of history, but a truly popular art derived from the inherent instincts and primitive passions of the *Volk*. Although much of it was bizarre and confused, *Rembrandt* was the first book in decades that German artists actually wanted to read, according to the turn-of-the-century art historian Cornelius Gurlitt.[32] As such, it became a direct inspiration for a number of important cultural undertakings, including the artists' colony at Worpswede (see Chapter 5). Moreover, in its rejection of the unthinking adoption of historical forms and desire to reconcile utility and beauty, it prefigured the rhetoric of twentieth-century functionalism. Finally, though Langbehn was not in the same league as Nietzsche, he also managed to come up with some memorable aphorisms of his own, such as 'the professor is the German national disease'; or 'the true artist can never be local enough'.

Langbehn helped to pave the way for a succession of widely-read art pedagogues, who each in their own way tried to communicate to the general public the value of simplicity and spontaneity in artistic creativity, and to elevate the standing of folk art and vernacular traditions against the prevailing pomposity of the Empire's official culture. Arguably the most important of these was Alfred Lichtwark (1852–1914), the long-serving director of Hamburg's art gallery, whose tireless efforts to provide an aesthetic education for the general public and particularly for children, are still fondly remembered in the city. Lichtwark's concept of encouraging the artistic 'dilettante' led to a broad art education movement in Wilhelmine Germany, which was also furthered by the avuncular and accessible writings of Ferdinand Avenarius (1856–1923), publisher of the cultural journal *Der Kunstwart* since 1887; and Paul Schultze-Naumburg (1869–1949), whose essays on architecture and the landscape helped to sensitize many middle-class Germans to issues of town-planning and conservation.

As we shall see, the revolt against historicism inspired by this disparate group of cultural critics and pedagogues took a different guise in each of the arts, and nowhere was it clear cut; aesthetically or politically. With hindsight, it is possible to see that the voices of renewal and regeneration fell into two broad camps: those who sought distinctively German solutions, and those whose approach was more cosmopolitan. The former hoped either to re-establish continuity with earlier folk values or to build on the traditions of idealism, by emphasizing the unique power and depth of the German imagination. In contrast, the latter tended to embrace approaches that were self-consciously novel, urban and international. The gulf between these two positions would become apparent only later; for the time being the distinctions were blurred by a shared contempt for the excesses of the *Gründerzeit* and a common distaste for academic formalism.

Despite the frequent invocations of the German *Volk* in the rhetoric of the cultural critics and reformers, it should not be forgotten that a preoccupation with the primitive and the irrational was a common feature of European cultural life by the 1890s, as the century at last began to lose its sparkle, and alternatives to European rationalism were much in demand. One only has to think of the use of myth and folk song in the compositions of Dvorak and Stravinsky, or to recall Paul Gauguin's reason for setting sail to the South Seas (to escape 'everything that is artificial and conventional') to be reminded of this. The 1880s had been a 'stuffy decade' right across the continent.[33] It was not only in Germany that the values associated with nineteenth century civilization or their traditional modes of expression – the written word, figurative art, tonal music – were being called into question.

'One by one, the generation which had helped to create the nineteenth century went to their graves, and those who had until then felt themselves to be the young ones, now became the ancients', Anton von Werner wrote in his memoirs of the late 1880s.[34] Throughout Europe the self-satisfied cult of material progress, and with it much of the post-Enlightenment orthodoxy, was confronted by a new mood of scepticism and anti-intellectualism, in which the power of intuition and 'thinking with the blood' were upheld as alternatives to the coldly rational approach of the scientist. Today, much of this makes for uncomfortable reading, since the instrumentalization of such ideas in the twentieth century brought unprecedented barbarity and suffering. Without such radical critiques of modernity, however, the artistic modernism considered canonical today would simply not have been possible.

Naturalism in literature

The first of the late nineteenth-century movements for cultural renewal to make an impact in Germany was Naturalism. Two themes have dominated research into German Naturalist writers: on the one hand, the extent of their socio-political engagement and their relationship to socialism; on the other, the role of new scientific ideas, particularly theories of race and evolution, in their work. It is the latter which has been most influential in recent years, as literary historians have attempted to explain the later accommodation of former Naturalists with Nazism.[35] In comparison, it has largely been taken for granted that the apparently sudden upsurge of Naturalist writing in the 1880s was in sharp reaction to the cultural values of the *Gründerzeit* and the political priorities of the imperial government. Naturalism is thus portrayed as a 'revolution', which shocked the establishment and marked the breakthrough of modernism in Germany.

This was, of course, also the line put about by the Naturalists themselves, in lectures such as Max Halbe's 'The Revolution in Modern Drama' (1885), and in numerous polemical publications like Karl Bleibtreu's *The Revolution in Literature* (1886) or Arno Holz's *The Revolution in Poetry* (1898). Although it is certainly true that a diffuse anti-*Gründerzeit* sentiment was a defining characteristic of Naturalism, the 'revolutionary' nature of the movement must be treated with some caution. As a number of studies have made clear the boundaries between the Naturalists and other writers of the time were fluid and indistinct.[36] This was partly for semantic reasons. The term 'Naturalism' was first used by its opponents, while its adherents had previously been happy to call themselves 'Young Germans' or 'Realists'. Partly because of this, the terms 'Realism' and 'Naturalism' are often applied inconsistently, and sometimes even appear interchangeable, although as we shall see, there were characteristics of Naturalism that were largely absent in Realism. The inconsistency is also a consequence of the different usage of the terms in literary and art historical discourse.[37]

The boundaries between Naturalists and other writers were, however, far from clear-cut on the grounds of style and content either. As we have seen, contemporary settings and 'social' themes were not entirely absent from *Gründerzeit* literature. In addition to the work of Realist writers, it is possible to find specifically Naturalistic elements in a range of pre-1889 plays. Some of the works of the prolific Richard Voss (1851–1918), for example, contained psychologically-complex studies of female characters; while popular dialect plays and musicals often presented theatre-goers with tales of ordinary people, confronting the sort of issues – alcoholism, prostitution, the burden of history and inheritance – which would become stock themes of Naturalist drama. The Naturalist insistence on detailed stage directions and accurate settings was not so novel either, since it had been a feature of the otherwise very different Meiningen court theatre. In poetry, meanwhile, the seminal early Naturalist anthology *Moderne Dichter-Charaktere* ('Modern Personalities in Poetry', 1885), contained works by Ernst von Wildenbruch and other *Gründerzeit* poets. Wildenbruch was also able to adopt a superficial Naturalist style for his plays *Die Haubenlerche* ('The Crested Lark', 1890) and *Meister Balzer* ('Master Balzer', 1892), before returning to more conventional forms later in the decade.

In various respects, therefore, Naturalism was less 'revolutionary' than it sometimes appears, and its highpoint was certainly shortlived, spanning only the late 1880s and early 1890s. It is nevertheless regarded as a significant chapter in German cultural history, not least because of the half-decade of manifestos, essays and journals that preceded it. These came from the pens of literati like Heinrich Hart (1855–1906), who published six editions of the short-lived but influential *Kritische Waffengänge* ('Critical Jousts', 1882–4) with his brother Julius (1859–1930), Karl Bleibtreu (1859–1928), and Michael Georg Conrad (1846–1927), founder of the Munich publication *Die Gesellschaft* ('Society') in 1885. This journal, which had a circulation of around 1000, directed most of its fire against Munich's 'literary Pope' Paul Heyse, the author of nearly 150 novellas and later the first German to win the Nobel Prize for Literature. Among the manifestos was the 'Ten Theses on the Modern in Literature' (1887) drawn up by the young academic Eugen Wolff (1863–1929) for the *Durch* group in Berlin, which had been founded in the previous year, and included the Hart brothers, Wilhelm Bölsche (1861–1939) and Bruno Wille (1860–1928) amongst its members.

Although the 'Ten Theses' were not in themselves particularly radical, they did mark one of the first appearances in print of the term *die Moderne*.[38] This key word of the last hundred years, which Wolff had previously used in the title of an 1886 lecture, and which was already in circulation as an adjective, was from the beginning both vague and multifaceted. Wolff used it to highlight a contrast with the aesthetic ideals of the Ancient world; for others in the 1880s it implied the use of scientific methods; or the creation of a specifically German art.[39] As we shall see, it was to remain an elusive yet over-used term for many years to come. The theorists of the 1880s paved the way for a generation of twenty-something Germans, who had been attracted to Berlin or Munich as students, and had become aware of Zola, Ibsen and Tolstoy, to attempt to put such ideas into practice. These included Hermann Conradi (1862–90), Conrad Alberti (1862–1918), Karl Henckell (1864–1929), Arno Holz (1863–1929) and Johannes Schlaf (1862–1941). Holz's first collection of poems *Buch der Zeit* ('Book of the Age', 1885) is widely regarded as the most important anthology of Naturalist poetry. Together with Schlaf he was able to capture with great accuracy the milieu of working-class and artisanal North East Berlin; most notably in the play *Die Familie Selicke* ('The Family Selicke', 1889).

Ultimately, however, none of these young writers were really able to live up to their own revolutionary rhetoric. This was not altogether surprising. For a start, Naturalist theory was so contradictory that it was impossible to meet all its demands. As Roy Cowen has remarked 'there were nearly as many Naturalisms as Naturalists',[40] and it was not long before literary critics and cultural commentators were dissecting the movement into a variety of competing strands, of which the pronounced and sometimes bitter Berlin–Munich rivalry represented only one aspect.[41] Also, Naturalist theory was much clearer about what it was against than what it was for. It was easy enough to condemn the formalism and unoriginality of much *Gründerzeit* writing – '1600 authors and no literature!'[42] as Leo Berg despaired – but it was more difficult to put something of lasting value in its place.

For all the differences between the works of individual authors, however, it is possible to highlight some common themes of German Naturalist writing around 1890. Their novels, poems and plays were invariably hostile to authority (church, state, employers) and authority figures (priests, judges, army officers, teachers); critical of the bourgeois family and its hypocrisies; and sympathetic to figures on the edge of society (the unemployed, alcoholics, criminals, pimps and especially prostitutes). They also reflected a preoccupation with sexual drives and with revolutionary ideologies, whether Marxist, Nietzschean or Darwinian in nature. Although the Church came in for much criticism, these new faiths frequently gave Naturalist works an air of fervent religiosity. At the same time, the dominant tone was pessimistic: the biological determinism of Darwin and the economic determinism of Marx combined to restrict the freedom of movement of Naturalist characters who, shaped by their oppressive environment, could not escape the shackles of their destiny.[43]

Of course, much of this came directly from the German Naturalists' foreign role models, but it was also a consequence of their own experience of big city life in the 1880s. Arriving in Berlin or Munich, these young men from provincial middle-class backgrounds were simultaneously attracted and repelled by the modern metropolis, and fascinated by the fate of the 'losers' in their rapidly changing society.[44] For a time, some chose to live in working-class districts – Holz in Wedding, Hauptmann in Moabit – and took their notebooks everywhere, recording observations and snatches of overheard conversations in the manner of Zola. The aim was to capture the authentic voice of common people, and to present this 'slice of life' with scientific precision (Holz even came up with the pseudo-scientific formula 'Art = Nature –X'). Accordingly, characters were given accents and stutters, and seldom finished sentences, whether on the printed page or on the stage. The eponymous 'heroes' of Gerhart Hauptmann's first novella *Bahnwärter Thiel* ('Thiel, the Level-crossing Keeper', 1887), Johannes Schlaf's *Meister Ölze* ('Master

Ölze', 1892) or Hauptmann's later *Fuhrmann Henschel* ('Driver Henschel', 1898) were inarticulate and ordinary, a world away from the heroes of the *Gründerzeit*.

In addition to this consciously anti-heroic stance, the Naturalist opposition to *Gründerzeit* values was also reflected in an anti-idealistic aesthetic, which was directed less at the actual works of Goethe, Schiller or Kant, than the vulgarized version of their ethos that permeated not only the educated middle classes in Imperial Germany, but which was seemingly embraced by everyone from the Kaiser to the leaders of the socialist labour movement. The famous line from Goethe's *Epilogue to Schiller's 'Bell'* ('Ins ewige des Wahren, Guten, Schönen'), which could be found engraved on theatres, opera houses and art galleries across the Empire, was particularly subject to vulgarization. As Robert Musil remarked, some people 'could utter the words "the true, the good and the beautiful" as often and as casually as someone else might say "Thursday".'[45] The eagerness of Naturalist writers to embrace the uglier aspects of modern life no doubt had much to do with this.

The Naturalist portrayal of 'real life' in all its forms provoked predictable outrage amongst Church groups, morality campaigners and conservative cultural critics in Germany, as it did everywhere else. In the *Kaiserreich*, however, the all-highest endorsement of 'the True, the Good and the Beautiful' as the only true basis for art, gave the confrontation between the Naturalists and the authorities a political edge that was often lacking elsewhere, and put the issue of censorship near the top of the political agenda. Officially, there was no censorship in the Empire, although books and pictures that transgressed the articles of the Imperial Criminal Code dealing with lèse-majesté (99–101), incitement (130), blasphemy (166), obscenity (184), and 'gross mischief' (360/11) could be charged once they had been published or exhibited.

These articles presented dangers for writers and artists, particularly if they lived in a culturally conservative state that interpreted and implemented the criminal code vigorously. Hermann Bahr, Richard Dehmel, Max Dreyer, Paul Ernst, Ludwig Fulda, Otto Erich Hartleben, Ludwig Thoma, Frank Wedekind and Oskar Panizza were amongst the more prominent writers to suffer in this way, although on many occasions attempts to prosecute members of the avant-garde were blocked by the courts or ended in discharge. In 1890, at the height of the Naturalist 'revolution', the young novelists Conrad Alberti, Hermann Conradi and Wilhelm Walloth were all involved in an infamous court action in the Kingdom of Saxony. They were charged with blasphemy and obscenity, but the 27-year old Conradi died of pneumonia before his case could be heard. In such trials much depended on the individual judge, and outcomes were difficult to predict.[46] On this occasion, the Leipzig judge fined Alberti 300 RM, Walloth 150 RM, confiscated the unsold copies of their books, and ordered the destruction of the printing plates. Of course, it must be remembered that such trials and verdicts were relatively commonplace throughout Europe, and continued well into the twentieth century.

The main focus of the censorship debate in 1890s Germany was the so-called Lex Heinze; a legislative bill that was first introduced to parliament in 1892 but did not come in to force until June 1900. Its initial intention had been to tighten up the laws on prostitution and immoral behaviour – Heinze was a Berlin criminal and pimp – but, with the encouragement of the Kaiser and the Centre party, a paragraph was added on immorality in art and the theatre. This was designed to prevent exhibitions and performances that were 'likely to cause annoyance through grossly offending the sense of modesty and morality'. It was a paragraph that aroused fierce debate. For much of the 1890s, and especially in the spring of 1900, writers, publishers and artists campaigned against it, and eventually succeeded in removing the most threatening proposals.[47] Even so, in most parts of the Empire dramatists still faced the long-standing hurdle of pre-performance vetting of their plays.[48] This was justified on the grounds that theatrical productions, unlike books or pictures, could have a dangerous and immediate effect on a crowd.[49]

It was also a play that prompted the Berlin Chief of Police to make the infamous remark: 'Die janze Richtung passt uns nicht!' [50] The comment was made not in reference to one of Naturalism's more political pieces, but rather *Sodoms Ende* ('Sodom's End') by the largely-forgotten Hermann Sudermann (1857–1928), which was due to receive its premiere at the Lessing Theatre on 26 October 1890. The play was finally performed a fortnight later, after the ban was lifted by the Prussian Home Secretary Herrfurth, although he in turn was summoned to explain his decision to a far from happy Wilhelm II, and was dismissed not long after. Where public performances of plays were forbidden, a legal loophole allowed closed performances of plays for members of private associations. This was the background to the founding of the 'Freie Bühne' or Free Stage in early 1889; a theatrical association which had no theatre, sets, costumes or indeed actors of its own, and relied on established theatres to accommodate its productions. The Free Stage, inspired by the model of the Parisian Théâtre Libre, was led by the literary historian and critic Otto Brahm and included a number of other important figures from the world of publishing and journalism: Maximilian Harden and Theodor Wolff amongst them. This ensured that their productions received much more press coverage than might have been expected from a closed, private society.

The Free Stage Association also published a weekly journal, the *Freie Bühne*, from 1890.[51] This was intended as a mouthpiece for the many literary groups in and around Berlin, so its editor Otto Brahm often featured articles with contradictory messages. It was published by Samuel Fischer (1859–1934), who had founded the Fischer Verlag in 1886 and quickly became Germany's leading publisher of modern literature; including the works of Zola, Ibsen, Tolstoy, Dostoyevsky and Thomas Mann. On 20 October 1889, the Free Stage presented the controversial premiere of *Vor Sonnenaufgang* ('Before Sunrise') by Gerhart Hauptmann (1862–1946) at Berlin's Lessing Theatre. This 'social drama' in five acts, set in the coalfield of Hauptmann's native Silesia, was preoccupied with the difficulty of maintaining human relationships in harsh surroundings. The Free Stage repeated the success of *Before Sunrise* with productions of Sudermann's *Honour*, and Holz and Schlaf's *The Family Selicke.* Hauptmann himself quickly followed up *Before Sunrise* with *Die Weber* ('The Weavers'), which was written in 1890–1, premiered as a Free Stage production at the Neues Theater in February 1893, and which then enjoyed a long public run at the Deutsches Theater in 1894.

The Weavers was set against the backdrop of the Silesian weavers' uprising of 1844, which had left a traumatic mark on the Hauptmann family's collective memory. The play eloquently expressed the despair that led to the revolt, and the horror that ensued, but its ultimate message was open to interpretation. Certainly the authorities saw the play as an invitation to insurrection and class warfare. For a time it was banned, and the subject of a long court battle, which ultimately went Hauptmann's way on the grounds that the seat prices at the Deutsches Theater were too high for the sort of people who might be tempted to riot. *The Weavers* was even debated in the Prussian parliament, where the Home Secretary Köller invoked the 'holiest wealth of the nation' and the 'health of the people' against the play.[52] When the theatre nevertheless decided to go ahead with public performances, Wilhelm II cancelled his box in protest. Hauptmann, however, was no revolutionary – he had sympathy for the poor and the suffering, but endorsed no solutions to end their plight – and *The Weavers* was not acclaimed unreservedly by the radical left either.

One of the principal spokesmen on cultural affairs for the socialist labour movement, Franz Mehring (1846–1919), was angered by the unremitting gloom of Naturalism. While Mehring and other figures in the SPD welcomed the new-found interest of writers and artists for the 'social question', they bemoaned the absence of an uplifting message or an indication of where salvation might lie, which they felt was the duty of a truly committed art. This provoked a long-running theoretical debate between Mehring and Holz, and a rather fractious relationship between the two movements throughout the 1890s. It was the 'outsider' status of workers in the Empire of the 1880s that had first attracted the Berlin Naturalists to socialism. For a time, under Bismarck's repressive Anti-Socialist laws, the young writers could identify with people who appeared to be struggling against the same enemy. As soon as the Anti-Socialist laws lapsed, however, and the SPD began to resemble a political party like any other, much of this appeal disappeared. The Naturalists did not have much time for the resolutions, leaflets and subscriptions of everyday party politics. In any case, it had always been the fifth, rather than the fourth estate, which had really interested them: not class-conscious, self-taught proletarians, but the prostitutes, tramps and thieves of the Berlin *demi-monde.* Moreover, for all their disgust at *Gründerzeit* values, the Naturalists generally shared the established view of the artist or poet as someone standing above the everyday machinations of politicians: the isolated individual, whose creative output was to be judged on its originality rather than its social function. They were also deeply conscious of the antipathy their predominantly bourgeois readers and audiences had to 'tendentious' literature.

This antipathy was readily apparent in the diary entry of the future Imperial Chancellor Hohenlohe-Schillingsfürst, who attended the premiere of Gerhart Hauptmann's play *Hanneles Himmelfahrt* ('Little Hannah's Ascension') in the winter of 1893–4. He wrote: 'A hideously sorry effort, social democratic-realistic, but at the same time with a sickly sentimental mysticism, sinister, a strain on the nerves, purely and simply dreadful . . . Afterwards we went to Borchardt's, to restore our human spirits with champagne and caviar.'[53] Of course, this 'dream play' was already a long way from

The Weavers. By 1894 the highpoint of Hauptmann's Naturalism, and Naturalism in general, had already passed. Indeed, it has been claimed by some literary historians that Hauptmann was never actually a Naturalist at all.[54] Certainly, he was too good a writer to ever be limited to one stylistic approach and most of his subsequent work was well away from the aesthetics of Naturalism. On the other hand, he did return to Naturalist idioms periodically, and never disowned his early work, which most would regard as quintessentially Naturalist.

Hauptmann's short sojourn in working-class Moabit had come to an end in 1885, when he moved with his wife to the village of Erkner, south-east of Berlin. This set a trend that was followed by most other Berlin Naturalists by 1890. Here they led comfortable middle-class lives, even if their works were critical of just such circumstances. The most prominent group of Naturalist émigrés from inner-city Berlin were the writers and intellectuals who became known as the Friedrichshagener *Dichterkreis*, or Writers' Circle. The Friedrichshagen Circle, which was parodied in Hauptmann's play *Einsame Menschen* ('Lonely People', 1890) and Holz's *Sozialaristokraten* ('The Social Aristocrats', 1896), was never a fully fledged artists' colony, but rather a loose grouping of intellectuals, who settled just a few miles from Hauptmann's Erkner in Friedrichshagen, a small town on the banks of the Müggelsee.[55]

The core of the Friedrichshagen Circle was formed by men who had been involved in the *Durch* group in the mid- to late-1880s. These included Wilhelm Bölsche, not only editor of the *Freie Bühne* but a self-styled scientist who helped to popularize Darwin, Haeckel and the study of nature, by lecturing to workers' groups and writing books;[56] Bruno Wille, a poet, preacher and utopian anarchist, who felt that egalitarianism ran counter to the message of Darwin;[57] the Hart brothers, who in addition to their literary activities established the prototype commune known as the New Community; and the Kampffmeyer brothers, later to play a leading role in the German Garden City Association, who were the first to settle in Friedrichshagen after inheriting a villa in the town. These core members, who all moved to Friedrichshagen around 1890, were joined from time to time by friends and associates like Wilhelm Hegeler (1870–1943), author of *Mother Bertha* (1893); the anarchist writers Gustav Landauer (1870–1919) and Erich Mühsam (1878–1934); the painter Fidus (1868–1948); the Swedish dramatist August Strindberg (1849–1912); and the monocled but penniless 'cultural pessimist' Arthur Moeller-Bruck (1876–1925).[58] Friedrichshagen, the 'Müggelsee Republic', also attracted political activists with no literary ambitions, like the SPD Reichstag members Max Schippel and Georg Ledebour, or the producers of the journal *Der Sozialist*, who included Albert Weidner (1871–1946), Wilhelm Spohr (1868–1959) and Hermann Teistler (1867–1937).

The Friedrichshagener were responsible for the one positive achievement of the shortlived relationship between Naturalism and the labour movement: a version of the Free Stage idea, but more accessible to working-class people, known as the 'Freie Volksbühne' ('Free People's Stage'). It was founded in 1890 and gained 4000 members in its first year, each paying just 50 pfennigs per month in membership fees to watch plays like Hauptmann's *Before Sunrise* and Ibsen's *Enemy of the People.* By the end of 1892 the membership had reached 8000, but the rapidly deteriorating relationship between the Party and the poets led to an acrimonious split. The Friedrichshagener were unceremoniously replaced on the theatre's board by loyal SPD members, and under Franz Mehring's leadership the Free People's Stage moved away from Naturalism and towards the classics. At the same time the closest allies of the Friedrichshagener in the Party – the radical, Nietzsche-influenced *Jungen* – were expelled. The Party's attitude was obvious from a statement issued at the time: 'Anyone is welcome to join us as a comrade and colleague if they have the same goals as us: the spreading of knowledge amongst the people; the furtherance of the common good; the cultivation of "the True, the Good and the Beautiful" in every area of public and intellectual life'.[59]

The Friedrichshagener responded immediately, establishing both a rival theatre association – the New Free People's Stage[60] – and a new political grouping, the 'Association of Independent Socialists', although the latter survived only three years. A faction sympathetic to Naturalism did remain within the SPD, but at the 1896 party conference in Gotha a dispute over the direction of the newspaper supplement *Die Neue Welt* ('The New World') developed into a full-scale debate on the Party's attitude to Naturalism and culture in general. *Die Neue Welt*'s serialization of Hegeler's *Mother Bertha* and Hans Land's *The New God* shocked many ordinary readers, whose progressive political views were often coupled with highly conventional attitudes on questions of morality and taste. The debate was inconclusive, and a week later in his essay 'Art and the Proletariat' the party's Franz Mehring drew a line under the discussion, although not before condemning Naturalism as a 'School of Decadents'.[61]

By this time most of the Friedrichshagener had in any case moved on, and were exploring a range of novel aesthetic approaches, including Symbolism, Impressionism, Aestheticism and Art Nouveau. In common with other self-proclaimed modernists – such as Oskar Panizza and Frank Wedekind in Munich – they soon turned their backs on Naturalism's attempts to be a mirror on the world, and instead began to celebrate artifice and distortion: to search for a style 'whose only limitation was the fantasy and audacity of the artist'.[62] While this illustrates the short life of German literary Naturalism, it also shows how its assault on *Gründerzeit* culture unleashed important new energies and ideas. As for the Friedrichshagen circle, its significance was by no means just literary. The contribution of these bohemian intellectuals to other Wilhelmine reform movements will feature in Chapter 5.

Naturalism in painting

At the height of literary Naturalism, a number of German painters who had been inspired by the mid-nineteenth-century French Realists[63] Courbet and Millet – including Max Liebermann (1847–1935) and Fritz von Uhde (1848–1911) – were dubbed 'Naturalists' by hostile critics, and the tag stuck, even though the painters' approach was rather different from, and in part pre-dated, the poets and playwrights of 1880s Berlin and Munich. Today it is possible to view German Naturalist painting simply as the teutonic variant of nineteenth-century European Realism, although some historians have attempted to distinguish between the two. Richard Hamann and Jost Hermand, for example, define Naturalist painting as 'Realism on the attack',[64] while others see the difference as essentially generational. Certainly, one could argue that Liebermann went further than Courbet or Millet in depicting the 'ugly' realities of life, but it is also true that German Naturalist painters did not share their literary counterparts' fondness for political posturing and pamphleteering.

Liebermann, who came from a wealthy Jewish family and lived for many years at one of imperial Berlin's prime addresses, may have had no manifesto and no political axe to grind, but from his very first major painting, *Die Gänserupferinnen* ('Goosepluckers', 1872), it was obvious Liebermann was different from other *Gründerzeit*

Figure 8 Max Liebermann, Goosepluckers *(1872)*

painters. By raising a banal, and rather unpleasant, everyday activity to the level of high art, Liebermann caused a sensation in the world of 'the True, the Good and the Beautiful'. Although his painting was not inspired by any desire to make social comment – Liebermann himself described its subject as 'absolutely nothing';[65] a means to a painterly end – the seriousness with which the artist treated his theme was perceived as provocative. Unlike Liebermann's later works, the painting was not based on personal observation; it was just as much a studio creation as the paintings of Werner or Makart, and employed models rather than 'genuine' goose pluckers. Even so, it is often described as the first work of German Naturalism because its non-anecdotal and non-sentimental treatment of a 'genre' subject was in such stark contrast to the work of contemporaries like Munkacsy, Ortlieb or Knaus, whose scenes of idyllic rural life enjoyed great popularity at the time; and also because the portrayal of real women was still so rare in German art.

Liebermann did not attempt to cash in on this early *succès de scandale,* as he flitted between Weimar, Paris, Barbizon and Munich in search of a personal style. *The Potato Harvest* (1875) and *Workers in the Turnip Field* (1876) were clearly derivative of Millet, while his admiration for Frans Hals and Dutch genre painting led him to the Netherlands. It was here that some of Liebermann's most important work was produced. The artist was attracted by what he perceived to be the honesty and simplicity of Dutch life, which he compared favourably to the hollow bluster of the German *Gründerzeit.* Many of Liebermann's Dutch paintings were coolly objective pictures of labour – weavers, cobblers, food preservers and fishing-net menders – which made no attempt to romanticize or monumentalize, and which treated their subjects with quiet dignity rather than false pathos. The predominantly female workers were shown in their milieu, absorbed in the silent ritual of their daily tasks and eschewing eye contact with the viewer. Both the choice of subject matter, and the subdued black-grey-green palette of the artist, were deemed 'dirty' by *Gründerzeit* art critics. Liebermann was dubbed a 'son of darkness', and even an 'apostle of ugliness' by the prominent critic Adolf Rosenberg.

There has been much art historical speculation on the 'message' of Liebermann's Dutch paintings.[66] Although he always refrained from political sloganeering, the very fact that female labour was a recurring theme of these paintings has inevitably aroused interest:[67] the status of the working class and the position of women were, after all, two of the great issues of the later nineteenth century. It is clear that Liebermann did not see his paintings as a critical indictment of working conditions or practices: there is little sign of boredom or exhaustion, or indeed of modern production methods. Rather than the classical proletariat, these were pre-industrial labourers, in a country that was still comparatively undeveloped in industrial terms. Some have suggested that the paintings represented Liebermann's endorsement of the co-operative ideals of the early German socialist Ferdinand Lassalle; others see them as a celebration of the artist's own Prussian work-ethic: Liebermann was a notoriously diligent painter, who believed in 'self-realization through work' and wrote in an 1879 letter that 'work, and work alone, can make people happy'.[68] It should not be forgotten, however, that he chose his motifs on aesthetic rather than political grounds. Liebermann was a detached observer – albeit a humane and liberal one – not a man with a message.

On the other hand, the political impact of his paintings cannot be denied. This was particularly apparent with one of Liebermann's rare attempts to tackle a religious subject, his portrayal of the 12-year old *Jesus in the Temple* (1879), which created such a furore among

Bavarian Catholic parliamentarians when it was exhibited in Munich that the picture had to be moved to a side room. The portrayal of a Jesus as an ordinary, halo-less lad, in an interior based on an Amsterdam synagogue, appears to have caused genuine offence to some people, although the intemperate rhetoric of its critics is hard to understand today.[69] There were also some who took advantage of the controversy to launch openly anti-semitic attacks on the artist. The notorious Prussian court preacher Adolf Stoecker was amongst those who attacked the very idea of a Jew painting a 'Christian' subject. However, Liebermann was by no means the only Naturalist painter to face the wrath of churchmen and politicians. In an 1890 debate the Bavarian Centre deputy Eugen Jäger condemned Fritz von Uhde's portrayal of the Sermon on the Mount (1887) in equally strident terms.

The hostile reception of Liebermann's 'Jesus' painting was repeated a decade later when controversy surrounded the artist's portrait of Hamburg's long-serving mayor, Carl Friedrich Petersen (1809–91). Liebermann had gained the commission through the gallery director Alfred Lichtwark, who had bought the artist's *Net Menders* for Hamburg in 1889. The painting was completed in the summer of 1891, but when it went on show in 1893 it was condemned as unworthy and unfinished. Liebermann's technique, which increasingly involved a palette knife and thick, unblended layers of paint, had become so associated with toiling labourers that it was deemed an insult to the esteemed patrician, who was portrayed as a frail old man. The Petersen family hated it, and the episode became a Hamburg *cause célèbre*: it was not until 1902 that the picture went on display at the city's art gallery. In the long term, however, it did Liebermann no harm at all, and portraiture became his stock-in-trade after 1900.

For all the public criticism of his work, Liebermann was greatly admired by young German artists, and many in the late nineteenth century attempted to follow in his footsteps. His Dutch subjects were particularly imitated. The preoccupation with such humble themes was apparent at major German art exhibitions from the late 1880s onwards. Hermann Pleuer (1863–1911) and Hans Baluschek (1870–1935), for example, focused on railway yards; Friedrich Kallmorgen (1856–1934) and Carlos Grethe (1864–1913) both made their name by painting scenes from Hamburg's docks. Franz Skarbina (1849–1910) moved on from Liebermannesque Dutch scenes to invigorating city streetscapes in Berlin and Paris. Lesser

Ury (1861–1931) was another painter to capture street life in a Naturalist manner.

The only German Naturalist to achieve a similar status to Liebermann, however, was the aforementioned Fritz von Uhde; a former cavalry officer, who became known as a 'poverty painter' in the 1880s, even though his *plein air* scenes of rural life were generally more up-beat than Liebermann's. He specialized in paintings on religious themes, and was particularly fond of placing Bible stories in contemporary Bavarian settings. Thus in *Grace* or *Come, Lord Jesus, be our Guest* (1885) a working class family is about to sit down to a humble dinner of bread and soup, when Jesus takes the words of a traditional Protestant grace literally and joins them at the table; while in *Suffer little Children to come unto Me* (1884) the biblical passage is enacted in a spartan Bavarian classroom, as poorly dressed urchins line up to meet their bedraggled Saviour.[70] Uhde came from a prominent Protestant family, and was a practising Christian himself, but this did not stop some from attacking his work as 'blasphemous' and 'socialist', which he most certainly was not. Eventually, having set everything from the Nativity to the Last Supper in contemporary Bavaria, Uhde moved on from Biblical themes to paint a series of attractive domestic studies, in the light and airy style of his earlier *Playroom* of 1889. By the 1890s, both Uhde and Liebermann were viewed in Germany as the standard-bearers of a modern approach to art, which included not only Naturalism, but Symbolism and Impressionism too. That this was so, was largely the result of their involvement in the Secessionist movements of Munich and Berlin respectively.

The Secessions

The revolt of disaffected artists against the academy is a familiar narrative in the history and mythology of modern art, from the Salon des Refusés (1863/73) and the Salon des Indepéndants (1884) in Paris, to the 'Modernista' in Spain (1892), the 'Shiro-uma' in Japan (1895) and 'Mir Iskusstwa' in Russia (1899). Until the last decades of the nineteenth century private galleries and dealers were rare, and the academy exhibitions (often known as 'salons' after the Paris example) were vital for artists' livelihoods. For young painters in particular, the salon offered the principal opportunity to make their mark; to win travel bursaries, medals and prizes. Moreover, despite the increasing number of bourgeois collectors, the state remained a major purchaser of art in its own right, and many of those purchases were made at the salon. Although salons became larger and more frequent as the century wore on, they could not keep pace with the numbers of artists wishing to exhibit.[71] This had two consequences: more artists found their work rejected by selection juries; and those who had work accepted were often little happier, since their paintings were placed too far up the crowded walls to be noticed.

When revolts occurred, therefore, the motivation was seldom purely aesthetic: economic self-interest, personal antagonisms, and generational conflict all played a part; and, given the 'royal' status and traditions of most academies, they could easily develop a political dimension as well. Such revolts rarely lasted more than a decade, however, and where they did survive, they had a tendency to become more 'respectable' and less tolerant with every passing year. In the German states, the exhibition societies that set themselves up in opposition to the annual salon called themselves Secessions,[72] following the example of the first such revolt in Munich (1892). Secessions also took place in Düsseldorf, Weimar, Dresden, Stuttgart and Karlsruhe, but the most important were those in Vienna (1897) and Berlin (1898).

As the name implies, these were groups of artists who 'seceded' from the salon, and chose to exhibit their work elsewhere. Their exhibitions are often said to mark the breakthrough of modern art in the German states, but this should not be misunderstood. Certainly, large-scale historical paintings and imitative 'old masterly' works all but disappeared at Secession shows: their predominantly bourgeois clientele had different requirements than the state-sponsored purchasers at academic salons. In general, however, the modernity of the Secessions had less to do with the style or subject of their own members' work, which varied greatly in both approach and quality, than with the foreign artists they introduced to Germany; their new forms of presentation; and their acceptance of graphic and applied art alongside (the traditionally more exclusive) fine art. Above all, the importance and modernity of the Secessions lies in the very act of secession itself. In a society that regarded rebellion and disorder with deep hostility, the challenge thrown down by the Secessionists, with their rhetoric of individual artistic freedom, had implications that went beyond the purely aesthetic.

In one sense it was fitting that the first Secession should take place in Munich, because the Bavarian capital had been the leading

German art centre for most of the nineteenth century. It had impressive collections, built up by the Wittelsbach dynasty but on display in public museums, large exhibition halls, good rail connections, a relatively low cost of living and an attractive hinterland. The city guarded its 'capital of art' status fiercely. As Maria Makela has made clear, however, the city was not an obvious setting for an artists' revolt. For a start, the Munich salon was no longer in the hands of the academy or the state, but had been run by the artists themselves since 1863. The artists were organized in an independent and democratically run guild, the Münchener Künstlergenossenschaft, which was attached to the General German Artists' Guild. Moreover, the exhibitions appeared to be very successful. The 1888 salon had produced record profits and the proportion of rejected pictures was comparatively low.

There were signs, however, that Munich was becoming a victim of its own success.[73] In the words of a retrospective article from 1907, 'an almost grotesque disparity between artistic supply and demand' had set in.[74] Too many mediocre journeymen artists were taking advantage of their rights as members of the guild, and the exhibitions were becoming something of a 'bazaar', in which thousands of pictures of variable quality were piled high and sold off cheaply. It also appeared that the vital overseas buyers were beginning to find Munich pictures provincial and outdated. Sales at the 1891 salon were poor, and local artists were hardest hit. The artists' guild was divided in its response. Some favoured a strict limit of three works per artist, and a reduction in the number of foreign works. Others, however, felt this would merely exacerbate the problem, cutting Munich off from the new trends in European art, and condemning it to permanent mediocrity.

The latter view was outvoted, but found strong support amongst two groups of artists: high-profile painters like von Uhde and Franz Stuck, who resented having to compete for valuable wall space with the 'art proletariat'; and the aesthetically adventurous, whose works ran the risk of jury rejection. It was these two groups who formed the core of the Secession in 1892. A break-away may well not have occurred, however, had it not been for the powerful backing of two key individuals: Adolf Paulus, the long-serving and respected business manager of the guild, who had been forced out in the winter of 1891–2; and the Munich publisher Georg Hirth, whose enthusiasm for the German Renaissance was waning, but who remained a vigorous and influential figure in the Bavarian art world. The first meeting of the rebels took place in April 1892, when the name Munich Association of Visual Artists was chosen. The catchier 'Munich Secession', which was favoured by press and public alike, was formally adopted later that year. The association soon had over 100 members, including Ludwig Dill (1848–1940), Wilhelm Trübner (1851–1917), and Leopold von Kalckreuth (1855–1928). Most were aged between 29 and 43, while the painters who remained with the guild tended to be either much older or younger than this.[75]

Georg Hirth ensured that the Secessionists received plenty of positive coverage in the pages of his newspapers. Meanwhile, Adolf Paulus began to plan their first exhibition. The concept was to hold annual shows that would be small, international in scope, and elite in character. Indeed, as Makela notes, 'the new association repudiated the democratic ethic of the Genossenschaft, frankly stating that fairness and equality for all were not its governing principles. Rather, the Secession would limit its membership to "true" or "genuine" artists and its exhibitions to the "absolutely artistic".'[76] A self-conscious elitism was common to all the Secessions, as it was to much of the turn-of-the-century avant-garde. While the academic salons continued to uphold a belief in art's didactic role, the Secessionists had little interest in uplifting, inspiring or entertaining the masses.

In their literature, the Secessionists made no attempt to define what was 'genuinely' or 'absolutely' artistic, but they consistently stressed the importance of artistic 'freedom' and creative 'honesty' above stylistic criteria. Each of the Secessions consisted of disparate individuals, seeking their own creative path and with varying degrees of success. Their tolerance of different aesthetic approaches was by no means unlimited – all of the Secessions struggled to come to terms with Expressionism, for instance, prompting the creation of 'new' Secessions around 1910 – but it was still in stark contrast to the narrow aesthetic codes of the official salons. Having contributed to the Berlin salon of 1893, the Secessionists' first Munich exhibition opened in July of that year. In many ways the most innovative aspect of the show was the installation. Whereas the official Munich salon displayed up to 3000 paintings, covering the walls like 'stamps in an album' (Peter Paret), the Secession showed just 900 objects, 650 of which were paintings hung in a single row. Moreover, while paintings in the salon were hung against boldly patterned wallpaper surrounded by architectural plasterwork, the Secession opted for a sober, neutral background. Makela suggests this was an 'integral factor in the perceived modernity of the Secession'.[77] It certainly gave the undertaking a more elite and exclusive atmosphere than the official salon. This was important, because for all their rhetoric against the 'bazaar' and the treatment of art as a commodity, many Secessionists had made a cool calculation that their sales chances would improve in a more select setting, especially when accompanied by the notoriety of rebellion.

The first Munich Secession shows included many foreign works, but the leading Impressionists and Post-Impressionists were not amongst them. Most of the talking points, therefore, were provided by German artists: Liebermann and Uhde, but also Franz Stuck (1863–1928),[78] whose work combined elements of Makart and Böcklin with an air of decadence. Indeed, Stuck's *Sin* (1893) has been described as 'perhaps the most notorious work of art to have been produced in *fin-de-siècle* Munich'.[79] Since Stuck painted essentially the same scene on eighteen occasions (eleven times as 'Sin', four times under the title 'Sensuality' and three times as 'Vice') the motif of the bare-breasted *femme fatale* with a serpent curling around her seductive shoulders owed much of its notoriety to its omnipresence. Stuck was able to make a fortune from such paintings – set in a Nietzschean world beyond good and evil, but also situated uneasily between high art and low kitsch – despite the rise of a populist and puritanical Catholicism in Bavaria at this time.[80]

Stylistically, the first exhibitions of the Munich Secession were dominated by two approaches: Naturalism and Symbolism. Apart from Stuck's erotic allegories, most of the latter had rural settings, and attempted to evoke emotion through the lyricism of nature. The melancholic paintings of Leopold von Kalckreuth enjoyed particular popularity. Themes from the natural world, presented in a flat, decorative manner, were also the favoured subject matter of a number of Munich Secession artists who would shortly become associated with *Jugendstil* graphics and applied art, such as Otto Eckmann (1865–1902) and Richard Riemerschmid (1868–1957). Two of the mainstays of the Munich Secession exhibitions, Uhde and Liebermann, both moved away from Naturalism and adopted an increasingly impressionistic style in the 1890s. The transformation in Liebermann's work was particularly dramatic, since the lightening of his palette and the loosening of his brushwork was accompanied by a change in subject matter. Rather than rural labourers, the old and the poor, he began to focus on the urban bourgeoisie: families at the zoo, on the beach, in restaurants and beer gardens. These were much brighter and more colourful paintings than his earlier works, though they lacked the freedom and vivacity of French Impressionism. Whatever the reasons for Liebermann's change of direction,[81] his new approach influenced a number Secessionists, including Lovis Corinth (1858–1925) and Max Slevogt (1868–1932), who would both later join him in Berlin. In 1894 Corinth and Slevogt were amongst ten artists who seceded from the Secession. It would be the first of many splits, not least because of Uhde's uncanny ability to turn friends into enemies.

The Munich Secession's importance as a bridgehead for modern art in Germany is easily exaggerated. Makela argues, however, that we should not dismiss its importance, just because it failed to exhibit 'those artists of the 1890s who today dominate our canon'.[82] Many of the key figures in early twentieth century art – Wassily Kandinksky, Paul Klee, Franz Marc and others – were trained in turn-of-the-century Munich, and all were frequent visitors to the Secession. Despite initial alarm, the Bavarian authorities quickly came to terms with the Secession. In truth they had little alternative, since the fear of losing ground to Berlin was pervasive in the closing years of the century. With hindsight it is clear that the city's role as the artistic capital of Germany was coming to an end.

The imperial capital had none of Munich's cultural flair or tradition. Its Royal Academy of Arts dated back to 1696,[83] but its reputation had declined, and it was only in the 1880s that new signs of life were detected in the Berlin art world. The city's artists had gained a capable and combative leader in Anton von Werner, whose major 'Proclamation' paintings were now behind him, and who was devoting more time to administration and teaching. Werner combined his academic position – he was Director of the College of Fine Arts and a member of the Academy's Senate – with the leadership of the independent Association of Berlin Artists, which was attached to the General German Artists' Guild.

It was Werner who masterminded the compromise in 1892 that gave the artists' association a joint share in the running of the Berlin salon for the first time. The compromise removed, for the time being at least, the danger of a Munich-style split. It came, however, at a price: the Berlin artists had to accept a much stronger level of official supervision than existed in Munich. Under the new system, the salon juries formed jointly by the academy and the artists' association were only advisory bodies, with their recommendations subject to the confirmation of the *Kultusminister*, and ultimately to the King of Prussia himself. This was one reason why the conflicts surrounding the Berlin Secession were to prove more highly politicized than had been the case in Munich.

The Berlin Secession, which was not founded until 1898, had a long prehistory in which three events were of particular relevance. The first was the founding of an independent exhibition society known as The XI in February 1892, by eleven artists including Liebermann, Franz Skarbina and several other future Secessionists. The society had its origins in a pub and was inspired by the example of the Belgian 'Les Vingts' of 1884, but its members did not secede from the Association of Berlin Artists, and they continued to submit works to the salon. The XI's spring exhibitions gained a certain notoriety and fashionability in avant-garde circles, but the standard was uneven, and the group split up in 1897.

More significant was the controversy that blew up around an exhibition of fifty-five works by the Norwegian Edvard Munch (1863–1944), which opened under the auspices of the Association of Berlin Artists on 5 November 1892. One year before his proto-Expressionist masterpiece *The Scream*, Munch's works were already far more radical than anything yet seen in Berlin, and the response was savage. His paintings were condemned as 'daubings', reflecting the 'excesses of Naturalism'.[84] The only positive reviews came from outside the art establishment, principally from members of the Friedrichshagen writers' circle and other literary bohemians who had befriended Munch in the 'Zum Schwarzen Ferckel' bar. With Werner's encouragement, members of the Association voted to close the exhibition.

The controversy did Munch little harm. He was well aware the publicity could work in his favour, and wrote to his family: 'I could hardly get better advertising!'[85] He decided to stay in Germany and his paintings went on show in Munich, Düsseldorf and Cologne instead. Over the next two decades he sold more pictures in Germany than anywhere else. Ironically, the artists' association came off much the worse. Its membership had been split right down the middle, and even some who had little time for Munch's work were embarrassed by Werner's handling of the affair. Forty-eight of the minority group, including Liebermann and Skarbina, published a declaration in the liberal *Vossische Zeitung* newspaper explaining their actions and condemning the decision. This act was to have serious repercussions for Skarbina, who was a professor at the Berlin College of Fine Arts. Anton von Werner accused him of uncollegiality, and informed the Prussian *Kultusminister* and Wilhelm II. As a result, Skarbina was forced to resign his position.

For a short while it appeared as if secession was imminent in the winter of 1892–3, but at this point few Berlin artists were prepared to risk life outside the *Verein* or the salon. It would be another six years before the imperial capital would experience a secession of its own. During these years the city's progressive artists gained some important new forms of support. The number of private galleries was growing, as was the market for Naturalist, Symbolist and Impressionist works. The new Swiss-born Director of the National Gallery, Hugo von Tschudi (1851–1911), proved to be more sympathetic to contemporary art than his predecessor, and was even prepared to purchase works by Frenchmen. Moreover, in 1895, a fresh and innovative journal for modern art and literature appeared in Berlin: *Pan* may have had fewer than 1000 subscribers, but for five years it stimulated an interest in avant-garde paintings amongst Germany's wealthy elites.[86]

The immediate incident that provoked the founding of the Berlin Secession in May 1898 was the salon jury's decision to decline *Grunewaldsee* (1895), a moody Brandenburg landscape by Walter Leistikow (1865–1908). Leistikow had been a member of the XI and was a close friend of Liebermann; he was also to become the driving force behind the Berlin Secession, which began with some sixty-five members.[87] Liebermann was elected President, Leistikow its First Secretary. After several months of fruitless negotiations, in which the two men tried to gain some sort of autonomy for the new organization within the salon system, arrangements were made for an independent exhibition to take place in May 1899. The practical details were handled by the cousins Bruno (1872–1941) and Paul Cassirer (1871–1926), who had recently opened their own art gallery and publishing business in Berlin, and who were to become important promoters of modern art in Wilhelmine Germany. The Secession's own small gallery was erected in Berlin's Kantstrasse, and was just about finished in time to host the first exhibition that opened on 20 May.

As Paret makes clear, the Secession's debut – a survey of late nineteenth-century German art, with 380 works by the likes of Leibl, Böcklin, Uhde, Stuck and other representatives from the Munich and Dresden Secessions – was far from shocking. Its black-tie opening was a highly respectable social occasion, with the Lord Mayor of Charlottenburg and the President of the Academy of Arts in attendance. The Imperial Chancellor, Hohenlohe, was an early visitor, and sales of both entrance tickets and paintings exceeded expectations. Encouraged by this success, however, the Secession took more risks with its subsequent exhibitions, showing a higher proportion of foreign works, including Impressionist and post-Impressionist paintings by the likes of Pissarro and Renoir (1901); Monet, Manet, Kandinsky and the controversial Munch (1902); and Cézanne, Gauguin and van Gogh (1903). The exhibitions recorded good sales and attendance figures but the critical reception remained divided, and hostility to the Secession was growing amongst a section of Berlin's artistic community. Indeed, sixteen of the Secession's own members, including Skarbina, left because of the perceived favouritism towards foreign artists. Ironically, the unrest amongst Berlin artists was further exacerbated by the salon's attempts to emulate the Secession's commercial success by reducing the number of pictures on display, and by accepting more foreign works. For the city's large 'art proletariat' the high prices and column inches devoted to Impressionism and other 'foreign fads' were felt to be a kick in the teeth for their own honest endeavours.

Despite the move towards Impressionism instigated by the likes of Liebermann, Uhde, Corinth and Slevogt, who became known in some quarters as the 'German Impressionists',[88] it remained a style that was perceived to be uniquely French, and therefore alien to German culture. The fact that leading Secessionists such as Liebermann and Cassirer were Jewish was not lost on some of the opponents of Impressionism, but the unease went well beyond the *völkisch* right. For some, such as the Heidelberg professor Henry Thode (1857–1920),[89] the essentially visual nature of Impressionist art contrasted unfavourably with the 'deeper' exploration of emotional and intellectual themes to be found in the work of 'German' artists like Böcklin and Klinger. The *Gründerzeit* search for a distinctive national style remained a pressing preoccupation of German cultural commentators and producers up to the era of Expressionism, and beyond. For others, the problem was even more fundamental. The commercialization of the art market, with its new breed of private dealers and wealthy collectors; its fashionable, trend-seeking magazines; and its rapid, market-driven turnover in styles, raised serious questions about the role of art in a capitalist society. Why should a lucky few become rich, while the majority of artists struggled to earn a living? Why should novelty be valued above ability? There would be no easy answers to such questions.

Wilhelm II's objections to 'Secessionism' were more straightforward. He simply did not like it, and made no secret of the fact.

Berlin's military commander banned officers in uniform from visiting the Secession gallery as a result. In February 1904 painting, and Secessionism in particular, was the subject of a surprisingly well-informed two-day Reichstag debate in which German parliamentarians of all parties revealed themselves to be a good deal more open-minded than their ruler. The Reichstag debate was triggered by the controversy surrounding Germany's contribution to the 1904 World's Fair in St Louis, Missouri. The tragicomic St Louis affair, which has been analysed in detail elsewhere, was the consequence of a dramatic government 'U-turn', in which both Werner and the Kaiser were involved.[90]

The civil servants responsible for the initial planning of the German show had hoped to secure the support of all the country's arts associations, including the Secessions, to ensure that the exhibition was a commercial and critical success. Their notion of a broadly based 'Art Parliament' to select the works for St Louis represented an important departure from previous practice. For earlier World Exhibitions, the General German Artists' Guild had been entrusted with the selection of art exhibits, which it had done by allocating wall space to its regional guilds on the basis of membership figures. This ostensibly fair system had consistently resulted in mediocre exhibitions, but the Artists' Guild had no intention of giving up its privilege quietly. It was particularly unwilling to allow the Secessions an equal say in the choice of exhibits. When Wilhelm II was informed of the situation by Werner he predictably shared the Guild's anger, and insisted on the scrapping of the 'Art Parliament'. The Home Secretary had little option but to backtrack; and the Guild's previous role was restored. To add insult to the Secessionists' injury, Werner was given a personal role in co-ordinating the exhibition, which the Secessions boycotted entirely. The pictures which finally crossed the Atlantic were a predictable mixture of large historical paintings, genre scenes, landscapes and portraits, together with some 'classics' from public collections. No artist had more works in the show than Werner, who rather unwisely took six of his own large canvases. As Paret notes, however, the German contribution did not stand out – positively or negatively – in St Louis, and German painters ended up with a fair share of prizes, including a 'Grand Prize' for Menzel and a gold medal for Werner.

The traditionalists' victory was achieved at a heavy cost. For a start, the notoriously fractious Secessions were united as never before. At a meeting in Weimar in December 1903 they formed a new umbrella association as a progressive rival to the Guild. The 'Deutsche Künstlerbund', or German Artists' League, was established under the patronage of the Grand Duke of Saxe-Weimar, with Leopold von Kalckreuth as its president. Kalckreuth, who had served as President of the Karlsruhe Secession as well as participating in the Munich Secession, was a conservative monarchist from an old noble family, and his appointment made it more difficult for the Secessions' enemies to brand them 'radicals' and 'socialists'. Secondly, the Kaiser's intervention in the preparations for St Louis was savaged in the satirical press and by leading newspaper columnists. For moderate and conservative critics of Wilhelm II, the affair provided a welcome opportunity to criticize, with little risk of being branded unpatriotic or disloyal.

This was apparent in the Reichstag debate of 15–16 February 1904, in which speakers from the bourgeois parties lined up with the socialists to attack the hapless Home Secretary, who had little joy in attempting to defend the government's actions. Even the Centre party – a frequent critic of 'Secessionism' in the recent past – accepted that the Secessionists should have been involved at St Louis, and the Chairman of the Centre faction expressly praised a painting by Liebermann. Although constitutional realities meant the matter could go no further, the press coverage of the debates at home and abroad ensured that exhibitions of German art at future World Fairs were indeed more balanced. For a time, the Kaiser's public remarks on aesthetic issues became less outspoken too, and the long-planned 'Century of German Art' exhibition at the Berlin National Gallery passed off without a hitch in 1906. The gallery's director, von Tschudi, sidestepped a potentially explosive confrontation by choosing 1875 as the cut-off point for the exhibition, which featured some 2000 works loaned by 600 institutions and individuals. The National Gallery director proved less agile two years later, however, when the so-called 'Tschudi Affair' once more thrust Emperor Wilhelm's views into the spotlight.

The affair followed an offer to sell a private collection to the National Gallery.[91] Before a decision was taken, Tschudi invited the Kaiser and the Berlin museums chief Wilhelm Bode to inspect the collection, but he also included some extra pictures by nineteenth-century French artists that were available from the dealer Paul Cassirer. Tschudi had hoped the Kaiser would not notice, but precisely these pictures caught Wilhelm's eye. He was not impressed and refused to permit the purchase of the pictures *en bloc*, although he did appear to agree to the purchase of four less objectionable works out of royal funds. After Tschudi had obtained the four paintings, however, Wilhelm declined all knowledge of the matter, and the gallery director was left with an embarrassing 400,000 RM shortfall. The money was soon raised by private donations, but the affair provided Tschudi's enemies with welcome ammunition. Under pressure from Werner, the Prussian *Kultusminister* arranged for Tschudi to spend a year in Japan on 'sick leave': it seemed unlikely that he would ever return to his job, but Tschudi pre-empted any decision on his future by accepting a mischievous Bavarian offer to become Director General of Munich's Pinakothek instead.

The real significance of this episode, however, lies in the fact that Tschudi and other supporters of modernism were able to continue to run important German galleries, despite the Kaiser's objections. As James Sheehan puts it: 'Treue, Swarzenski, Pauli, and Sauerlandt [gallery directors in Dresden, Frankfurt, Bremen, and Halle respectively] all kept their jobs. . . . All these men survived because they found powerful allies, sometimes . . . in the city government, sometimes in the ministries, more often among wealthy private patrons who had been won over to the modernist cause.'[92] Even Tschudi's replacement in Berlin, Ludwig Justi, was a pro-modernist, albeit a more tactful one.

That conservative, art-loving monarchs did not have to become embroiled in such embarrassing episodes, can be seen from the example of neighbouring Austria, where the venerable Emperor Franz Joseph showed much more patience towards the 'Union of Austrian Visual Artists', as the Viennese Secession was officially known. Its short but remarkably productive life cannot be discussed in any detail here.[93] One aspect, however, requires some mention, since the Viennese contribution to new ideas in architecture and design was felt throughout Europe, and particularly in Germany, in the last years of the nineteenth century. From the beginning, the Viennese Secession embraced applied art as well as fine art, dismissing the traditional distinctions between high and low art. This was a feature of the German Secessions too, but in Vienna the Secession building was itself designed as a manifesto and a showcase for the new ideas in applied art and architecture, which were summed up in the Secession's motto *Der Zeit ihre Kunst. Der Kunst ihre Freiheit* ('To the age its art. To art its freedom'). Indeed, with the exception of Gustav Klimt (1862–1918), the Vienna Secession is today better remembered for its architects and designers than for its painters.

It was fitting that the revolt against architectural historicism made an early breakthrough in the Habsburg capital. The Viennese Ringstrasse development had represented the apogee of nineteenth-century academic architecture, with its Classical parliament; its Gothic town hall; its Renaissance university; and its Baroque theatre, all built within a few years by a small group of architects. During the 1890s one of them, Otto Wagner (1841–1918), had begun to distance himself from historicism. In his plans for Vienna's future urban development (1890–3); his lectures at the Viennese academy, where he was head of the architecture school; and in a series of suburban railway stations (1897–1901), Wagner showed a refreshing willingness to experiment with new structural and decorative forms. His buildings and books attracted the attention of architectural publications across the continent.

The architect of the Viennese Secession building, Joseph Maria Olbrich (1867–1908), had worked in Wagner's studio and was determined to take his mentor's ideas further. Olbrich's 'temple of art' took less than ten months to build, and housed its first exhibition at the end of 1898. The building was a Secessionist *Gesamtkunstwerk*, employing the talents of a wide variety of members. Its eye-catching dome, which represented a gilded laurel tree, rather than a cabbage as local cynics suggested, was a self-conscious symbol. In the classical world the laurel was associated with victory, dignity and purity. Here it also symbolized the Secession's hopes for renewal, a 'Sacred Spring' that would reunite art and life.[94] At first, the building was not warmly received by the general public: it was compared to a 'Buddist temple'; the 'Mahdi's grave'; a public convenience; and a mosque. As early as March 1899, however, the perceptive Hermann Bahr wrote: 'Six months ago, everyone was laughing at the new home of the Secession. Today it is already the pride and joy of the Viennese. I fear that in another six months it will be the template for keen copyists to build churches, hotels and villas in "Secessionist style".'[95] He was right. The building succeeded in making the Secession a household name in Vienna, and suddenly the *Sezessionsstil* was on everyone's lips.

Jugendstil in applied art and architecture

Sezessionsstil was just one of many terms used to describe the new style in applied art and architecture which blossomed across Europe in the 1890s: 'Art Nouveau', 'Modern Style', *Stile Inglese, Mouvement Belge, Paling Stijl* ('Eel Style'), and *Style Nouille* ('Noodle Style') all had backers, while in Germany the term *Jugendstil* quickly found favour. The variety of names given to the phenomenon indicates both its pan-European impact and the diversity of its roots, which stretched as far back as the 1880s, and as far afield as Japan. The two names which are used most frequently today, Art Nouveau and *Jugendstil*, both stem ostensibly from business ventures:[96] the former from the 'Maison de l'Art Nouveau', the Paris shop established by Hamburg-born art dealer Samuel Bing on 26 December 1895; the latter from the Munich journal *Jugend*, first published on 1 January 1896 by the tireless Georg Hirth, whose earlier endorsement of the German Renaissance style was now dismissed as a 'white lie', born out of necessity.

Subtitled an 'illustrated weekly for art and life', *Jugend* carried articles on politics, fashion and sport, as well as original works of art and literature. The front cover and masthead of each edition was different, but humour, parody, and satire always featured prominently on the inside pages. As with the Munich Secession, Hirth stressed that artistic 'freedom' rather than 'style' was the key, and propagated the value of subjective emotion over the cold rationality of contemporary life. From the very first issue, he claimed *Jugend* was open to all aesthetic approaches. It was ironic, therefore, that the journal's name should become so closely associated with one particular style of illustration and typography that even the proverbial man in the street soon began to speak of a *Jugend-Stil*.[97] For Hirth, this was a mixed blessing. While he welcomed the impressive circulation figures,[98] and rewarding commercial spin-offs, he recognized the dangers of an all too close association with the fortunes of a single style, especially one that was already being dismissed as an aesthetic dead-end by many critics. It was perhaps for this reason that the journal was so reticent about using the term in its own pages.

The pictorial content of the journal did indeed cover quite a wide range of styles, even if certain motifs recurred with particular frequency: dynamic dancers, pale maidens, and Spring landscapes among them.[99] However, the graphic art that 'framed' many of *Jugend*'s pages, designed by the likes of Otto Eckmann and Hans Christiansen, tended to be more homogenous. Multicoloured plant roots and tendrils, stylized snakes, swans' necks and flowing female locks curled sinuously around the pages, and even the individual columns. Illustrations were often framed too, so that the distinction between the 'frame' and the 'picture' was blurred. The curvilinear floral form, variously referred to as the 'wavy line', the 'whiplash' or the 'irritated earthworm', which was derived from nature and appeared to express the dynamism of the 'life-force', became – along with the more severe, geometric patterns prevalent in Vienna[100] – the definitive decorative device of *Jugendstil.* It was not, however, invented in the pages of the *Jugend.* The Belgians Victor Horta (1861–1947) and Henry van de Velde (1863–1957) had been following the 'cult of line' in their architecture and furniture design since around 1892. They in turn had derived inspiration from a wide range of sources, including Japanese textiles and prints; the furniture and book illustrations of the British Arts and Crafts designer Arthur Mackmurdo (1851–1942); as well as painters like Paul Gauguin, Henri de Toulouse-Lautrec and the Dutch Symbolist Jan Toorop.[101]

In fact, avant-garde artists and designers all over the western world began to employ the 'wavy line' in the 1890s.[102] By turning to nature rather than history for inspiration, they hoped to find a genuinely new decorative form, which had no connection with the world of the academy or the 'style masquerade' of nineteenth-century historicism. For craftsmen and architects, there was the added hope that the new ornamentation would be 'organic' rather than merely 'applied': that it would grow out of the intrinsic form of the object, reflecting both its function and the materials it was made from. This would fulfil at least one of the demands of William Morris (1834–96) and the British Arts and Crafts movement, whose influence on European designers was on the rise at this time, as was the 'organic architecture' of the Chicago architect Louis H. Sullivan (1856–1924), and the 'structural rationalism' of the French theorist Eugène Viollet-le-Duc (1814–79). In Germany, interest in the decorative and structural forms of the natural world became apparent through works like Moritz Meurer's *The Study of Natural Forms at Schools of Applied Art* (1889) and Ernst Haeckel's *The Art Forms of Nature* (1899). In 1891 the museums of applied art in Dresden and Berlin both staged exhibitions inspired by Meurer's work, and schools of applied art began to introduce classes on natural forms alongside the historicist contemplation of 'Our Fathers' Works'.[103]

It was characteristic of Art Nouveau in all its national variants that the definition of 'art' was expanded to include magazine illustrations, posters and the design of humble objects for everyday use. As the writer Otto Julius Bierbaum noted, 'Modern man doesn't want to know about "high" art any more; he doesn't want to run through museums and exhibitions; to stand and stare in amazement, only to come home feeling empty.'[104] Instead of the 'ivory tower' of the academy, or the gold-framed 'cemetery' of the gallery, the 'living world' was to be the focus of aesthetic attention. Art was to be placed in the service of society, ennobling the modern world and impregnating it with beauty. For a short while at least, it appeared as if the ugly realities of everyday life, with all its conflicts and crises, could be cured by aesthetic means. In practice, of course, little impact was made on the streets of Germany's cities, but in the private sphere of the home, where the owner could rule as a Nietzschean master of all he surveyed, a complete aestheticization of life seemed almost within reach.

The founding of journals like *Pan* (1895), *Jugend* (1896), *Dekorative Kunst* (1897), *Deutsche Kunst und Dekoration* (1897) and *Die Insel* (1899)[105] created new openings for German artists. This was particularly the case in Munich, where most of these titles were based and where a number of Secessionist painters started to experiment with graphic and decorative art, tapestry and weaving. Some, like Richard Riemerschmid (1868–1957)[106] and Peter Behrens (1868–1940),[107] went further still: branching out into furniture design and architecture in pursuit of the Holy Grail of the 'total work of art'. This became a recurring theme in the years around 1900, reflecting not only the influence of Wagner and Nietzsche, but also that of the Victorian art critic and theorist John Ruskin (1819–1900).

In 1897 Riemerschmid and Behrens were among the founder members of Munich's United Workshops for Art in Handicraft (*Vereinigte Werkstätten für Kunst im Handwerk*), along with Paul Schultze-Naumburg, August Endell (1871–1925), Hermann Obrist (1863–1927), Bernhard Pankok (1872–1943), Bruno Paul (1874–1968) and several dozen others. Their inspiration was 'the Arts and Crafts ideal of a community of craftsmen with their own workshops, able to produce a full range of everyday objects and so stamp daily life with an integral artistic unity'.[108] The United Workshops became a commercially successful limited company, producing both expensive 'designer' originals, and more modestly priced ensembles for the wider market. The Munich example was emulated a year later by Riemerschmid's future brother-in-law Karl Schmidt, who established the 'Dresden Workshops for Handicraft' in Saxony. Schmidt (1873–1948), a master-craftsman who had served some of his apprenticeship in Britain and was inspired by the ideas of William

Morris and C. R. Ashbee's 'Guild of Handicraft', was an enthusiastic campaigner for social reform, and a supporter of Friedrich Naumann's National Social Association. As in Munich, 'named' artists were commissioned to partake in the whole production process, with the aim of overcoming the separation of design and production which had come to characterize most modern manufacturing, and which was blamed for the ornamental 'excesses' of nineteenth-century historicism. In return, the artists were to be rewarded with a cut of the profits.

The social concerns of Karl Schmidt were shared by many *Jugendstil* artists, who saw the fight against ugliness as a moral and political crusade. Certainly, there was more to *Jugendstil* than a flight into 'regressive floral inwardness'.[109] The expansion of art into hitherto neglected areas of everyday life; the conviction that decorative form should grow out of functional necessity; and the self-conscious novelty of their aesthetic approach; all created at least a rhetorical affinity with the politics of social reform. Some, like Henry van de Velde – who moved to Germany in 1899 and remained until World War One – maintained close links to organized socialism. Even so, there was always a tension between *Jugendstil*'s egalitarian aspirations and its aesthetic elitism. Otto Eckmann once famously proclaimed 'we must use the snob, in order gradually to reach the people', but the work of leading *Jugendstil* designers always lay beyond the financial reach of ordinary households. Like their British Arts and Crafts cousins, the German movement remained reliant on bourgeois and aristocratic patronage.

Nowhere was this more apparent than in Darmstadt, which supplanted Munich as the focal point of German *Jugendstil* at the turn of the century.[110] The Grand Duke of Hesse-Darmstadt, Ernst Ludwig (1868–1937), had shown a consistent interest in the arts since his accession in 1892. Of course, a patriarchal interest in cultural life was expected of any ruler, but Ernst Ludwig – a grandson of Britain's Queen Victoria – was a genuine enthusiast for the Arts and Crafts movement, and had commissioned a breakfast room by M. H. Baillie-Scott and a reception room by C. R. Ashbee for his own palace. With the Mathildenhöhe project of 1899, however, Ernst Ludwig went one stage further. A whole district on the outskirts of the Grand Duchy's capital was to be developed as a showcase for the new ideas in architecture and design. To this end he invited seven young artists to Darmstadt to form the nucleus of the new community. The artists represented a variety of crafts and came from all corners of the German-speaking world. Each was given a monthly income and a plot of land. J. M. Olbrich was placed in overall charge and, like Peter Behrens, was awarded a professorial chair.

Ernst Ludwig's motives were mixed. In part, he was indulging a personal hobby: as a passionate Wagnerian, he wanted to sponsor a *Gesamtkunstwerk* of his own. He also felt obliged to offer symbolic and practical support to craftsmen at a time of structural change in the local economy. Above all, he sought to justify the Grand Duchy's continuing existence by 're-branding' it as a centre of cultural innovation within the Empire. In this he was encouraged and supported by the Darmstadt wallpaper manufacturer and publisher Alexander Koch, whose 1898 memorandum *Darmstadt: An Artists' Town?* pre-empted the project. The Darmstadt artists exhibited together in their own room at the 1900 Paris world exhibition and were warmly praised, but their efforts were mainly channelled towards the production of 'A Document of German Art' for the summer of 1901. An address issued by the seven artists in November 1899 outlined the aims of the project, which was intended to give 'a lasting picture of modern culture and modern artistic sensibilities'. It was to feature a mixture of permanent and temporary buildings, as well as shows of visual art and theatrical productions, but without the fairground distractions of other exhibition sites.

The 'Ernst-Ludwig-Haus', which formed a symbolic Acropolis at the centre of the Mathildenhöhe development, housed artists' workshops and studios, thereby implying that this was to be a community ruled by artists. Olbrich designed the long, low, flat-roofed building, whose arched entrance was flanked by two giant figures representing 'strength' and 'beauty'. The Austrian architect also designed most of the private houses for the individual artists, a gallery, theatre, music pavilion and a monumental gateway. Indeed, the only major building not by Olbrich was an idiosyncratic house designed, furnished and decorated by Peter Behrens. Although he had received no architectural training, Behrens was to become one of Germany's leading twentieth-century architects, and, to use Nikolaus Pevsner's phrase, a 'pioneer of modern design'. Behrens's house at the Mathildenhöhe was his first attempt at architecture, and combined the organic curves of Munich *Jugendstil* with the vernacular brick solidity of his native Hamburg. Inside, the music room resembled a sacred space, with a gilded ceiling and mystical geometric patterns inspired by Nietzsche's *Zarathustra.* Behrens's Nietzscheanism was also evident in *Das Zeichen* ('The Sign'), the stage-dedication play to mark the formal opening of the 'Document of German Art' exhibition on 15 May 1901 on which he collaborated.[111] *The Sign* was very much in the tradition of Wagner's *Parsifal*, with all the pathos and trappings of holy ritual: long flowing robes designed by Behrens himself; a fanfare; choral singing; and a mystical 'prophet' descending from the golden portal of the Ernst-Ludwig-Haus to receive a crystal, symbolizing the new life and new art.

In general, 'A Document of German Art' received mixed reviews. Inevitably its portentous title and opening ceremony promised more than it could deliver. Those who were not involved resented the implication that only the Darmstadt group was at the forefront of German art. Others criticized the fact that despite frequent references to 'the people', the houses, furniture and fittings were suited to upper-middle-class wallets alone. As an aestheticized island dependent on royal patronage the entire undertaking had a rather unworldly, dreamlike air, and was seen by some as a peculiarly inappropriate way to mark the opening of the new century. On the other hand, it undoubtedly helped to bring the new art to the attention of the general public and to raise the international profile of German architects and designers, who had hitherto been overshadowed by their British, French and Belgian counterparts.

Ironically, however, the highpoint of German *Jugendstil* also turned out to be its swansong. By the time the exhibition closed, manufacturers were already mass-producing furniture, tableware, cutlery and all manner of kitsch in the style of Behrens, van de Velde and other *Jugendstil* designers. Although they had always sought a wider public, there was little rejoicing at this newfound popularity, over which they had no control. For a start, only a superficial approximation of the *Jugendstil* aesthetic was achieved: crude imitations of the 'whiplash' applied to existing models, with little concern for the intrinsic form or function. Far from abandoning their production in historical styles, manufacturers had merely added a new style to their pattern-books. Despite the efforts of the 'workshops' in Munich, Dresden and Vienna, the dream of reuniting design and production seemed as distant as ever. Most of the leading *Jugendstil* figures were quick to distance themselves from their 'sins of youth'. The sort of decorative art that trumpeted its style rather than its content, its novelty rather than its quality, quickly fell into disrepute.[112] In contrast, the rhetoric of sober simplicity and functional honesty, which had ushered in the new style but had become lost along the way, would return with renewed vigour in the 1900s.

Aestheticism in literature and music

Although the term *Jugendstil* is generally associated with applied art and architecture, some authors have made a case for the existence of a literary or a musical *Jugendstil* too. As far as the latter is concerned, the principal case was made by Hans Hollander, who pointed out, amongst other things, that one of the first editions of *Jugend* featured a handwritten copy of the song *We both want to Jump* by Richard Strauss (1864–1949); 'a musical ornament' in which 'text and music, everything is in movement'.[113] A 1987 exhibition on the musical life of turn-of-the-century Munich was organized under the title *Jugendstil-Musik?* and its catalogue featured essays on Max Reger (1873–1916), Hans Pfitzner (1869–1949) and Gustav Mahler (1860–1911), as well as Strauss, whose first opera *Salome* (1905) took a theme favoured by many *Jugendstil* artists.[114]

The literary figures most often claimed for the style are the poets Rainer Maria Rilke, Richard Dehmel and Stefan George, but elements of *Jugendstil* have also been detected in the early work of other well-known writers, including Hofmannsthal, Wedekind and Thomas Mann.[115] Certainly, the *Jugendstil* vision of an aestheticized world lived on in the pages of literature, and particularly lyric poetry, long after its decline in the applied arts, but the existence of a literary *Jugendstil* remains a matter of scholarly dispute. That Rilke and Dehmel enjoyed close personal links to the style and its practitioners is easily established, but it is more difficult to define themes or linguistic patterns in their work as distinctively *Jugendstil*. In a 1971 study, Edelgard Hajek quoted a series of unidentified poems with 'typical' *Jugendstil* motifs, only to reveal that all were in fact written in the early nineteenth century.[116]

Rainer Maria Rilke (1875–1926), who nearly became an academic art historian and as a young man wrote well-regarded essays on the Worpswede artists and the sculptor Auguste Rodin, experienced the breakthrough of *Jugendstil* in Munich in 1897. A year later, in Berlin, he wrote enthusiastically about van de Velde's redesign of the Keller and Reiner galleries, and collaborated with the *Jugendstil* painter Ludwig von Hofmann. The artist illustrated Rilke's 'Songs of the Girls' for *Pan* (1898), before the poet returned the compliment by composing a cycle of fourteen poems inspired by Hofmann's sketches. According to Karl Webb, Rilke's enthusiasm for *Jugendstil* was a result of recognizing kindred spirits at work.[117] Certainly, Rilke's early poems did not appear out of place when published in

Jugend, Pan, and *Ver Sacrum* between 1897 and 1902. As an idealistic and sensitive individual, with aristocratic pretentions and a tendency to mysticism, the young Rilke shared many of *Jugendstil*'s characteristics. Appearances were important – he liked to dress like a duke, with a cane and pale leather gloves – and he was as perturbed by the ugliness of everyday life as any designer or painter. On the other hand, the themes of his early poems were hardly unique to *Jugendstil*: alienation from the modern world; the construction of a private paradise; the sanctification of nature; life, death and aesthetic renewal.

Webb's argument, however, does not rely solely on Rilke's thematic preferences. He gives examples, for instance, of the poet's 'tendency to imitate in verbal descriptions typical scenes from the art of *Jugendstil*',[118] and of his attempts to adopt the style's basic element, the 'whiplash' or 'wavy-line', as both a motif and a structural feature of his writing-style. To be sure, Rilke's early poetic language was self-consciously decorative, and he was prepared to alter syntactic structure for stylistic effect, but whether such literary aestheticism is best considered as a form of *Jugendstil* remains open to doubt. Certainly, he soon distanced himself from the movement and its main figures. While Rilke is now widely regarded as one of the great poets of the twentieth century, his slightly older contemporary Richard Dehmel (1863–1920) is rarely read today. In the first decade of the century, however, Dehmel was arguably Germany's most admired contemporary writer. His biography is itself a cultural history of Imperial Germany in microcosm: a convinced Nietzschean and Darwinian, he had close personal ties to the Naturalists of Berlin; was a frequent visitor to Friedrichshagen; and was a formative influence on the Expressionist generation. His links with *Jugendstil*, however, are particularly strong.

His first collection of poems, *Erlösungen* ('Redemptions'), was published in 1891, but he did not come to the attention of the general public until 1896, when his poem *Venus consolatrix* led to a court case and a conviction for 'injuring religious and moral feelings'. At around the same time, although married to the children's writer Paula Dehmel (1862–1918), he embarked on a celebrated affair with Ida Auerbach (1870–1942), whom he married in 1901. Dehmel recounted the story of the affair in the epic poem *Zwei Menschen* ('Two People'), which was serialized in *Die Insel* from 1900, and which suggested that the love of two people could not only overcome individual alienation, but gain an insight into the mysteries of the cosmos too. Henceforth the couple became something of a living 'total work of art' in

Jugendstil, openly embodying the freer, more sexual approach to love often associated with the *fin-de-siècle.* Their Hamburg apartment was furnished and decorated with the works of Behrens, van de Velde, and other *Jugendstil* figures. Ida even wore special dresses designed by her husband and by van de Velde. Although Dehmel counted many visual artists amongst his circle of friends, including Max Klinger and Edvard Munch, his closest bond was with Behrens, whom he met in 1899 when both were working for the journal *Pan.* Their relationship was based on mutual admiration. Behrens was happy to design book covers and a special typescript for the poet, and his woodcut of Dehmel graced the *Selected Poems* collection of 1901. For Dehmel meanwhile, Behrens was nothing less than a Nietzschean superman, capable of expressing himself in any artistic medium. Later, when the Dehmels moved to a detached home in the Hamburg suburb of Blankenese, Dehmel attempted to emulate Behrens's Darmstadt house by designing many of the fixtures and fittings himself.[119]

Dehmel's writing, however, is less easy to categorize as *Jugendstil*, even though his poems often appeared in journals like *Jugend* and *Ver Sacrum.* For a start, he showed an interest in aesthetic theory that was largely absent from the 'hands-on' *Jugendstil* artists and designers. His theoretic writings, full of the power and pathos of later Expressionist manifestos, reflected his conviction that art was replacing religion in the modern world. In one essay, for instance, he argued that theatres should be built for the working class rather than new churches, since the latter were destined to remain empty. His belief in the spirituality of the aesthetic sphere is apparent from the titles of some of his poems: *Jesus der Künstler* ('Jesus the Artist'), *Rembrandts Gebet* ('Rembrandt's Prayer'), *Predigt ans Grossstadtvolk* ('Sermon to the people of the City') and so on. Some of these were ostensibly lyrical studies of nature, but they were also works endowed with complex spiritual and metaphysical meanings.

Dehmel's poems were non-Naturalistic and deliberately formalistic – *Two People* consisted of 36 'songs', each with 36 lines – which could be equated with *Jugendstil*'s striving for form. Like other *fin-de-siècle* writers, Dehmel took their appearance very seriously indeed: as Hans-Ulrich Simon has noted, 'around 1900 a beautiful book aroused more interest than a good book . . . words were regarded as visual events'.[120] The themes of his poetry, however, were extremely varied, and did not shy away from contemporary urban life, including the situation of the working class. There was, moreover, an emotional intensity and rawness in them that was often lacking in the stylized world of *Jugendstil*, but which so impressed the first generation of Expressionists.

Dehmel's second wife Ida was a former companion of the third Wilhelmine poet sometimes subsumed under the heading of *Jugendstil*: Stefan George (1868–1933). George's personal links to visual and applied artists were limited, although Melchior Lechter (1865–1937) who supplied many book illustrations and developed his own typeface for George, is sometimes considered a *Jugendstil* figure. George, who first came to the attention of artistic and literary circles with his self-published collection *Hymns* in 1890, founded the *Blätter für die Kunst* in 1892. This privately produced journal was not widely available, but nevertheless became the focal point of a close-knit community of admirers. After his 1897 collection *Das Jahr der Seele* ('The Year of the Soul'), George withdrew himself even further from public life, and the cultish aspects of his following became apparent. Amongst the young writers to fall under his spell were Ludwig Klages, Karl Wolfskehl, Friedrich Gundolf and Max Dauthendey. George's poetry, which gloried in the magic and sensuality of language, sometimes adopted the wave-like rhythm of *Jugendstil* art and shared its preference for style over content. Indeed, though they became more philosophical and mystical over the years, George's poems were generally less concerned with the communication of a specific meaning than with a love of linguistic experiment for its own sake, which took him to unchartered territory in the history of German literature, and close to the borders of abstraction. Some of his early poems were even written in his own artificial language, *lingua romana*, and throughout his life he declined to use capital letters for nouns.

Needless to say, the aloof George had little interest in terms like *Jugendstil* or Symbolism, or the vagaries of artistic fashion. Nor did he share the social concerns held however superficially by many *Jugendstil* artists: for once, the cliché of the inward-looking and apolitical German artist is appropriate. Even so, it is perhaps unfortunate that George is today remembered more for his infamous 'Circle' of disciples than his poetry, which contained much that was innovative. The rapidly growing body of literature on George – in which he is variously portrayed as a religious charlatan, as a homoerotic and paedophiliac pied piper, and as a precursor to Hitler – has examined his legacy in great depth.[121] However, his influence on the wider cultural community was probably less profound than the proliferation of such works implies.

Whether *Jugendstil* is the appropriate term or not, it is clear that a self-consciously stylized, mannered and decorative approach to language was one of two major tendencies within Wilhelmine Germany's literary avant-garde. The other was Naturalism. Although Rilke, Dehmel and George owed a considerable debt to French and Belgian Symbolism, they also drew much inspiration from the world of visual and applied art. Their approach, for which Aestheticism or 'aesthetic fundamentalism' (Stefan Breuer) is perhaps the most accurate description, also embraced 'experimental conservatives' like Hugo von Hofmannsthal, Rudolf Alexander Schröder, Rudolf Borchardt and Hermann Hesse. All of these writers shared a faith in the power of language and the importance of art, not only for society at large, but for its own sake too. Indeed, it was no coincidence that these years saw much avant-garde art literature and art move away from the grasp of the general public, becoming more esoteric and inaccessible in the search for aesthetic perfection. Germany was by no means unique in this regard, but as Thomas Nipperdey notes: 'German authors were – in comparison to the British, say – more individualistic, anti-conventional, despairing, ecstatic, pretentious, experimental.'[122] Thus, when Wilhelm II launched his regular attacks on modern aesthetic values, he was no doubt voicing the views and concerns of many ordinary Germans. As we shall see in Chapter 5, however, the real surprise was how many people declined to follow him.

5 *'Wilhelminism' and its Discontents*

Introduction

As a scholarly term 'Wilhelminism' (*Wilhelminismus*) leaves much to be desired. Its meaning is vague; its usage inconsistent. Nevertheless, its regular appearance in recent works of political, literary and art history would seem to indicate that many find it indispensable.[1] Hans-Ulrich Wehler once dismissed it as a label that concealed 'the interplay of pressure groups, quasi-autonomous institutions and politicians who lacked formal political responsibility' in Imperial Germany.[2] More usually, however, it has been employed to denote the apparent congruence between Wilhelm II as an individual and the age to which he gave his name. As such, its seductive appeal is obvious: a single word that stands for operatic gesture and sentimental yearning; for pomp and pathos; for 'romantic modernity' and 'nervous idealism';[3] even for the peculiarly adjective-laden language of Wilhelm's bombastic speeches, so enthusiastically emulated by Heinrich Mann's Diederich Hessling and other *Untertanen*.[4]

The danger, of course, is that such a label is as likely to obscure as to enlighten when applied indiscriminately to the diverse products of a complex and transitory age. Few would agree with Nicolaus Sombart's assertion that 'for all the variety, clash and confusion of Wilhelmine Germany, the era was also exceptionally unified in its physiognomy, in its style, in the variety of its expressions, as are few periods in history'.[5] Here, therefore, Wilhelminism is used more narrowly to refer only to the Empire's official culture in the reign of Wilhelm II. Some aspects of this were dealt with in Chapter 2, and further examples follow. This chapter seeks to demonstrate, however, the extent to which the character and values of Wilhelm II's official culture became contested and opposed in the years around 1900: not only from within the ranks of the socialist labour movement and of organized Catholicism, but amongst patriotic middle-class Protestants too. The challenge came in a variety of forms, not only from the pens of satirists and cartoonists who savaged the Kaiser and his pet projects with unprecedented ferocity; but also from a bewildering array of cultural critics, prophets, and reform leagues, each clamouring to be heard; and from the rapid emergence of a new mass culture, based on commercial calculation rather than aesthetic contemplation. Each of these is featured over the following pages.

Wilhelm II's *Kunstpolitik*

'The broad and varied area which comes under the jurisdiction of the *Kultusministerium* – art, research, medicine etc. – is something I have always followed with lively interest, and always sought to promote'.[6] When the former Kaiser's memoirs were published in the 1920s, this solitary bland sentence represented virtually the only comment on the many cultural controversies that had stirred during his reign. Some have taken this as a sign that Wilhelm's apparent interest in aesthetic issues was never more than skin-deep. When the Kaiser spoke, Rudolf Pfefferkorn has suggested, he was merely expressing the views of others, such as Anton von Werner.[7]

However, as Peter Paret and Martin Stather have shown,[8] the extent of Wilhelm's handwritten notes in the margins of the many art-related papers and architectural plans laid before him, often at his own request, would seem to indicate otherwise; as would his frequent attempts to exercise his own modest creative abilities. He also once said that if he had not been an emperor, he would have liked to have been a sculptor.[9] Wilhelm's personal intervention in numerous building projects, from monuments and churches to post offices and railway stations, is well documented, as is his involvement in the St Louis and Tschudi affairs. It is known that he paid regular unofficial visits to the studios of artists and sculptors; was an enthusiastic painter,[10] poet and composer;[11] and dabbled in the design of furniture, yachting trophies and uniforms.

There is also no shortage of anecdotes that appear to reveal that he was a man of firm aesthetic preferences. On a visit to the

Düsseldorf Exhibition of Industry in 1902, for instance, Wilhelm refused to enter a room showing the work of the *Jugendstil* designer Henry van de Velde, telling his entourage: 'No, no gentlemen, I decline to be made seasick!'[12] On another occasion Leistikow's Secessionist painting *Grunewaldsee* was dismissed by the Kaiser on the grounds that he did not recognize it: 'I know the Grunewald', he declared, 'and besides, I am a hunter'.[13] The best compliment a contemporary work of art could receive, Wilhelm believed, was: 'That is nearly as good as the art of 1900 years ago'.[14] Wilhelm II was not a great collector of art, but in an officially approved 1912 study of Hohenzollern cultural policy, the art critic Georg Malkowsky explained that for Wilhelm 'nothing could be further from his thoughts than a personal, aestheticizing patronage: he pursues a genuine art policy (*Kunstpolitik*)'.[15] According to Malkowsky, this *Kunstpolitik* was rather different from conventional patronage of the arts: '*Kunstpolitik* is the official cultivation and promotion of artistic creativity which grows out of national consciousness and which expresses the national idea', he wrote.[16]

Wilhelm spelt out his views on the ideological and didactic function of art in one of his many long and opinionated speeches. 'Art should contribute to the education of the people', he argued. 'Even the lower classes, after their toil and hard work, should be lifted up and inspired by ideal forces.' And he continued: 'when art, as often happens today, shows us only misery . . . then art commits a sin against the German people. The supreme task of our cultural effort is to foster our ideals. If we are and want to remain a model for other nations, our entire people must share in this effort, and if culture is to fulfil its task completely it must reach down to the lowest levels of the population. That can be done only if art holds out its hand to raise the people up, instead of descending into the gutter.'[17]

One practical consequence of such views was the Prussian government's programme to encourage monumental painting in schools, universities and libraries, which was overseen by the Prussian *Landeskunstkommission*, a body with a larger budget than the National Gallery.[18] These large-scale paintings, depicting heroic, uplifting deeds from the classical world or, less often, from German history, provided painters like Georg Bleibtreu (1828–92), Hermann Prell (1854–1922), Hermann Knackfuss (1841–1915), and Peter Janssen (1844–1908) with years of work and a comfortable standard of living before World War One, especially as they received commissions from town halls and German embassies as well.

Another practical example of the Kaiser's didactic *Kunstpolitik* was the 'Avenue of Victory' or Siegesallee in Berlin's Tiergarten. From the beginning, the Siegesallee was Wilhelm's personal project: a gift to the people of the imperial capital, first announced on his 36th birthday in 1895. A team of twenty-seven Berlin sculptors under the command of Reinhold Begas worked for six years to produce thirty-two groups of marble figures drawn from Prussian history. Each group of figures featured one of Wilhelm's noble ancestors, together with a small supporting cast of generals, bishops and administrators, chosen in consultation with the director of the Prussian state archives.[19]

It was to celebrate the opening of the Siegesallee on 18 December 1901, that Wilhelm gave his best-known speech on the subject of aesthetics, an extract of which has already been quoted. The Kaiser suggested to the assembled sculptors and artists that art, like nature, exists 'according to eternal laws that the Creator himself observes, and which can never be transgressed or broken without threatening the development of the universe. . . . Before the magnificent remnants of classical antiquity we are overcome with the same emotion; here too, an eternal, unchanging law is dominant: the law of beauty and harmony.'[20] Like others of his generation, the Kaiser had received his aesthetic education in the spirit of German idealism and in particular from Friedrich Theodor Vischer's five-volume *Ästhetik*. When he used words like 'beauty' and 'harmony' in his speeches he made no effort to define their meaning because he felt it was common knowledge, and in a way it was. Even at the end of the nineteenth century most middle-class Germans would have seen things in much the same way. Of course, Wilhelm's stubborn defence of the 'eternal laws' of aesthetics had a political background as well. As a believer in the divine right of kings he perceived any threat to the 'eternal laws' to be a challenge to his throne.

The times, however, were changing. As we saw in Chapter 4, the existence of 'eternal verities' no longer found universal acceptance. Thus, although David Blackbourn has urged us not to underestimate the role of the Kaiser as an arbiter of taste – 'Given that young men were prepared to grow their moustaches in the royal style and even to imitate William's rasping voice, it would be surprising if the All-Highest denunciations of green horses and degenerate prose had found no echo'[21] – the striking thing is just how faint this echo proved to be. Not only did 'green horses and degenerate prose' continue to be produced, they became accepted well beyond the avant-garde, and even found supporters at the heart of the imperial establishment. Indeed, the reception of the Siegesallee showed how broad the opposition to Wilhelminism was becoming. For a start, its unveiling was met with a host of critical cartoons in Germany's satirical press. Thomas Theodor Heine's drawing in *Simplicissimus,* for instance, was captioned 'Little Willy plays Berlin'. It depicted a battalion of tin soldiers marching down an avenue of wooden trees and toy statues, just set up by a disembodied hand.[22] Similarly, a popular cabaret song of 1904 had a Berlin policeman showing off the Siegesallee to a tourist: 'Dummies on the right, dummies on the left' he sang, in a broad Berlin accent.[23]

Secondly, the commentaries in some of the Empire's most influential middle-class journals, like *Jugend, Die Zukunft* and *Der Kunstwart,* were damning. Ferdinand Avenarius's eminently respectable and patriotic *Kunstwart,* which in principle shared Wilhelm's views on art's didactic role and on Germany's distinctive cultural mission, was dismayed by the banality of the Siegesallee.[24] Later, after the further débâcle of the St Louis affair, a resigned Avenarius wrote: 'It is perhaps just as well that the Emperor thinks and speaks about art as he does; a ruler who would assert true leadership in the arts would make it more difficult for us Germans . . . to develop independent judgements.'[5] It is the growing community of *Kunstwart* readers, and others of their ilk, who are the main focus of this chapter. In the course of 1903 surreal advertisements for the oral hygiene product 'Odol' began to appear in middle-class journals such as *Jugend,* depicting the Siegesallee lined not with heroic Hohenzollerns, but with bottles of mouthwash.[26] Not only did this suggest that advertising was already becoming an art form in its own right, but it also indicated the commercialized nature of the modern culture that emerged in Germany in the later Wilhelmine years. Contrary to the product's claims, the advertisements must have left the Kaiser with a bitter taste in his mouth.[27]

Wilhelmine satire

Wilhelm's pomposity soon made him a target of satire. One of the earliest such works was an essay in *Die Gesellschaft* entitled *Caligula: A Study of Roman Imperial Madness* (1894) by the liberal historian and pacifist Ludwig Quidde (1858–1941), which sold over half a million copies and was reprinted thirty-four times when published in pamphlet form.[28] The essay was presented as a scholarly biography of the Roman emperor and boasted copious footnotes, but was nevertheless clearly an attack on Wilhelm II's own caesarian aspirations. His work confronted the authorities with a dilemma that would recur frequently in the Wilhelmine era, since a prosecution on the grounds of *lèse-majesté* would have amounted to a judicial admission that Germany's emperor really did resemble the mad Roman ruler. Quidde escaped prosecution.

Another early and persistent critic of Wilhelm, Maximilian Harden, also used humour and satire in his attacks on the emperor. Harden particularly mocked the monarch's fondness for travel and what would now be called 'photo-opportunities', dubbing him *Filmhelm* and the *Reisekaiser.* Harden, however, was not a great humourist, and his *Die Zukunft* generally offered few laughs. For humour, middle-class Wilhelmine readers turned instead to journals like *Kladderadatsch* and *Simplicissimus*, as well as the more general *Jugend*, and the less political *Fliegende Blätter*;[29] while working-class readers favoured the socialist equivalent, *Der wahre Jakob.*[30] The 'grandfather' of German political satire was *Kladderadatsch*, a Berlin-based satirical weekly founded in 1848 by David Kalisch. It continued publication until 1944, but was arguably past its peak by the turn of the century, when its circulation was around 50,000. Politically, *Kladderadatsch* began as a radical liberal paper, but in the 1870s it adopted a strongly pro-Bismarck – and hence anti-Catholic and anti-socialist – line. In its politics and its humour it closely resembled the British *Punch.* Its rival *Simplicissimus*, co-founded by the publisher Albert Langen (1869–1909) and the artist Thomas Theodor Heine (1867–1948), was first published in Munich in 1896. The two journals reflected the different character of the cities in which they were based: the Munich paper (which was actually printed first in Leipzig and later in Stuttgart) had a much more vulgar, direct and less subtle humour than its laconic Berlin competitor.[31]

The success of *Simplicissimus* – its circulation grew from 15,000 in 1898 to about 86,000 in 1908 – was principally a result of its fine cartoons and illustrations. These were notable not only for their content, but also for their stylistic innovations. As Makela, Peter Jelavich and others have pointed out, satire and parodic humour were an important aspect of modernism as it emerged in Munich in the 1890s, and the *Simplicissimus* illustrators, such as Heine, Olaf Gulbransson (1873–1958), and Bruno Paul (1874–1968) played their part. Each had their own personal style, but they nevertheless shared something of a common approach, based on simplification and exaggeration. It is a testament to the quality of the journal's illustrators that they had more impact than the literary contributors, who included some of turn-of-the-century Germany's finest writers: Thomas and Heinrich Mann, Ludwig Thoma, Rilke, Dehmel and Frank Wedekind, whose contributions financed his unremunerative work as a playwright.[32]

For both *Kladderadatsch* and *Simplicissimus* recurring targets included the army, its reserve officer system and militarist sentiment in general; 'monument mania'; cultural politics, such as the Secessions; and the hypocrisy of the Catholic Church. The Kaiser only became a regular target during his 1898 trip to Palestine, when *Simplicissimus* found that political satire 'paid', in the form of a growing circulation. The farcical aspects of Wilhelm's 'crusade' were ridiculed in illustrations by Heine and a Wedekind poem, for which the writer was sentenced to a seven-month stay in the Saxon fortress of Burg Königstein. Both Heine and Langen also received periods of *Festungshaft*, although this was a good deal less unpleasant than prison, and was cushioned by the large increase in sales. Part of the journal's success was due to its appeal across the class spectrum. Its cheap cover price meant many workers purchased copies, but it also gained a more unexpected following amongst young army officers. Eventually, in 1910, the Prussian Minister of War had to issue an order requiring all officers to sign a pledge not to read the subversive journal.[33]

One must be careful, of course, not to exaggerate the political impact of the satirists. Although the paper and its writers played an active role in the campaign against the Lex Heinze, their political engagement generally stopped with the defence of liberties in the civil and cultural sphere: they did not actively campaign to achieve social justice or more fundamental political reforms. Indeed, it is possible to portray the Wilhelmine satirists as a stabilizing and therefore ultimately conservative force in German society, acting as a 'safety valve that helped alleviate political discontent . . . in a politically inconsequential manner'.[34] It is clear, however, that Kaiser Wilhelm did not share this view, and nor did many other conservative Germans.

The opening chapters of Heinrich Mann's famous novel *Der Untertan* ('Man of Straw') also first appeared in *Simplicissimus*. If satire 'consists most fundamentally in contrasting a person's stated values with his or her actual practices',[35] then *Der Untertan* was satire at its best. It followed two other social novels – *Im Schlaraffenland* (1900) and *Professor Unrat* (1905) – and was finished in 1914, but not published in full until 1918. The name of the novel's repulsive antihero Diederich Hessling means something like 'the ugly little German', and the character certainly embodied all the worst features of the Wilhelmine middle classes: an arrogant and aggressive tyrant, yet servile and sycophantic toward people in positions of authority. It should not be forgotten, however, that like all good satire *Der Untertan* was based on exaggeration: the novel has scant sympathy for any of its characters and did not aspire to be a sensitive or balanced portrayal of a whole society.

As we have seen, the social reality of Imperial Germany was complex and fractured; divided along lines of class, confession and region into a variety of very different socio-cultural milieus, and even within the Protestant *Bürgertum* the figure of Diederich Hessling personified only one strand. As Thomas Nipperdey reminds us, success and social advancement for the middle classes in Wilhelmine society was generally based on achievement, rather than craven sycophancy.[36] Society, moreover, was changing rapidly in the later years of Wilhelm II's reign. One expression of this was the growth of cabaret as a cultural phenomenon in Germany's major cities after 1900. Peter Jelavich, whose studies of the *Kleinkunst* culture of Munich and Berlin have opened up a new area of historiographical interest, has termed cabaret 'an unstable but vital combination of satire and parody dealing with love, fashion, art, and politics'.[37] Political cabaret, as opposed to variety and music-hall entertainment, began in Germany in 1901, with the opening of three shortlived but influential establishments.

The first of these was Ernst von Wolzogen's 'Buntes Theater' (Motley Theatre) in Berlin, whose debut performance took place on 18 January 1901, the thirtieth anniversary of the founding of the German Empire. Wolzogen (1855–1934) was the half brother of the Wagnerian Hans von Wolzogen, and termed his cabaret *Überbrettl*, implying that Nietzsche's *Übermensch* would be treading the boards of his stage. The cabaret enjoyed early commercial success, and moved into a new purpose-built theatre in November 1901, although it did not enjoy a long life. Their most scandalous piece was a song set to the patriotic tune of 'The Watch on the Rhine' entitled *Der Marschallstab* ('The Marshall's Baton'), which alluded to the vanity of Field Marshall Alfred von Waldersee, commander of Germany's military task-force in China.[38] If this was just about as political as

Wolzogen's cabaret got, then a more sophisticated tone was struck by another Berlin cabaret established in 1901. 'Schall und Rauch' (Sound and Smoke) was founded by Max Reinhardt (1873–1943), later to become acclaimed as a genius of the theatre, and 'stood at the beginning of a new theatrical sensibility and practice, which revolutionized the stage by stressing exuberant play'.[39] In May 1901 it staged a parody of Hauptmann's *Die Weber* at the Deutsches Theater, specially edited for a fictitious and rather thick German prince, Serenissimus, who sat in the very box cancelled by Wilhelm in 1894. On the stage, the weavers' hovel was transformed into a comfortable bourgeois home, and at the end of the play Serenissimus came on to the stage to award the actors medals.

The most famous cabaret in Wilhelmine Germany was not in Berlin, however, but in Munich, where the 'Elf Scharfrichter' (Eleven Executioners) appeared almost every night between April 1901 and December 1903. The masked 'executioners' performed their own songs and texts, rather than employ professional actors in the manner of Wolzogen or Reinhardt. Their audience sat at tables in an intimate environment and the walls were decorated with *Jugendstil* graphic art. Indeed, the connections between the cabaret and Munich's journals *Jugend* and *Simplicissimus* were readily apparent, not least in the persona of Frank Wedekind, who quickly replaced one of the original executioners and became a full member himself. The 'Elf Scharfrichter' often performed political material; including a piece inspired by the Siegesallee and other Wilhelmine monuments, *Das Denkmal* by Otto Falckenberg and Paul Schlesinger (June 1902). They sought to evade the censors by staging closed performances for invited 'guests' (who paid an inflated cloakroom fee in lieu of an entrance charge), but soon lost that right and had to subject their songs and sketches to the Munich police for pre-performance censorship. Even so, this did not prevent them from making further political comment. In November 1903 a straight-faced performance of Kaiser Wilhelm's musical composition *Sang an Aegir* brought the house down.

Wilhelmine reform movements

In 1902 Heinrich Driesmans wrote: 'Innumerable are those who seek to reform our circumstances. Reform is the catchword of our age.[40] Three-quarters of a century later, the historian Thomas Nipperdey concurred: 'Wilhelmine society was a society of reform movements and of reforms.'[41] Even so, comprehensive studies of the movements for cultural and social reform in Wilhelmine Germany are still comparatively rare.[42] One reason for the long-standing historiographical neglect is undoubtedly the bewildering variety and diversity of causes that came together under the broad and vague banner of 'reform'. Historians have generally preferred to focus on individual organizations or specific areas of reform – such as clothing, lifestyle and sexuality; youth and education; the environment, architecture and town planning – rather than undertake the much more difficult task of overall synthesis and interpretation. This is understandable, especially since all the efforts of contemporaries to bring the various reformist strands under a common umbrella ended in abject failure. Rather than a single coherent entity we are dealing with a host of autonomous leagues (*Bünde*),[43] each with their own recipe for cultural and/or social renewal.

Even so, a number of common characteristics can be identified. The reform leagues founded in the decades either side of 1900 were composed predominantly – but not solely – of urban, middle-class Germans from Protestant backgrounds. They opposed the aesthetic values, authoritarian rituals and 'hurrah patriotism' of *Wilhelminismus*, but were nevertheless proudly nationalistic. They were pained by the excesses of capitalism, but firmly rejected Marxism too. Under the influence of cultural pessimism and the late nineteenth-century reaction against materialism, positivism and historicism, the reform leagues therefore favoured an elusive 'third-way' between capitalism and communism. In practice, this could mean anything from a broadly progressive German Fabianism to a *völkisch* proto-fascism, but always with a pronounced tendency to seek aesthetic or cultural answers to what were essentially economic or political questions. This does not mean, however, that the reformers should be dismissed as politically irrelevant. As Nipperdey – one of the few major historians to treat the Wilhelmine reform movements seriously – noted: 'Revolutions and reforms began in the sciences, in the arts, in lifestyles, rather than in politics. But politics were not left untouched.'[44]

Lifestyle reform (Lebensreform)

The origins of the reform leagues lay in the numerous closely related strategies for self-improvement that emerged in Europe during the nineteenth century, such as abstinence, dietary reform, vegetarianism, natural health and homoeopathy. The reformers therefore began with the idea of reforming society through the individual, and as such reflected the enduring influence of German idealism and its notion of the perfectibility of the individual through self-cultivation (*Bildung*). As one Wilhelmine reformer, Friedrich Landmann, put it: 'Lifestyle reform is above all reform of the self; it has to begin with one's own body and in one's own home.'[45] In the particular German context, this is often portrayed as recognition of the difficulties of achieving reform through the political system, and as part of the *Bürgertum*'s withdrawal into the personal sphere. The fact that three of the failed revolutionaries from 1848–9 – Gustav Struve (1805–70), Eduard Baltzer (1814–87) and the composer Richard Wagner – were later all prominent advocates of vegetarianism would seem to lend weight to this case.

In 1867 Baltzer had established a vegetarian association and a journal; a year later the first conference of German vegetarians took place in Baltzer's hometown of Nordhausen. Wagner wrote a famous pro-vegetarian tract and frequently dined at one of Europe's first vegetarian restaurants, established in Bayreuth in 1871. He also spoke in support of the anti-vivisection cause – vegetarians and natural health activists were often involved in the campaigns against the 'twin evils' of vaccination and vivisection – and posthumously became something of a role model for the Wilhelmine reformers, especially since his hero Tannhäuser wore sandals. This should not blind us to the fact, however, that the pioneers of modern vegetarianism and natural health came from a wide variety of national backgrounds. The ascetic Leo Tolstoy was just as much a role model for German reformers as Wagner, and key impulses also came from Britain, France and Switzerland. The latter, for instance, produced the 'sun doctor' Arnold Rikli (1823–1904), and the inventor of müsli Max Bircher-Benner (1867–1939). In any case, since the Wilhelmine reformers ultimately went well beyond the sphere of the individual, the 'retreat of the *Bürgertum*' argument should not be pursued too far.

Early German *Lebensreformer* (the term itself did not appear until the 1890s) also included the poet Johannes Guttzeit (1853–1935), who combined his vegetarian diet with a wardrobe of simple peasant clothes, and who founded one of the first lifestyle reform leagues in 1884; Gustav Jäger (1832–1917), who propagated all-woollen clothing as a way to better health; Sebastian Kneipp (1821–97) the Catholic priest whose herbal water cures are still on sale today; and

Adolf Just (1859–1936) who chose to spend several years living in a wooden hut near Brunswick. The latter founded the natural health spa 'Jungborn' in the Harz mountains; one of many establishments offering 'sunlight and fresh air' cures which, despite the much-touted achievements of 'scientific' medicine, sprang up across Central Europe during the second half of the nineteenth century.

More than a decade earlier Carl Braun, a keen supporter of homoeopathy, had opened a shop and mail-order business supplying organic food, wholemeal bread and vegetable oil to the wealthy middle classes of Berlin (1887). This was in many ways the prototype *Reformhaus*, although that name did not come into use until the businessman Karl August Heynen opened the 'Reformhaus Jungbrunnen' in Wuppertal (1900). By 1925 there were around 200 *Reformhäuser* in Germany and they remain a familiar sight on German high streets today. In 1893 the vegetarian restaurant 'Ceres' in Berlin was the venue for the founding of the 'Vegetarische Obstbau-Kolonie Eden' at Oranienburg.[46] This large-scale orchard and market garden enterprise was set up on a co-operative basis: the Eden logo featured three trees, standing for lifestyle reform, land reform and social reform. To discourage property speculation all of Eden's 440 hectares were held in common ownership. Individual growers leased their plots and houses from the colony, and their produce was packaged and marketed collectively. The settlers and their families were expected to lead healthy lifestyles. The sale or serving of alcohol and tobacco was banned, as were gaming halls, brothels and betting shops. The early years of the Eden experiment were a struggle. To fertilize the sandy soil 30,000 hundredweight of horse-dung had to be transported from Berlin each year, and the undertaking was dogged by persistent financial difficulties. It survived, however, and has continued to function in some form until the present day.

Naturism

In May 1901 one of the Eden settlers, Karl Mann, opened Berlin's first 'sunlight and fresh-air sport baths', offering lawn tennis and sand baths as well as sun loungers and a massage room. Mann, who also published the 'body beautiful' journal *Kraft und Schönheit* ('Strength and Beauty'), was convinced of the health benefits of nakedness, but stressed its moral value too. It would, he argued, combat hypocrisy and prudery, and reduce the need for pornography and prostitution. The police were not fully convinced, however, and refused to allow permission for a 'ladies section' on the site. At around the same time naked bathing became popular in secluded spots on the North Sea and Baltic coasts, and authors like Heinrich Pudor (1864–1943) and Richard Ungewitter (1868–1958) began to celebrate a new 'naked culture' (*Nacktkultur*) in numerous papers and pamphlets. These stressed the aesthetic as well as health benefits of nudity, but also explored notions of 'racial hygiene' and purity. A more erotic charge was carried by the journal *Die Schönheit* ('Beauty'), published by Karl Vanselow (1876–1959) from 1903 to 1932, which was shunned by many naturists as 'pornographic'. Undeterred, Vanselow set up a 'Garden of Beauty' at Werder on the Havel and staged 'Beauty Evenings' at which his future wife, the London-born Olga Desmond, performed naked dances. However, like all early naturist societies, Vanselow's enterprises suffered from a gender imbalance: there were too many men and simply not enough women.

The title of Imperial Germany's foremost naturist, however, probably belongs jointly to the Munich painter Karl Wilhelm Diefenbach (1851–1913) and his loyal disciple 'Fidus'. After many years of ill-health, the long-haired Diefenbach had become a virtual hermit in a tumbledown cottage at Höllriegelskreuth in Bavaria. Here he experimented with a variety of alternative treatments, including a vegetarian diet and prolonged spells of nudity, and was dubbed by sceptical locals the 'kohlrabi apostle'. In 1887 he was visited by the young Lübeck art student Hugo Höppener (1868–1948), who had gone to study at the Munich academy. Höppener, who had also endured a youth scarred by illness and had benefited little from conventional medicine, was persuaded to abandon Jäger's 'wool cure' and live the Diefenbach way instead. In November 1888, however, the two men were observed walking naked in a quarry, and were charged with immoral behaviour. Diefenbach was sentenced to six months; his young follower, whom Diefenbach christened 'Fidus', to three months.[47]

The court case gave the painter and his young disciple cult-status in avant-garde circles. Indeed, Fidus went on to become one of Wilhelmine Germany's best-known lifestyle reformers, whose rather fey illustrations of naked androgynous youths and *Jugendstil* angels were to adorn numerous reformist tracts; journals like *Pan*, *Jugend* and *Simplicissimus*; and some important literary works too. His most famous picture, the *Lichtgebet* ('Prayer to Light') depicts a naked blonde-haired figure with upstretched arms, as if in communion with the sun. It was first painted in 1890 and repeated in eight different versions over the following decades, one of which ended up on the wall of Martin Bormann's Munich apartment during World War Two.

Figure 9 Fidus, High Watch *(better known as* Prayer to Light*) (1894)*

The popularity of the *Lichtgebet* motif – reproduced as a postcard it became an icon of the German youth movement – reflects the importance with which Wilhelmine reformers regarded the sun and its rays as a metaphor for life and health. In fact, while the notion of a 'place in the sun' is generally associated with the Empire's colonial aspirations, it was an equally important preoccupation amongst domestic reformers, and featured prominently in the art and literature of the time. Cäsar Flaischlen, for instance, proclaimed 'Have the sun in your heart!' in a collection of poems entitled *Vom Alltag und Sonne* ('Of the Everyday and the Sun', 1898); and Georg Heym wrote in his diary in 1906: 'I find myself believing more and more firmly in Helios, in the light, the sun, the holiness of the whole natural order.'[48] The reformist 'Freyabund' (1908) called its journal *Der Lichtfreund* ('Friend of the Light'), while the lifestyle-bible *House in the Sun* (1895), by the Swedish artist-designer Carl Larsson, was also immensely popular in Germany, as people attempted to break free from the gloomy interiors of the *Gründerzeit.* Inspired by the same notion, reformist architects such as Walter Gropius propagated what became known as the glass 'curtain-wall', flooding factories, department stores and schools with 'healthy' sunlight. Indeed, one architectural historian has spoken of a 'craze for light' in 1900s Germany.[49]

In some cases, the Wilhelmine sun worship took on a cultic and pseudo-religious character. The midsummer solstice, for instance, was once again celebrated as a major festival, with bonfires and parties across Central Germany sponsored by the publisher Eugen Diederichs (1867–1930) and his 'Sera Circle'. Fidus, who was introduced to the occult and theosophical ideas by Wilhelm Hübbe-Schleiden (1846–1916) in the 1890s, produced many plans for temples and stone circles. The purpose of these fantasy structures, with their eclectic mix of Egyptian, Indian and prehistoric forms, was never spelt out and none were built, even though Fidus was always prepared to adapt them to the demands of the time. In the 1890s, for instance, they stood for the 'regeneration of mankind' and the 'sacred spring' of *Jugendstil*; in the 1910s he offered them to Rudolf Steiner and the anthroposophists;[50] and by the 1940s he was still trying to get them accepted as crematoria for fallen Nazi heroes. One is reminded of Heinrich Hart's retrospective observation on the Wilhelmine reformers: 'The object of our longing was unclear, as is all springtime longing (*Frühlingssehnsucht*), but it was in a sense of spring that we lived and worked.'[51]

Clothing reform

The Wilhelmine clothing reformers were pre-empted by the nineteenth-century natural health campaigners like the aforementioned Gustav Jäger and Heinrich Lahmann (1864–1931), founder of the 'Weisser Hirsch' sanatorium in Dresden and author of *The Reform of Clothing* (1889). These and other early clothing reform publications were aimed predominantly at men's clothing, and polemicized against the stand-up collar, the 'Prince Albert' frock coat, and the top hat. In the 1890s, however, the focus shifted towards female dress. Here the demand was for dresses without stays and the abolition of the corset, which not only restricted movement and made breathing difficult, but could even damage internal organs. The medical discourse against the corset was given a *völkisch* spin in publications like Paul Schultze-Naumburg's *Die Kultur des weiblichen Körpers als Grundlage der Frauenkleidung* ('The Culture of the Female Body as a Basis for Women's Clothing', 1901) and Heinrich Pudor's *Reform-Kleidung* ('Reform Clothing', 1903), which claimed the fertility of the German race was being threatened by the disfiguring dictates of French fashion houses. The women's movement also addressed the issue of crinolines and the corset. At the International Congress of Women's Organizations in Berlin (1896) there were several debates on clothing issues, resulting in the establishment of a 'General Association for an Improvement in Women's Clothing' later that year, and an exhibition in Berlin attracted over 8000 visitors in 1897.

The first 'reform dresses' were coarse and unshapely (*Reformsäcke*) but around 1900 a number of Secessionist and *Jugendstil* artists began to develop their own designer dresses: Pankok, Schultze-Naumburg, van de Velde, Behrens and Fidus all came up with designs. Henry van de Velde's wife, Maria Sethe, wrote about them, and modelled many of the dresses herself. Curiously, the wife of another leading architectural reformer of the time, Hermann Muthesius's wife Anna, was also prominent in the dress reform movement. The connection between architecture and clothing had earlier been made by the public health campaigner Max von Pettenkoffer, who wrote in 1876: 'The hat is the roof of one's clothing, and the roof is the hat of one's house.'[52] Indeed, the links between the reform movements in architecture and clothing at the turn of the century – both stressed the importance of hygiene, functional 'honesty', sobriety, and material quality – represent a fascinating and largely unexplored chapter in the history of early German modernism.

The 'General Association' split in 1903, but one of its successors – the 'Free Union for an Improvement in Women's Clothing' – soon had over 3000 members in twenty branches, and its own journal, *Die neue Frauentracht* ('The New Women's Costume'). Further splits followed,[53] but the simple linen or cotton reform dress gained steadily in popularity, especially amongst the first female professionals; the wives of vicars and professors; and women's rights activists such as Gertrud Bäumer. Of course, in the *haute couture* world of Paquin and Worth, Doucet and Drecol, the corset lived on, although even in Paris young rebel designers like the Frenchman Poiret began to abandon the 'hour-glass' ideal. If one discounts Amelia Bloomer's baggy breeches, which became popular amongst German women cyclists, Poiret's pantaloons (1912) were the first high-fashion trousers for women.

In the 1900s, under the influence of the youthful hiking societies (*Wandervogel*), a distinctive 'alternative look' also became well-established amongst reform-minded German males. It involved sandals (or stout walking shoes for the more serious hiker), long woollen socks, cotton knee breeches or *Lederhosen*, and loose tunics or night-shirts, often worn with a neckerchief. At the youth movement's famous 1913 gathering on the Hohe Meissner, one of the organizers, Christian Schneehagen, distributed copies of a pamphlet that suggested that the new partnership between the sexes also required a common approach to questions of clothing. In fact it was already apparent that, even without official co-ordination, the dress of male and female hikers was becoming steadily more similar.

Wandervogel *and other youth organizations*

Compared to other aspects of Wilhelmine reformism, the youth movement, and especially the hiking *Wandervogel*, has attracted considerable interest from historians, so this section offers only the briefest of introductions.[54] For a start, it is important to remember that the concept of 'youth' as we understand it today did not exist in the nineteenth century. The 1896 edition of the popular reference work *Meyers Konversations-Lexikon*, for example, offered the following entry under the heading 'Youth': 'see Age'.[55] Youth was at most a physiological and legal category. Despite the efforts of Wilhelmine educationalists like Georg Kerschensteiner, the vast majority of Germans went straight from childhood to the world of work and adult concerns. Indeed, study of nineteenth-century autobiographies suggests that the main concern of adolescents was to reach adulthood as soon as possible.

The rise of the *Wandervogel* movement occurred at a time, however, when the word 'youth' was suddenly on everyone's lips. Not only had a *Jugendstil* appeared in the arts, but *Jungen* had become active in the SPD, in the Evangelical Social Congress, and even in the German Pharmacists' Association. As the writer Stefan Zweig (1881–1942) recalled: 'The whole generation decided to become more youthful. In contrast to the world of my parents, everyone was proud to be young: suddenly . . . the beards began to disappear.'[56] Whether inspired by the accession of the 'young Emperor', or the onset of a new century – which the Swedish author Ellen Key heralded as the 'century of the child' – the 1900s saw the rise of numerous youth organizations, although not all were as free from adult control as the first *Wandervogel*. The turn-of-the-century infatuation with youth was by no means unique to Germany, but Germany was an unusually 'young' country in two ways: not only had the Empire been created just three decades before, but it also possessed a remarkably youthful demographic profile. Later, Arthur Moeller van den Bruck would attempt to draw some political conclusions from this in his book *Das Recht der jungen Völker* ('The Rights of Young Nations', 1919).

The 'Wandervogel, Ausschuss für Schülerfahrten' was officially established in the Berlin suburb of Steglitz in November 1901, although pupils at the local grammar school had been taking part in informal hikes since 1896, organized by the Berlin University student Hermann Hoffmann (1875–1955) and his charismatic deputy Karl Fischer (1881–1941). Hoffmann soon left for a career in the diplomatic service, but under Fischer the Steglitz boys' country rambles quickly developed from day-trips to fortnight-long expeditions undertaken during the school holidays. The hikes involved sleeping in barns, singing campfire songs and eating frugally. Their terminology, a curious mixture of grammar school Latin and archaic German, included the greeting 'Heil!' which probably came from Austrian student circles. Encouraged by progressive teachers like Ludwig Gurlitt (1855–1931) and Hermann Lietz (1868–1919) the idea caught on quickly in schools throughout Germany, although it remained a predominantly urban, middle-class and Protestant phenomenon. The total number of *Wandervögel* grew from around 100 in 1901 to some 25,000 in 1914, with a further 10,000 or so adult leaders and supporters.

However from 1904, when the Steglitz group divided into Fischer's 'Alt-Wandervogel' and Siegfried Copalle's 'Steglitzer Wandervogel', the history of the movement is a complicated saga of leadership disputes and secessions, over such thorny issues as alcohol consumption, homosexuality and, above all, the participation of girls, elementary school (that is to say, working-class) boys and Jews.[57] In 1906 the 'Bund Deutscher Wanderer' was founded, and in 1907 the 'Wandervogel, Deutscher Bund'. The latter was the first group to allow female members, although most of the others followed a year or two later. 1910 saw the formation of both the 'Jung-Wandervogel' and the 'Wandervogel Vaterländischer Bund'. An umbrella organization was created in 1913 with the establishment of the 'Wandervogel e.V. Bund für deutsches Jugendwandern' (sometimes known as the 'United Wandervogel') but the unity was only partial, and in any case proved shortlived.

By this time, moreover, a wide variety of rival youth groups had been established. The major Christian churches organized their own youth associations, as did the socialist labour movement and the Jewish community. Some of these included hiking amongst their activities. A German branch of Baden Powell's Boy Scouts was founded in 1911; and in the same year the imperial authorities set up the quasi-military 'Jungdeutschlandbund', under the leadership of serving army officers. In total, these groups numbered some two million members by 1914 and therefore vastly outnumbered the membership of the 'free' *Wandervogel* societies, which were themselves less autonomous than is sometimes suggested.[58]

The politics of the *Wandervogel* – the extent, on the one hand, of the movement's emancipatory potential and, on the other, of its hostility to western liberal values – has been much discussed, especially in light of the political polarization that occurred in the movement after 1918. It is clear, however, that their 'contrived air of aimlessness' (Stachura) did not lend itself to serious political activity before World War One. As Laqueur puts it: 'They were vague in their diagnosis and even less clear in their proposals for remedying the situation. But they felt strongly and sincerely about it'.[59] In general, neither the middle-class *Wandervogel*, not its equivalents in the labour movement's youth organizations, were ever really able to transcend the cultural boundaries of their class or upbringing. Certainly, the *Wandervogel*'s distaste for the chauvinistic sabre-rattling of *Wilhelminismus*, and its genuine desire to liberate members 'from petty egoism and careerism, to oppose artificial conventions, snobbery, and affectation'[60] did not stop many contemporary bourgeois prejudices from surfacing in their debates and publications.

Like other Wilhelmine reformers, the *Wandervogel* leaders had little difficulty in accepting the notion of a distinctively German cultural mission. This was expressed through a veneration of the natural and man-made landmarks of the countryside; a revival of folk tales and songs – gathered together by Hans Breuer (1883–1918) in the immensely-popular song book *Der Zupfgeigenhansl* (1909) – and the studious propagation of 'German' virtues, such as simplicity, honesty, idealism and comradeship. Ultimately, however, the *Wandervogel* struggled to channel its idealism towards an appropriate cause, and much of it evaporated in the windy rhetoric of the Hohe Meissner gathering, to which we will return in Chapter 6. The positive achievements of the Wilhelmine youth movement – other than the hiking 'experience', which undoubtedly left a lasting impression on many participants – lay mostly in the area of educational reform.

Reformist teachers and pedagogic theorists were attracted to the *Wandervogel* idea from the start, and some such as Hermann Lietz and Gustav Wyneken (1875–1964) tried to harness its energy for their own reform projects. Wyneken, who established the Free School Community (*Freie Schulgemeinde*) at Wickersdorf in 1906, believed that youth had less to do with age than with attitude. He was seldom free from scandal, however, because of his radical views and his homosexuality. In 1910 the Ministry of the Interior in the state of Saxe-Meiningen withdrew the licence for Wickersdorf, prompting a widespread outcry. Wyneken turned to journalistic activities for a time, editing the pioneering student magazine *Der Anfang* in 1913–14. Like its equally shortlived successor, Eugen Diederichs's *Der Aufbruch* (1915), it was amongst the first journals to posit the notion of a distinctive 'youth culture'. It may only have had about 800 subscribers in 1913, but it could boast a teenage Walter Benjamin amongst its contributors.

Artists' colonies and communities

European artists had been gathering together in rural retreats since the early 1800s but, inspired by the *plein air* Barbizon painters in France, artists' colonies experienced a new lease of life in the later nineteenth century. The aesthetic and social costs of rapid urban growth and industrialization spurred many painters to head for the countryside, where they sought a more natural lifestyle and a more tangible sense of community, without having to set sail for the South Sea islands. Munich, nineteenth century Germany's art capital, was surrounded by a ring of small towns and villages in which artists rubbed shoulders with local farmers and craftsmen: places like Holzhausen on the Ammersee; or Dachau, to the north-west of the city, where Ludwig Dill, Adolf Hölzel and Fritz von Uhde could often be found. Dachau was sited'on flat, marshy moorland, and its misty, moody atmosphere was particularly attractive to the outdoor painters of Realism and Naturalism.

The topographical situation of the best-known artists' colony in turn-of-the-century Germany, at Worpswede north of Bremen, was similar. However, while artists had been coming to Dachau for most of the nineteenth century, Worpswede was a genuine backwoods community, lacking even the most modest amenities. The first artist to 'discover' the village on the Teufelsmoor, with its peat bogs and avenues of birch trees, was the Naturalist painter Fritz Mackensen (1866–1953). Mackensen paid his first visit in 1884 and decided to settle in 1889, along with a fellow student from the art academies of Düsseldorf and Munich, Otto Modersohn (1865–1943). Over the next few years they were joined by two further student friends: Fritz Overbeck (1869–1909) and Hans am Ende (1864–1918), together with the younger Heinrich Vogeler (1872–1942). Vogeler, who had come straight from the Düsseldorf academy at the age of 22, may have been the junior member when the Worpswede Artists' Association was formally established in 1894, but he was the first artist to purchase a property in the village. The ramshackle old farm-house which he bought in 1895 and christened the 'Barkenhoff' quickly became the focal point of the artists' colony; hosting not only the communal print workshop with its ancient etching press, but also banquets, recitals, poetry readings and open-air theatre.

As master of the Barkenhoff, Vogeler rebuilt the house, adding monumental gables to the north and south, and laying out a garden with decorative urns and potted laurels. When the poet Rilke stayed on his first visit to Worpswede in 1898 he remarked in a letter that 'every brick and every chair' in the house was a product of Vogeler's aesthetic intentions; the house was truly a total work of art, by a man who 'planted trees as an author plants letters'.[61] Vogeler's quest to unite art and life in aesthetic harmony led him to design book covers, theatre sets, dresses, furniture, rugs and even Worpswede's railway station. His principal talent, however, lay in illustration, where he combined fine line drawings or etchings with decorative *Jugendstil* graphics.[62]

The Worpswede artists enjoyed their big breakthrough in 1895, first in Bremen and then at the International Art Exhibition held in Munich. For the next decade or so they were able to command high prices for their studies of the north German landscape and its weather-beaten inhabitants. Their paintings were more decorative than Liebermann's Dutch works, and had a symbolic depth that appealed to admirers of Böcklin. In the era of Langbehn's *Rembrandt* and a growing *Heimatkunst* movement, their work could appeal to progressives and conservatives alike. Personally, however, the Worpswede artists soon began to drift apart, and although they continued to live in the village, the communal activities declined. The Artists' Association was dissolved as early as 1899.

Some new life was breathed into the Worpswede community at the turn of the century by the presence of a young painter called Paula Becker, who had arrived in 1897 to study with Fritz Mackensen. Her fresh and unsentimental gaze fell on the people of the village rather than her fellow artists or the landscape. In 1901 – the year of three weddings and a funeral for the Worpsweder[63] – she became Otto Modersohn's second wife. Over the next six years Paula Modersohn-Becker (1879–1907) divided her time between Worpswede and Paris, where she was captivated by the work of Cézanne, Gauguin and van Gogh. Although a naturally confident woman, who strengthened her resolve with frequent readings of Nietzsche's *Zarathustra*, Modersohn-Becker always struggled for recognition. Of the 700 paintings and nearly 1000 drawings she completed, only three were sold during her short lifetime, and she was not even mentioned in Rilke's *Worpswede* essays. In this her fate was typical of many women artists in Imperial Germany. In other respects, however, she was far from typical. First, because she was an important and innovative painter, whose self-portraits in particular have become part of the canon of early modernism; and secondly, because she died at the tragically young age of 31, just weeks after giving birth to her first child. The fact that she had predicted her early demise in diary entries lends an almost unbearable poignancy to much of her work.[64]

In 1905 Vogeler completed a lasting monument to the Worpswede community in the form of the painting *Summer Evening*, which depicted eight of the group at an impromptu music recital on the terrace of the Barkenhoff. At first glance it seems an idyllic scene, but it is clear from the distant stares and preoccupied expressions that the 'fairy-tale' was coming to an end. Some moved away from the village altogether. Vogeler stayed, but entered a mid-life crisis, prompted by a drop in demand for his work and the slow break-up of his marriage. This led him to volunteer for military service in 1914, and it was the experience of World War One that changed him from a dreamy aesthete to a committed socialist. From 1918, the Barkenhoff became a centre of left-wing activism.

What Worpswede was for painters, Friedrichshagen was for writers. As we saw in Chapter 4, the little town south-east of Berlin became home to a colourful collection of literary and political 'refugees' in the 1890s; people seeking an alternative lifestyle, but within easy reach of the comforts and attractions of modern urban civilization. It comes as no surprise therefore, to find a host of *Lebensreform* undertakings emanating from the 'Müggelsee Republic'. The best-known of these was the New Community ('Neue Gemeinschaft') established by the Hart brothers in 1900. The New Community began as a loose and informal group, meeting in Friedrichshagen pubs, but in 1901 it moved to an apartment in Wilmersdorf, and in 1902 to Schlachtensee, where it took over a former sanatorium. This was to be transformed into an earthly paradise: a place with a 'genuinely humanitarian culture', offering 'a life in the light'. Appropriately, the New Community's symbol was a rising sun.

The fifty or sixty members, predominantly writers and artists, paid a nominal monthly subscription. This entitled them to use the accommodation, partake in communal meals, and to take advantage of the other facilities, which included a library, artists' studios and an outdoor theatre. Within the community they were also expected to contribute in some way to the provision of meals and accommodation. The members were encouraged to address each other with the informal 'du', and to treat each other as brothers and sisters. The New Community had its own journal; staged lectures, and organized regular excursions and festive events on a variety of themes. The latter were not intended as parties, but as a serious attempt to 'compose a work of art out of people'. Indeed, the whole community was to be a 'living work of art'.

The New Community attracted hundreds of curious visitors, some of whom gave guest lectures. Amongst the visitors were Henry van de Velde, Theodor Herzl, Magnus Hirschfeld and Erich Mühsam. Paula Modersohn-Becker, who did not suffer fools gladly, noted after her visit: 'There seems to me to be a lot of vanity: longhaired artists, [too much] powder, and excessive corsetlessness.'[65] Women, in fact, were rather peripheral figures in the New Community. Although wives were taken on outings and could contribute to debates, they were generally expected to perform much the same role as bourgeois housewives. Predictably, much of the communal cooking and cleaning fell to the 'womenfolk'. There were exceptions – Paula Dehmel, Lou Andreas-Salomé,[66] and Else Lasker-Schüler,[67] were accepted more or less as equals – but on the whole women had little to gain from the New Community.

Julius Hart, the New Community's co-founder, had published an anthology of poems under the title *Die Insel der Seligen* ('The Isle of the Blessed'). The same title was used by Max Halbe (1865–1944) for his comic play loosely based on the New Community and the wider Wihelmine reform movement. The play was set in a 'back to nature' commune, in which both naturism and Buddhism were practised zealously, but where the vegetables failed to grow. The commune ultimately fails because it has 'too many philosophers and insufficient potato-diggers', and the New Community met with much the same fate. After a dispiriting succession of squabbles, intrigues and accusations, the undertaking was wound up in 1904. Not only had the members failed to do their share of digging, but most had taken advantage of the community's facilities without paying. Despite generous donations from well-wishers, the New Community was a financial disaster.

Four years earlier, the New Community's foundation day had also seen the birth of another Friedrichshagen enterprise, Bruno Wille and Wilhelm Bölsche's 'Giordano-Bruno-Bund'. The League was named after a religious freethinker in fifteenth-century Rome, and was established as an umbrella organization for Germany's growing band of freethinkers, humanists, theosophists and other religious dissidents. Many members of the Giordano-Bruno-Bund, including Wille and Bölsche, endorsed the doctrine of Monism, which Ernst Haeckel had revived in 1892, and which sought to eliminate the dichotomy between science and religion; body and soul. Haeckel, who was made Honorary Chairman of the League, believed Darwin's discoveries brought a single, unified world-view within mankind's grasp, and he gained a wide audience for his views in *Die Welträtsel* ('Riddles of the Universe', 1899).[68] The book's mixture of science and mysticism fitted closely with Bölsche's own works on the natural world, and both he and Wille were founder members of the 'Monistenbund' (Monist League) in 1906. It campaigned 'for the progress of mankind towards freedom and self-determination under the rule of reason', and against all forms of religious dogmatism.

It is often suggested that in adopting the new paradigms supplied by Haeckel and Nietzsche, the Friedrichshagener moved away from Naturalism and socialism to become elitist *Sozialaristokraten* in the later 1890s. Although there is some truth in this, they remained very different from the George Circle, and continued to seek contact with Berlin's working class. Bölsche and Wille were frequent lecturers for the workers' education associations, for instance, and they helped to establish the 'Free High School' in 1902. Moreover, their fundamental outlook remained overwhelmingly optimistic: 'The Friedrichshagener were radical cultural optimists, forward-thinking evolutionists, who looked into the future with enthusiasm and without any self-doubt'.[69]

In his autobiography Max Halbe wrote that Friedrichshagen was a state of mind rather than a place.[70] At the distant end of this Friedrichshagen imagination stood the village of Ascona, a tiny community on the Swiss side of Lake Maggiore, in the canton of Ticino. Ascona offered Wilhelmine reformers a lakeland landscape even more attractive than the Müggelsee, and a much better climate, but in the 1900s its transient population were still recognizably Friedrichshagener. Some, such as Landauer, Mühsam and Lasker-Schüler, flitted between the two. For others, such as Henri Oedenkoven and Ida Hofmann, Ascona became a home for some twenty years. Oedenkoven, a wealthy Belgian, and Hofmann established a natural health sanatorium, 'Monte Verità', near the village in 1900.

Their regime was strictly vegetarian and abstinent, with plenty of sun, fresh air and water, together with generous helpings of *Parsifal*. At various times it attracted the likes of Hermann Hesse, D. H. Lawrence, Max Weber and C. G. Jung, as well as a succession of *Naturmenschen* – long-haired, bare-legged, sandal-wearing 'seekers after truth' – who passed through the small community, which became the 'semi-official meeting place for all Europe's spiritual rebels':[71] people such as Otto Gross (1877–1919), a brilliant psychoanalyst, but also an anarchist, drug addict and sexual revolutionary;[72] the hairshirted guru Gusto Gräser, who had spent much of the 1890s with the naturist Karl Diefenbach; or the spirited young women known to bemused locals as the 'three witches': Else Lasker-Schüler, the dancer Mary Wigman and the painter Marianne Werefkin. It was little wonder that a host of writers chose Ascona as the basis of novels and plays.

The Wilhelmine period also threw up three or four dozen less famous model communities and colonies, many of which survived well into the 1920s. Some were anarcho-socialist in character, inspired by the likes of Peter Kropotkin (1842–1921), William Morris (*News from Nowhere*, 1890) or Gustav Landauer (*Die Siedlung*, 1909). Others – like the 'Siedlungsgemeinschaft Heimland', established in 1909 by readers of Theodor Fritsch's anti-semitic *Hammer*, or Willibald Hentschel's 'Mittgard' colony – were openly racist, and refused to allow 'non-aryan' members. There were also, of course, communities based on religion, and several women-only communities. Despite their philosophical differences, however, these undertakings all had much in common. Each sought to re-establish communitarian values at a time of rapid social atomization, and did so in rural locations, on the basis of a more natural and self-sufficient lifestyle (organic farming, vegetarianism, naturism, homoeopathy). Each was anti-capitalist and anti-materialist in its rhetoric; stressed youth as a value in itself; and developed a calendar of celebratory events or rituals. Moreover, the problem of 'too many philosophers, insufficient potato-diggers' was common to all such communities, whether left or right.

The Heimat *movement*

Although *Heimat* associations were established in many regions of the new Empire in the 1870s – to preserve local identities, customs and landmarks, and to research local history – it was not until the 1890s that serious attempts were made to develop an ideology or programme out of this vague but comforting concept, which was briefly mentioned in Chapter 1. Given the different motivations of the individuals involved, it is not surprising that the *Heimat* movement was from the beginning a loose and disparate coalition of interests ranging from literature to conservation.[73] This is reflected in the many turn-of-the-century neologisms which took the *Heimat*-prefix: *Heimatkunst*, *Heimatschutz*, *Heimatkunde*, and so on.

For the Alsatian writer Friedrich Lienhard (1865–1929), the principal goal was *Heimatkunst*: an earthy new German literature and art, rooted in the diversity of regional cultures and dialects, and heralded as an antidote to both Wilhelmine pomp and the aesthetic affectations of the literary avant-garde. In 1900 Lienhard teamed up with the literary historian Adolf Bartels (1862–1945) to establish the journal *Heimat,* which had a pronounced anti-urban agenda. Bartels attempted to put his literary theories into practice in his own novel *Die Dithmarscher* (1898); a heroic tale of everyday farming folk. His political outlook was shared by Heinrich Sohnrey (1859–1948), a teacher who published the rural revivalist *Deutsche Dorfzeitung* from 1896, and who diligently recorded disappearing country customs for posterity. Literary *Heimatkunst* took its inspiration from Realist writers like Theodor Storm, whose work was characterized by a strong sense of place and a genuine regard for 'real' people. In visual art, the romantic landscapes of Hans Thoma (1839–1924) – an artist from humble Black Forest farming stock who was long shunned by the German academic art establishment[74] – were held up as exemplary, as were Fritz Boehle's farming paintings. Prominent proponents of *Heimatkunst* included M. G. Conrad, the Naturalist pioneer, who wrote in 1901: 'The secret of art lies in the secret of the blood and the soil.'[75]

Not all *Heimatkunst* novels had country settings – Johann Kinau (1880–1916), who wrote under the pseudonym Gorch Fock, was admired for his sea-faring tales – but there was certainly a proliferation of 'hearth-and-homeland' literature in the Wilhelmine era: books like *Jörn Uhl* (1901) by Gustav Frenssen (1866–1945), which sold 130,000 copies in its first year; or *Der Wehrwolf: Ein Bauernchronik* ('The Werewolf: A Peasant Chronicle', 1910) by Hermann Löns (1866–1914), set on the author's beloved Lüneburg Heath at the time of the Thirty Years War. It was the high sales figures for such works, rather than the ideological posturings of Bartels and Lienhard, which spawned thousands of trivial *Heimat* novels in their wake. Clearly, many readers felt a need for stable literary settings and values at a time of rapid social and economic change.

It would be wrong to assume, however, that the authors of such books were all conservative anti-modernists. Before World War One, Frenssen was like Conrad a left-liberal urban intellectual, while the most popular author of witty Bavarian dialect tales was none other than Ludwig Thoma; the *Simplicissimus* writer, scourge of Wilhelm II and outspoken critic of authoritarianism. Nor were they all male: the best known *Heimat* writer of the Eifel region was Clara Viebig (1860–1952), with novels like *Kinder der Eifel* ('Children of the Eifel', 1895), and other women writers such as the lyric poets Helene Voigt-Diederichs and Lulu von Strauss und Torney were also successful in the genre. It is, moreover, salutary to compare the reputation of turn-of-the-century German *Heimat* writers with their equivalents in other national contexts. In his highly-influential *Selections from Scrutiny* the British literary critic F. R. Leavis reminded his readers 'of those unfashionable writers who celebrated village life and arts', and argued that some – like the British rural romanticist Richard Jefferies (1848–87) and others in 'The English Tradition' – were important in paving the way for modernism. In Germany, however, writers who worked very similar themes are automatically portrayed as reactionary or even 'crypto-fascist'. As Martin Green puts it: 'As we move from the English Department floor to the German Department floor of the language and literature building, we find that these ideas change color, looking acid in one context, alkali in the other.'[76]

Of course, no one could deny that many of the champions of *Heimatkunst* held deeply conservative and racist views, or that other aspects of the *Heimat* movement were motivated by a blind and undifferentiated hatred of Germany's evolving modern urban culture; but one must be careful not to fall into the self-same trap, by tarring all *Heimat* activists with the same, 'anti-modern' brush. Until recently, this was certainly the fate of the *Heimatschutz* strand of the movement. The Berlin professor of music Ernst Rudorff (1840–1916) who coined the term *Heimatschutz* in 1897, was indeed a died-in-the-wool reactionary, who had attacked the coming of the railways because it made it more difficult to find stable-boys. However, the threat to the natural world posed by industrialization and urbanization was undeniably real, and not all the solutions pursued by the *Heimatschützer* were escapist or romantic.

With the rise of environmental history as an academic discipline, and with 'green' issues fashionably prominent in political discourse, recent years have seen a proliferation of research into the pioneers of German environmentalism.[77] These works focus mainly on the Wilhelmine years, because it was in the first decade of the twentieth century that the key early achievements were recorded. These included the first mass protest against a large engineering project in an environmentally-sensitive location (the unsuccessful campaign in 1903–4 to stop the Laufenburg rapids in Baden from being lost as part of a hydro-electric power scheme); the first organized attempts to create national parks in Germany (the 'Verein Naturschutzpark', founded in 1909, purchased some 4000 hectares of land on Lüneburg Heath between 1910 and 1920); the first campaigns against the over-development of areas of outstanding natural beauty for tourism; and the first town and country planning legislation to offer real protection for the German landscape, the Prussian 'Law against the Disfigurement of Places and Outstanding Landscapes' of 1907.

Such legislation was the principal achievement of the 'Bund Heimatschutz', the first mass movement in the history of German conservation and environmentalism, which was founded as an umbrella organization for a host of smaller associations in 1904, and which claimed over 100,000 individual and affiliated members by 1906.[78] Once the Bund Heimatschutz had been established, the likes of Rudorff and Bartels took a back seat, and were quickly eclipsed by more pragmatic figures, including Paul Schultze-Naumburg and the conservationist Hugo Conwentz (1855–1922). Unlike Rudorff and other late nineteenth-century cultural pessimists who could see only decadence and decay on the horizon, Schultze-Naumburg's pre-war writing was characterized by a genuine, if rather naive, optimism that his pedagogic efforts could really make a difference.[79] Of course, his attitude to the natural world was – in common with other Wilhelmine environmentalists – aesthetic and sentimental rather than ecological. This had less to do with the shortcomings of scientific knowledge in turn-of-the-century Germany than with the priorities of a grammar-school education: like other Wilhelmine reformers, Schultze-Naumburg tended to seek solutions in the world of culture rather than civilization.

Historians have generally viewed this predominantly aesthetic approach as the *Heimatschutz* movement's fatal weakness. In a recent study, however, William Rollins contends that 'a strongly aesthetic attitude toward the land was in some ways the most radical and effective form that environmentalism in Wilhelmine Germany could take',[80] not least because at the turn of the century scattered scientific findings 'stood little chance of overturning the immense cultural consensus in favour of industrial expansionism'. For Rollins, aestheticism 'constituted a central ground of perception and discussion from which real problems could be addressed'.[81] Moreover, since the emotional concept of *Heimat* is much more powerful as a rhetorical tool than the rather sterile notion of the 'ecosystem', even contemporary scientific environmentalists should take note. The latter aspect of Rollins's views has not found universal acceptance, but the Wilhelmine *Heimatschützer* are certainly no longer dismissed as blind reactionaries. It was, after all, largely their achievement that Article 150 of the 1919 Weimar constitution proclaimed: 'The monuments of art, history, nature and the landscape enjoy the protection and the care of the state.'

Land reform and the garden city movement

Both the land reform movement ('Verein für Bodenreform', 1894; 'Bund Deutscher Bodenreformer', 1898) and the German Garden City Association ('Deutsche Gartenstadtgesellschaft', 1902) had their roots in 1890s Berlin, particularly in the bohemian milieu of Friedrichshagen. Although German land reformers drew important inspiration from abroad,[82] their principal motivation came from the crisis on their own doorstep. Germany's cities at the turn of the century were characterized not only by chronic over-crowding, but also wild land speculation on their peripheries, as developers bought up large tracts of land in the expectation of future profit. Reformers argued that the housing crisis in the Empire's cities would not be solved until land ceased to be treated as a speculative commercial commodity. They disagreed, however, on how this was to be achieved. Some, such as Michael Flürscheim (1844–1912), favoured the nationalization of all land, and its subsequent leasing back to the highest bidder. Others called for a tax on profits made from land or property sales, which should be re-invested in co-operative housing schemes and in the employment of more housing inspectors. This more moderate course was advocated by Adolf Damaschke (1865–1935), the best-known of the Wilhelmine land reformers and a close associate of the left-liberal politician Friedrich Naumann.[83]

People like Damaschke and Franz Oppenheimer, author of the co-operative classic *Freiland in Deutschland* (1894), became popular figures in reformist circles,[84] not least because their work appeared to give the notion of a 'third-way' between capitalism and communism real credibility. In a cover design for the journal of the League of German Land Reformers the illustrator Fidus attempted to express this in graphic terms. He depicted a country crossroads with three possible routes. To the right, a path signposted 'capitalism' heads straight to the cliff's edge; to the left, a path marked 'communism' is a long and winding road to some distant hills; only the third way, that of 'land reform', heads straight to a sunlit paradise. This uncharacteristically clear statement from the woolly-headed Fidus may have lacked sophistication, but it captured perfectly the essence of the land reform movement's appeal to middle-class Germans. Ironically, given the artist's latent but later well-documented anti-semitism, the German land reform movement's greatest successes were to come in Palestine. Oppenheimer was an important influence on Theodor Herzl's Zionist movement, and was commissioned to establish the first co-operative settlement, or *Kibbutz*, near Nazareth in 1911. Although such settlements then spread rapidly in Palestine, they made little headway in Germany, even in the changed political climate of the 1920s.[85]

A consistent feature of the land reform movement's programme in the 1900s was its call for the establishment of co-operatively owned 'garden cities'. The garden city is generally associated with the name of Ebenezer Howard (1850–1928), the British author of *Tomorrow: A Peaceful Path to Real Reform* (1898). This surprise best-seller, which was renamed *Garden Cities of Tomorrow* from its second edition onwards, led directly to the establishment of the world's first garden city at Letchworth in 1903. However, the garden city idea developed contemporaneously in a number of places, and the German writer Theodor Fritsch (1852–1933) claimed to have got there first in his *Die Stadt der Zukunft* ('The City of the Future', 1896), which pre-empted Howard by nearly two years. Even so, when the German Garden City Association was founded in the autumn of 1902, its programme was closer to Howard than to Fritsch, who was recognized as a *völkisch* anti-semite of the worst kind.

The association was another enterprise to emerge from the Friedrichshagen writers' circle. The Harts, the Kampffmeyers, Fidus, Bölsche, Landauer and Weidner all signed up to its first declaration; as did the land reformer Oppenheimer, and the *Heimatschützer* Schultze-Naumburg. Not only were there close personal links between the *Heimatschutz* and garden city movements; both also developed along a similar trajectory. The visionary literati soon fell by the wayside when practical lobbying work was called for, and the pragmatists took over. Alongside founder-member and Social Democrat Hans Kampffmeyer (1876–1932), a group of progressive architects and town-planners soon set the tone in the Garden City Association: men like Richard Riemerschmid, Hermann Muthesius (1861–1927), Theodor Fischer (1862–1938) and Joseph Stübben (1845–1936), who drew their influences from the British Arts and Crafts movement and from the more aesthetic approach to town planning represented by Camillo Sitte and Raymond Unwin. Despite much press coverage, however, the association failed to create a 'German Letchworth', and Howard's original conception – an economically independent settlement of 32,000 souls, built on a co-operatively owned green-field site – was realized nowhere in Germany before 1918.

Nevertheless, the garden city activists could draw some consolation from seeing at least some of their ideas put into practice at the model community of Hellerau, planned between 1906–8, and built in 1909–12. Hellerau was the brainchild of the furniture manufacturer Karl Schmidt, whom we encountered in Chapter 4. Despite the early demise of *Jugendstil*, Schmidt's Dresden workshops had flourished in the 1900s,[86] and in 1906 their three sets of Riemerschmid-designed 'machine furniture' were a major success at the third German exhibition of applied art. The Dresden site had little room for expansion, however, and the forward-thinking Schmidt decided to combine the construction of a new factory for 500 workers, with the establishment of a community along garden city lines. It was to be built on 130 hectares of undulating farm- and moorland some five miles north-west of the Saxon capital. Riemerschmid was entrusted with the planning of the town's four zones (cottage, villa, factory and welfare) as well as the design of the factory and many of the cottages, which incorporated features requested by Schmidt's employees in a series of questionnaires. The cottages were attractive examples of Germany's pre-war reform architecture: simple, functional, but homely and colourful (ochre walls, white window-frames, green shutters and red-tiled roofs) and employing local materials. The detached or semi-detached villas, designed by Muthesius, were larger and more imposing, but also eschewed historicist ornamentation. The whole community was linked by winding country lanes, and had three main focal points: the factory; the market square; and the festival playhouse designed by Heinrich Tessenow (1876–1950). The playhouse, Hellerau's cultural centre, accommodated the educational institute of the Swiss 'music and movement' pioneer Emile Jaques-Dalcroze (1856–1950), whose contribution to dance reform is considered below.

Hellerau was not a garden city in the true sense of the term: it was never economically or administratively autonomous; its population in 1914 was only 2000; and even today it remains more a village than a town. On the other hand, Ebenezer Howard was impressed when he visited in 1912, and Hellerau differed in significant ways from other model communities established by paternalist employers like Krupp in Essen, Lever at Port Sunlight, or Cadbury at Bournville. Housing was provided on long-term secure leases, under which workers could not be evicted but could chose to leave at any time.[87] To prevent speculation, leases could not be sold at a profit. The land on which the community was built did not belong to Schmidt or his company, but to a co-operative, in which many of Germany's prominent reformers owned shares.

Figure 10 *Deutsche Werkstätten Furniture Factory, Hellerau (1909). Architect: Richard Riemerschmid*

Ironically, comparatively few of the cottages were taken by Schmidt's employees, who mostly preferred to stay in Dresden, and were instead occupied by reform-minded middle-class aesthetes, who soon turned Hellerau into a sort of up-market artists' colony: people such as Jakob Hegner (1882–1962), the son of a wealthy Viennese industrialist, who translated and published the work of the French writer Paul Claudel (1868–1955). When one of Claudel's plays was premiered at the Hellerau festival playhouse in 1912, the audience included George Bernard Shaw, Serge Diaghilev, Upton Sinclair, Darius Milhaud, Gerhart Hauptmann, Oskar Kokoschka and Max Reinhardt.[88] Claudel's own verdict on Hellerau was that it amounted to a *laboratoire d'une humanité nouvelle*.[89]

The Werkbund

The leading players in the Hellerau project, including Friedrich Naumann and other left-liberal activists, were all members of the German Werkbund (DWB). This organization was established in 1907 to resolve the issue on which *Jugendstil* had foundered: namely, the proper role of artists and craftsmen in an age of machine mass-production. On the occasion of its fiftieth anniversary in 1957 the first President of the Federal Republic of Germany, Theodor Heuss, described the DWB as 'one of the greatest and most productive achievements of recent German history'.[90] Heuss was somewhat biased, since he had been involved with the organization since its inception, but it was an eye-catching claim none the less. Certainly, the breadth of the DWB's membership and preoccupations – 'from sofa cushions to town planning' in Muthesius's memorable phrase – made it more interesting and less esoteric than many other Wilhelmine reform leagues, and the involvement of industrialists and politicians lent its discourse a more worldly air.[91]

The reconciliation between art and industry, which the organization proposed, was to be on the latter's terms. Its membership included major industrial firms as well as individual businessmen and artists; united in the hope that an 'ennobling' of modern industrial production would not only boost German exports, but would also increase the self-respect of industrial workers, and thereby help to restore social harmony to the German people. The best-known example of the organization's ethos in action is Peter Behrens's work with the electrical engineering giant AEG between 1907 and 1914. He designed not only industrial products, but also the firm's logo, publicity material, factory buildings and workers' housing: in short, a complete 'corporate identity'. Behrens further secured his place in the design history books by employing all three of the future giants of European modern architecture – Walter Gropius (1883–1969), Mies van der Rohe (1886–1969) and Le Corbusier (1887–1965) – in his studio near Potsdam before 1914. Gropius's own project, the Fagus factory at Alfeld (1911–14) became an icon of modernism in its own right, and introduced many of the design principles he was to pursue as director of the Bauhaus school in the 1920s.

Not all the products of Werkbund design were so unashamedly modern, but even so, Werkbund architecture is well summed up by Nipperdey's phrase 'modern buildings for modern people, proud of their modernity'.[92] The organization's work found relatively widespread acceptance amongst the general population and its publications, such as the annual DWB yearbooks, were highly regarded. They were published in Jena by Eugen Diederichs, that patriarch of the Wilhelmine reform movement, whose list of authors represented a fascinating cross-section of European cultural and spiritual life at the turn of the century. The Diederichs-Verlag was, to quote the title of a recent monograph, a 'meeting place of modern spirits',[93] and much the same could be said of the Werkbund itself. It is interesting to note, therefore, that the DWB received some backing from governing circles, as the choice of Behrens to design the German embassy in St Petersburg (1912), or of the Deutsche Werkstätten to fit out the interiors of thirteen imperial naval vessels before 1914 would seem to indicate.

Figure 11 *Fagus factory, Alfeld an der Leine (1911–14). Architect: Walter Gropius*

Certainly German modernists in architecture and design did not experience the same level of official disapproval as their equivalents in the fine arts. The state-financed 'Standing Exhibition Commission for German Industry', established to co-ordinate German exhibits at international exhibitions, was generally sympathetic to modern design. The 1904 St Louis world's fair, which had provoked such controversy with regard to painting, showed Germany at the forefront of new ideas in the applied arts. Former Secessionists like Behrens and Bruno Paul were not only allowed to participate, but were appointed to Prussian state posts – heading the schools of applied art in Düsseldorf (1903) and Berlin (1906) respectively – despite the latter's satirical cartoons for the 'subversive' *Simplicissimus.* Hans Poelzig held a similar position in Breslau, as did van de Velde in Weimar. Another DWB founder member, Hermann Muthesius, had been a Prussian civil servant for many years, including a famous stint as an embassy attaché in London between 1896 and 1903, when his task was to investigate current British approaches to applied art and architecture. He subsequently initiated a wide-ranging reform of art and craft education in Prussia.

The DWB aesthetic was based on the notion of *Sachlichkeit*; a term which is variously translated as 'sobriety', 'objectivity' or 'matter-of-factness', and is more usually associated with the *Neue Sachlichkeit* of the 1920s. The old *Sachlichkeit* was one of the reformers' favourite antidotes to *Wilhelminismus*, and as such found favour far beyond the discourse of architects and industrial designers. For instance, naturists were wont to defend their nudity as *sachlich*, and clothing reformers praised the *Sachlichkeit* of the reform-dress. When Avenarius attempted to broaden his '*Kunstwart* community' into a mass movement in 1902, he termed his 'Dürerbund' a *Partei der Sachlichen.*[94] Furthermore, despite the late nineteenth century backlash against positivism and rationalism, one only has to look at the 'Zeppelin mania' of the 1900s to see that the *Sachlichkeit* of scientists and engineers continued to enjoy enormous respect in Wilhelmine Germany, where technocratic solutions – from 'Taylorism' and 'scientific management' in the workplace, to eugenics and 'racial hygiene' – were often embraced with naive enthusiasm.

Dance and theatre reform

The revolt against historicism in architecture and design was mirrored in the world of dance by the growing opposition to classical ballet. The ballet, with its strict routines and narrow aesthetic codes, not to mention its close associations with aristocratic patronage, seemed out of step with the spirit of the new century. Around 1900 a number of young female dancers – from the beginning, the new dance was conceived and performed by women, in a spirit of emancipation – began to explore novel and more 'natural' forms of dance, which resembled neither classical ballet nor the sort of dancing to be seen in comic opera or variety shows. Their individualistic approach, which was variously termed 'free-', 'soul-' (*Seelentanz*), or 'expressive-' dance (*Ausdruckstanz*), was pioneered well away from the opulent surroundings of the royal ballets and court theatres, in the music halls and cabaret clubs of Paris, London, Berlin and Munich.

The American Loïe Fuller (1862–1928), for instance, was a dancer in Paris before forming her own company in the mid-1890s. She caused a sensation across Europe with her 'Serpentine Dance', which involved the rapid waving of coloured veils to produce an abstract blur of colour, enhanced by the use of electric lighting. It was essentially a celebration of movement for its own sake, and won many artistic admirers including Rodin, Toulouse-Lautrec and seemingly everyone with any connection to *Jugendstil*. Another female dancer to attract the bohemian avant-garde was Saheret, whose dances were so frenetic and animalistic that she was described as a 'barbarian' and an 'ape'. Such dancers were never likely to find widespread acceptance in high art circles, but their influence on a younger generation of classically trained dancers soon became apparent.

First of all Isadora Duncan (1878–1927) arrived in Europe from San Francisco, mystically clothed in white draperies and dancing barefoot to open-mouthed audiences. She wore neither corset nor make-up, and her bodily contortions appeared improvised. The impression of natural spontaneity was in fact rather misleading: Duncan was an intellectual dancer, who thought long and deep about her art. She first read Nietzsche in Berlin in 1902 and his work left a lasting impression. Duncan stayed in Berlin, established a dance school with her sister Elizabeth (1904), and became an enthusiastic *Lebensreformer*, vegetarian and regular pilgrim to Ascona. Another dance reformer who devoured Nietzsche in the 1900s was Rudolf Laban (1879–1958), who ran a school for expressive dance in Munich; mixed with painters like Kandinsky and Jawlensky; and offered summer schools at Ascona from 1913. Laban is widely acknowledged as the father of modern dance. Like many in the turn-of-the-century avant-garde he was fascinated by primitive cultures and their ritualistic dances. He would often travel into the Bavarian countryside to watch the peasants perform their traditional *Schuhplattlertanz*, whose dissonant, natural rhythms he embraced as the antithesis of classical ballet. His best-known disciple was Mary Wigman (actually Marie Wiegmann, 1886–1973), a graduate of Emile Jaques-Dalcroze's Hellerau institute, who was tempted away by Laban's more radical spirit of adventure.[95]

Jaques-Dalcroze (1865–1950) was Laban's great rival in the years before World War One. Today, Laban's fame is the greater, but until the 1920s Jaques-Dalcroze was the major figure in European dance reform. He had started out as a music teacher in Geneva, where he had developed the concept of 'rhythmic gymnastics': a form of collective dance very different from the martial drills of the German gymnastics movement. He viewed rhythmic gymnastics not only as the basis of dance and theatre reform, but also as a pedagogic tool for the general population. In this sense, Jaques-Dalcroze's institute in the model community of Hellerau was not a conventional dance school, but a university of the new lifestyle, which 'aimed at a spiritualization of the body; at having freedom, health, nature, triumph over the artificial clothes and shoes and postures and hair styles of 1900'.[96] The institute had nearly 500 students by 1913–14, all meals were vegetarian, and provision was made for regular sunbathing. Some students nevertheless complained it was too much like a convent.

Whatever the merits of Jaques-Dalcroze's pedagogic methods, his Hellerau institute produced some of the major figures of twentieth-century dance: not only Wigman, but Suzanne Perrottet (1889–1983), and the young Pole Myriam Ramberg (1888–1982). Ramberg, who choreographed Nijinsky in Stravinsky's *Rite of Spring*, became the doyenne of British ballet under the name Marie Rambert. The institute's most memorable pre-war production was Gluck's *Orpheus and Eurydice*, which was performed at the Hellerau festival in both 1912 and 1913, in front of an audience amounting to a 'Who's Who' of twentieth-century dance: Pavlova, Diaghilev, Nijinsky and Laban.

The new ideas emanating from the world of dance were also felt in the German theatre. Whether Classical or Naturalist, German stage productions around 1900 were widely viewed as wordy and heavy going, with little visual flair, spectacle or movement. As Peter Jelavich has shown, modernist dramatists and directors in turn-of-the-century Munich sought fresh inspiration from the physical and visual theatricality of variety shows. The individual most closely associated with the 're-theatricalization' of the stage was Max Reinhardt, who took over the direction of the Deutsches Theater in Berlin in 1905. He encouraged visual and gestural spectacle to such an extent that colour and motion sometimes appeared to become more important than words. In Munich in 1910 Reinhardt devised the first major theatre-in-the-round production for a mass audience in modern times.[97]

Conclusion

This rapid survey of Wilhelmine reform movements, although far from comprehensive, should at least indicate why Germany was considered a 'laboratory of the modern world' long before the Weimar Republic, and why it has been dubbed 'the modernist nation par excellence' by one recent historian.[98] Our survey has also attempted to show that while the reformers may have begun with the individual, they did not flinch from addressing fundamental social and political questions too. A willingness to engage in political activity – lobbying officials, writing pamphlets, organizing public meetings – is not a characteristic frequently associated with the Wilhelmine middle classes, but the reformers did all that and more. Even if relatively few became involved in electoral politics, and fewer still posed a direct challenge to the power structures of the Empire, the stereotype of the unpolitical German aesthete, seeking introspection instead of social engagement, is surely unhelpful and inaccurate.

The reform movements discussed in this chapter represented a very diverse range of interests and enthusiasms: some could be characterized as essentially cultural or artistic (and feature frequently in histories of European modernism), while others would more usually be described as 'social'. Yet artists and aesthetes, of one sort or another, played a prominent role in all of them. Taken together, these movements can be seen as a substantial – if splintered – force for change in early twentieth-century Germany. This is perhaps best illustrated by the fact that 'Wilhelmine' figures lay behind many of the developments usually associated with 'Weimar' culture and society in the 1920s; a theme we shall return to at the end of the book.

In view of this influence, it may appear surprising that the Wilhelmine reformers have not received a more sympathetic press.

In part, of course, it was because their impact was much greater in the 'marginal' sphere of culture than in politics, where the illusions and evasions of the reformist discourse were easily and cruelly exposed. Thus, while the reformers' relatively enlightened approach to issues of personal health and education; their sensitivity to the natural environment; and their concern for habitable cities might win grudging respect, their political naivety and elitist attitude toward the 'masses' counts against them. Indeed, their view of the labour movement, which was at best patronizing, and at worst contemptuous, was not so very different from that of Diederich Hessling. Of course, the reformers were not solely responsible for the deep divide that had developed between Imperial Germany's middle and working classes; nor was that divide wholly insurmountable – individual SPD members did work alongside bourgeois reformers in the Garden City Association, the League of German Land Reformers, and the Association for Natural Health Care, to name but three – but the relative lack of co-operation undoubtedly lessened the prospects of success.

A second reason for the Wilhelmine reformers' less than shining reputation lies in their preference for distinctively German solutions to the problems of modernity. This lent their discourse a nationalist tone, however quick they were to condemn the 'hurrah patriotism' of *Wilhelminismus*. The vulgarized Social Darwinism and racial preoccupations of a small but by no means insignificant section of the reform milieu is particularly unsettling.[99] It took many forms, from the crude aryan mysticism and anti-semitism of the 'General German Cultural League' (1906), to the comparatively rational scientific discourse of the 'Society for Racial Hygiene' (1905), whose members included Ernst Haeckel and Gerhart Hauptmann.[100] Located somewhere between these two poles was the 'Werdandibund', founded in 1907 by Henry Thode and the Berlin professor of architecture Friedrich Seesselberg as a sort of *völkisch* version of the Werkbund.[101]

The reformist crusade for renewal and regeneration certainly possessed its 'dark sides' (Geoff Eley) or 'dark strands' (Thomas Nipperdey), and these were to grow darker still when the Great War failed to provide Germany with the victory it expected. Even so, it is important to emphasize that not everyone who sought cultural renewal on the basis of the *Volk* ended up in the arms of Adolf Hitler. Moreover, just as the progressive and emancipatory energies contained within the lifestyle reform, *Heimat* or *Wandervogel* movements have often been obscured by the lazy application of the 'anti-modern' or 'cultural pessimist' label, so the very real dangers inherent in the 'rational' pursuit of scientific and technological advancement are frequently underestimated or ignored. As Eley, Jeffrey Herf and others have pointed out, there is nothing innately liberal or democratic about the appliance of science.[102] Indeed, arguably the darkest side of the reform milieu lay not in its tendency to seek individual or aesthetic antidotes to social and economic ills, but in its increasing fascination with technocratic or scientific panaceas, such as the new science of eugenics.[103] As one recent study of Wilhelmine reformers concludes: 'Like the broad tapestry of Western modernity to which it unquestionably belongs, their story contains both shadows and bright prospects, a perilous texture from which our future too must one day be woven.'[104]

The challenge of commercial and popular culture

No doubt the more zealous lifestyle reformers and outspoken modernists appeared rather cranky to the proverbial man or woman in the street, but whether they knew it or not, all Germans at the turn of the century were participating in a cultural revolution of unprecedented proportions. The rapid development of a commercial popular culture was made possible by technological change,[105] but predicated on changes in the organization of capitalism and mass education. New printing techniques and almost universal literacy facilitated an explosion of printed matter. This consisted of, on the one hand, piles of pulp fiction – such as the seventy adventure novels of Karl May (1842–1912), whose much-loved character Old Shatterhand first appeared in *Through the Desert* (1892), or the romantic novels of Hedwig Courths-Mahler (1867–1950) – and on the other, of newspapers and illustrated magazines. Between 1885 and 1913 daily newspaper circulation in Germany doubled,[106] making Hegel's earlier observation that newspapers served modern man as a substitute for morning prayers appear more prescient than ever.

Moreover, the sensation-seeking press was already subjecting the Hohenzollern family to a very modern gaze. This first became apparent during the illness of Friedrich III, when the conflicting views of doctors on how to treat his throat cancer were reported openly, and the right-wing press attacked Empress Victoria for trusting the advice of British rather than German specialists. Little deference was apparent. Indeed, just months after the Kaiser's death, extracts from his private diaries were published in the *Deutsche Rundschau*. A similarly modern note was struck on the death of Bismarck in 1898. Surreptitious photographs were taken of the ex-Chancellor on his deathbed, to the horror of the Bismarck family. Although the aspiring paparazzi Willy Wilcke and Max Priester were arrested when they tried to sell the prints through newspaper advertisements – they were sentenced to six and three months imprisonment respectively – a retouched print of one of their snaps was reproduced countless times in the following years.

The proliferation of newspapers and magazines was largely due to the increase in commercial advertising, with vast sums expended in the 1890s and 1900s to launch new brands – both indigenous (Manoli cigarettes, Hag coffee, Bahlsen biscuits) and foreign (Coca-Cola, 1896) – on the German market. No company, Coca-Cola included, spent more money on advertising in Germany than the Dresden manufacturer Lingner, whose 'Odol' mouthwash was mentioned at the start of this chapter. The 'Siegesallee' advertisement was just one in a long line of humorous and surreal images employed to create a demand for a type of product only invented in 1892. Lingner, a collector of Secessionist art and friend of Richard Strauss, defended his original and subversive advertising as a 'cultural act', although there were many cultural critics who viewed the proliferation of advertising as a tragic defeat at the hands of materialism. There was, however, precious little they could do to stop it. In the Wilhelmine era, advertising not only took over increasing column inches in the print media, but also became an intrusive feature of the landscape for the first time. The characteristic 'face' of the twentieth-century's consumer society was beginning to form.

The triumphal march of the national and international brands, made possible by rising incomes – real wages in Germany rose by 13 per cent between 1900 and 1914 – was a significant factor in the decline of German particularism. Regional differences in diet and custom eroded rapidly after the turn of the century. The emergence of market-dominating brands was accompanied by a concentration process in the retail sector too. The long, slow demise of the small shopkeeper was exacerbated by the belated appearance in Germany of huge department stores, several decades later than in Britain or France. Such buildings, with their vast light-filled atria and electrically illuminated window displays; their escalators and lifts; and above all, their huge range of goods at seductively affordable prices, were veritable temples to consumerism. Of course, for many Germans the majority of articles remained tantalizingly out of reach, but 'window-shopping' nevertheless became a popular form of free entertainment. An afternoon in Wertheim or the Kaufhaus des Westens offered a multitude of sights and aromas, and was a good deal cheaper than an evening in the theatre. Arguably it was here, rather than on the production lines of Wilhelmine Germany's 'cathedrals of labour', that the true site of modernity was located: 'In those early years I came to know the "city" only as the theatre of "shopping". . . . A chain of impenetrable mountains, nay caverns of commodities – that was "the city",' Walter Benjamin recalled.[107]

Long before Benjamin wrote his famous essay on 'The Work of Art in the Age of Mechanical Reproduction', it was becoming apparent that most people's aesthetic world was shaped by the art of the advertisement and the mass-produced print, rather than by unique and unrepeatable gallery paintings. Some *Jugendstil* artists had welcomed this as an opportunity to aestheticize everyday life: van de Velde had designed packaging for the health product Tropon; Mucha, Gulbrannson and Heine all produced advertisements for Henkell sparkling wine; and Schmidhammer and Stuck for Odol.[108] After *Jugendstil*'s rapid demise, the challenge of encouraging aesthetically pleasing packaging and advertising was taken up by the Werkbund. The advertisements of Behrens for AEG, or Bernhardt for Kaffee Hag, were discussed with deep seriousness in specialist journals and exhibited by the new German Museum for Art in Trade and Industry.

The paramount chronicler of this evolving commercial culture was Georg Simmel (1858–1918), a philosopher and sociologist whose lectures at Berlin University were popular among both students and the public at large. In works like the *Philosophy of Money* (1900), the *Philosophy of Fashion* (1905), and *The Metropolis and Mental Life* (1903), Simmel became one of the first academics 'to experiment in even a tentative way with what would later be called "the phenomenology of everyday life"'.[109] Despite sharing many of the misgivings of the cultural pessimists towards modern life – 'the impoverishment of emotional sensitivity, the loosening of the sense of affiliation, and the diminished feeling of continuity with the past and of respect for traditional values'[110] – Simmel attempted to avoid value judgements, seeing promise as well as threat in modernity: 'He valued chiefly the modern emphasis on freedom and encouragement of experimentation, which created many more opportunities of the expression and cultivation of individual preferences and potentialities.'[111]

Thus while the cultural pessimists had speculated on 'solutions' to modernity, Simmel and that other Wilhelmine pioneer of sociology, Max Weber (1864–1920), essentially accepted the existence of modern commercial-technological culture and concentrated their efforts on comprehending it instead. Simmel's work sparked a series of theoretical debates on fashion, consumerism and commodity culture, which highlighted commodity fetishization as a central cultural fact of modernity. These debates 'were an important part of the first sustained and often sophisticated discussions of the nature of culture in a consumer-oriented capitalist economy',[112] and as such laid the intellectual foundations for later theorists of mass culture like Bloch, Lukács, Benjamin and Adorno. Although non-German thinkers addressed such issues too, the rapid and uneven nature of German modernization made these debates particularly acute. Not all participants shared Simmel's detached coolness. For some, such as Werner Sombart (1863–1941), culture appeared 'to be disintegrating into something flat and standardized as it got more and more caught up in the processes of capitalist mass production . . . it seemed that culture was becoming inherently meaningless and despiritualized and consequently was losing touch with people's inner lives'.[113] For defenders of 'the True, the Good and the Beautiful', this was a deeply depressing development.

Of course, not all of the new commercial culture developed in direct or conscious opposition to the Kaiser and his values. Indeed, something of a love affair developed between the Emperor and the new medium of film, so that Wilhelm II, who thrived on playing to the camera and was known to cancel events if it was not *Kaiserwetter*, has been dubbed 'Germany's first film-star'. Even so, in the long run, the commercial values of the cinema or advertisements could only undermine the 'eternal verities' that Wilhelm and many other Germans sought to uphold. The origins of German cinema are significant, because it was in Berlin that moving pictures were first shown to a paying audience anywhere in the world. On 1 November 1895, nearly two months before the more famous Lumière screening in Paris, the brothers Emil and Max Skladanowsky, who owned a patent on a mechanical film-winding system, staged a 'bioscope' performance at the Wintergarten variety theatre. Another German, Oskar Messter (1866–1943), built the first modern film projector and camera a few months later. It was Messter who also made the first newsreels ('Messter-Woche', 1897) and issued the first catalogue of films, which listed some eighty-four titles in total.

For the next ten years or so, most films were shown in circus tents and at travelling fairs. Since the films on offer did not change regularly, there seemed little money to be made from establishing permanent venues. It was only when the first film rental and exchange companies were established that purpose-built cinemas, offering a different programme every week, began to appear. Thus while there were only a handful of cinemas in Germany before 1905, by 1910 there were over 500; and in 1914, when the daily film attendance reached nearly one and half million, the Empire boasted around 2500 cinemas. Most of the audiences consisted of working-class Germans – women in the afternoons, men in the evenings – who were able to devote more time and income to entertainment and leisure pursuits as the economy grew rapidly in the 1900s.

Despite the Kaiser's enthusiasm, cinema was viewed 'not as a prop for established social and political order but rather as a dangerous threat to it' in Wilhelmine Germany.[114] Civil servants and politicians regarded it as morally dubious, and devoid of artistic merit: 'by focusing on the seamy underside of life rather than the noble and beautiful, it was feared that popular films corrupted the aesthetic sensibilities of the viewer'.[115] Film censorship began on an ad hoc basis around 1906, with a number of cities passing local by-laws permitting pre-performance police checks. Subsequently most of the major German states standardized procedures, establishing central boards of censors, so that by 1914 most of the Empire was covered by legislation. There were still inconsistencies, however, and many films banned in Bavaria could be freely seen in Berlin. The need for film censorship was something on which the representatives of government and the middle-class reform movements were generally in agreement. Indeed, the reformist 'Dürerbund' co-founded a 'cinema reform movement' in 1905. The widespread hostility to the cinema was apparent from a draft bill presented to the Reichstag in 1914, which would probably have passed had war not intervened. It stated: 'The attraction of the cinema for youth and for the undereducated classes . . . represents a moral threat to the nation that must absolutely be resisted.'[116] Given that the most popular and profitable films in pre-war Germany were violent action stories and prurient explorations of sexual themes, the opposition was perhaps understandable. Certainly, few yet considered the movie as an art form.

As World War One neared its climax, Germany's military leadership somewhat belatedly discovered the uses of cinema: as entertainment for the troops and as a propaganda tool. It began, secretly, to produce films itself, and took the lead in the formation of the 'Universum Film AG' in late 1917, which was backed by substantial private capital, and which quickly expanded by buying up existing film-making and distribution companies. Under the abbreviated name 'Ufa', the company would come to dominate the German film industry in the 1920s, though it would seldom be free from financial worries. In the cinema, as in the world of commodities, novelty was everything. The nature of the capitalist marketplace became reflected in other areas of cultural production too. Artistic fads and fashions, like commercial ones, were to come and go with increasing frequency in the years after 1900. Symbolism, Fauvism, Cubism and Futurism were among them, but the most important in Germany was Expressionism.

6 *Expressionism, Nationalism and War*

Introduction

Virginia Woolf once famously observed that 'in or about December, 1910, human character changed',[1] whilst the poet Gottfried Benn also cited 1910 as 'the year when all the timbers started creaking'.[2] This was the year, it is suggested, which saw the 'emancipation of dissonance' across the arts.[3] If this was the case, it was likely to have been at least in part because of discoveries and developments in the natural sciences. After the discovery of X-rays (1895), radioactivity (1896), and the electron (1897) the physicist Max Planck outlined what became known as quantum theory in 1900, and five years later another future German Nobel prize winner, Albert Einstein (1880–1952), proposed his special theory of 'relativity'. Arguably the most important aspect of Einstein's work was that it amounted to a denial of any absolute frame of reference, and thus called into question the very nature of scientific laws, or as Michael Biddiss has put it 'opened up vast vistas of uncertainty'.[4]

Much the same could be said of the work of Sigmund Freud (1856–1939), the Viennese specialist in nervous ailments, who invented 'psychoanalysis' in the 1890s and whose publications *The Interpretation of Dreams* (1899) and *Three Essays on Sexuality* (1905), revealed the power of the subconscious. His work was epoch-making – even if *The Interpretation of Dreams* took eight years to sell its first 600 copies – because it called into question the entire conventional terminology of sanity, morality and rationality. Scientific and intellectual change was to have a great influence on the last major movement in Imperial German culture, Expressionism, which forms the initial focus of this chapter. The cultural historian Egon Friedell described Expressionist art as 'the theory of relativity in paint',[5] while the Expressionist painter Wassily Kandinsky (1866–1944) recalled that Becquerel's discovery of radiation (the disintegration of atomic nuclei), 'was in my soul the same as the disintegration of the world. Everything became uncertain, wobbly and soft . . . To me, science seemed destroyed'.[6] Meanwhile, Arnolt Bronnen's Expressionist play *Vatermord* ('Patricide', 1917) dramatized the Freudian Oedipus complex by featuring a teenage boy having sex with his mother on stage and then stabbing his father. The 'dream plays' of Strindberg or the first act of Reinhard Sorge's *Der Bettler* ('The Beggar', 1911) also suggest a Freudian influence, and as Walter Sokel points out: 'Even those Expressionists who were not conversant with the actual works of Freud and Jung could not but be familiar with the climate of thought that had given rise to psychoanalysis in the first place.'[7]

Much has been written on Expressionism in recent years, not least because it was one of the few 'isms' to make a significant impact on every major area of cultural activity in the first quarter of the twentieth century.[8] Painting, literature, music, architecture, dance and film all went through Expressionist phases, especially in central and northern Europe. Of course, not all Expressionists were German, but Germany was central to Expressionism. Critics point out, however, that as well as being a movement associated with a specific place and time – most of the important Expressionists were born between 1880 and 1895 – it was, and is, a manifestation of a recurring tendency in culture, in which psychological or emotional force periodically takes precedence over form. This explains why striking similarities can be found between Expressionism and earlier movements, such as *Sturm und Drang*, and why expressionistic works are still being produced today, characterized by a raw intensity, exaggeration and violent distortion.

There are many different accounts of the origin of the term 'Expressionism'. Some claim it dates from 1901, when the little-known French academic painter Hervé exhibited some nature studies in Paris under the heading of *expressionnisme*. The paintings were highly conventional, however, and the exhibition was quickly forgotten. Rather more historians suggest the term originated a few years later with the critic Louis Vauxcelles, who described the paintings of Matisse as expressionist. On the other hand, some Germans have argued that the word was first used at the Secession gallery in Berlin: when somebody asked whether a painting by Pechstein still came under the heading of Impressionism, the art dealer Paul Cassirer is said to have replied, 'no, it's Expressionism'.[9] Three things are clear: first, that the term was initially used in the visual rather than literary arts; secondly, that it was used principally by critics and dealers, rather than the painters themselves; and thirdly, that it came into use some time after many of the most famous Expressionist pictures had already been painted. Edvard Munch's quintessentially Expressionist *The Scream* (1893), for instance, predated the term by many years.

Whoever used the term first, it was clearly invented to point to a contrast: to define a youthful, avant-garde art that was based not on purely visual impressions like Impressionism, but on the artist's own psychic inner-state. The Expressionists believed it was the internal, rather than the external aspect of reality that was important. The purpose of art was not to reproduce what was already visible, but to make things visible for the first time. Expressionists wanted to extend the domain of art beyond the boundaries of the 'real world' to embrace imagination, dreams and premonitions. This turn to the internal and emotional was captured in Kandinsky's famous 1912 essay 'On the spiritual in art': 'When religion, science and morals are shaken – the last by Nietzsche's strong hand – and when external supports begin to topple, men turn their eyes away from externals and towards themselves.'[10] Since the material differences between the different forms of cultural expression were also merely 'externals', a true artist could employ almost any medium to convey his inner message, regardless of whether one had gained academic competence in a particular discipline.

As the Expressionist was no longer interested in trying to imitate nature, or aspiring to formal perfection, previously essential skills and techniques appeared to lose their relevance. Painters could express themselves without knowledge of draughtsmanship; dramatists could write plays without a mastery of plot construction. Many of the leading Expressionists were self-taught in their chosen medium, and the Expressionist generation brought forth an unusually large number of artistic all-rounders. There were composers, like Arnold Schönberg (1874–1951), who painted haunting self-portraits;[11] sculptors, like Ernst Barlach (1870–1938), who wrote plays; and painters, like Kandinsky and Kokoschka, who created idiosyncratic stage-works involving music, dance and drama.

As we have seen, however, German artists had been pursuing the Holy Grail of the *Gesamtkunstwerk* for many years, and one should try to resist the temptation of viewing Expressionism as a sudden eruption of new approaches. It did not come out of the blue, but developed over a period of more than a decade, incorporating elements of *Jugendstil* and aestheticism along the way. The Secessionist desire to break free from the shackles of the art academies and their conventions was amongst the baggage picked up by Expressionism en route. It borrowed too from the Fauves and Cubists in France, and from the Futurists in Italy: all of whom were the Expressionists' 'allies and spiritual kinsmen'.[12] It is important to stress, however, that an anti-modern reaction against the 'materialist' approach of Naturalism and the pre-war *Sachlichkeit* of the Werkbund was also instrumental in energizing Expressionism. Indeed, the historian Frank Trommler has recently called for a 'critical repositioning of expressionism with its antirealistic and antimaterialistic momentum'. It was, he points out, 'a movement against *Sachlichkeit,* rather than vice versa'.[13]

Generally, the interdisciplinary approach of Expressionist artists has not been matched in the historiography: there are vast, separate literatures for each of the different areas of creative activity. This is unfortunate, because cross-fertilization between the arts was a defining characteristic of Expressionism. The seminal move of Expressionist painters like Kandinsky and Marc towards abstraction, for instance, could not have occurred without the inspiration of music (Kandinsky once famously defined painting as 'composing with colours' and maintained a long correspondence with Schönberg). Recognizing that in music meaning can exist without narrative or description, they began to eliminate the subject from their paintings in the immediate pre-war years. They perceived that people could be moved by the colour, texture and form of paint on canvas, even if no descriptive purpose was served. Similarly, Expressionist theatre owed much to painters and their search for the true *Gesamtkunstwerk.* Kokoschka's *Murderer, Hope of Womankind,* written in 1907 and first performed two years later, consisted mostly of ecstatic shouts, cries and drumbeats rather than dialogue, and its vigorous physical drama had little in common with conventional theatre.[14] Kandinsky's *Yellow Sound,* written in 1909–10 but never performed at the time, also made language secondary to movement and music (in this case composed not by the painter, but by a professional musician).[15] In his music drama *The Lucky Hand* (1910–13) Schönberg attempted to go one step further, by designing the set and costumes as well writing the music and the libretto.

Although the historiography of Expressionism is as confused and complex as the movement itself, it is clear that many studies focus as much on its politics as on aesthetics. Expressionists had a tendency to identify with the political extremes. Of course, some regarded themselves and their art as 'above' politics, but they could and often did embrace radical positions on both the left and right of the spectrum. Examples of the latter include the painter Emil Nolde (1867–1956), who joined the Nazi party in the mid-1920s;[16] writers like Gottfried Benn (1886–1956) and Hanns Johst, who wrote the infamous and often-misquoted line 'whenever I hear the word culture . . . I release the safety-catch of my Browning',[17] and even Joseph Goebbels himself. The future National Socialist Minister of Propaganda wrote an expressionistic novel in the early 1920s called *Michael: A German Fate.*[18] Indeed, although many Expressionists, including Nolde, were later branded as 'degenerate' by the Nazis, Goebbels had initially proposed that Expressionism should be the official art of the Third Reich.

The illiberal and irrational aspects of Expressionism were first highlighted by the Marxist critic and theorist Georg Lukács (1885–1971), who famously wrote in 1934 that it had a 'poverty of content'. A similar verdict was reached by the left-wing writer and film critic Siegfried Kracauer, who suggested that Expressionism – especially the Expressionist cinema of the 1920s – reflected the collective soul of the German nation, including patterns of thought that had helped to nourish Nazism. This might seem far-fetched, but some aspects of Expressionism were certainly common to National Socialism too: a dislike of rationality, materialism and liberalism, the cult of youth, and a desire to renew society. After a period in which the Lukács line was prominent, Expressionism was rehabilitated after World War Two, and given a 'left-wing' (or at least an anti-fascist) interpretation, which relied much on Nazi hostility to their work after 1933. In general this was every bit as misleading and simplistic as the earlier Marxist view had been. Undoubtedly, Expressionism's messianic pathos, its fascination with the emancipatory power of madness, and its desire to rebel against convention and authority, made for a potentially dangerous cocktail, but the seriousness of the hangover should not be exaggerated.

Expressionist painting

In the 1890s, avant-garde art had moved into two apparently different directions: pure colour and the geometry of space were explored by the French Post-Impressionists; while van Gogh and Munch attempted to express emotional and mental states in form and colour. The latter path lead more directly to Expressionism, but the influence of Cézanne and Matisse would also be felt in Germany before World War One. The history of German Expressionist painting is largely associated with two groups of artists: Die Brücke ('The Bridge') in Dresden and Der Blaue Reiter ('The Blue Rider') in Munich.

The former was founded in 1905 by four young students of architecture: Ernst Ludwig Kirchner (1880–1938); Erich Heckel (1883–1970); Karl Schmidt-Rottluff (1884–1976) and Fritz Bleyl (1880–1966). If Kirchner was the Brücke's dominant and arguably most gifted personality, it was the mediator Heckel who kept the group together until 1913. Heckel, the most business-minded of the four young men, rented a butcher's shop in a Dresden suburb for the group to use as a communal studio. Their first exhibition took place in a lamp factory showroom in 1906. It was not a great popular success, but sixty-eight people signed up to pay for a year's subscription to their portfolio of prints, at 12 RM a time. The group's choice of name has been explained in various ways: some believe it came from the French Symbolist painter Gustave Moreau, the teacher of Matisse who claimed to be a 'bridge' between generations; others suggest it referred to the bridge across the Elbe in Dresden, which the artists crossed every day on their way to college. More probably, however, it comes from Nietzsche's *Zarathustra*; a work frequently declaimed by Heckel, and a major influence on the whole group. The Brücke artists also derived great inspiration from Dresden's fine public collections of old masters, and from the 'primitive' art on display in the city's ethnographic museum. In particular the carvings of the Palau islanders made a great impression on Kirchner. However, rather than heading for the South Seas themselves, the Brücke artists sought the natural pleasures of their native Saxony instead.

As we saw in Chapter 5, Dresden was to become an important centre of *Lebensreform* activity in the later Wilhelmine years, with a host of 'natural health' sanatoriums, Germany's first garden city, a school for rhythmic gymnastics and a major international exhibition

Figure 12 Ernst-Ludwig Kirchner, Bathers at Moritzburg *(1909, reworked 1926)*

on the theme of hygiene. Accordingly, bathing, natural health cures and the culture of the body were all reflected in the Brücke artists' works. They took every opportunity to venture out of the city to the nearby countryside, and especially to the Moritzburg lakes, where they bathed naked and where many of their best-known paintings were done. These were works of great spontaneity and freedom, in which studied draughtsmanship made way for dynamic brushstrokes and intensity of colour (paint was applied straight from the tube, rather than mixed on the palette). In the summer they travelled further afield, to places like Dangast, Nidden and Fehmarn on the North Sea and Baltic coasts.

In common with other Wilhelmine *Lebensreformer*, the Brücke artists loathed pretension, affectation and the materialism of contemporary life. They particularly objected to the popular view of artists as conceited men in velvet jackets, who frequented the salons of rich society women. They painted their girlfriends and acquaintances rather than professional models, and refused to turn them into classical goddesses. Taking great pleasure at antagonizing and shocking Dresden's stuffier burghers, the Brücke chose to set up its studios in working-class districts, and by flaunting an open, uninhibited attitude to sexuality. They dated dancers and performers, and frequently made the heightened reality of the circus or the music hall a subject of their art. This may seem to contradict their 'back to nature' sensibilities, but as Wolf-Dieter Dube points out: 'Both forms of life, the natural and the artificial, were ways by which fossilized bourgeois attitudes could be overcome, ways to the "new human being".'[19]

The Brücke artists explored a variety of media. Today they are as well-known for their jagged, angular woodcuts, etchings and lithographs as their oil paintings, and they tried their hand at sculpture too. Printing, and especially the woodcut, found favour not only because it provided something to do during the long cold winters: rebellious artists have often turned to unfashionable or neglected techniques, and the woodcut suited the Brücke for a variety of reasons. For a start, it was a simple, direct, and economical way of expressing the essence of a subject; secondly, it enabled them to communicate their message to a wider audience; and thirdly, it consciously evoked the cultural heritage of Dürer and his age. A Kirchner woodcut was featured on the cover of the group's first publication in 1906. Inside was a statement that amounted to the first Expressionist manifesto: 'As youth, we carry the future and we want to create for ourselves freedom of life and movement against the long-established older forces. Everyone who directly and authentically conveys that which drives him to creation, belongs with us.'[20]

In this spirit, the group was joined for a short while by a number of other artists, including Emil Nolde (originally Emil Hansen from Nolde in Schleswig), Max Pechstein (1881–1955), and Otto Müller (1874–1930), a cousin of Gerhart Hauptmann. It was only after Kirchner and his friends had left Dresden for the imperial capital in the autumn of 1911, however, that the Brücke really gained national prominence. It was in Berlin that Kirchner painted his memorable images of urban life and prostitution, such as *Five Women in the Street* (1913) and *Women at Potsdamer Platz* (1914). Such works are often cited as an example of the Expressionist artist's sense of alienation in the 'dehumanized' city. Matthias Eberle, for instance, writes: 'A free and natural relation between the sexes, something Kirchner depicted in so many paintings, seems impossible in the big city. . . . This can happen, it appears, only outside the city, outside civilization, in the primitive untouched paradises of the world.'[21]

As Charles Haxthausen has pointed out, however, this dark view contrasts strikingly with the predominantly positive reading of the Berlin works before 1933, and Kirchner himself described his Berlin style as an attempt to capture 'the ecstasy of initial perception', rather than an expression of emotional estrangement. Haxthausen concludes: 'Kirchner's street scenes would then function not as the negative antithesis of his erotic Baltic idylls but as a glorification of those same primordial energies within the modern metropolis.'[22] This is surely right. Kirchner, like most other Expressionists, made a conscious choice to live in big cities, and enjoyed the seductions on offer. Over the years a romantic aura has grown up around the Brücke, at least part of which is the stuff of myth. For all the youthful anti-capitalist and 'back-to-nature' posturing, their lifestyle did not deviate all that much from the bourgeois norms they were said to reject. Like many city-dwellers, they often sought leisure and relaxation in the countryside, and in the summer would pack their bags for long vacations by the coast. Such undertakings were seldom communal, however, and none of the artists was willing to relinquish the attractions of modern city life for very long. Moreover, although they often posed as bohemian rebels, challenging conventions and lambasting modern society, they relied almost entirely on the patronage of bourgeois collectors and enthusiasts to earn a living.[23] Indeed, despite their anti-bourgeois rhetoric, many Expressionist artists were very interested in such material things as sales figures and profit margins. As Robin Lenman, Robert Jensen and others have recently shown, the artists often cultivated their relationships with dealers and critics in most calculating ways.[24] This was particularly apparent with the second major group of pre-World War One Expressionists in Germany, the 'Blaue Reiter'.

The Blue Rider grew out of a pair of artists' associations involving the Russian-born Kandinsky in his adopted home of Munich in the 1900s. The first was the 'Phalanx' (1901–4); and the second the Munich New Artists' Alliance (1909–11), whose members included Kandinsky's partner Gabriele Münter (1877–1962), Franz Marc (1880–1916) and another Russian emigré Alexei Jawlensky (1864–1941). It had none of the cohesion of the Brücke, however, and in December 1911 a picture by Kandinsky was rejected by the association's exhibition jury. Kandinsky, Münter and Marc resigned on the spot, and immediately set about staging their own exhibition in another part of the same Munich gallery. It opened on 18 December 1911 under the mysterious title 'First Exhibition of the Editors of the

Blue Rider', and toured Germany over the following months, culminating in a Berlin showing at Herwarth Walden's new 'Sturm' gallery.

Walden (actually Georg Lewin, 1878–1941), a publisher, art dealer, pianist and energetic impresario of avant-garde causes, was vital for the success of the Blue Rider artists. Indeed, he was instrumental in creating and marketing the very notion of Expressionism. In addition to Kandinsky, Münter and Marc, works by August Macke (1887–1914) and Paul Klee (1879–1940) were included in the show, which was quickly followed up by a second Munich exhibition in the spring of 1912, featuring foreign artists like Picasso and Braque. Whereas the Brücke was deeply rooted in German traditions, the Blue Rider was truly international in its membership and influences. As their exhibition title suggested, Kandinsky and Marc planned to edit a series of publications under the Blue Rider moniker. The first and, as it transpired, only work to appear was the legendary *Blue Rider Almanac* (May 1912), which included articles on visual art, music (contributions came from Schönberg, Berg and Webern) and theatre, together with reproductions of original work by many of the leading avant-garde artists of the day. As an artists' association, the Blue Rider did little else, but individually its members were responsible for some of the classic works of early twentieth-century modernism.

The Blue Rider artists each pursued their personal aesthetic visions, so a single 'house style' is difficult to identify. The influence of folk art, with its bold use of colour and scant concern for realism is often cited, along with that of contemporaries like Cézanne and Matisse. However, as Irit Rogoff notes, 'Perhaps the most important and allusive common denominator is their attempt to find pictorial form for concepts such as mysticism, piety, spirituality and religion.'[25] The Blue Rider artists in particular turned to nature as a source of spiritual inspiration. Franz Marc, whose celebrated paintings of horses helped to give the group its name,[26] venerated animals as 'uncontaminated' creatures, in touch with the rhythms of the cosmos. Similarly, the Swiss Paul Klee attempted to adopt a child's perspective on the adult world, while Kandinsky sought spirituality through studies of the natural landscape, attempting to capture its essence through lines and colours which increasingly bore little resemblance to recognizable reality. Both Kandinsky and Marc began to use colour in a purely expressive way, associating each colour with particular emotions and symbols. As Marc put it in a letter of February 1911: 'There are no "subjects" and no "colours" in art, only expression.'[27]

Figure 13 Wassily Kandinsky, final study for the cover of The Blaue Reiter Almanac *(1911)*

In retrospect, the landmark move to abstraction may appear to have been inevitable. However, as Kandinsky himself recalled, this development took place only gradually, 'by way of innumerable experiments, despair, hope, discoveries'.[28] Kandinsky acknowledged the debt to music by giving his abstract paintings titles like *Improvisation No. 19* (1911) and *Dreamy Improvisation* (1913), while Marc was more descriptive: *Struggling Forms, Cheerful Forms, Playing Forms* and *Broken Forms* (all 1914). Understandably, many people experienced the abandonment of figuration as an anarchic provocation, but the Blue Rider painters do not seem to have aroused the same levels of public hostility as composers of avant-garde music in the years around 1914.

In short, German Expressionist painters embodied many of the qualities and contradictions of modernism as a whole: proclaiming a new vision, yet turning to primitive folk art for inspiration; fiercely critical of bourgeois materialism, yet smart enough to secure the best prices for their work; anti-urban, yet fascinated by the city and unwilling to move far away from metropolitan life. The Expressionists demonstrated that criticisms of rationality and materialism could be just as much an expression of modernity as of conservatism; and whilst much has been made of the movement's apocalyptic strain (see below), it is important not to lose sight of the more prosaic aspects of the Expressionist phenomenon. As Thomas Nipperdey has argued, revolution in the arts went hand-in-hand with a fundamental change in middle-class consciousness.[29] The breakthrough of Expressionism would not have occurred without new private art dealers and many new patrons, like the bankers August von der Heydt and Karl Ernst Osthaus (1874–1921) in the industrial towns of Hagen and Wuppertal respectively. Osthaus, who bought his first Renoir in 1901, had purchased works by van Gogh, Gauguin, Heckel, Kirchner and Kokoschka before 1914,[30] just as other bourgeois patrons commissioned buildings from Werkbund architects or attended concert performances of works by Arnold Schönberg.

Expressionist music

The earliest documented use of the word Expressionism in musical discourse dates from as late as 1919, and the term is generally applied to works from the 1920s, like Alban Berg's operas *Wozzeck* (begun in 1914, but not finished until 1925) and *Lulu* (1928–35), or the work of his Austrian compatriot Anton von Webern (1883–1945). No pre-World War One composer claimed the title 'Expressionist' for himself. Even so, the relationship between Berg and Webern's teacher Arnold Schönberg – who lived in Berlin between 1911 and 1915 – and the Blaue Reiter meant that a connection is often made between the so-called Second Viennese School and pre-war Expressionism. Schönberg's Expressionist phase is said to lie between the melodic Wagnerian works of his youth and the development of the 'twelve tone system' of composition in the early 1920s, and therefore to include works like the monodrama *Erwartung* ('Expectation', 1909) and the song-cycle *Pierrot Lunaire* (1912). Some musicologists reject this practice. Christopher Hailey, for instance, has written: 'As a category, musical Expressionism may be a useful "adjective", but it is bad history.'[31] Yet the dissonant and contorted music composed by Schönberg in the late 1900s certainly sounds like an aural equivalent of Expressionist painting, to the untrained ear at least. It provoked great antagonism amongst the concert-goers of Europe and culminated in the infamous Vienna *Skandalkonzert* of 31 March 1913, when police had to be called to restore order.[32]

Schönberg's *Erwartung*, in which an unnamed woman is found wandering alone at night in a forest, searching for a lover may or may not be 'all in the mind', but its naked emotion and eerie splendour seems archetypically Expressionist. As Thomas Harrison points out, the 30-minute work is actually an account of the single second of emotion when the woman discovers her lover's dead body.[33] Moreover, Schönberg's own writings from the time reveal many similarities with the rhetoric of Expressionism: 'I believe that art comes not of ability but of necessity', he wrote in 1911.[34] Both as a composer and a painter, Schönberg was an outsider, and largely self-taught. On the other hand, for all his iconoclastic tendencies, it is well-known that Schönberg considered himself a conservative composer. His work was generally based on strict formal principles.[35]

Expressionist literature

As a literary term, 'Expressionist' first came into circulation around 1911, initially in lyric poetry. It reached the theatre somewhat later, but then lasted well into the 1920s. Frank Wedekind, dubbed 'the first Expressionist' by the critic Rudolf Kayser in 1918, and August Strindberg, who was the most frequently performed playwright on the German stage in the immediate pre-war years, prepared the ground for Expressionist drama. Richard Dehmel, who had supplied the text for Schönberg's *Verklärte Nacht* (1899) and was memorably portrayed by Kokoschka in the journal *Der Sturm* ('Storm'), performed a similar role for Expressionist poets. In literature, even more than in painting, the connections between *Jugendstil* and Expressionism were considerable.[36] Even so, literary historians have generally portrayed Expressionism as a sudden uprising of revolutionary force. There is little consensus as to the primary nature of that rebellion – generational revolt against the father; social revolt against the authoritarianism and materialism of Wilhelmine society; or cultural revolt against the stale orthodoxies of German literary life – although it is generally accepted that what began as an aesthetic uprising ended by being associated with political revolution.

Many of the best-known German Expressionist poets emerged from a literary circle established in 1909 by the writer Kurt Hiller (1885–1973). The 'Neue Club', as it was known, developed from a University of Berlin student society. The Neue Club was not a university institution, although most of its members were students. It met on Wednesday evenings to discuss aesthetic and literary questions. The club had no formal programme, apart from a Nietzsche-inspired mission to promote creative individualism, but it became a rallying point for the new generation of writers who would later become known as Expressionists. They included Jakob van Hoddis (actually Hans Davidsohn, 1887–1942); Ernst Blass (1890–1939), co-founder of the literary cabaret 'GNU' in 1911; Erwin Loewenson (1888–1963); and Georg Heym (1887–1912).

In 1910 the Neue Club began to stage performance evenings under the title Neopathetic Cabaret. Jakob von Hoddis read out his eight-line poem *Weltende* ('End of the World') – 'The Marseillaise of the Expressionist Revolution'[37] – and Georg Heym recited his works from the second evening onwards. Soon, the Cabaret was attracting many of the German avant-garde's movers and shakers: Herwarth Walden, Franz Pfemfert, Karl Kraus, Ernst Rowohlt and many more. The Neue Club's Kurt Hiller also edited the first major anthology of Expressionist poems *The Condor* ('a radical collection of radical verses') in 1912. Although Kurt Pinthus's 1919 anthology *Menschheitsdämmerung* ('Twilight of Mankind') is more widely remembered, Expressionist poetry was by then already on the wane. In 1911–12 the journalist Simon Guttman hatched a plan to bring together the Neue Club and the painters of the Brücke to collaborate on a joint periodical, *Neopathos*. Although Schmidt-Rottluff designed the covers for the last two Neopathetic Cabaret programmes, and Kirchner produced a famous portrait of Georg Heym, together with a series of illustrations for Heym's posthumous collection of poetry *Umbra vitae*, nothing else came of the plan. Heym drowned in a skating accident on the River Havel and the Neue Club disbanded shortly after.

Before his tragically early death, Heym had been sufficiently prolific – about two-thirds of his entire output dates from the last two years of his life, and half of that was produced in his last eight months[38] – to ensure his lasting reputation as one of German Expressionism's key poets. Heym's father was a senior judge, so his poetic rebellion can be read as both socio-political and generational. In fact, few of Heym's poems had overtly political messages; most were abstract and metaphysical, with a strong sense of pathos, as in the couplet which became his epitaph: *Kurz ist das Leben / Und wenige Sterne* ('Life is short and few are its stars'). Heym, whose first collection *Der ewige Tag* ('The Eternal Day') was published by Ernst Rowohlt in 1911, had a powerful visual imagination, and was often inspired by paintings. Poems like *Laubenfest* ('Allotment Party') and *Vorortbahnhof* ('Suburban Station'), for instance, recall the works of the Berlin Naturalist Hans Baluschek. They also reveal the poet's love–hate relationship with the Prussian capital, which he was said to observe with 'X-ray eyes'.

Heym was by no means the only Expressionist poet to die young. The Austrian Georg Trakl (1887–1914) – the 'great genius of negativity'[39] whose dark poetry explored themes like incest, persecution and madness – died of a cocaine overdose in his mid-twenties. The canon of early Expressionist poets also includes the Prague-born writer Franz Werfel (1890–1945), who moved to Leipzig in the autumn of 1911, and whose first collection of poems *Der Weltfreund* ('Friend to the World') appeared a few months later; Else Lasker-Schüler, one of few prominent female Expressionists;[40] and Gottfried Benn, a young doctor who became one of Germany's leading writers of pessimistic poetry and prose after World War One, but was unknown when his *Morgue* cycle of poems appeared to uncomprehending reviews in 1912. One newspaper wrote: 'Disgusting! What an unbridled imagination, devoid of all mental hygiene, is here laid bare; what sordid delight in the abysmally ugly.'[41]

In the theatre, the German Expressionists were influenced not only by Strindberg, Wedekind and the music dramas of Kokoschka and Kandinsky, but by the director Max Reinhardt's new production ideas at the Deutsches Theater. Thus noise, spectacle, movement and physical gesture all became key features of Expressionist theatre.

The Italian Futurist Marinetti inspired August Stramm (1874–1915) to develop a condensed and economic form of poetic language – staccato sentences of just one or two words – that is sometimes referred to as the 'Telegram Style' and which also became a defining characteristic of Expressionist drama.[42] In this way the 'single emotional word replaces the involved conceptual sentence as the basic unit of Expressionist language',[43] although long monologues can also be found in the works of playwrights like Stramm, Reinhard Sorge (1892–1916), and Georg Kaiser (1878–1945), whose *Von morgens bis mitternachts* ('From Morning to Midnight', 1912) is still performed today. These dramatists also explored the expressive possibilities of punctuation – especially the exclamation mark! – and the full-throated scream. The latter even gave its name to a sub-category of Expressionist theatre, the *Schreidrama.*

Apart from linguistic innovation, other features of early Expressionist plays included an episodic structure, powerful imagery, and a preoccupation with 'types' rather than carefully drawn characters. Where Naturalism had focused on the assemblage of external detail to capture a particular milieu and to build character, Expressionist theatre featured archetypes and caricatures: old man, young woman, the peasant, the clown, the prostitute and so on. As Walter Sokel has noted: 'Expressionist drama is theme-centered rather than plot- or conflict-centered. This factor constitutes the most marked break with the tradition of the "well-made play".'[44]

A favourite theme was the revolt of youth, which featured in the first genuinely Expressionist play, Sorge's *Der Bettler* ('The Beggar') of 1911, as well as Walter Hasenclever's *Der Sohn* ('The Son', 1914), and Arnolt Bronnen's *Vatermord* ('Patricide', 1917). One leading Expressionist dramatist who was perhaps surprisingly slow to rebel against his parents was Fritz von Unruh (1885–1970), who was born into a leading aristocratic family and attended cadet school with Kaiser Wilhelm II's sons. Unruh, who was close friends with the artistically inclined Prince August Wilhelm, served as a Prussian officer between 1906 and 1911. His career as a dramatist, which was aided by Max Reinhardt, took off in rather conventional style with *Jürgen Wullenweber* (1908), but moved in a more Expressionist direction with *Offiziere* ('Officers', 1912). After the war, in which he was seriously wounded at Verdun, he became one of the Weimar Republic's leading playwrights.

The influence of German Expressionist theatre, with its grotesque distortions, exaggerations and sense of visual style, was arguably more lasting than that of Expressionist poetry, architecture or music. The so-called Theatre of the Absurd, Brecht's epic theatre of the Weimar Republic, and much of today's avant-garde theatre are amongst its heirs.[45] Expressionism had less impact on prose fiction, although the artist and illustrator Alfred Kubin (1877-1959), an often-overlooked member of the Blue Rider group, produced an early Expressionist novel in *Die andere Seite* ('The Other Side', 1909), which was said to have impressed Franz Kafka. At this time Kafka (1883–1924) was in Prague, contemplating German-language classics like *The Judgement* (1912), *Metamorphosis* (1915), and *The Trial* (written in 1914–15, but only published posthumously in 1926). Literary historians are divided on Kafka's own Expressionist credentials, but the dominant themes of his work were certainly those of the Expressionist age.

'Storm' and 'Action': apocalypse now?

A popular cliché suggests that early German Expressionists spent their lives sitting in cafés, like the Café des Westens on Berlin's Kurfürstendamm, attempting to change the world from a sedentary position. No doubt there is some truth in this – Herwarth Walden renamed that particular establishment 'Café Megalomania' – but they were also extremely active in the founding of new journals and publishing houses, including Walden's own *Der Sturm* and Franz Pfemfert's *Die Aktion* ('Action'). Such names were, of course, programmatic.

Walden founded the Sturm publishing house in Berlin in 1910.[46] Its journal *Der Sturm*, subtitled a weekly for 'culture and the arts', became the biggest and best avant-garde journal in Germany. Later there was also a Sturm theatre and a Sturm art gallery, which opened in 1912 with Germany's first exhibition of Italian Futurism. The journal focused primarily on visual art, but there were also literary contributions from Lasker-Schüler, Benn, and many others, while Kokoschka provided both texts and images. *Der Sturm* enjoyed a fruitful rivalry with *Die Aktion*, which was founded by the pacifist Franz Pfemfert (1879–1954) in February 1911, as a weekly for politics and literature, but which also covered visual art from time to time. Pfemfert and Walden shared a deep personal antipathy, based on clashing temperaments and zealous proprietorial pride, but nevertheless had much in common (including a number of their contributors).[47] Pfemfert was a highly principled man of the Left, and his paper became a forum for pacifists, anarchists and socialists of all hues, including both Karl Liebknecht and Rosa Luxemburg. Unsurprisingly, *Die Aktion* experienced many struggles with the censors during World War One.

In November 1912 the Sturm gallery staged an exhibition of a group of young Berlin artists who called themselves *Pathetiker*, after the literary Neopathetic Cabaret. Some fifteen of the paintings were by the hitherto unknown Ludwig Meidner (1884–1966), who may have worn his influences – Futurist painting and Georg Heym's poetry[48] – on his sleeve, but whose visions of urban devastation made an immediate impact. Meidner's paintings from this time are nowadays generally referred to as his 'apocalyptic landscapes', after the eschatological titles given by the artist to many of these works. They are often cited as examples of Expressionism's anti-urban *Angst* and of a prescient foreboding of coming conflict. As Charles Haxthausen notes, 'Art historians, like their colleagues in German literary studies of this period, have tended to see in the artistic treatment of Berlin symptoms of *ein Leiden an der Stadt*, a chronic state of suffering and alienation brought on by urban experience',[49] but this aspect should not be exaggerated.

Figure 14 Ludwig Meidner, Apocalyptic Landscape *(1912–13)*

A good case in point is Ludwig Meidner, who is invariably characterized as an artist deeply troubled by the bustle and bombast of Berlin life, but whose own writings seem to give a wholly different picture. Of Berlin, he wrote: 'We were so in love with that city . . . beautiful, magnificent, unique, even sublime, and inexpressibly delightful.'[50] He recalled of that time: 'I was very poor but not at all unhappy; I was charged with energy, full of mighty plans; I had faith in a magnificent future.'[51] Recent research offers an explanation for this apparent contradiction. Paintings that now bear names like 'Apocalyptic Landscape' once had more prosaic titles. Indeed, Meidner's self-compiled inventory of 1915 contained only one 'apocalyptic' title: the paintings were called things like *Landscape with Fire-Damaged House.* It would seem that the artist chose to re-title many of his works before the retrospective exhibition of 1963–4 that rescued him from obscurity. As Haxthausen explains, it was as if Meidner wished 'to capitalize retroactively . . . on a prophetic gift which was confirmed by two world wars'.[52] Stripped of their 'apocalyptic' titles, many of Meidner's paintings from 1911–14 can be read in very different ways. The buildings seemingly in a state of collapse, for instance, might not represent cataclysmic destruction at all, but rather an attempt to capture the optical effect of the gaslit city.[53]

A rather different approach to Meidner is pursued by Carol Eliel, who points out that '[e]tymologically, the word apocalypse does not stand for a catastrophe but a revelation, disclosing the hidden side of a cosmic crisis and the nature of its causes'.[54] For Meidner, as for many Expressionists, a modern apocalypse was perceived as both necessary and desirable, since it would usher in a fresher, purer world. Some claimed to see portents of the imminent apocalypse in a series of unrelated events – the Messina earthquake (1908); the appearance of Halley's Comet (1910) and the sinking of the Titanic (1912) – which were all beyond mankind's control. Franz Marc, who painted his own vision of catastrophe in *The Fate of Animals* (1913), famously expressed apocalyptic views in his letters of 1914. On 26 September, for example, he told Kandinsky he was profoundly thankful for the war: 'There was no other way to the era of the spirit. Only so could the Augean stable, the old Europe, be cleansed.'[55] Meidner's favourite poet Georg Heym had expressed similar sentiments a few years earlier: 'if someone would only begin a war, it need not be a just one. This peace is so rottenly oleaginous and greasy, like the surface of old furniture'.[56]

We will return to the Nietzschean notion of the cathartic and regenerative apocalypse, which the Expressionist generation adopted with such tragic enthusiasm, at the end of this chapter. The example of Ludwig Meidner shows, however, just how difficult it is to determine the mood or mentality of any individual at a given point in history. How much more difficult it must be, therefore, to establish a common 'spirit of the age' (*Zeitgeist*) amongst whole communities or nations. Even so, some historians have not shied away from attempting to define a distinctive Wilhelmine mentality.[57] In a 1986 book, for instance, Martin Doerry argued that the young Expressionist poets and painters did not need to invent or propagate a sense of imminent catastrophe; but merely 'diagnosed' a state of mind which was all around them.[58] According to Doerry four 'constants' – aggression, an authority-fixation, a desire to assimilate, and a search for harmony – marked out the Wilhelmine mentality, which was 'one of the decisive causes of the German Empire's crisis'.[59] Self-criticism and understatement were not amongst the Wilhelminians' strengths; the grandiose pronouncement, preferably evoking pathos, most certainly was.

Doerry adopts a term coined by the Naturalist writer Hermann Conradi in 1889 – *Übergangsmenschen* ('people in transition') – to characterize the Wilhelmine Germans.[60] It is certainly true that Germans born in the second half of the nineteenth century experienced change at an unprecedented pace. Such a rapid technological, social and economic transformation was bound to affect patterns of perception and behaviour. It was perhaps not surprising then, that many contemporary observers of the 'restless Empire', including Simmel and Freud, diagnosed an anxious excitability, an excess of imagination, and a tendency to succumb to wild fears and longings; as new and defining features of their age. Medics spoke of neurasthenia, but the word most contemporaries used to describe such phenomena was 'nervousness' (*Nervösität*), which was variously said to be a product of secularization, increasing acquisitiveness, the revolution in transport and communications, increasing noise levels, or the growth in competitive sport, which made even leisure a strain.[61] As Freud put it in 1908: 'All is hurry and agitation; night is used for travel, day for business, even "holiday trips" have become a strain on the nervous system. . . . The exhausted nerves seek recuperation in increased stimulation and in highly spiced pleasures, only to become more exhausted than before.'[62]

In recent years, a number of intellectual and cultural historians have focused on the 'nervousness' discourse, and some have used it to characterize the Wilhelmine epoch as a whole. It was, it is suggested, 'the age of nervousness'.[63] While the value of the 'history of mentalities' approach remains open to question,[64] few would disagree that the tone of cultural discourse in Germany became more fractious and bitter in the years immediately before World War One, as political tensions at home and abroad – exacerbated by the SPD's success in the 1912 Reichstag elections, the second Moroccan Crisis and the Balkan War – began to mount.

Nationalism and chauvinism in later Wilhelmine culture

As we have seen, questions of national identity and national mission had figured prominently in German cultural discourse throughout the nineteenth century, and in the lifetime of the Empire a wide range of cultural approaches – officially sanctioned and otherwise – were defined or defended using the rhetoric of nationalism. From the 1890s onwards, the revolution in transport and communications and the emergence of an incipient consumer culture began to undermine the Empire's particularist traditions, and to develop a new sense of national identity 'from below'. As Peter Fritzsche puts it: 'in the first years of the twentieth century people in Germany became more and more alike'.[65] This 'vernacular nationalism', which expressed populist impatience with the rulers of the Empire, proved difficult to control. In the last years of peace it was to leave its mark on the cultural sphere as well.

Until 1911 the north German landscape artist Carl Vinnen was identified with the more progressive forces in the German art world. Originally from Bremen, he had been a member of the Worpswede artists' colony; he had championed Paula Modersohn-Becker; and had become a member of the Berlin Secession. In the mid-1900s, however, his career began to stagnate. He felt himself to be a victim of fashion and the growing power of the art dealers. The large sum paid by the Bremen Kunsthalle for a work by van Gogh acted as a catalyst for a flurry of angry essays, articles and personal letters to leading cultural figures. In 1911 a volume was published which brought together Vinnen's essays and letters, with a selection of responses, under the title *Ein Protest deutscher Künstler* ('A Protest by German Artists'). The 'Protest' included the names of 140 artists, critics and others unhappy with what they perceived to be the overwhelming French aesthetic influence on German visual culture, although by no means all who responded agreed with every aspect of Vinnen's analysis.

Vinnen's 'Protest' is often mentioned as an example of the increasingly chauvinist tone in German cultural life before World War One. It is important to stress, however, that not all the signatories were cultural and political reactionaries: Käthe Kollwitz was amongst them, as were nine full and sixteen associate members of the Berlin Secession. Also, Vinnen's tract was much milder in tone than one might imagine: it recognized the positive contribution of French artists to German art and condemned 'chauvinistic German jingoism'. Even so, although it raised some genuine issues, its analysis was not very sophisticated, and its economic arguments easily refuted. Moreover, though Vinnen tried hard to be balanced, others took up the message that a nation's culture could only be raised 'through artists of its own flesh and blood' with fewer scruples. In response, the German Artists' League published a booklet, *German and French Art*, containing the views of seventy-five artists, critics, dealers and gallery directors who disagreed with Vinnen. Just as Kollwitz's support for Vinnen might have raised eyebrows, so Arthur Moeller van den Bruck was an unexpected signatory to the counter-blast.[66]

Thereafter little was heard of Vinnen again, but the repercussions of his petition were considerable. The famous Cologne 'Sonderbund' exhibition of modern art in 1912, for instance, was at least in part conceived 'to demonstrate that the young German painting had strong roots in the "Germanic" artists van Gogh and Munch as well as in the French masters';[67] and pro-modern critics like Karl Scheffler (editor of the journal *Kunst und Künstler* from 1907) became more vocal in their belief that a spiritually superior Germany was destined to replace France as the home of artistic innovation. Many of the contributors to Vinnen's volume were also prominent in what has become known as the '*Parsifal* Debate' of 1912–13. The thirtieth anniversary of Wagner's death saw the copyright on the composer's last and most sacred work expire. Wagner's dying wish, that *Parsifal* only be performed at Bayreuth, fell with it. As 1913 approached, the campaign to 'save' *Parsifal* spread far beyond the Bayreuth Circle. A 'Committee for the Protection of *Parsifal*' was established in every major city; a petition calling upon the Reichstag to restrict the piece to Bayreuth was signed by 18,000 people; even Richard Strauss was mobilized to lobby parliament. As Frederic Spotts comments, 'Only in Germany and only with Wagner could such an eventuality have ranked as a cataclysm.'[68] Nothing came of the protests, and the Reichstag declined to intervene, but the affair was seldom out of the newspapers during 1913.

The debate aroused such passions because *Parsifal*-at-Bayreuth had become an important symbol of German cultural identity. It was no coincidence that it was this particular Wagner music-drama which was performed at Bayreuth on 1 August 1914. The '*Parsifal* Debate', however, was only one of a series of events in 1913 that gave cultural chauvinists a platform for their views. The last full year of peace was a year of anniversaries: the centenary of the Battle of Leipzig (the *Völkerschlacht* of 1813); the centenary too of the historic meeting of the East Prussian Landtag in Königsberg; and Kaiser Wilhelm II's Silver Jubilee, which was marked by a week of celebrations in June. As Wolfram Siemann wryly remarks, all such events contributed to a climate in which it became easier to pass an Army Bill through the Reichstag.[69]

In Breslau, on the eastern fringe of the Empire, a giant reinforced concrete dome, the 'Century Hall', was designed by Max Berg (1870–1947) to host large-scale celebrations, and in particular an historical pageant to be written by Gerhart Hauptmann and directed by Max Reinhardt. The production opened in May 1913, but was immediately surrounded by controversy. Hauptmann had chosen to portray the monarchs of 1813 as marionettes on the stage of a 'world theatre'. The Prussian Crown Prince, conservative politicians and veterans' associations complained loudly about the pageant's 'un-German feeling', which was said to challenge the 'unity of throne and people'. Certainly, Hauptmann's coolly ironic text did not please all the audience, and when the Crown Prince threatened to withdraw as patron of the celebrations, the production was closed early. Even so, perhaps the most illuminating aspect of this little episode was the fact that an 'oppositional' figure like Hauptmann was invited to become involved in the first place. By 1913 modernists like Berg, Hauptmann and Reinhardt were already on the inside; their aesthetic values accepted by large sections of the middle class, if not yet by all the conservative Prussian elite.

Predictably, 1913 also witnessed the highpoint of the *Hermannsschlacht* boom, with over sixty performances of Kleist's patriotic play, which was well suited to commemorate the centenary of what contemporary Germans called the 'Wars of Liberation' against Napoleonic France. The 1813 anniversary festivities continued in August, with a major festival at the 'Liberation Hall' (1863) in

Kelheim on the Danube, organized by the Bavarian authorities, and with most of the German rulers present. The highpoint of the year, however, was to come in the centenary month of October, with the ceremony to unveil the *Völkerschlacht* monument, built close to the original Leipzig battlefield site. For this, 43,000 gymnasts ran in relay across Germany, each carrying a symbolic oak branch as a baton.[70] The routes had been measured with military precision so that the runners would all arrive at the same time, and took in national monuments, historic battlefields, the graves of Bismarck and Jahn, and the Zeppelin works at Friedrichshafen along the way.

Plans to build a monument to the Battle of Leipzig had been around since 1815, but the dynastic rulers of the German states had shown little enthusiasm. This was hardly surprising since many of them had spent much of the war on Napoleon's side. In the 1890s the plans were revived by an architect called Clemens Thieme, who in 1894 had set up an association called the German Patriotic League to lobby for a monument. Thieme launched a competition to attract designs, and eventually one by the ubiquitous Bruno Schmitz was selected, even though it had failed to win first prize. Building work on the monument began in 1900 and was only just completed in time for the centenary celebrations in October 1913, which gives some indication of its mammoth dimensions. It was the biggest monument in Europe at the time of construction, and for Schmitz it represented a final and complete break from academic historicism. The language of its architecture was emotional rather than rational: designed to make the individual feel small and insignificant, yet at the same time empowered by belonging to a national community of vast potential. The irony of its location – Saxony was one of the states which had spent most of the Napoleonic Wars on the side of the French and had not deserted Napoleon until the penultimate day of the battle – was not so much forgotten as buried beneath the colossal weight of the monument's 91-metre high walls.

It cost some 6 million RM to build; almost all of which was raised from the general public, through raffles, lotteries and donations. In this sense it was a genuinely popular monument; a fact perhaps emphasized by Wilhelm II's premature departure from the 11 October opening ceremony. However, it is clear that not all the citizens of Leipzig were behind the project. Thieme's Patriotic League had made little secret that it believed the Empire was under threat not only from external enemies, but also from the 'masses led astray

Figure 15 Völkerschlacht monument, Leipzig (1900–13). Architect: Bruno Schmitz

by the social question' and the 'religious absolutism' emanating from Rome. Accordingly, the SPD instructed its members to boycott the fund-raising lotteries, with the slogan 'Eyes open, Pockets closed!'[71] Thus, if the original conception for a *Völkerschlachtdenkmal* had been to honour those who had fought for freedom and fatherland in 1813, the 1913 version became what Nipperdey calls 'a monument of national concentration', directed as much against the enemy within as the enemy without.[72]

Much of Germany's youth seemed to be on the march in the second week of October 1913. As the patriotic gymnasts made their mass relay to Leipzig, several thousand other youngsters – described by one observer as 'veggie faces, rusk eaters, raspberry juice students'[73] – were heading to an alternative celebration on a hill near Kassel. The gathering on the 754-metre Hohe Meissner, officially titled the first 'Free German Youth Conference', was planned by more progressively minded members of the German middle classes as a conscious alternative to the nationalist pomp of the events in Leipzig. The hilltop location in central Germany was carefully chosen, offering both 'unspoilt' natural surroundings, and good railway connections. The weekend of 11–12 October was cold and foggy in the hills of Hesse, however, and the Hohe Meissner gathering was on a much smaller scale than Leipzig, attracting only 2500 participants. Even so, fourteen different *Wandervogel* and educational reform organizations were present, representing a broad coalition of pacifist, environmentalist, vegetarian and abstinent students, who rejected the drinking and duelling ethos of the fraternities.

Amongst the 'honorary guests' invited to the Hohe Meissner were reformist grandees such as Ferdinand Avenarius and Eugen Diederichs, and the educationalist Gustav Wyneken, whose speech warned against 'sabre-rattling' and the danger of being 'seduced into armed conflict with a neighbouring people'. Wyneken reminded his young audience that the heroes of 1813 had been 'citizens of the world', for whom common humanity was more important than any nation. Further messages of support, later published in a *Festschrift*, came from some of the leading figures in German cultural and intellectual life: Gerhart Hauptmann, Ludwig Thoma, Friedrich Naumann and the philosophers Paul Natorp and Ludwig Klages. Participants later recalled how, just as the speeches began, the clouds cleared, and the 'Meissner Formula' – a brief statement of intent written by Avenarius and agreed by all the participant groups – was greeted by shafts of warm sunlight. The formula asserted youth's demand to be recognized as an independent estate, entitled to self-determination and responsibility.[74] Its message appears to have been warmly received, despite its 57-year old author's less than youthful appearance.

Before we leave 1913 one further episode merits brief attention. To mark Wilhelm II's Silver Jubilee and the centenary of the

Völkerschlacht, a major retrospective exhibition was planned in Berlin for the artist Anton von Werner, whose seventieth birthday was approaching. Arrangements were already far advanced when the show was cancelled without explanation. Gradually, however, it became known that the exhibition had been called off on the orders of 'higher authorities', which felt that Werner's large-scale depictions of the Franco-Prussian war might antagonize French public opinion, and provoke a diplomatic incident. The German bourgeois press was outraged, and printed headlines such as 'Anton von Werner sacrificed', 'An unparalleled scandal', and 'The dangerous Anton von Werner'. As Peter Paret notes, subsequent attempts by embarrassed civil servants to lie their way out of a tight spot by shifting the blame on to Werner only made things worse: 'That the government had made a mistake and then lied to protect itself was obvious.'[75] A mass demonstration was planned in the artist's support, but was called off at Werner's own request, and the storm soon blew over. Even so, the affair demonstrated how, on the eve of the Great War, political tensions at home and abroad were beginning to have a direct impact on German cultural life.

August 1914

The First World War, the '*Urkatastrophe* of the twentieth century',[76] that began in the first week of August 1914, destroyed the Wilhelmine world and had a profound effect on the course of German history. It had a particularly devastating impact on the Expressionist generation, claiming the lives of Marc and Macke, Stramm and Sorge, and many more. As Armin Wegner once put it: 'Seldom has a generation bled to death so quickly.'[77] It was, of course, a tragic irony that so many artists and writers would fall victim to a war they had longed for. They had wanted to live dangerously, to experience a heightened reality that would release primal energies and purify the decadent materialism of bourgeois life. Instead, they died a wretched death in the most degrading of circumstances: 'The Great War was a travesty of the unanchored idealism of 1910, a nihilism without heroic dimension, a dashing of oneself on the reef merely out of fear of the open sea.'[78]

Some realized their tragic mistake. Shortly before his death in battle, Franz Marc wrote: 'I often think how in my childhood and teens I was sorry not to be living at a time when history was in the making – now it's upon us and is more terrible than anyone could have imagined.'[79] The blame for such fatal illusions was, and still is, often placed at the door of Friedrich Nietzsche. Indeed, no sooner had the Great War begun, than a London bookseller had dubbed it the 'Euro-Nietzschean War',[80] and the French intellectual Romain Rolland (1866–1944), was writing: 'One superman is a sublime spectacle. Ten or 20 supermen are unpleasant. But hundreds of thousands who combine arrogant extravagance with mediocrity or natural baseness become a scourge of God which is ravaging Belgium and France.'[81] Undoubtedly, Nietzsche's influence on the Expressionist generation was considerable. They embraced his notions of the artist as warrior superman and the regenerative power of apocalypse with great enthusiasm. Some of them even took their copies of *Zarathustra* into the trenches.[82]

However, this influence was not limited to artists and writers who worked in an Expressionist style, and it did not apply only to Germans: Robert Graves in England, d'Annunzio in Italy and Drieu La Rochelle in France were all self-styled Nietzschean warriors for a time. Thomas Mann, who viewed the war as a 'purification, a liberation, an enormous hope', seemed to suggest in his pre-war novella *Death in Venice* (1912) that the whole continent was just waiting 'for the chance to cast aside all notions of order, containment, scruple in the name of some entry into intense, incandescent experience'.[83] In fact, the notion that the world had 'grown old and cold and weary' (Rupert Brooke) and needed an explosion of youthful energy was one of two tragic delusions common to middle- and upper-class Europeans right across the continent in 1914 – the other was that the war was going to be short – and its roots cannot be traced to any single individual.

As Klaus Vondung has illustrated, the practice of viewing war as a regenerative apocalypse or a 'Last Judgement' on the nation's enemies had a long pre-Nietzschean tradition in German culture. Ernst Moritz Arndt had employed this sort of eschatological imagery in 1813, for instance, as had fellow poet Emanuel Geibel in 1870.[84] If the use of apocalyptic language did become more widespread and intense in the early years of the Great War than in previous conflicts, it was due as much to an army of Protestant pastors and professors who toured Germany lecturing on the 'meaning' of the conflict as it was to Nietzschean Expressionists. The Nobel Prize winning philosopher Rudolf Eucken (1846–1926), for instance, gave at least two lectures a week on this subject throughout 1914–15, and other professors were not far behind.[85] The rectors and senates of Bavaria's universities issued a joint statement in August 1914, which proclaimed: 'Students! The muses are silent. The issue is battle, the battle forced on us for German *Kultur*.'[86]

In October 1914, ninety-three of Germany's leading professors, writers, artists and scientists published an 'Appeal to the world of Culture', expressing their support for a war 'forced on Germany' and condemning the black propaganda of Germany's enemies. The signatories included Behrens, Hauptmann, Humperdinck, Liebermann, Liszt, Planck, Reinhardt and Richard Dehmel, who volunteered for the army at the age of 51.[87] Other writers who spoke out in favour of the war included Wedekind, Musil, Hofmannsthal, Hesse and Alfred Döblin. It should not be forgotten, however, that the British authors J. M. Barrie, Arnold Bennett, G. K. Chesterton, Arthur Conan Doyle, John Galsworthy, Thomas Hardy, Rudyard Kipling and H. G. Wells all pledged to assist their country's war effort in a more co-ordinated way, at a secret meeting with London government officials on 2 September 1914.[88] In all the participant nations, writers and artists attempted to portray the conflict as a 'war of the cultures', in which the future shape of European culture and society was at stake.

It was hardly surprising, therefore, that the outbreak of war was greeted as a welcome opportunity for cultural rebirth by German *Lebensreform* leaders such as Avenarius, Diederichs and Wyneken. Forgetting his wise words on the Hohe Meissner, Wyneken travelled around Germany giving enthusiastic lectures on 'The War and Youth'; while Avenarius's poem 'Greetings to the Free Germans', written to mark the first anniversary of the Hohe Meissner, concluded: 'to die a soldier's death does not hurt'. The absurdity of such a claim was, of course, brought home very rapidly to the youthful volunteers in the fields of Flanders. At the Battle of Langemarck on 11 November 1914, four reserve corps containing many Free Germans – who appear to have joined up with as much alacrity as the 'paramilitary' gymnasts from the *Völkerschlacht* Monument – were wiped out in a futile show of courage.[89] As Peter Stachura notes: 'The battle became a legend in the history of the German Youth Movement, including the Hitler Youth, serving to epitomise the unparalleled idealism and willingness for self-sacrifice of German youth in the national cause'.[90] In total, some 7000 members of the independent youth movement lost their lives in the war, including Christian Schneehagen, the organizer of the Hohe Meissner gathering.

When war was declared, the leaders of Germany's marginalized groups – workers, women, Jews and homosexuals – were quick to demonstrate their patriotism and reliability too. The campaigner for homosexual rights Magnus Hirschfeld, for instance, announced that the war was to defend teutonic 'honesty and sincerity' against the 'smoking jacket culture' of Britain and France, and admitted that the omnipresence of uniforms and guns acted as a sexual stimulant.[91] Even permanently sceptical intellectuals like Max Weber pronounced the war 'great and wonderful'.[92] The question why so many people succumbed to 'war euphoria' in the long hot summer of 1914 has fascinated generations of historians. It is clear that it was not simply a product of the pressure to conform in an authoritarian society. Study of first-hand recollections of the 'August miracle' – or a glance at some of the 50,000 war poems written on every single day that month[93] – reveals a genuine sense of exhilaration, even amongst those well aware of the dangers of 'hurrah patriotism'.

Principally, of course, it was the new spirit of national togetherness that thrilled a people who had grown weary of the conflicts between capital and labour, agriculture and industry, tradition and modernity. The 'civil truce' produced by the 'August miracle' was particularly welcome to educated middle-class Germans, who had little to gain from either a socialist revolution or a conservative reaction. At last, and perhaps for the first time since its foundation, the Empire seemed to be a true *Volksgemeinschaft*, a national community united in harmony. The cultural historian Modris Eksteins puts in the following terms: 'In early August Germans wallow in what appears to them to be the genuine synthesis of past and future, eternity embodied in the moment, and the resolution of all domestic strife. . . . Life has achieved transcendence. It has become aestheticized.'[94] Although the sense of *Volksgemeinschaft* did not last much beyond 1916, it survived long enough for a host of optimistic intellectuals to draw some high-flown conclusions about the nature of German society, and in particular the differences between German culture and western civilization. These were often referred to as the 'Ideas of 1914': a phrase first coined by the economist and sociologist Johann Plenge (1874–1963); and formulated in more detail by the Germanophile Swede Rudolf Kjellen (1864–1922) and the left-liberal theologian Ernst Troeltsch (1865–1923), who both wrote popular essays on the subject.

Essentially, the 'Ideas of 1914' claimed concepts such as community, sacrifice, spirit, discipline and duty as intrinsically German. The popularity of this dubious thesis had much to do with its vagueness. The 'Ideas' were sufficiently malleable to fit into both a 'progressive' and 'reactionary' discourse. Left-liberals and 'ethical socialists' could contrast the communitarian German approach with the selfish, plutocratic mentality of Anglo-American society. Conservatives, meanwhile, could emphasize a positive contrast with the demagogic 'Ideas of 1789'. Either way, however, the 'Ideas of 1914' owed more to wishful thinking than scientific observation, for the apparent national consensus soon began to dissolve.[95]

Indeed, recent research has emphasized the extent to which the 'war euphoria' of August 1914 was from the start limited to a relatively narrow section of German society. Whilst the educated middle classes and the military caste celebrated, 'depression, frustration and fear' hung over working-class districts of the Empire's cities and across great swathes of the German countryside.[96] A village pastor from a community near Frankfurt wrote: 'All the village was filled with sorrow during the last week of July. . . . No euphoria, no patriotic songs'.[97] Case studies of a number of German cities, including Hamburg, Darmstadt and Freiburg, highlight the fact that the excited crowds which thronged city streets in late July and early August were motivated as much by a desire to find out what was going on as by nationalist fervour.[98] Special extra newspaper editions were the only source of up-to-date information in a society without radio or television. The mood of these crowds, whose size owed much to the fine summer weather, was ambivalent and changeable. Although patriotic songs were sung, so were anti-war anthems. The conservative Berlin daily *Die Post* reported with disappointment in late July: 'Only a small part of the tens of thousands who paraded up and down [Unter den] Linden was patriotically minded, or dared to bear witness to this feeling.'[99]

If the actual declaration of war was greeted with excitement and relief, it appears to have been caused by a release of accumulated nervous tension, rather than a widespread desire for war. This is born out by the number of volunteers for the German army in 1914–15: not, as contemporary accounts suggested, a matter of millions, but actually a rather modest 308,000 souls.[100] The first week of August saw hoarding, profiteering and a wave of redundancies, as well as patriotic cheers. In the pubs, many people were asking 'why is there to be so much suffering for an Austrian archduke?'[101] Particular historical attention has been focused on the reaction of working-class Germans to the outbreak of hostilities. Peace demonstrations promoted by the socialist press in at least thirty-two German towns and cities in late July had summoned three-quarters of a million people onto the streets. Even while these demonstrations were taking place, however, the SPD leadership was involved in secret negotiations with the imperial government. As a result, the party instructed its newspapers to tone down their anti-war rhetoric. On 1 August 1914, in an about-turn which left many ordinary party members distressed and disoriented, the socialist press came out in support of a war to defend German culture from 'Tsarist barbarism'. With peace demonstrations now banned, the SPD leadership urged party members not to partake in illegal gatherings. Fear of violent confrontation no doubt played a part, but most socialist politicians had become convinced of the justness of Germany's cause. Loyalty to the Empire, they argued, did not have to imply blind obedience to the Emperor. This view, which found expression in the Reichstag vote to approve war credits on 4 August, was probably more widely shared than later critics of the SPD leadership would care to admit.

However, those who hoped the fragile unity of August 1914 would usher in a more harmonious and homogenous society were to be disappointed. The war would leave Germany even more divided than before. A huge gulf developed between those who experienced the trenches and those who remained at home; while existing divisions between town and country, rich and poor, old and young, were all exacerbated by terrible shortages of food and fuel. Supplies began to run out as early as the autumn of 1914 and became critical early in 1915.[102] Despite rationing, cheese, butter, eggs and other staples were only available on the socially divisive black market after 1916. 'Eventually, these conditions destroyed the fabric of an orderly society and undermined its very legitimacy.'[103] By the so-called 'turnip winter' of 1916–17 – captured in a chillingly bleak painting by Hans Baluschek (*Winter in Wartime,* 1917) – the fissures in German cultural and intellectual life were equally apparent. The patriotic professors had fallen out over the issue of war aims and annexations; the 'warrior artists' had long since discovered that Nietzschean virtues like courage and initiative meant little against the machinery of modern warfare; and the Wilhelmine reform movement was in a state of terminal disintegration, collapsing under the weight of its own contradictions.

The latter had always been the broadest of churches, of course, but by 1917 the process of political and philosophical polarization was well underway. In May of that year Eugen Diederichs, for two

Figure 16 Hans Baluschek, Winter in Wartime *(1917)*

decades the doyen of *Lebensreform* publishers, invited the great and the good of German cultural life to a behind-closed-doors conference at Burg Lauenstein in Thuringia. Representatives of many of the Wilhelmine reform leagues responded, along with individual artists, and intellectuals such as Max Weber. The staging of such an event at this time demonstrated not only the enduring faith in the existence of a distinctive and coherent 'German culture', but also the conviction that culture still had a pivotal role to play in the nation's fortunes. Looking back over the lifetime of the Empire it is remarkable how resilient this belief had been, surviving all the aesthetic revolts and secessions of the previous half-century. At the same time, however, Diederichs's gathering also served to highlight how little consensus was now left in German cultural life. It was as if the 'cultural war' unleashed on Germany's enemies in 1914 had begun to turn in on itself. It was to become a civil war instead.

Although there would be two further meetings at Burg Lauenstein, it was already apparent in May 1917 that the mutually hostile ideological positions associated with 'Weimar Culture' had now been formed, in outline at least.[104] Some participants, such as the theologian and erstwhile socialist Max Maurenbrecher, were moving rapidly to the *völkisch* right, while others such as the young writer Ernst Toller, were travelling equally swiftly in the opposite direction. Toller's wartime odyssey – from the euphoria of 1914, through the disillusionment of the war's middle years, to the radical political activism of 1918[105] – may have been typical for many in the Expressionist generation, but similar experiences led others to draw very different conclusions. Later, in the increasingly polarized cultural conflicts of the Depression years, prominent Wilhelmine reformers could be found on both sides of the barricades: cosmopolitan and *völkisch*, pro- and anti-modernist. In reality, of course, Weimar cultural politics was never quite a simple clash of polar opposites, but the complicated process by which former allies and colleagues could become bitter enemies, often without seeming to move very far from their original positions, can only be explained by detailed study of individual circumstances.

Continuities and discontinuities

In the opening chapter of his acclaimed book *Weimar Culture: The Outsider as Insider*, Peter Gay makes an eye-catching admission: 'the

Republic created little; it liberated what was already there'.[106] Although the vitality and pluralism of Wilhelmine cultural life described in the previous chapters suggests that 'liberation' was hardly necessary, the implications of Gay's statement are significant. Most 'Weimar Culture', it suggests, was not conceived in the fresh air of liberal democracy, but in the altogether mustier atmosphere of the Second Empire. Nor is Gay alone in this view. Walter Laqueur, for instance, concedes that Weimar Culture 'antedates the Weimar Republic by at least a decade',[107] and Detlev Peukert agrees: 'the features that are commonly singled out as typical of Weimar had already begun to take shape around the turn of the century'.[108] Even so, it is Weimar rather than the Empire that remains synonymous with modernity and 'the birth of modernism'.[109] The reasons for this lie partly in historians' desire to emphasize the uniqueness of Weimar Culture, 'in order to enhance the drama before its demise in 1933' as Frank Trommler puts it,[110] but also in the real and significant changes that took place in Germany as a result of World War One and the revolutions of 1918–19. It is appropriate, therefore, for this book to conclude with a necessarily brief look at some of the continuities and discontinuities in German cultural history before and after 1918.

Peter Gay's thesis centred on a cultural changing of the guard, in which the 'outsiders' of the Empire became the 'insiders' of Weimar. This is sustainable only up to a point. As we have seen, many figures associated with the avant-garde of early modernism were already on the inside well before 1918: the architects and designers Behrens, Poelzig and Paul; the writer Hauptmann; the theatre director Reinhardt; the composer Strauss; and the painter Liebermann among them (the latter finally even received a medal from the Kaiser). This picture is backed up by James Sheehan's recent study of *Museums in the German Art World*: 'Ludwig Justi, Tschudi's successor at the National Gallery in Berlin, remained in office under the Weimar Republic. Max Sauerlandt, another member of the . . . "museum modernists", returned from military service to his post as director in Halle. . . . Similarly, Ernst Gosebruch (Essen), Walter Kaesbach (Erfurt), Emil Waldmann (Bremen), Georg Swarzenski (Frankfurt), and Gustav Pauli (Hamburg) held important posts before and after the war.'[111] A comparable pattern can be observed across a range of cultural institutions, from theatres to opera houses.

Continuities can also be found in terms of style too. As we have seen, the major movement in German culture before World War

One had been Expressionism, and things appeared little different in the years immediately after the conflict: '[a]ll that was novel about Expressionism in this period was the extent of its acceptance and its success', Willett notes.[112] In fact, even this appears questionable, since the Expressionist artists Kandinsky, Jawlensky and Marc had 'all crossed the museum "threshold" well before the war',[113] with their work on show in public galleries in Aachen, Barmen, Elberfeld and Hagen, to name but four. Moreover, though Expressionism soon ran out of steam as a creative force and was largely overtaken by a *Neue Sachlichkeit* ('New Objectivity' or 'Sobriety') by 1923, that movement's novelty is also open to debate. Certainly, in architecture and design, there was much to link the 'new' *Sachlichkeit* with its pre-war namesake. The most famous expressions of *Neue Sachlichkeit* in design – Walter Gropius's Bauhaus school (established in 1919),[114] and the Werkbund's Weissenhof model housing estate in Stuttgart (1927)[115] – both had strong and well-documented links to pre-war developments, while the *Neue Sachlichkeit* photographer August Sander had found his objective documentary style before 1914 too. Frederic Schwartz has claimed that the new *Sachlichkeit* 'wanted nothing to do with the piety and pathos of the old one',[116] but this will seem strange to anyone who has ever read the literature emanating from the Bauhaus.

Of course, some continuities were unavoidable. The lives and careers of architects and writers, painters and composers, do not fit neatly into the comparatively rigid structures of political historiography. Cultural historians have long highlighted the limitations of working within a temporal framework determined solely by political events. Indeed, in purely cultural terms, the period from the 1890s to the 1930s is perhaps best viewed as a single entity: the era of 'classical modernity' as Peukert has called it, which hit its crisis-point around 1930.[117] It is clear, however, that wars and revolutions cannot be removed from the equation altogether. It would be perverse, for instance, to deny the massive impact of World War One on German culture, not only as a powerful force on the creative imagination, but as a breeding ground for hatred, and as a laboratory for new technologies as well. Similarly, for all the undoubted continuities, the establishment of the republic did alter the character of German *Kultur.*

Ultimately, the most novel aspect of Weimar Culture was not a change in personnel, or in style, but in the context of cultural production and consumption. The republic 'did not so much liberate the modern movement as shift it on to a new, much wider and less personal plane where for the first time it could affect the lives of whole communities, not just small cultural elites', as John Willett pus it.[118] The Empire's avant-garde and traditionalists alike had, for the most part, addressed their work to the educated middle classes, and their definition of culture had remained largely static. This common understanding of what culture meant was even shared by those, such as manual workers, who did not enjoy easy access to its pleasures. The consensus began to breakdown before World War One, but it was not until after 1918 that substantial numbers of cultural producers and theorists proved willing or able to take up the challenge posed by the masses.

The 1920s saw a rapid and massive extension of cultural activities, based largely on technological innovations such as the cinema, radio, the pocket camera, and new printing techniques. With the growth of picture palaces and dance halls, sport and leisure, fashion and advertising, commercial popular culture gained a new prominence. As we have seen, a mass market had already begun to develop in the Empire, and 'neither the consumer culture of the twenties and thirties nor the theories which sought to account for it grew out of thin air'.[119] However, whereas popular culture had previously been dismissed as vulgar and materialistic by both left- and right-wing critics, some on the left now saw an egalitarian authenticity beneath its brash facade. For all their stylistic or political differences, many of the key names in Weimar Culture – Brecht, Weill, Piscator, Gropius, Hindemith – shared a common desire to affect the lives of people well beyond their own class or milieu. The Weimar years were therefore important in widening both the audience and the definition of culture.

As this book has attempted to demonstrate, Imperial Culture was seldom divorced from political pressures and impulses. Even so, comparatively few cultural producers became actively involved in party politics; the close ties between the pre-war Werkbund and organized left liberalism were an exception rather than the rule. All this was to change, briefly and dramatically, in the revolutionary turmoil of 1918–19: Toller, Walden, Hiller, Brecht, Cassirer, were amongst many who rallied under the banner of the Independent Social Democrats (USPD); others, such as the Dadaists Grosz and Heartfield, joined the Communist KPD, or – like the Expressionists Pechstein and von Unruh – signed up to the majority SPD. Famously, the writers Toller, Landauer and Mühsam even held government posts in the shortlived Bavarian socialist republic (*Räterepublik*), where they were assisted by two writers – Schumann and Polenske – from the hitherto rather stuffy bourgeois journal *Der Kunstwart*.

By comparison, the long list of progressive cultural figures who signed a declaration in support of the Democratic People's League (Demokratische Volksbund) in late November 1918 has been virtually forgotten. This centrist political party summoned into life by the liberal industrialist Walther Rathenau was still-born, but the signatories read like an A–Z of Imperial Culture: Behrens, Dehmel, Hauptmann, Liebermann, Muthesius, Oppenheimer, Paul, Tschudi and so on.[120] This impressive line-up shows that cultural producers did not automatically gravitate to the political extremes – most of the signatories were happy to transfer their allegiance to the newly founded German Democratic Party (DDP) a few weeks later – but it also offers a tantalizing glimpse of the political potential accumulated within the leadership of Germany's Imperial Culture. This potential may have remained unfulfilled before 1918, but it indicates once more that the image of the introspective German artist, seeking inwardness rather than social engagement, owes more to myth than reality.[5]

Notes

Notes to the Introduction

1. P. Gay, *Weimar Culture: The Outsider as Insider* (Harmondsworth: Penguin, 1974); W. Laqueur, *Weimar: A Cultural History* (London: Weidenfeld and Nicolson, 1974); J. Willett, *The New Sobriety: Art and Politics in the Weimar Period* (London and New York: Thames and Hudson, 1978).
2. For introductions to the historiography of Imperial Germany see R. Chickering, 'The quest for a usable German Empire', in R. Chickering (ed.), *Imperial Germany: A Historiographical Companion* (Westport and London: Greenwood, 1996), pp. 1–12; R. J. Evans, *Rethinking German History* (London: Unwin Hyman, 1987) chs 1–3; and R. Moeller, 'The Kaiserreich Recast?', in *Journal of Social History*, 17 (1984), 655–83.
3. Published in English as H.-U. Wehler, *The German Empire* (Leamington Spa: Berg, 1985).
4. Historians such as Richard J. Evans, David Blackbourn and Geoff Eley.
5. For example, the 'cultural' section of volume 3 of Wehler's mammoth *Deutsche Gesellschaftsgeschichte: von der Deutschen Doppelrevolution bis zum Beginn des Ersten Weltkriegs, 1849–1914* (Munich: Beck, 1995), looks only at churches, schools and publishing houses.
6. G. Eley, 'Introduction', in G. Eley (ed.), *Society, Culture and the State in Germany, 1870–1930* (Ann Arbor: University of Michigan Press, 1996), p. 41.
7. C. E. McClelland, 'The wise man's burden: the role of academicians in Imperial German Culture', in G. D. Stark and B. K. Lackner (eds), *Essays on Culture and Society in Modern Germany* (Arlington: Texas University Press, 1982), p. 45.
8. D. Langewiesche, 'German Liberalism in the Second Empire', in K. Jarausch and L. E. Jones (eds), *In Search of a Liberal Germany* (1989), p. 234.
9. See J. J. Sheehan, *Museums in the German Art World: From the End of the Old Regime to the Rise of Modernism* (Oxford: Oxford University Press, 2000).
10. The 'false generosity' (Pierre Bourdieu) of nineteenth-century cultural

institutions is highlighted by Sheehan, *Museums in the German Art World*, p. 116. Many German art galleries and museums did not open on Sundays or in the evenings, the only times when most of the general public would be able to visit.

11. For the so-called 'Naturalism Debate' at the SPD congress of 1896, which marked the climax of a five-year dispute within the party, see H.-J. Schulz, *German Socialist Literature, 1860–1914* (Columbia, SC: Camden House, 1993).
12. The nineteenth-century Italian politician D'Azeglio is alleged to have said after his country's unification, 'We have made Italy, now we must make Italians'.
13. See, for instance, F. Stern, *The Politics of Cultural Despair: A Study in the Rise of Germanic Ideology* (Berkeley and London: University of California Press, 1961); G. L. Mosse, *The Crisis of German Ideology: Intellectual Origins of the Third Reich* (London: Weidenfeld and Nicolson, 1966); and also his *Nationalization of the Masses: Political Symbolism and Mass Movements in Germany from the Napoleonic Wars through the Third Reich* (New York: Fertig, 1975). For a more recent work in this vein see A. K. Wiedmann, *The German Quest for Primal Origins in Art, Culture and Politics, 1900–1933* (Lampeter: Mellen, 1995).
14. The label was used frequently by R. Hamann and J. Hermand in their five-volume series *Epochen deutscher Kultur von 1870 bis zur Gegenwart* (Frankfurt: Fischer, 1977), see, for instance, vol. 4, p. 365.
15. See D. Blackbourn and G. Eley, *The Peculiarities of German History* (Oxford: Oxford University Press, 1984).
16. Blackbourn and Eley, *The Peculiarities of German History*. See also D. Blackbourn and R. J. Evans (eds), *The German Bourgeoisie* (London: Routledge, 1991); J. Kocka and A. Mitchell (eds), *Bourgeois Society in Nineteenth-Century Europe* (Oxford: Berg, 1993); J. Kocka (ed.), *Bürger und Bürgerlichkeit im 19. Jahrhundert* (Göttingen: Vandenhoeck & Ruprecht, 1987); G. Cocks and K. Jarausch (eds), *The German Professions, 1800–1950* (Oxford: Oxford University Press, 1990); D. Hein and A. Schulz (eds), *Bürgerkultur im 19. Jahrhundert. Bildung, Kunst und Lebenswelt* (Munich: Beck, 1996), and many more.
17. See W. H. Bruford, *The German Tradition of Self-Cultivation: 'Bildung' from Humboldt to Thomas Mann* (Cambridge: Cambridge University Press, 1975).
18. See, for instance, G. Craig, *The Politics of the Unpolitical: German Writers and the Problem of Power, 1770–1871* (Oxford: Oxford University Press, 1995).
19. G. Craig, *Germany, 1866–1945* (Oxford: Oxford University Press, 1978), p. 215.
20. W. J. Mommsen, 'Culture and politics in the German Empire', in Mommsen, *Imperial Germany, 1867–1918: Politics, Culture and Society in an Authoritarian State* (London: Arnold, 1995), p. 120.
21. The latest author to put forward this view is K. Repp, *Reformers, Critics and the Paths of German Modernity: Anti-Politics and the Search for Alternatives, 1890–1914* (Cambridge, MA and London: Harvard University Press, 2000).

22. Such as Stark and Lackner (eds), *Essays on Culture and Society in Modern Germany*; also G. Chapple and H. Schulte (eds), *The Turn of the Century: German Literature and Art* (Bonn: Bouvier, 1981); and F. Forster-Hahn (ed.), *Imagining Modern German Culture, 1889–1910* (Hanover, NH: University Press of New England, 1996).
23. G. Craig, *Germany, 1866–1945*; V. Berghahn, *Imperial Germany, 1871–1914: Economy, Society, Culture, and Politics* (Providence and Oxford: Berghahn, 1994); R. Burns (ed.), *German Cultural Studies: An Introduction* (Oxford: Oxford University Press, 1995).
24. Mommsen, *Imperial Germany, 1867–1918.*
25. K. Friedrich, 'Cultural and Intellectual Trends', in J. Breuilly (ed.), *Nineteenth-Century Germany: Politics, Culture and Society, 1780–1918* (London: Arnold, 2001), p. 97.
26. J. Winter, *Sites of Memory, Sites of Mourning: The Great War in European Cultural History* (Cambridge: Cambridge University Press, 1995), p. 4.
27. E. Kolinsky and W. van der Will (eds), *The Cambridge Companion to Modern German Culture* (Cambridge: Cambridge University Press, 1998).
28. This point is emphasized by P. Burke in *Varieties of Cultural History* (Cambridge: Polity, 1997), p. 201.
29. R. Williams, *Keywords: A Vocabulary of Culture and Society* (London: Fontana, 1976), p. 76.
30. A. Kroeber and C. Kluckhohn, quoted by Burke, *Varieties of Cultural History*, p. 1. See also N. Dirks, G. Eley and S. Ortner (eds), *Culture / Power / History: A Reader in Contemporary Social Theory* (Princeton: Princeton University Press, 1993).
31. C. Geertz, *The Interpretation of Cultures* (London: Hutchinson, 1975), p. 89.
32. P. Willis, quoted by J. Retallack, 'Wilhelmine Germany', in G. Martel (ed.), *Modern Germany Reconsidered* (London: Routledge, 1992), p. 48.
33. *Der Grosse Brockhaus*, vol. 10 (Leipzig: Brockhaus, 1931), p. 692.
34. Quoted by R. Williams, *Keywords*, p. 79.
35. The first proponents of reception theory and reception history, in the late 1960s and 1970s, were literary specialists such as Hans Robert Jauss and Wolfgang Iser. Its uses for the historian are explored by M. Thompson, 'Reception theory and the interpretation of historical meaning', in *History and Theory*, 32 (1993), 248–72. See also W. Kemp (ed.), *Der Betrachter ist im Bild. Kunstwissenschaft und Rezeptionsästhetik* (Berlin: Reimer, 1992).
36. Within the field of Imperial Culture it has been the reception of literature in the *Kaiserreich* (and particularly the works of canonical authors) that has been most frequently subject to analysis, with contemporary newspaper and journal reviews providing the principal source material. However, the response of 'ordinary' readers remains more difficult to gauge, and the literary historian Hugh Ridley has described reception aesthetics as 'an attractive dream'. See H. Ridley, *The Problematic Bourgeois: Twentieth-Century Criticism on Thomas Mann's Buddenbrooks and The Magic Mountain* (Columbia, SC: Camden House, 1994), p. 18.
37. M. Jefferies, *Politics and Culture in Wilhelmine Germany: The Case of Industrial Architecture* (Oxford and Washington, DC: Berg, 1995).

38. P. Paret, *Art as History: Episodes in the Culture and Politics of 19th-Century Germany* (Princeton: Princeton University Press, 1988), p. 9.

Notes to Chapter 1: The Historical Context

1. Alsace-Lorraine, annexed from the French in 1871, had a special administrative status in the Empire, comparable to that of a colonial possession.
2. D. Blackbourn, *The Fontana History of Germany, 1780–1918* (London: Fontana, 1997), p. 265.
3. There were two main exceptions: 1871 saw the introduction of a copyright law for the whole Empire, thereby extending the 1867 North German Confederation law. It covered not only written works and theatrical pieces but also illustrations and musical compositions. A new copyright law for works of literature and music was issued in 1901, and in 1907 similar legislation was introduced for works of visual art and photography. The other main exception was the imperial press law of 1874.
4. See M. John, 'Constitution, administration, and the law', in R. Chickering (ed.), *Imperial Germany: A Historiographical Companion* (Westport and London: Greenwood, 1996), pp. 185–214. Also W. J. Mommsen, 'The German Empire as a system of skirted decisions', in Mommsen, *Imperial Germany, 1867–1918* (London: Arnold, 1995).
5. See D. Blackbourn and G. Eley, *The Peculiarities of German History* (Oxford: Oxford University Press, 1984).
6. G. Eley, 'German history and the contradictions of modernity', in G. Eley (ed.), *Society, Culture and the State in Germany 1870–1930* (Ann Arbor: University of Michigan Press, 1996), p. 87.
7. See H.-U. Wehler, 'Wie "bürgerlich" war das Deutsche Kaiserreich?' in his essay collection *Aus der Geschichte lernen?* (Munich: Beck, 1988); T. Nipperdey, *Wie modern war das Kaiserreich? Das Beispiel der Schule* (Opladen: Westdeutscher Verlag, 1986).
8. Stanley Suval suggests that 'almost a third of the German voters had at least some tenuous organizational connection which buttressed their political preferences'. S. Suval, *Electoral Politics in Wilhelmine Germany* (Chapel Hill and London: University of North Carolina Press, 1985), p. 34.
9. R. Koshar, 'The *Kaiserreich's* Ruins', in G. Eley (ed.), *Society, Culture, and the State in Germany 1870–1930* (Ann Arbor: University of Michigan Press, 1996), p. 497.
10. Blackbourn, *The Fontana History of Germany*, p. 159.
11. For a short overview of the topic and suggestions for further reading see D. S. White, 'Regionalism and particularism', in Chickering, *Imperial Germany: A Historiographical Companion*, pp. 131–55. A recent study of particularism in mid-nineteenth century Germany is Abigail Green's *Fatherlands: State-building and Nationhood in Nineteenth-Century Germany* (Cambridge: Cambridge University Press, 2001).
12. The phrase was coined by C. Applegate, *A Nation of Provincials: The*

German Idea of Heimat (Berkeley and London: University of California Press, 1990).

13. A. Confino, *The Nation as a Local Metaphor: Württemberg, Imperial Germany and National Memory, 1871–1918* (Chapel Hill and London: University of North Carolina Press, 1997).
14. M. Walker, *German Home Towns: Community, State, and General Estate, 1648–1871* (Ithaca and London: Cornell University Press, 1971).
15. C. Applegate, 'Localism and the German bourgeoisie', in D. Blackbourn and R. J. Evans (eds), *The German Bourgeoisie* (London and New York: Routledge, 1991), pp. 229–30. See also E. Boa and R. Palfreyman (eds), *Heimat: A German Dream* (Oxford: Oxford University Press, 2000).
16. W. Brepohl, *Industrievolk im Wandel von der agraren zur industriellen Daseinsform, dargestellt am Ruhrgebiet* (Tübingen: Mohr, 1957); K. Rohe, 'Regionalkultur, regionale Identität und Regionalismus im Ruhrgebiet', in W. Lipp (ed.), *Industriegesellschaft und Regionalkultur* (Cologne: Heymann, 1984).
17. See T. Nipperdey, *Deutsche Geschichte, 1866–1918*, vol. 1 (Munich: Beck 1990–2), ch. 13; also R. J. Evans, 'Religion and society in modern Germany' in his essay collection *Rethinking German History* (London: Unwin Hyman, 1987), pp. 125–55; J. Sperber, *Popular Catholicism in the Nineteenth Century* (Princeton: Princeton University Press, 1984); D. Blackbourn, *Class, Religion and Local Politics in Wilhelmine Germany: The Centre Party in Württemberg before 1914* (New Haven and London: Yale University Press, 1980); H. Walser Smith, *German Nationalism and Religious Conflict: Culture, Ideology, Politics, 1870–1914* (Princeton: Princeton University Press, 1995).
18. See the detailed statistics in G. Hübinger, 'Confessionalism', in Chickering (ed.), *Imperial Germany: A Historiographical Companion*, p. 158.
19. Nipperdey, *Deutsche Geschichte, 1866–1918*, vol. 1, p. 488.
20. The number of those actually leaving the churches was very small – just a few thousand per year – but for many church attendance became a less regular occurrence.
21. Blackbourn, *The Fontana History of Germany*, p. 285.
22. See D. Blackbourn's *The Marpingen Visions: Rationalism, Religion and the Rise of Modern Germany* (London: Fontana, 1995).
23. The most recent account of the *Kulturkampf* in English is by R. J. Ross, *The Failure of Bismarck's Kulturkampf: Catholicism and State Power in Imperial Germany, 1871–1887* (Washington, DC: Catholic University of America, 1998).
24. Ross, *The Failure of Bismarck's Kulturkampf*, p. 77.
25. Blackbourn, *The Fontana History of Germany*, p. 262.
26. But the proportion of Catholics voting for the party never again reached its height in the *Kulturkampf* years. See E. L. Evans, *The German Center Party, 1870–1933: A Study in Political Catholicism* (Carbondale: Southern Illinois University Press, 1981); J. K. Zeender, *The German Center Party, 1890–1906* (Philadelphia: American Philosophical Society, 1976); D. Blackbourn, 'The Centre Party and its constituency', in his

collection *Populists and Patricians: Essays in Modern German History* (London: Allen and Unwin, 1987).

27. It was Pope Leo XIII who formally declared an end to the struggle in May 1887.
28. Quoted by R. J. Evans, *The Feminist Movement in Germany, 1894–1933* (London: Sage, 1976), p. 13. The Civil Code did at least recognize women as independent legal subjects, and accepted that a wife's earnings from employment should remain legally hers.
29. Evans, *The Feminist Movement in Germany*, p. 16.
30. In 1901 there were only 7892 divorces in the whole of the Empire. In 1913, just 152 of every 100,000 marriages were terminated by the courts. See V. Berghahn, *Imperial Germany, 1871–1914* (Providence and Oxford: Berghahn, 1994), p. 78.
31. See J. Remak, *The Gentle Critic* (New York: Syracuse University Press, 1964); A. Bance, *Theodor Fontane: The Major Novels* (Cambridge: Cambridge University Press, 1982). A dozen of Fontane's 14 novels had a woman as the main character.
32. J. Quataert, *Reluctant Feminists in German Social Democracy, 1885–1917* (Princeton: Princeton University Press, 1979), p. 23.
33. The laws of association had previously been somewhat more liberal in the free cities of Hamburg and Bremen, and the southwestern states of Baden and Württemberg.
34. A few thousand women property owners (mostly rich spinsters or widows) were entitled to vote in local elections in some parts of the Empire.
35. D. Bänsch in H. Scheuer (ed.), *Naturalismus: Bürgerliche Dichtung und soziales Engagement* (Stuttgart: Kohlhammer, 1974), p. 136. For women writers see C. Diethe, *Towards Emancipation: German Women Writers of the Nineteenth Century* (New York and Oxford: Berghahn, 1998).
36. See D. S. Linton, 'Between school and marriage: young working women as a social problem in late Imperial Germany', *European History Quarterly* (1988), 387–408.
37. Evans, *The Feminist Movement in Germany*, p. 19.
38. See Evans, *The Feminist Movement in Germany*; also B. Greven-Aschoff, *Die bürgerliche Frauenbewegung in Deutschland, 1894–1933* (Göttingen: Vandenhoeck & Ruprecht, 1981).
39. See J. Quataert, *Reluctant Feminists in German Social Democracy, 1885–1917* (Princeton: Princeton University Press, 1979).
40. The real figure was probably no more than a quarter of a million, since many corporate and affiliated members were counted twice, but the Empire still boasted the world's third largest women's movement.
41. J. Quataert in Eley, *Society, Culture and the State in Germany 1870–1930*, p. 52.
42. A. T. Allen, *Feminism and Motherhood in Germany* (New Brunswick: Rutgers University Press, 1991).
43. See C. Koonz, *Mothers in the Fatherland: Women, the Family and Nazi Politics* (London: Methuen, 1987).
44. Allen, *Feminism and Motherhood*, p. 244.

45. See Evans's essay 'Liberalism and society: the feminist movement and social change' in his collection *Rethinking German History*.
46. Evans, 'Liberalism and society: the feminist movement and social change', p. 238.
47. U. Frevert, *Women in German History* (Oxford: Berg, 1989), p. 113.
48. The female workforce numbered 7.79 million out of 23 million in 1882, 9.74 million out of 31.26 million in 1907. This was a higher proportion than in Britain or the USA, but lower than in Austria or France. See Berghahn, *Imperial Germany*, p. 66.
49. See R. J. Evans and W. R. Lee (eds), *The German Family* (London: Croom Helm, 1981).
50. Those who survived birth and their first year could expect to live a decade longer than these figures. See Berghahn, *Imperial Germany*, p. 321.
51. Berghahn, *Imperial Germany*, pp. 78–9.
52. In 1871 the cities were Berlin, Breslau, Cologne, Dresden, Hamburg, Königsberg, Leipzig and Munich. The German statistical definition of a city, as a community with a population over 100,000, was introduced in 1887. See J. Quataert, 'Demographic and Social Change', in Chickering, *Imperial Germany: A Historiographical Companion*, p. 105.
53. Cologne's population increased by 282 per cent; Essen by 438 per cent; and Kiel by 468 per cent, between 1871 and 1910. Figures from Berghahn, *Imperial Germany*, p. 44.
54. See A. Lees, *Cities Perceived: Urban Society in European and American Thought, 1820–1940* (Manchester: Manchester University Press, 1985).
55. Cologne was the last major city to do this in 1875. See B. Ladd, *Urban Planning and Civic Order in Germany, 1860–1914* (Cambridge, MA and London: Harvard University Press, 1990).
56. See R. J. Evans, *Death in Hamburg* (Oxford: Clarendon, 1987).
57. Agriculture's share of the Gross National Product was rather smaller, at around 25 per cent in 1913.
58. See K. Barkin, *The Controversy over German Industrialization* (Chicago: University of Chicago Press, 1970).
59. Berghahn, *Imperial Germany*, p. 123.
60. One of the key features of German industry was its geographical dispersal. Some regions – Upper Silesia, Saxony, the Rhineland – began to develop significant levels of industry much earlier than 1850, but it was not until then that the major industrial region of the Ruhr, with its coal, iron and steel industries, really 'took off'. Between 1870 and 1913 German industrial capacity increased eightfold (benefiting in part from its 'latecomer' status), whereas Britain's only doubled. Germany's lead was particularly apparent in the sectors of the 'second industrial revolution', such as chemicals and electrical engineering. See W. O. Henderson, *The Rise of German Industrial Power, 1834–1914* (London: Temple Smith, 1975).
61. The influential idea that German society was fragmented into self-contained 'milieus', which acted as effective vehicles for political mobilization but which simultaneously lessened the prospects for political reform, is closely identified with the German social scientist M. Rainer

Lepsius. See his essay 'Parteiensystem und Sozialstruktur: Zum Problem der Demokratisierung der deutschen Gesellschaft', in G. A. Ritter (ed.), *Deutsche Parteien vor 1918* (Cologne: Kiepenheuer & Witsch, 1973).

62. W. J. Mommsen, 'Culture and Politics in the German Empire', in Mommsen, *Imperial Germany, 1867–1918*, pp. 119–40.
63. J. Röhl, *The Kaiser and his Court: Wilhelm II and the Government of Germany* (Cambridge: Cambridge University Press, 1994), p. 70.
64. Röhl, *The Kaiser and his Court*, p. 77. The figures are from around 1910.
65. There was no imperial honours system as such, but all the states (with the exception of the three city states) had their own well-developed programme of awards. All Germans with awards were listed in the *Deutscher Ordens-Almanach*, which expanded from 1322 pages in 1904 to 1734 in 1908. By 1914 over 100,000 Germans possessed an order of some sort or other. See A. Thompson, 'Honours uneven: decorations, the state and bourgeois society in Imperial Germany', *Past and Present*, 144 (1994), 171–204.
66. W. J. Mommsen, 'Economy, society and the state', in Mommsen, *Imperial Germany*, p. 114.
67. See M. Gräfin Dönhoff, *Kindheit in Ostpreussen* (Berlin: Siedler, 1988), p. 195.
68. F. L. Carsten, *A History of the Prussian Junkers* (Aldershot: Scolar, 1989), p. 1.
69. Quoted by J. Remak in *The Gentle Critic*, p. 23.
70. See E. K. Bramsted, *Aristocracy and the Middle Classes in Germany: Social Types in German Literature, 1830–1900* (Chicago and London: University of Chicago Press, 1964).
71. See H. Gollwitzer, *Die Standesherren* (Göttingen: Vandenhoeck & Ruprecht, 1964).
72. From a letter of 1881, quoted by J. Remak in *The Gentle Critic*, p. 30.
73. Carsten, *A History of the Prussian Junkers*, p. 127.
74. Such as Count Schaffgotsch's Schloss Koppitz; Prince Hohenlohe-Ingelfingen-Oehringen's rebuilt Schloss Sawentzitz; or Prince Hans Heinrich XI zu Pless's new palace near Komnitz. Perhaps the most impressive of all the Silesian palaces, however, was Schloss Neudeck (1868–75): a 'Silesian Versailles' built for Count Guido Henckel von Donnersmarck.
75. See J. Retallack, *Notables of the Right: The Conservative Party and Political Mobilization in Germany, 1876–1918* (Boston, Mass.: Unwin Hyman, 1988).
76. See Wehler's *The German Empire, 1871–1918* (Leamington Spa: Berg, 1985); or the third volume of his *Deutsche Gesellschaftsgeschichte: von der Deutschen Doppelrevolution bis zum Beginn des Ersten Weltkriegs, 1849–1914* (Munich: Beck, 1995).
77. See Blackbourn and Eley, *The Peculiarities of German History*, for a full discussion of these issues.
78. The titles which enabled thousands of middle-class Germans to advance up the social ladder – *Medizinalrat* for a doctor; *Kommerzienrat* for a businessman, and so on – were based on the archaic system of

court advisors (*Hofräte*) and privy councillors (*Geheimräte*). It was suggested that in this way the bourgeoisie was infused with 'feudal' values, but as Alastair Thompson points out: 'private individuals . . . saw honours primarily in the light of what the state could do for them, rather than what they could do for the state' (Thompson, 'Honours uneven', p. 189). See also K. Kaudelka-Hanisch, 'The titled businessman', in Blackbourn and Evans, *The German Bourgeoisie,* pp. 87–114.

79. See Blackbourn and Evans, *The German Bourgeoisie*; also, J. Kocka and A. Mitchell (eds), *Bourgeois Society in Nineteenth-Century Europe* (Oxford: Berg, 1993); J. Kocka (ed.), *Burger und Bürgerlichkeit im 19. Jahrhundert* (Göttingen: Vandenhoeck & Ruprecht, 1987); G. Cocks and K. Jarausch (eds), *The German Professions, 1800–1950* (Oxford: Oxford University Press, 1990); D. Hein and A. Schulz (eds), *Bürgerkultur im 19. Jahrhundert. Bildung, Kunst und Lebenswelt* (Munich: Beck, 1996), and many more.
80. A view advanced by Blackbourn and Eley in *The Peculiarities of German History.*
81. The various meanings of these terms are discussed by J. Kocka, 'Bürgertum und bürgerliche Gesellschaft im 19. Jahrhundert: Europäische Entwicklungen und deutsche Eigenarten', in J. Kocka (ed.), *Bürgertum im 19. Jahrhundert: Deutschland im europäischen Vergleich,* vol. 1 (Munich: Beck, 1988).
82. See K. Vondung (ed.), *Das wilhelminische Bildungsbürgertum: Zur Sozialgeschichte seiner Ideen* (Göttingen: Vandenhoeck & Ruprecht, 1976).
83. Blackbourn and Evans, *The German Bourgeoisie,* p. xiv.
84. See M. Hettling and S.-L. Hoffmann (eds), *Der bürgerliche Wertehimmel. Innenansichten des 19. Jahrhunderts* (Göttingen: Vandenhoeck & Ruprecht, 2000).
85. A view famously advanced by the French sociologist Pierre Bourdieu in *Distinction: A Social Critique of the Judgement of Taste* (London: Routledge, 1984).
86. W. J. Mommsen, 'Culture and Politics in the German Empire', in Mommsen, *Imperial Germany, 1867–1918,* p. 138.
87. See W. H. Bruford, *The German Tradition of Self-Cultivation* (Cambridge: Cambridge University Press, 1975).
88. Quoted by V. Ullrich, *Die nervöse Grossmacht: Aufstieg und Untergang des deutschen Kaiserreichs, 1871–1918* (Frankfurt: Fischer, 1997), p. 285.
89. Some 90 per cent of children did not advance beyond the free elementary *Volksschulen,* which were usually segregated on lines of gender and confession, and where class sizes could be huge: sometimes over 100 pupils of different ages in a single room (although pupil–teacher ratios did improve steadily throughout the period). The standard leaving age was 14, although the number of pupils staying longer – in so-called 'continuation schools' or in occupational training schools – increased eightfold between 1850 and 1914. Those who continued with their education had two main choices: the grammar school (*Gymnasium*), or the various types of *Realschulen,* which offered a more practical

curriculum but which were generally less prestigious. Since both levied fees, it was extremely difficult for the son of a manual worker to acquire a secondary education. See J. Albisetti, 'Education', in Chickering, *Imperial Germany: A Historiographical Companion,* pp. 244–71.

90. E. M. Butler, *The Tyranny of Greece over Germany* (Cambridge: Cambridge University Press, 1935).
91. M. Naumann, 'Bildung und Gehorsam', in Vondung, *Das wilhelminische Bildungsbürgertum,* p. 34.
92. G. Craig, *Germany, 1866–1945* (Oxford: Oxford University Press, 1978), p. 180.
93. W. J. Mommsen, 'Culture and Politics in the German Empire', p. 139.
94. See Mommsen, 'Culture and Politics in the German Empire'; also Hermann Glaser, *Bildungsburgertum und Nationalismus: Politik und Kultur im Wilhelminischen Deutschland* (Munich: DTV, 1993).
95. Suval, *Electoral Politics in Wilhelmine Germany.*
96. Charles Maier, *Recasting Bourgeois Europe* (Princeton: Princeton University Press, 1975), p. 30.
97. See Suval, *Electoral Politics in Wilhelmine Germany.*
98. See J. J. Sheehan, *German Liberalism in the Nineteenth Century* (Chicago and London: University of Chicago Press, 1978); D. Langewiesche, *Liberalism in Germany* (Basingstoke: Macmillan, now Palgrave Macmillan, 2000); A. Thompson, *Left Liberals, the State, and Popular Politics in Wilhelmine Germany* (Oxford: Oxford University Press, 2000).
99. D. Langewiesche, 'German Liberalism in the Second Empire', in K. Jarausch and L. E. Jones (eds), *In Search of a Liberal Germany: Studies in the History of German Liberalism from 1789 to the Present* (New York: Berg, 1990), p. 219.
100. Mommsen, 'Culture and politics in the German Empire'; see also his essay collection *Bürgerliche Kultur und politische Ordnung* (Frankfurt: Fischer, 2000).
101. Langewiesche, 'German Liberalism in the Second Empire', p. 234.
102. T. Nipperdey, *Wie das Bürgertum die Moderne fand* (Berlin: Siedler, 1988), p. 63.
103. The number of Catholic newspapers grew from 126 in 1870, to 446 in 1912.
104. R. J. Evans, 'Religion and society in modern Germany', in his collection *Rethinking German History,* p. 149.
105. Blackbourn, *The Fontana History of Germany,* p. 301.
106. Nipperdey, *Deutsche Geschichte, 1866–1918,* vol. 1, p. 440. See also H. Heitzer, *Der Volksverein für das katholische Deutschland im Kaiserreich, 1890–1918* (Mainz: Grünewald, 1979).
107. W. Laqueur, *Young Germany: A History of the German Youth Movement* (New York: Basic Books, 1962), p. 70.
108. The phrase was used by the Centre politician Peter Spahn in a Reichstag debate of February 1904, quoted by Mommsen, 'Culture and politics in the German Empire', in *Imperial Germany,* p. 133.
109. See G. A. Ritter, 'Workers' culture in Imperial Germany: Problems and points of departure', in *Journal of Contemporary History,* 13 (1978).

110. L. Abrams, *Workers' Culture in Imperial Germany* (London: Routledge, 1992), p. 192.
111. For an introduction to the 'rough' or deviant side of German working-class life see Evans (ed.), *The German Working Class, 1888–1933* (London: Croom Helm, 1982).
112. The best-known proponents of *Alltagsgeschichte* are Hans Medick, Alf Lüdtke, Lutz Niethammer and Franz Brüggemeier. Landmark publications include Niethammer and Brüggemeier's 'Wie wohnten die Arbeiter im Kaiserreich?' in *Archiv für Sozialgeschichte*, 16 (1976); also J. Reulecke and W. Weber (eds), *Fabrik, Familie, Feierabend. Beiträge zur Sozialgeschichte des Alltags im Industriezeitalter* (Wuppertal: Hammer, 1978); G. Huck (ed.), *Sozialgeschichte der Freizeit. Untersuchungen zum Wandel der Alltagskultur in Deutschland* (Wuppertal: Hammer, 1980); R. J. Evans, *Kneipengespräche im Kaiserreich* (Reinbek: Rowohlt, 1989).
113. As Rainer Hauff notes: 'Although the financial possibilities and the cultural assumptions of the upper and lower social classes were poles apart, a workers' opposition to the decor and furnishings of the propertied classes never materialized' (R. Hauff, *Gründerzeit: Möbel und Wohnkultur* (Westheim: Rhein-Verlag-Haaff, 1992), p. 211).
114. See V. Lidtke, *The Alternative Culture: Socialist Labor in Imperial Germany* (Oxford: Oxford University Press, 1985); Abrams, *Workers' Culture in Imperial Germany*; A. Hall, *Scandal, Sensation and Social Democracy: The SPD Press and Wilhelmine Germany* (Cambridge: Cambridge University Press, 1977); G. A. Ritter (ed.), *Arbeiterkultur* (Königstein: Hain, 1979); B. Emig, *Die Veredelung des Arbeiters: Sozialdemokratie als Kulturbewegung* (Frankfurt: Campus, 1980); W. Hagen, *Die Schillerverehrung in der Sozialdemokratie: zur ideologischen Formation proletarischer Kulturpolitik vor 1914* (Stuttgart: Metzler, 1977).
115. The SAPD's vote declined slightly in 1881; thereafter, however, the party managed to increase its share of the vote at each Reichstag election held before the law was allowed to lapse in 1890.
116. Lidtke, *The Alternative Culture*, p. 17.
117. 1 May, the international workers' day since 1889, took on a mystical, almost religious character in German labour movement culture (the May Day festival had, of course, a long pre-socialist tradition). The day was marked by large-scale public events in the big cities of the Empire, but did not touch some rural communities at all. The 18 March celebrations are now almost totally forgotten, but in the late nineteenth century they were every bit as important. This was the day on which the labour movement remembered both the Berlin uprising of 1848 and the Paris Commune of 1871. Highpoints of the 18 March celebration were in 1873 (the 25th anniversary of the 1848 revolutions) and in 1898 (the 50th anniversary). Thereafter, the day declined in importance, as did 31 August, the anniversary of the death of Lassalle in 1864.
118. A view famously advanced by G. Roth's *The Social Democrats in Imperial Germany: A Study of Working-Class Isolation and National Integration* (Totowa, NJ: Bedminster, 1963).
119. Lidtke, *The Alternative Culture*, p. 6.

120. Lidtke, *The Alternative Culture*, p. 10.
121. Quoted by Lidtke, *The Alternative Culture*, p. 197.
122. Lidtke, *The Alternative Culture*, p. 19.
123. Quoted by W. L. Guttsman, *Art for the Workers: Ideology and the Visual Arts in Weimar Germany* (Manchester: Manchester University Press, 1997), p. 34.

Notes to Chapter 2: Official Culture

1. The Prussian monarchical anthem *Heil Dir im Siegerkranz* was generally played – to the tune of the UK's 'God Save the Queen' – at occasions when the Kaiser was in attendance. Max Schneckenburger's 1840 poem *Die Wacht am Rhein*, which was set to music by Karl Wilhelm in 1854, also enjoyed widespread popularity without becoming an official anthem. Hoffmann von Fallersleben's poem *Deutschland, Deutschland über alles*, united with the familiar melody of Joseph Haydn's 1797 imperial anthem, did not become Germany's national anthem until 1922.
2. For a time it was considered whether the ancient crown of the Holy Roman Empire could be used, with a coronation in an historic setting, such as Aachen or Frankfurt. However, neither Wilhelm I nor the National Liberals were enthusiastic since the crown had too many Catholic associations, and in any case was unlikely to be allowed to leave Vienna. A new Imperial crown was designed but only ever existed as a wooden model.
3. The only mention of an Imperial flag in the 1871 constitution was in the section on shipping and navigation, which provided for the creation of an ensign for the naval and merchant fleets (Article 55). The ensign combined the black and white colours of Prussia with the red of the hanseatic cities. An Imperial order of 8 November 1892 declared formally that a horizontal tricolour of the same colours should be regarded as the national flag. The black, red and gold flag was deemed to be too closely associated with both liberal nationalism and the idea of a 'greater Germany' to be used by the new Empire.
4. The phrase was used as early as 1871 by Edmund Jörg, and more recently by T. Schieder in *Das deutsche Kaiserreich von 1871 als Nationalstaat* (Göttingen: Vandenhoeck & Ruprecht, 1992), first published in 1961.
5. 'Germanization' policies – for instance the compulsory use of the German language in schools – could be imposed with less reticence on the Empire's ethnic minorities.
6. See D. Blackbourn, *The Fontana History of Germany, 1780–1918* (London: Fontana, 1997), p. 265.
7. E. R. Huber in T. Schieder and E. Deuerlein (eds), *Reichsgründung, 1870–71* (Stuttgart: Sewald, 1970), p. 175.
8. A. von Werner, *Erlebnisse und Eindrücke* (Berlin: Mittler, 1913), p. 30.
9. Werner's father was a carpenter. The family name dated back to an ennoblement in the early eighteenth century.

10. Werner's own estimate, see *Erlebnisse und Eindrücke*, p. 32. Toeche-Mittler put the total number of participants at 1391 in his 1896 booklet 'Die Kaiserproklamation in Versailles am 18. Januar 1871', which included a list of all who were present.
11. Werner, *Erlebnisse und Eindrücke*, p. 33.
12. 18 January was the anniversary of Elector Friedrich III's self-coronation as the first King of Prussia in 1701. Werner thought he had been invited to a ceremony to commemorate that event.
13. The various versions are discussed by Werner in *Erlebnisse und Eindrücke*, p. 34.
14. As late as the evening of 17 January, Wilhelm had been insisting he should receive the title 'Emperor of Germany' (*Kaiser Deutschlands*) – which was unacceptable to the rulers of the other German states – rather than 'German Emperor' (*Deutscher Kaiser*).
15. Although photographs were taken in the Palace of Versailles on the day of the Proclamation, none were taken of the ceremony itself.
16. Appropriately, the exhibition took place in the Berlin arsenal, under the auspices of the Berlin Museum and the German Historical Museum. The catalogue, *Anton von Werner. Geschichte in Bildern*, was edited by D. Bartmann (Munich: Hirmer, 1993), who had earlier written a monograph on Werner, *Anton von Werner. Zur Kunst und Kunstpolitik im Deutschen Kaiserreich* (Berlin: Deutscher Verlag für Kunstwissenschaft, 1985).
17. P. Paret, *Art as History: Episodes in the Culture and Politics of 19th Century Germany* (Princeton: Princeton University Press, 1988).
18. T. W. Gaehtgens, *Anton von Werner: Die Proklamierung des Deutschen Kaiserreiches. Ein Historienbild im Wandel preussischer Politik* (Frankfurt: Fischer, 1990).
19. Similarly, the gilded figure on the top of the column was originally conceived by the sculptor Friedrich Drake (1805–82) in 1865 as a Borussia – the female personification of Prussia – but after 1871 she became a Victoria. She faced pointedly towards France from the centre of the Königsplatz until 1938, when the column was moved to its present position and extended on Hitler's orders.
20. Werner, *Erlebnisse und Eindrücke*, pp. 71–2.
21. The painting was destroyed during World War Two.
22. Paret, *Art as History*, p. 178.
23. In his 1913 memoirs, for instance, he speaks out against anti-semitism and makes no secret of his admiration for French culture. See Werner, *Erlebnisse und Eindrücke*.
24. Werner, *Erlebnisse und Eindrücke*, pp. 356–57.
25. Bartmann, *Anton von Werner*, p. 120. This view is further strengthened by the fact that the final scene of Wolfgang Liebeneiner's 1940 film *Bismarck* is a carbon copy of the Friedrichsruh version, with Paul Hartmann playing the Chancellor in a white dress-coat.
26. Gaehtgens, *Anton von Werner*, p. 71.
27. Paret, *Art as History*, p. 169.
28. Paret, *Art as History*, p. 165.
29. The first panoramas date from the late eighteenth century, but they

enjoyed a renaissance across Europe in the 1870s and 1880s. They were particularly popular in France and Belgium. See S. Oettermann, *Das Panorama: Die Geschichte eines Massenmediums* (Frankfurt: Syndikat, 1980). Also D. Sternberger, *Panorama, oder Ansichten vom 19. Jahrhundert* (Frankfurt: Insel, 1978).

30. It took between 15 and 25 minutes to revolve. The project cost around 1 million RM, 100,000 of which went to Werner. On the ground floor of the building was a restaurant, decorated by murals displaying the 'lighter' side of military life. The waitresses wore traditional Alsatian costumes.
31. The demise of the Sedan Panorama, however, also reflected a generational change. The 'Wars of Unification' were pivotal events in the lives of Germans born in mid-century, but subsequent generations needed new heroes and new horizons. The building was demolished in 1904 and the final resting place of the paintings is unknown.
32. See M. Arndt, *Die Goslarer Kaiserpfalz als Nationaldenkmal: Eine ikonographische Untersuchung* (Hildesheim: Lax, 1976).
33. Quoted by Arndt, *Die Goslarer Kaiserpfalz*, p. 6.
34. Arndt, *Die Goslarer Kaiserpfalz*, p. 7.
35. The popular legend that the medieval Emperor Barbarossa was not dead, but merely sleeping in anticipation of the rebirth of the Empire, had become a common subject in nineteenth-century poetry and visual art, and blossomed again towards the end of the century. The legend itself was, however, somewhat inconsistent. It originally referred to Friedrich Barbarossa II, and only later became attached to his grandfather, Friedrich Barbarossa I, who drowned on a crusade in 1190 and whose 'red beard' was an invention of the seventeenth century. The Kyffhäuser was only one of at least three sites in Germany that laid claim to the sleeping emperor.
36. Quoted by Arndt, *Die Goslarer Kaiserpfalz*, p. 12.
37. Quoted in E. Mai and S. Waetzoldt (eds), *Kunstverwaltung, Bau- und Denkmal-Politik im Kaiserreich* (Berlin: Mann, 1981), p. 55.
38. Arndt, *Die Goslarer Kaiserpfalz*, pp. 26–33.
39. See O. Dann (ed.), *Religion – Kunst – Vaterland. Der Kölner Dom im 19. Jahrhundert* (Cologne: J. P. Bachem, 1983), and particularly the essay by T. Nipperdey, 'Der Kölner Dom als Nationaldenkmal'. Nipperdey's essay, which first appeared in the *Historische Zeitschrift*, 233 (1981), was also published in his essay collection *Nachdenken über die deutsche Geschichte* (Munich: Beck, 1986).
40. The idea that the Gothic style originated in the German lands was propagated by Goethe in his 1773 essay 'Von deutscher Baukunst'. In the 1840s Franz Mertens proved that the style actually originated in Northern France, although this did not stop some Germans from continuing to lay claim to it.
41. T. Nipperdey in Dann, *Religion – Kunst – Vaterland*, p. 111.
42. For the procession see W. Hartmann, *Der historische Festzug: Seine Entstehung und Entwicklung im 19. und 20. Jahrhundert* (Munich: Prestel, 1976), pp. 37–41.
43. A decade after the completion of the cathedral in Cologne, similar cel-

ebrations marked the opening of Ulm Cathedral, where the foundation stone had been laid in 1377. Ulm was seen as the Protestant counterpart to Cologne, and gave the Lutheran church a rare chance to mount a major procession of its own.

44. Quoted in Dann, *Religion – Kunst – Vaterland*, p. 167.
45. See C. Tacke, *Denkmal im sozialen Raum: Nationale Symbole in Deutschland und Frankreich im 19. Jahrhundert* (Göttingen: Vandenhoeck & Ruprecht, 1995); and A. Dörner, *Politischer Mythos und symbolische Politik: Der Hermannmythos; zur Entstehung des Nationalbewusstseins der Deutschen* (Reinbek: Rowohlt, 1996). As Tacke's work in particular shows, there was nothing peculiarly German about delving far back into history for national symbols: at the same time as the Hermann Monument was being built, the French were building monuments to Vercingetorix.
46. Although in fact Bavaria's King Ludwig I was a generous contributor.
47. Including some large sums from the United States, where an almost identical Hermann Monument was built (Neu-Ulm, Minnesota, 1897), Greece, Britain (Prince Albert was a keen supporter of the project) and many other countries. Heinrich Heine was also amongst the contributors, despite the sarcastic tone of his comments on the monument in *Germany: A Winter's Tale.*
48. Interestingly, the 11 March 1871 edition of *Punch* carried a cartoon of Wilhelm I – in the guise of Hermann – entering Paris.
49. A. Dörner, *Politischer Mythos und Symbolische Politik* (Reinbek: Rowohlt, 1996), p. 155. He points out that in addition to Heinrich von Kleist's famous 1809 play *Die Hermannsschlacht,* which did not receive its premiere until the 1860s and only gained widespread critical recognition in the 1870s, Hermann also features in plays by Rudolf Brockhausen and Gustav Wacht; as well as Heinrich Hoffmann's opera, with a libretto by Felix Dahn; and a collection of poems, *Armins Lieder,* edited by Hans Ferdinand Massmann (1839). Between 1872 and 1915 there were well over 50 literary re-workings of the Hermann story: see G. Unverfehrt, 'Arminius als nationale Leitfigur' in Mai and Waetzoldt, *Kunstverwaltung, Bau- und Denkmal-Politik,* pp. 315–40.
50. The first book in English to take German monuments seriously was G. L. Mosse's *The Nationalization of the Masses* (New York: Fertig, 1975). Mosse was able to gain his information from a couple of valuable German sources: Nipperdey's 1968 essay 'Nationalidee und Nationaldenkmal in Deutschland im 19. Jahrhundert', since re-published in T. Nipperdey, *Gesellschaft, Kultur, Theorie: Gesammelte Aufsatze zur neueren Geschichte* (Göttingen: Vandenhoeck & Ruprecht, 1976); and the essay collection edited by H.-E. Mittig and V. Plagemann, *Denkmäler im 19. Jahrhundert. Deutung und Kritik* (Munich: Prestel, 1972). Subsequently, a large number of studies have appeared in Germany, both on monuments in general, and on specific structures: R. Alings, *Monument und Nation: das Bild vom Nationalstaat im Medium Denkmal* (Berlin: de Gruyter, 1996); W. Hardtwig, *Geschichtskultur und Wissenschaft* (Munich: DTV, 1990); H. Scharf, *Kleine Kunstgeschichte des deutschen Denkmals* (Darmstadt: Wissenschaftliche Buchgesellschaft,

1984); A. Laumann-Kleineberg, *Denkmäler des 19. Jahrhunderts im Widerstreit* (Frankfurt: Lang, 1989).

51. For the history of the monument see L. Tittel, *Das Niederwalddenkmal, 1871–1883* (Hildesheim: Gerstenberg, 1979). Also P. Mazón, 'Germania triumphant: the Niederwald National Monument and the liberal moment in Imperial Germany', *German History*, 18 (2000) 2, 162–92.
52. This did not stop an Elberfeld anarchist group from attempting to assassinate Wilhelm I during the ceremony. It was, however, a rather sorry tale: the chief plotter fell ill; his deputies managed to place the dynamite but the dampness of the fuses meant it failed to explode. They then made the futile, and ultimately fatal, gesture of throwing the explosives at the building where a celebration banquet was being held. They were arrested and two were executed in Halle in February 1885.
53. Tittel examines the financing of the monument in great detail. It is clear that enthusiasm for the monument amongst the general population was limited, especially in areas of the Empire with resentments against Prussia: Hanover, Bavaria, the Hanseatic cities, and of course Alsace-Lorraine, which contributed just 83 RM. The fact that the project had to be salvaged by the Imperial government was a deep embarrassment to all concerned. In the Reichstag, both the Centre and Social Democrats voted against the 400,000 Mark rescue package (*Das Niederwalddenkmal*, Chapter 5).
54. See L. Gall, 'Die Germania als Symbol nationaler Identität im 19. und 20. Jahrhundert', in *Nachrichten der Akademie der Wissenschaften in Göttingen: 1. Philologisch-historische Klasse*, 1993. Bismarck would have preferred Wilhelm I to be portrayed as the central figure. Failing that, Charlemagne would have been Bismarck's choice. Ironically, later monuments to Bismarck often portrayed him together with Germania.
55. See Gall, 'Die Germania als Symbol nationaler Identität', p. 50.
56. The stamp's design was chosen after a competition judged by Wilhelm II. The winner was Paul Eduard Waldraff, an employee of the Imperial Printing Works, who based his Germania on the popular actress Anna Führing. Führing had played Germania in a procession to mark the opening of the Berlin Kaiser-Wilhelm-Monument in 1897.
57. Mosse, *The Nationalization of the Masses*, pp. 44–5.
58. See the essay by H.-E. Mittig in Mittig and Plagemann, *Denkmäler im 19. Jahrhundert*.
59. And, indeed, overseas: Schmitz built a war memorial in Indianapolis (1888–93) and won a prize for his unbuilt design for the Victor-Emanuel-Monument in Rome (1883).
60. Quoted in J. Müller, 'Das Deutsche Eck bis zur Einweihung des Kaiser-Wilhelm-Denkmals', *Koblenzer Beiträge zur Geschichte und Kultur*, 3 (1997), 51.
61. Quoted by W. Hardtwig in *Geschichtskultur*, p. 287.
62. Quoted by W. Hardtwig in *Geschichtskultur*, p. 256.
63. Quoted by W. Hardtwig in *Geschichtskultur*, p. 288.
64. Quoted by Mosse, *The Nationalization of the Masses*, p. 67.

65. The design was only chosen after two competitions and considerable public debate.
66. This was perhaps the inspiration for the famous scene in Heinrich Mann's novel 'Man of Straw' (*Der Untertan*).
67. In an article in the *Rheinische Kurier* newspaper on 13 April 1871. Heyl was later rewarded by becoming a freeman of Rüdesheim in 1898. A street in the town was also named after him.
68. It remains so today, and although the railway to the monument was replaced by a chair lift in 1954, little else has changed for the hordes of tourists for whom the monument is literally and metaphorically the high point of their Rhine holiday.
69. Quoted by L. Tittel, 'Monumentaldenkmäler von 1871 bis 1918', in Mai and Waetzoldt, *Kunstverwaltung, Bau- und Denkmal-Politik*, p. 235.
70. See Tittel, 'Monumentaldenkmäler von 1871 bis 1918', pp. 257–9.
71. The aforementioned Kuby was not just a businessman, but also an ardent nationalist, with a seat in the Landtag and a political agenda of his own.
72. Not only are these monuments used as meeting points by right-wing extremists, but much controversy surrounds their upkeep and restoration. The best example is the Kaiser-Wilhelm-Monument in Koblenz, which was blown up by the Americans in 1945. In 1987 a wealthy lawyer and publisher, Werner Theisen, announced he was willing to pay for a copy of the equestrian statue, and to mount it on the plinth, which had remained bare for over 40 years. The offer was initially declined by the local and regional authorities, but the majority of local opinion was in favour. After much debate, the gift was accepted, and a newly cast statue was put in place on 2 September 1993.
73. See, for example, F. Schellack, *Nationalfeiertage in Deutschland von 1871 bis 1945* (Frankfurt: Lang, 1990) or his essay in D. Düding *et al.* (eds), *Öffentliche Festkultur: Politische Feste in Deutschland von der Aufklärung bis zum Ersten Weltkrieg* (Reinbek: Rowohlt, 1988). More recently, Alon Confino in *The Nation as a Local Metaphor* has examined the ultimately unsuccessful attempt to establish Sedan Day in Württemberg.
74. The first all-German gymnastics festival was held at Coburg in 1860; the first all-German shooting festival at Gotha in 1861; and the first all-German choir festival at Dresden in 1865. The festivals of shooting societies (*Schützenfeste*) usually fell into two parts: a shooting competition and a public fair, with stalls offering food, drink and games.
75. Quoted by F. Schellack in Düding *et al.* (eds), *Öffentliche Festkultur*, p. 279.
76. Schellack suggests the Emperor's negative response was at least in part because of the liberal convictions of the men behind the proposal: certainly, the likes of Bluntschli and Holtzendorff were seen as dangerously left-wing by many at the Prussian court. Schellack, *Nationalfeiertage in Deutschland*, p. 72.
77. See P.-C. Witt, 'Die Gründung des Deutschen Reiches von 1871 oder dreimal Kaiserfest', in U. Schultz (ed.), *Das Fest: Eine Kulturgeschichte von der Antike bis zur Gegenwart* (Munich: Beck, 1988), p. 451.
78. See A. Herzig, 'Die Lassalle-Feiern in der politischen Festkultur der

frühen deutschen Arbeiterbewegung', in D. Düding *et al.*, *Öffentliche Festkultur*, pp. 321f.

79. Alsace-Lorraine, Saxony, Württemberg, Hamburg and Lübeck were amongst the states where the Emperor's birthday was not an official holiday. Bavaria, which had its own highly developed calender of dynastic celebrations, had particular problems with the Emperor's birthday.
80. Quoted by F. Schellack in D. Düding *et al.*, *Öffentliche Festkultur*, p. 287.
81. It was agreed during the unification negotiations of 1870 that these two states could retain the right to operate their own postal services.
82. See A. Seemann, 'Die Postpaläste Heinrich von Stephans', University of Kiel PhD dissertation, 1990.
83. The first plan bearing Wilhelm II's suggestions was for a post office in Memel (1890–1). See P. Seidel, *Der Kaiser und die Kunst* (Berlin: Reichsdruckerei, 1907).
84. E. Krickeberg, *Heinrich von Stephan* (Dresden and Leipzig: unknown publisher, 1897), p. 258.
85. See H. Marschall, *Friedrich von Thiersch: Ein Münchener Architekt des Späthistorismus, 1852–1921* (Munich: Prestel, 1982).
86. See P. Landau, 'Reichjustizgesetze und Justizpaläste', in E. Mai, H. Pohl and S. Waetzoldt (eds), *Kunstpolitik und Kunstförderung im Kaiserreich* (Berlin: Mann, 1982). The proliferation of new courthouses at this time was essentially a consequence of the increasingly public nature of justice.
87. See the essays in Mai and Waetzold, *Kunstverwaltung, Bau- und Denkmal-Politik* by K. Nohlen and H. Hammer-Schenk; also Nohlen's book, *Baupolitik im Reichsland Elsass-Lothringen* (Berlin: Mann, 1982).
88. Chairs in German Philology had been established at a few universities in the first half of the nineteenth century, but the eagerness of Germanists to become involved in political affairs had a deterrent effect on state authorities. In any case, German literary studies did not really take on a scholarly character until the second half of the century. The Strasbourg example was followed by Berlin University in 1877.
89. See W. Feldenkirchen, 'Staatliche Kunstfinanzierung im 19. Jahrhundert', in E. Mai, Pohl and Waetzoldt, *Kunstpolitik und Kunstförderung im Kaiserreich*, p. 49.
90. Quoted by W. Pape (ed.), *German Unifications and the Change of Literary Discourse* (Berlin and New York: de Gruyter, 1993), p. 7.
91. Quoted by M. Makela, *The Munich Secession: Art and Artists in Turn-of-the-Century Munich* (Princeton: Princeton University Press, 1990), p. 35.
92. This grew steadily in later years, although the Gallery continued to rely to a large extent on the Prussian royal purse. See C. With, *The Prussian Landeskunstkommission* (Berlin: Mann, 1986).
93. Virtually all Berlin-based institutions, whether Prussian or imperial, gained in power and prestige after 1871, although the able leadership of Richard Schöne, Director General of Berlin Museums from 1879 to 1905, and Wilhelm (von) Bode, who remained in post into the Weimar Republic, no doubt helped. The Kaiser-Friedrich-Museum was renamed the Bode Museum in honour of the latter.

94. See M. S. Cullen, *Der Reichstag: Die Geschichte eines Monumentes* (Berlin: Frölich & Kaufmann, 1983). Also U. Haltern, 'Architektur und Politik. Zur Baugeschichte des Berliner Reichstags', in Mai and Waetzoldt, *Kunstverwaltung, Bau- und Denkmal-Politik*, pp. 75–102.
95. As in the first competition, the reasons for the jury's selections were not made public, nor were they recorded for posterity.
96. The famous dedication of the Reichstag building to the German people (*dem deutschen Volke*) was only actually carved into the building's pediment in December 1916, using a typeface designed by Peter Behrens. The reason why it took so many years to complete this part of the design is not clear, but it may have been due to the opposition of Wilhelm II, who had suggested that a dedication to German unity (*Der Deutschen Einigkeit*) would be more appropriate.
97. See the article by T. Buddensieg, 'Kuppel des Volkes. Zur Legitimität eines demokratischen Symbols', in the *Frankfurter Allgemeine Zeitung*, 2 October 1992.
98. Quoted by M. Cullen in *Der Reichstag*, p. 36.
99. Cullen, *Der Reichstag*, p. 36.
100. Cullen, *Der Reichstag*, p. 185.
101. Cullen, *Der Reichstag*, p. 38.
102. Cullen, *Der Reichstag*, p. 203.
103. Cullen, *Der Reichstag*, p. 155.
104. Wilhelm II, for instance, famously rejected the award of gold medals to Wallot (1890), the artist Käthe Kollwitz (1898) and the sculptor of the Bismarck Monument in Hamburg, Hugo Lederer (1908).
105. G. Malkowsky, *Die Kunst im Dienste der Staats-Idee. Hohenzollernsche Kunstpolitik vom Grossen Kurfürsten bis auf Wilhelm II* (Berlin: Patria, 1912), p. 224.
106. Quoted by P. Seidel, *Der Kaiser und die Kunst* (Berlin: Reichsdruckerei, 1907), p. 9.

Notes to Chapter 3: The *Gründerzeit*

1. Some authors are even less specific. Rolf Linnenkamp, for instance, defines it as the period 1835–1918, that he divides into 'early-', 'high-' and 'late-' *Gründerzeit*, whilst Hans Otto talks about a 'first' and 'second' *Gründerzeit*, and Günter Ogger chooses 1830 and 1900 as his key dates. See R. Linnenkamp, *Die Gründerzeit 1835–1918* (Munich: Heyne, 1976); H. Otto, *Gründerzeit: Aufbruch einer Nation* (Bonn: Keil, 1984); and G. Ogger, *Die Gründerjahre: Als der Kapitalismus jung und verwegen war* (Munich: Knaur, 1982).
2. E. Friedell, *Kulturgeschichte der Neuzeit*, vol. 3 (Munich: Beck, 1931), p. 357.
3. Quoted by R. Hauff, *Gründerzeit. Möbel und Wohnkultur* (Westheim: Rhein-Verlag–Haaff, 1992), pp. 18–19.
4. Academic interest had started to develop a few years earlier. Today houses and apartments from the period are highly sought-after. *Gründerzeit* furniture gained further popularity in the 1990s as a conse-

quence of German reunification, since many more good pieces survived in GDR households than in the West.

5. An honourable, if tendentious, exception is volume 1 of Richard Hamann and Jost Hermand's *Epochen deutscher Kultur von 1870 bis zur Gegenwart*, entitled simply *Gründerzeit*, first published in 1965. Hamann (1879–1961) was probably the first writer to use the term in the context of art history, in his 1914 book *Die deutsche Malerei im 19. Jahrhundert*.
6. These include E. Mai and S. Waetzoldt (eds), *Kunstverwaltung, Bau- und Denkmal-Politik im Kaiserreich* (Berlin: Mann, 1981); E. Mai, H. Pohl and S. Waetzoldt (eds.), *Kunstpolitik und Kunstförderung im Kaiserreich* (Berlin: Mann, 1982); E. Mai, J. Paul and S. Waetzoldt (eds), *Das Rathaus im Deutschen Kaiserreich* (Berlin: Mann, 1982); E. Mai, S. Waetzoldt and G. Wolandt (eds), *Ideengeschichte und Kunstwissenschaft im Kaiserreich* (Berlin: Mann, 1983); E. Mai and P. Paret (eds), *Sammler, Stifter und Museen. Kunstförderung in Deutschland im 19. und 20. Jahrhundert* (Cologne: Böhlau, 1993); K. Nohlen, *Baupolitik im Reichsland Elsass-Lothringen* (Berlin: Mann, 1982); C. With, *The Prussian Landeskunstkommission* (Berlin: Mann, 1986).
7. Quoted in D. Bartmann (ed.), *Anton von Werner*, p. 26. The guild had been founded in 1856, with branches in 21 cities. It lobbied for regular exhibitions of German art – essentially historical paintings with patriotic themes – and for a national gallery to house the works of artists from all the German states.
8. See J. Link and W. Wülfing (eds), *Nationale Mythen und Symbole in der zweiten Hälfte des 19. Jahrhunderts* (Stuttgart: Klett-Cotta, 1991), p. 218.
9. Quoted by H. J. Schoeps, *Zeitgeist im Wandel* (Stuttgart: Klett, 1967), p. 12.
10. R. M. Meyer quoted by Walter Pape (ed.), *German Unifications and the Change of Literary Discourse* (Berlin and New York: de Gruyter, 1993), p. 1.
11. The line comes from the poem *Deutschlands Beruf* (1861).
12. Evident, for instance, in the way that Virchow claimed genetics was essentially a German concept, or in the way Ernst Haeckel 'germanicized' Darwin's teachings on evolution.
13. See P. U. Hohendahl, *Building a National Literature: The Case of Germany, 1830–1870* (Ithaca and London: Cornell University Press, 1989).
14. The best known of the cheap editions was 'Reclams Universal Library', begun by the Leipzig publisher Anton Philip Reclam in 1867. The first Reclam title was Goethe's *Faust*, which cost just two Groschen (a price which was to remain unchanged for the next 50 years). The biggest Reclam seller, however, was Schiller's *Wilhelm Tell*. In 1870 German book production passed 10,000 new titles per annum for the first time: by 1910 some 30,000 new titles were appearing yearly.
15. See K. Mattheier, 'Standardsprache als Sozialsymbol', in R. Wimmer (ed.), *Das 19. Jahrhundert. Sprachgeschichtliche Wurzeln des heutigen Deutsch* (Berlin and New York: de Gruyter, 1991).
16. In the course of the nineteenth century the educated middle classes of northern Germany had increasingly adopted *Hochdeutsch* as their first

language, and the use of Low German dialect had become associated with a lack of education and social status. This trend accelerated after 1871.

17. K. Mattheier, 'Standardsprache als Sozialsymbol', pp. 49–50.
18. M. Durrell, 'Standard language and the creation of national myths in nineteenth-century Germany', in J. Barkhoff, G. Carr and R. Paulin (eds), *Das schwierige neunzehnte Jahrhundert* (Tübingen: Niemeyer, 2000), p. 21.
19. Quoted by R. Chickering, 'Language and the social foundations of radical nationalism', in Pape, *German Unifications and the Change of Literary Discourse*, p. 70.
20. All statistics from R. Chickering, 'Language and the Social Foundations of Radical Nationalism', pp. 70–6. See also C. J. Wells, *German: A Linguistic History to 1945* (Oxford: Clarendon, 1985).
21. These included: 'Telephon' (*Fernsprecher* was better); 'Sektion' (*Abteilung*); 'poste restante' (*postlagernd*); 'Passagierbillet' (*Fahrschein*) and so on.
22. Durrell, 'Standard language and the creation of national myths', p. 18.
23. See K. Milde, *Neorenaissance in der deutschen Architektur des 19. Jahrhunderts* (Dresden: Verlag der Kunst, 1981).
24. Lübke's books, such as *Deutsche Kunst des 16. Jahrhunderts* (1853), and *Die Geschichte der deutschen Renaissance* (1871–73) highlighted the originality of German Renaissance architecture, which he suggested was more romantic and picturesque than that of Italy.
25. Hirth's best-known publications were the series *Der Formenschatz der Renaissance* (1877) and *Das Deutsche Zimmer vom Mittelalter bis zur Gegenwart*, which included *Das Deutsche Zimmer der Renaissance* (1880). Hirth was editor and later co-owner of the *Münchener Neuesten Nachrichten*, south Germany's leading newspaper. He was also the first man in Munich to own a telephone (1883).
26. The paintings were usually still-life, landscape or genre scenes. The latter usually had a moral message: that family loyalty, friendship, hard work and piety pay off in the end.
27. W. Brönner in E. Mai *et al.* (eds), *Kunstpolitik und Kunstförderung im Kaiserreich*, p. 374.
28. In this the influence of Jacob Burckhardt's classic *The Culture of the Renaissance in Italy* (1860) is readily apparent.
29. W. Dilthey, *Gesammelte Schriften*, vol. 17 (Göttingen: Vandenhoeck & Ruprecht, 1974), p. 269.
30. See M. Gregor-Dellin, *Das kleine Wagner-Buch* (Reinbek: Rowohlt, 1982), p. 69.
31. Treitschke (1834–96) was Professor of History at Berlin University and also a National Liberal member of the Reichstag.
32. See M. Lewis, *The Politics of the German Gothic Revival: August Reichensperger* (Cambridge, MA: MIT, 1993), p. 4. For the neo-Gothic in general see G. Germann, *Neugotik. Geschichte ihrer Architekturtheorie* (Stuttgart: DVA, 1974).
33. Quoted by V. Hammerschmidt, *Anspruch und Ausdruck in der Architektur des späten Historismus in Deutschland* (Frankfurt: Lang, 1985), p. 60.

34. Quoted by M. Brix and M. Steinhauser, 'Geschichte im Dienste der Baukunst', in M. Brix and M. Steinhauser (eds), *Geschichte allein ist zeitgemäss: Historismus in Deutschland* (Lahn-Giessen: Anabas, 1978), p. 272.
35. P. Paret, *Art as History: Episodes in the Culture and Politics of Nineteenth-Century Germany* (Princeton: Princeton University Press, 1988), p. 141.
36. See W. Hardtwig's *Geschichtskultur und Wissenschaft* (Munich: DTV, 1990).
37. A. Wittkau, *Historismus: Zur Geschichte des Begriffs und des Problems* (Göttingen: Vandenhoeck and Ruprecht, 1992), p. 27.
38. Hardtwig, *Geschichtskultur und Wissenschaft*, p. 236.
39. Quoted by P. Kohl and C. Fawcett in *Nationalism, Politics and the Practice of Archaeology* (Cambridge: Cambridge University Press, 1995), p. 13. In fact, to stretch Hobsbawm's analogy further, a historian like Treitschke, whose works helped to undermine liberal opposition to Bismarck and shaped the way middle-class Germans viewed their history for many years to come, was actually more like a 'pusher'.
40. For instance, the Schiller centenary celebrations in 1859, or Martin Luther's 400th birthday, which fell in 1883 and was marked by a series of events, monuments and publications, including Treitschke's *Luther and the German Nation.*
41. See G. Iggers, *The German Conception of History* (Middletown: Wesleyan University Press, 1968); Wittkau, *Historismus: Zur Geschichte des Begriffs und des Problems*; Hardtwig, *Geschichtskultur und Wissenschaft.*
42. Iggers, *The German Conception of History*, p. 17. Historicism was therefore in part a rejection of the Enlightenment faith in abstract 'reason' and the universal claims of the French Revolution. Some believe this had profound consequences for German politics. In particular the historicist belief that every state was unique, and embodied its own spirit and values, is often highlighted as significant for the course of German history in the nineteenth and twentieth centuries.
43. Iggers, *The German Conception of History*, p. 26.
44. The second of his *Untimely Meditations*, its German title was 'Vom Nutzen und Nachteil der Historie für das Leben'.
45. Volumes of decorative patterns and templates taken from a wide range of historical styles.
46. Especially at the 1867 Paris fair. Subsequent events took place in 1873 (Vienna); 1876 (Philadelphia); 1878 (Paris); 1879 (Sydney); 1887 (Melbourne); 1889 (Paris); 1893 (Chicago). Attendances rose from 7 million (Vienna) and 10 million (Philadelphia), to 27 million (Chicago) and an incredible 50 million in Paris (1900).
47. Quoted in Mai, Pohl and Waetzoldt (eds), *Kunstpolitik und Kunstförderung im Kaiserreich*, p. 115.
48. See B. Mundt, *Die deutschen Kunstgewerbemuseen im 19. Jahrhundert* (Munich: Prestel, 1974). A museum of applied art had been established in Berlin in 1867, but by a private association; it was later taken over by the Prussian state. Prussia's first state schools of applied art were established in Breslau (1876), Frankfurt (1879), Kassel (1882) and Düsseldorf (1883): by the 1900s there were over 30 of them.

49. Quoted in Brix and Steinhauser (eds), *Geschichte allein ist zeitgemäss*, p. 199.
50. In his *Studien zur Wirkungsgeschichte des deutschen historischen Romans 1850–75*, Hartmut Eggert listed 427 such novels (many of which came in two or three volumes) by 156 authors. See G. Hirschmann, *Kulturkampf im historischen Roman der Grunderzeit 1859–1878* (Munich: Fink, 1978), p. 7.
51. Quoted by Paret, in *Art as History*, p. 142. Scheffel also had great success with the epic poem *Der Trompeter von Säckingen*, a love story from the late seventeenth century that was later turned into an opera.
52. Quoted by E. Park, *Fontane's Zeitromane: Zur Kritik der Gründerzeit* (Frankfurt: Lang, 1997), p. 17.
53. Paret, *Art as History*, p. 185.
54. In the 15 years from 1869 the number of German theatres rose from around 200 to over 600, after they were granted freedom of trade by the Commercial Code of 1869/71. In Berlin there had been eight theatres in September 1869; by the end of the year there were 20. Of these, only the Royal Playhouse and the Opera House were in receipt of subsidy. Inevitably, the vast majority of the new venues offered trivial and lightweight commercial fare, although others like the Deutsches Theater (1883) and the Berliner Theater (1888) offered more heavyweight productions.
55. S. Kiefer, *Dramatik der Gründerzeit: deutsches Drama und Theater, 1870–1890* (St Ingbert: Röhrig, 1997), p. 115.
56. See J. Osborne, *The Meiningen Court Theatre, 1866–90* (Cambridge: Cambridge University Press, 1988). The Meininger staged a total of nearly 3000 performances in 41 European cities between 1874 and 1890. Of these, over 2000 were of plays by Shakespeare or Schiller. The Duke himself did not accompany the troupe on tour.
57. The company took more risks in its own theatre, where the Duke removed censorship restrictions, staging the first performance of an Ibsen play in Germany (*The Pretenders* in 1876) and premiering the same writer's *Ghosts* ten years later.
58. F. Spotts, *Bayreuth: A History of the Wagner Festival* (New Haven and London: Yale University Press, 1994), p. 60.
59. A. von Werner, *Erlebnisse und Eindrücke 1870–1890*, pp. 166–70.
60. F. Spotts, *Bayreuth: A History of the Wagner Festival*, p. 74.
61. See W. Hartmann, *Der historische Festzug: Seine Entstehung und Entwicklung im 19. und 20. Jahrhundert* (Munich: Prestel, 1976).
62. It was rare for industrial workers to participate, unless they were members of middle-class associations.
63. The upsurge of historical processions in the late nineteenth century was at least partly motivated by economic considerations. Just as towns sought to attract visitors by erecting monuments, so civic and business leaders were well aware of the benefits that could be gained by staging spectacular processions and pageants: in 1886 nearly 100,000 people travelled on special trains to Heidelberg to watch the university's jubilee procession. See W. Hartmann, *Der historische Festzug*, p. 42/ p. 136.

64. J. Osborne, *The Meiningen Court Theatre, 1866–90*, p. 13.
65. See G. Baumgartner, *Königliche Träume: Ludwig II und seine Bauten* (Munich: Hugendubel, 1981).
66. Herrenchiemsee was kept secret from the public, and little was known about it until after Ludwig's death.
67. The money, totalling 4 million RM, was in return for Ludwig's grudging support for the *Reichsgründung* in 1871, and reflected Bismarck's desire to keep the ineffectual Ludwig on the Bavarian throne for as long as possible. It came in part from the *Welfenfonds*; the confiscated treasury of the Hanoverian kings.
68. Quoted by Brix and Steinhauser, *Geschichte allein ist zeitgemäss*, p. 306.
69. See E. Mai (ed.), *Historienmalerei in Europa* (Mainz: von Zabern, 1990).
70. It was not surprising, therefore, that large-scale historical paintings were frequently commissioned in newly independent or united countries as part of the state-building process.
71. Quoted by M. Wagner, *Allegorie und Geschichte* (Tübingen: Wasmuth, 1989), p. 1.
72. F. Kugler quoted by Paret, *Art as History*, p. 23.
73. Art's new bourgeois patrons much preferred genre, landscape and still-life scenes, which could more easily be accommodated in domestic surroundings.
74. In other words, after the 'founders' rather than the act of 'founding'.
75. Quoted by Hamann and Hermand, *Grunderzeit*, p. 39.
76. Quoted by G. Blochmann, *Zeitgeist und Künstlermythos. Untersuchungen zur Selbstdarstellung deutscher Maler der Gründerzeit* (Münster: Lit, 1991), p. 17. This hero worship took a strange turn in the work of Paul Möbius, whose 'pathographies' of Rousseau (1889), Goethe (1898), Schopenhauer (1899) and Nietzsche (1902) emphasized the 'sickness' and 'degeneracy' of supposedly great men.
77. The idea was first mooted in 1807, but was not built until the 1830s. It employed a very broad definition of 'German', including Scandinavians, Dutchmen and Baltic Russians.
78. T. Carlyle, *On Heroes, Hero-worship and the Heroic in History* (London: Chapman and Hall, 1872), p. 1. Carlyle (1795–1881) enjoyed particular popularity in Germany, not least because of his familiarity with German history and literature.
79. By 1900 there were over 80 art associations in towns and cities across the Empire. In Frankfurt it had over 2000 members. Such associations enabled middle-class Germans to obtain original works, which were usually allocated to members by lottery.
80. According to Erwin Panofsky, German was the 'mother tongue' of Art History. In the *Grunderzeit* there were four Chairs in Art History. By 1912 there were 15 of them at universities, plus a further 11 in polytechnics. See T. Nipperdey, *Deutsche Geschichte, 1866–1918*, vol. 1 (Munich: Beck, 1990–2), p. 644.
81. Nipperdey, *Deutsche Geschichte, 1866–1918*, vol. 1, pp. 692–715. This was, of course, also a legacy of German idealism, which had assigned to art a crucial role in the human and moral development of the individual.

82. Quoted by M. Makela, *The Munich Secession* (Princeton: Princeton University Press, 1990), p. 15.
83. See S. Wichmann, *Franz von Lenbach und seine Zeit* (Cologne: Dumont, 1973).
84. An English expression that entered the German language in untranslated form at this time.
85. Blochmann, *Zeitgeist und Künstlermythos*, p. 85.
86. Quoted by Blochmann, *Zeitgeist und Künstlermythos*, p. 91.
87. The painting, also known by the name 'The Seven Deadly Sins', was later to fall into the possession of both Mussolini and Hitler.
88. Makart's *atelier* was broken up after his death in 1884, but it survives in photographs and in a watercolour by Rudolf von Alt (1885).
89. The funeral procession, led by 200 torchbearers in Spanish costume, attracted such large crowds that the Ringstrasse had to be closed to traffic.
90. At the age of 25 he had been offered a professorship at Karlsruhe; in 1860 he received a similar offer from Weimar; and in 1872 from the Viennese academy. He briefly accepted the latter post, which placed him in charge of the classes in historical painting, but left because of the all-pervasive influence of Makart in the Austrian capital.
91. Quoted by R. Hamann and J. Hermand, *Gründerzeit*, p. 35.
92. See Blochmann, *Zeitgeist und Künstlermythos*, p. 58.
93. The book proved enormously popular, reaching its 45th edition in 1926.
94. I. Koszinowski, 'Böcklin und seine Kritiker', in E. Mai, S. Waetzoldt and G. Wolandt (eds), *Ideengeschichte und Kunstwissenschaft: Philosophie und bildende Kunst im Kaiserreich* (Berlin: Mann, 1983), pp. 279–92.
95. Böcklin worked briefly for Count Schack, but his breakthrough came with his second move to Munich in 1871, where he was able to benefit from the economic boom by securing remarkably high prices for his work. He hoped the Villa Bellagio would become a museum after his death. Significantly, however, Böcklin's fame never extended far beyond the German-speaking world, and the Italians had little respect for a peculiarly German shrine.
96. Quoted by Koszinowski, 'Böcklin und seine Kritiker', p. 281.
97. N. A. Silberman in Kohl and Fawcett, *Nationalism, Politics, and the Practice of Archaeology*, p. 251.
98. The judgement of K. von Burg in *Heinrich von Schliemann – For Gold or Glory?* (Watford: Windsor, 1987).
99. In addition to Burg's book, Schliemann's reputation has taken a battering from the works of the Americans William Calder and David Traill. See Traill's *Schliemann of Troy: Treasure and Deceit* (London: Murray, 1995).
100. It is now accepted that the treasures, which resurfaced in 1990s Russia after disappearing from Berlin in 1945, are genuine, although not from the time of Homer's King Priam. It is likely, however, that Schliemann 'bundled' together objects uncovered at different times and in different trenches, to create his spectacular haul.
101. The importance of the classical world to nineteenth-century Germans

was indicated by the fact that the Empire maintained archaeological institutes in both Athens and Rome. Indeed, such was the prestige and dominance of classical archaeology in German universities and in the public mind, that researchers into German prehistory faced an uphill battle for recognition.

102. Quoted by Traill, *Schliemann of Troy*, p. 4.
103. Quoted by Spotts, *Bayreuth*, p. 130.
104. The reviews were mixed, to say the least. The stifling heat of the theatre in August, and the length of the performances, left many critics drained. The popular journal *Gartenlaube* pulled no punches, calling the whole Bayreuth enterprise 'a swindle and a fraud'. Quoted by Gregor-Dellin, *Das kleine Wagner-Buch*, p. 13.
105. Spotts, *Bayreuth*, p. 6.
106. Werner, *Erlebnisse und Eindrücke*, pp. 166–70.
107. Spotts, *Bayreuth*, pp. 76–7.
108. Gregor-Dellin, *Das kleine Wagner-Buch*, p. 78.
109. Letter to Liszt, quoted by Spotts, *Bayreuth*, p. 33.
110. Albeit less dramatically than Nietzsche's, whose love for the composer turned into an equally passionate hatred.
111. Spotts, *Bayreuth* , p. 51.
112. Spotts, *Bayreuth*, p. viii.
113. Spotts, *Bayreuth*, p. 91.
114. It should be noted, however, that Wagner did not use the term *Leitmotiv* himself, and certainly did not invent the concept, which had earlier appeared in the works of Weber and Liszt, amongst others.
115. As Peter Vergo has pointed out, Wagner actually preferred the term *Gesamtvolkskunst* or *Kunstwerk des Gesamtvolkes.* In practice he was less concerned about maintaining personal control over every aspect of the work than in developing its communal, ritualistic character. Later artists who adopted the term *Gesamtkunstwerk* concentrated on the former, rather than the latter meaning, and wrongly invoked Wagner's authority to support the idea that the arts were growing ever closer together. See Vergo's 'The origins of Expressionism and the notion of the *Gesamtkunstwerk*', in S. Behr, D. Fanning and D. Jarman (eds), *Expressionism Reassessed* (Manchester: Manchester University Press, 1993).
116. V. Plagemann, 'Bismarck-Denkmäler', in Mittig and Plagemann, *Denkmäler im 19. Jahrhundert*, pp. 217–52. H.-W. Hedinger, 'Bismarck-Denkmäler und Bismarck-Verehrung', in Mai and Waetzoldt, *Kunstverwaltung, Bau- und Denkmal-Politik*, pp. 277–314.
117. His 75th, in the year of his dismissal as Chancellor.
118. Pipes, ashtrays, beer tankards and many other items. See K. Breitenborn, *Bismarck: Kult und Kitsch um den Reichsgründer* (Frankfurt: Keip, 1990).
119. It now stands in the Tiergarten, half a mile from its original site, but still in the shadow of the similarly relocated Victory Column.
120. Even so, Bismarck monuments certainly had their opponents too: projects were hampered by strikes, boycotts and vandalism. Town councils in Catholic areas were known to have refused to back partic-

ular schemes. In Hagen the Bismarck tower was confronted by a monument to the left-liberal leader Eugen Richter – one of Bismarck's most stubborn opponents – just half a mile away.

121. The 'chain of beacons' never functioned as the students had hoped, since it proved difficult to produce a suitably giant flame.
122. Wilhelm Kreis had won a design competition in 1898–9, which had attracted 320 entries.
123. See M. Russell, 'The building of Hamburg's Bismarck Memorial, 1898–1906', *Historical Journal*, 43 (2000), 133–56.
124. See Plagemann 'Bismarck-Denkmäler'.
125. R. J. Evans (ed.), *Society and Politics in Wilhelmine Germany* (London: Croom Helm, 1978), p. 17.
126. See J. P. Stern, *On Realism* (London: Routledge, 1973); or L. Furst, *All is True: the Claims and Struggles of Realist Fiction* (Durham and London: Duke University Press, 1995).
127. See, for instance, W. J. Mommsen, 'Culture and Politics in the German Empire', in Mommsen, *Imperial Germany. 1867–1918: Politics, Culture and Society in an Authoritarian State* (London: Arnold, 1995), p. 128.
128. See D. Blackbourn and G. Eley, *The Peculiarities of German History* (Oxford: Oxford University Press, 1984).
129. For a full exploration of these themes see M. Swales, *Studies of German Prose Fiction in the age of European Realism* (Lampeter: Mellen, 1995).
130. Bethel Henry Strousberg (1823–84) was arguably the most famous *Gründer* of all. A converted East Prussian Jew, he rose from poor circumstances to become one of the richest men in the world before his spectacular fall from grace. He made his fortune building railway lines and became known as 'the man who buys everything'.
131. F. Spielhagen, *Sturmflut* (Leipzig: Staackmann, 1877), p. 95.
132. Although Kretzer came from a middle-class background, he went to work in a factory at the age of 13 when his father's business went bankrupt. His best-known work is probably the family saga *Meister Timpe* (1888). See K. Roper, *German Encounters with Modernity: Novels of Imperial Berlin* (Atlantic Highlands, NJ and London: Humanities Press, 1991).
133. Quoted by Park, *Fontane's Zeitromane*, p. 29.
134. The title of J. Remak's study of Fontane, published in 1964.
135. See H. Ridley, *The Problematic Bourgeois* (Columbia, SC: Camden House, 1994), p. 15. Ridley points out that in the book's very first scene, French, High German, Low German and prayer-book German all make an appearance.
136. M. Travers, *Thomas Mann* (Basingstoke: Macmillan, 1992), p. 18.
137. See F. Stern, *The Politics of Cultural Despair* (Berkeley and London: University of California Press, 1961).
138. Ridley, *The Problematic Bourgeois*, p. 24.
139. F. Forster-Hahn, *Imagining Modern German Culture*, pp. 71–90. This was partly possible because many of Menzel's paintings were not shown in his lifetime, at the artist's own insistence, and so were only discovered after his death.

Notes to Chapter 4: Cultural Critics and Revolts

1. The laureates included men like Adolf von Baeyer (1835–1917) and Karl Bosch (1874–1940) for their work on synthetic dyes; Wilhelm Röntgen (1845–1923) for the discovery of the X-ray (1895); Emil von Behring (1854–1917), who developed a vaccine against diptheria; and Robert Koch (1843–1910), whose institute was the epicentre of a bacteriological revolution which changed the course of medical history. Between 1901 and 1925 Germans won 10 of the 31 prizes for Physics and 9 of the 22 prizes for Chemistry. See T. Nipperdey, *Deutsche Geschichte, 1866–1918,* vol. 1 (Munich: Beck, 1990–92), p. 602.
2. Quoted by D. Blackbourn, *The Fontana History of Germany,* (London: Fontana, 1997), p. 283.
3. Strictly speaking, positivism was a philosophical school associated with the likes of Auguste Comte and Herbert Spencer, but the term is also used more generally to characterize the practice of approaching problems in the manner of the natural scientist: by searching, for instance, for precise chains of causation. To its critics, positivism implied a materialistic and mechanistic approach that failed to account for the inexplicable, the irrational and the non-logical.
4. Of course, Darwin's works, such as *On the Orgin of Species* (1859) and *The Descent of Man* (1871), were known to most people only in slogan form: 'natural selection', the 'struggle for life', and 'the 'survival of the fittest'. Darwin developed his theories with nothing more than the natural world in mind, but his followers and numerous popularizers did not hesitate to draw other conclusions from his work.
5. C. Kranz-Michaelis, *Rathäuser im deutschen Kaiserreich 1871–1918* (Munich: Prestel, 1976); and E. Mai *et al.* (eds), *Das Rathaus im Kaiserreich* (Berlin: Mann, 1982). For the cultural role of cities in general see W. J. Mommsen, 'Stadt und Kultur im deutschen Kaiserreich' in his collection *Burgerliche Kultur und politische Ordnung* (Frankfurt: Fischer, 2000).
6. See H.-U. Wehler, *The German Empire, 1871–1918* (Leamington Spr: Berg, 1985).
7. The phrase comes from Georg Herwegh, the poet and 1848 revolutionary.
8. F. Nietzsche, 'David Strauss, the confessor and writer', in *Untimely Meditations,* trans. R.J. Hollingdale (Cambridge, Cambridge University Press, 1983), p. 3.
9. F. Nietzsche, 'On the uses and disadvantages of history for life', in *Untimely Meditations,* p. 121.
10. Glagau wrote in the popular journal *Die Gartenlaube,* a family weekly founded by Ernst Keil in Leipzig (1853), which had a circulation of 378,000 in 1873. His essays were tainted by anti-semitism and xenophobia.
11. G. Iggers, *The German Conception of History* (Middletown: Wesleyan University Press, 1968), p. 175.
12. Quoted by I. Koszinowski in E. Mai, S. Waetzoldt and G. Wolandt (eds), *Ideengeschichte und Kunstwissenschaft* (Berlin: Mann, 1983), p. 281.

13. There is a vast literature on Nietzsche and his ideas. See S. E. Aschheim, *The Nietzsche Legacy in Germany* (Berkeley: University of California Press, 1992) for a recent overview.
14. Elisabeth Förster-Nietzsche (1846–1935) controlled her late brother's estate, was his official biographer and edited his works in a most selective manner. *The Will to Power*, which she assembled from Nietzsche's notes, was arguably as much her work as the philosopher's. She established the Nietzsche Archive in Weimar, and attempted to make her brother 'respectable', by stressing his patriotism, morality and good health. See H. F. Peters, *Zarathustra's Sister: The Case of Elisabeth and Friedrich Nietzsche* (New York: Wiener, 1985).
15. Such as R. Hinton Thomas, *Nietzsche in German Politics and Society, 1890–1918* (Manchester: Manchester University Press, 1983); and S. Taylor, *Left-Wing Nietzscheans: The Politics of German Expressionism, 1910–20* (Berlin and New York: de Gruyter, 1990).
16. See D. B. Allison (ed.), *The New Nietzsche: Contemporary Styles of Interpretation* (Cambridge, MA: MIT Press, 1985).
17. Quoted by Aschheim, *The Nietzsche Legacy in Germany*, p. 274.
18. F. Spotts, *Bayreuth* (New Haven and London: Yale University Press, 1994), p. 74.
19. P. L. Rose, *Wagner: Race and Revolution* (New Haven and London: Yale University Press, 1992), p. 39.
20. Michael Tanner, Thomas Grey and Dieter Borchmeyer are amongst those critics who do not endorse Rose's hypothesis.
21. Rose, *Wagner: Race and Revolution*, p. 68.
22. See W. Schüler, *Der Bayreuther Kreis: Wagnerkult und Kulturreform im Geiste völkischer Weltanschauung* (Münster: Aschendorff, 1971).
23. Quoted by Schüler, *Der Bayreuther Kreis*, p. 219.
24. Quoted from the memoirs of Robert Zedlitz-Trützschler by M. Stather, *Die Kunstpolitik Wilhelms II.* (Konstanz: Hartung-Gorre, 1994), p. 122.
25. F. Stern, *The Politics of Cultural Despair* (Berkeley and London: University of California Press, 1961), and G. Mosse, *The Crisis of German Ideology* (London: Weidenfeld and Nicolson, 1966).
26. J. J. Sheehan, *German Liberalism in the Nineteenth Century* (Chicago and London: University of Chicago Press, 1978), p. 254.
27. D. Blackbourn and G. Eley, *The Peculiarities of German History* (Oxford: Oxford University Press, 1984), p. 217.
28. Blackbourn, *Fontana History of Germany*, p. 395.
29. G. Eley, 'The German Right, 1860–1945: How it changed', in his essay collection *From Unification to Nazism* (Boston and London: Allen and Unwin, 1986), p. 236.
30. Nipperdey, *Deutsche Geschichte, 1866–1918*, vol. 1, p. 829.
31. See J. Herf, *Reactionary Modernism: Technology, Culture and Politics in Weimar and the Third Reich* (Cambridge: Cambridge University Press, 1984).
32. Quoted by M. Makela, *The Munich Secession* (Princeton: Princeton University Press, 1990), p. 78.
33. The phrase is from H. Stuart Hughes *Consciousness and Society: The Reorientation of European Social Thought* (New York: Knopf, 1958), p. 40.

34. A. von Werner, *Erlebnisse und Eindrücke* (Berlin: Mittler, 1913), p. 569.
35. See D. Kafitz, 'Tendenzen der Naturalismus-Forschung und Überlegungen zu einer Neubestimmung des Naturalismus-Begriffs', *Der Deutschunterricht*, 40 (1988) 2, 11–29.
36. For instance, in drama see S. Kiefer, *Dramatik der Gründerzeit: Deutsches Drama und Theater, 1870–1890* (St Ingbert: Röhrig, 1997); or for poetry, G. Mahal's essay 'Wirklich eine Revolution der Lyrik?' in H. Scheuer (ed.), *Naturalismus. Bürgerliche Dichtung und soziales Engagement* (Stuttgart: Kohlhammer, 1974).
37. See the section on 'Naturalism in painting' later in this chapter.
38. According to J. McFarlane, 'Berlin and the rise of Modernism 1886–1896', in M. Bradbury and J. McFarlane (eds), *Modernism* (Harmondsworth: Penguin, 1991; first published 1976). Others suggest, however, that the word first appeared in an article by the Hart brothers for the *Allgemeine Deutsche Universitätszeitung* in 1884. See J. Schutte and P. Sprengel (eds), *Die Berliner Moderne, 1885–1914* (Stuttgart: Reclam, 1987), p. 186.
39. The Harts, for example, proclaimed that a new literature should follow the cues 'national' and 'modern', while Friedrich Lienhard demanded a 'christian-german-modern' aesthetic. See A. Marshall, *The German Naturalists and Gerhart Hauptmann. Reception and Influence* (Frankfurt: Lang, 1982), p. 38.
40. Quoted by Marshall, *The German Naturalists and Gerhart Hauptmann*, p. 11.
41. Until 1889, the 'capital' of German Naturalism was undoubtedly Munich, due largely to Conrad. The political controversies surrounding the plays of Sudermann and Hauptmann, however, and the success of the Free Stage, gave Berlin the upper hand. In general, Munich Naturalism was less radical, politically and aesthetically, than in Berlin. See A. Strieder, *'Die Gesellschaft' – Eine kritische Auseinandersetzung mit der Zeitschrift der frühen Naturalisten* (Frankfurt: Lang, 1985).
42. Quoted by Marshall, *The German Naturalists and Gerhart Hauptmann* , p. 35.
43. See J. Osborne, *The Naturalist Drama in Germany* (Manchester: Manchester University Press, 1971).
44. The Hart brothers were from Westphalia, Hauptmann from Silesia, Holz from East Prussia
45. R. Musil, *Der Mann ohne Eigenschaften* (Reinbek: Rowohlt, 1970), p. 42.
46. In Baden, Bavaria, Oldenburg and Württemberg such cases were tried by jury.
47. R. Lenman, 'Art, society and the law in Wilhelmine Germany: the Lex Heinze', *Oxford German Studies*, 8 (1973). See also G. D. Stark, 'Cinema, Society and the state', in Stark and B. K. Lackner (eds), *Essays on Culture and Society in Modern Germany* (Arlington: Texas University Press, 1982).
48. Practice varied from state to state, and even from town to town. The Prussian constitution permitted freedom of expression in 'word, writing, print and picture', but not in performance. Conservative

dramatists like Heyse and Wildenbruch also suffered as a consequence of the 1851 Prussian Theatre Code, that remained in place until 1918.

49. Thus Ibsens's *Ghosts* was available to Germans in print as number 1828 in Reclam's Universal Library, but was not allowed to be performed on stage.
50. Police chief von Richthofen's comment 'that whole movement is out of place here!' was made in a thick Berlin accent to the theatre director Oscar Blumenthal in 1890. He had gone to the police to enquire why the play had not been granted a licence. See G. Schulz, 'Naturalismus und Zensur', in Scheuer, *Naturalismus,* p. 93
51. It became a monthly in 1894 and was renamed *Neue deutsche Rundschau.* In 1904 it became simply the *Neue Rundschau.*
52. Debate of 21 February 1895. See Schulz, 'Naturalismus und Zensur', pp. 105–6.
53. Quoted in H. J. Schoeps (ed.), *Zeitgeist im Wandel* (Stuttgart: Klett, 1967), p. 126.
54. See Marshall, *The German Naturalists and Gerhart Hauptmann,* p. 2.
55. Friedrichshagen, which had a population of around 10,000 in 1890, was already developing suburban characteristics, however, following the arrival of the Berlin suburban railway in 1886. In 1921 it was incorporated into Greater Berlin.
56. Bölsche's *Die naturwissenschaftlichen Grundlagen der Poesie* (1887) argued that literature must turn to the natural sciences and learn from their approach, if it was to reflect the spirit of the age. He was the author of some 60 books and around 650 essays. His pamphlets for the workers' science journal *Kosmos* were read by up to a million people, and he has been judged 'the single best-selling nonfiction author in the German language before 1933'. See A. Kelly, *The Descent of Darwin* (Chapel Hill: University of North Carolina Press, 1981), p. 6.
57. Wille preached and lectured for Berlin's community of religious freethinkers. He spoke frequently at SPD rallies before 1891, but was never a Party member.
58. In the early 1900s, before he aristocratized his name to 'Moeller van den Bruck'.
59. Schulz 'Naturalismus und Zensur', p. 112.
60. The New Free People's Stage was reunited with the Free People's Stage in 1913, with a joint membership of some 70,000 and a new theatre of its own the following year.
61. For a full discussion see H.-J. Schulz, *German Socialist Literature, 1860–1914* (Columbia, SC: Camden House, 1993).
62. P. Jelavich, *Munich and Theatrical Modernism* (Cambridge MA and London: Harvard University Press, 1985), p. 72.
63. Ironically the French critic Castagnary had used the term 'Naturalism' to describe the work of his friend and compatriot Courbet in 1857, but although some art historians have used it subsequently, most art history books prefer 'Realism'.
64. R. Hamann and J. Hermand, *Naturalismus,* p. 8.
65. B. Küster, *Max Liebermann: Ein Maler-Leben* (Hamburg: Ellert and Richter, 1988), p. 30.

66. By no means the least interesting aspect is why he chose to paint labourers in the Netherlands rather than in his own homeland. The long realist tradition of Dutch genre painting no doubt played a part, as did the artist's admiration of the Dutch people and social institutions. Some have suggested it was also a 'flight' from the industrial realities of Imperial Germany, but more significant was probably the desire to avoid any association with the *Lederhosen* art of Franz Defregger and his ilk.
67. See D. Schlapeit-Beck, *Frauenarbeit in der Malerei, 1870–1900* (Berlin: Elefanten Press, 1985).
68. Küster, *Max Liebermann: Ein Maler-Leben*, p. 53.
69. See P. Paret, *The Berlin Secession* (Cambridge MA and London: Harvard University Press, 1980), pp. 44–5; and Makela, *The Munich Secession*, p. 33.
70. See Makela, *The Munich Secession*, pp. 26–8 and p. 93.
71. In most art centres they were traditionally held every two or three years, but they became annual events from 1830 in Paris, and from 1889 in Munich.
72. General treatments of the Secessions include H.-U. Simon, *Sezessionismus. Kunstgewerbe in literarischer und bildender Kunst* (Stuttgart: Metzler, 1976); and the exhibition catalogue by S. Wichmann, *Secession: Europäische Kunst um die Jahrhundertwende* (Munich: Haus der Kunst, 1964).
73. By 1895 around 1180 painters and sculptors – over 13 per cent of the total number in Germany – lived in Munich. In comparison, Berlin, which was more than four times as populous, had only 1159. Düsseldorf followed with 335; Dresden, 314; Hamburg, 280; Frankfurt, 142; and Hanover, 88. Figures from Makela, *The Munich Secession*, pp. 14–15.
74. From *Kunst für Alle* (1907) quoted by M. Makela, *The Munich Secession*, p. 19.
75. Makela, *The Munich Secession*, p. 77.
76. Makela, *The Munich Secession*, p. 60.
77. Makela, *The Munich Secession*, p. 68.
78. The son of a miller, Stuck was ennobled in 1905 and was a millionaire by 1914. He designed his own neo-Classical villa on Munich's exclusive Prinzregentenstrasse in 1897–98.
79. Makela, *The Munich Secession*, p. 74.
80. This was largely the reason for the moralistic titles of Stuck's paintings – 'Temptation' was another favourite – which were chosen in an attempt to disarm the critics and censors.
81. Liebermann would not be drawn on the matter, but it has been suggested that the artist was concerned that his 'Dutch peasant' paintings might be identified as an endorsement of Langbehn's *Rembrandt as Educator* credo, which was proving so popular at this time. See Makela, *The Munich Secession*, p. 85. Liebermann's admiration for French Impressionism was obvious from his own collection of paintings, which included three works by Monet, five by Degas, two by Cezanne, and no fewer than seventeen by Manet.

82. Makela, *The Munich Secession*, p. 127.
83. In 1833 it had been divided into two sections: one for music and one for fine art (a literature section was only added in the Weimar Republic). Both sections controlled a teaching establishment: the Royal College of Music and the College of Fine Arts.
84. Quotes in D. Bartmann (ed.), *Anton von Werner: Geschichte in Bildern* (Munich: Hirmer, 1993), p. 104.
85. Quoted in Bartmann (ed.), *Anton von Werner: Geschichte in Bildern*, p. 104.
86. *Pan* was a co-operative enterprise involving, amongst others, the art critic Julius Meier-Graefe, the diplomat and art patron Count Harry Kessler, and the writers Otto Julius Bierbaum and Richard Dehmel. Much of the capital to establish the journal was put up by Germany's monarchs and princes. A later version of *Pan* appeared from 1911 to 1914, published by Paul Cassirer.
87. The membership stayed at around this level until the mid-1900s, when it began to increase gradually. Unlike the Association of Berlin Artists, the Secession also allowed female painters to become members.
88. The term is not very helpful, because the German painters' principal interest was not the play of light or the visual impression of an object.
89. Thode was another son-in-law of Richard Wagner, and close to the Bayreuth Circle.
90. See ch. 4 of Paret's *The Berlin Secession.*
91. See P. Paret, 'The Tschudi Affair', *Journal of Modern History*, 53 (1981), 4.
92. J. J. Sheehan, *Museums in the German Art World* (Oxford: Oxford University Press, 2000), p. 168.
93. Although the Secession continued to exist after this date, the loss of its leader Gustav Klimt and his supporters was a more fundamental blow than the splits endured by the Munich or Berlin Secessions.
94. 'Sacred Spring' (*Ver Sacrum*) was also the name of the Viennese Secession's exclusive journal, which was published between 1898 and 1903.
95. Quoted by Simon, *Sezessionismus*, p. 49.
96. Either, or both, of the terms may have been in use prior to this, but conclusive evidence is thin on the ground. One author has claimed to have found a reference to art nouveau as far back as 1856, but clearly that usage had nothing to do with the stylistic approach recognized as Art Nouveau today.
97. The first use of the term *Jugendstil* appears to have been in 1897. By 1900 its documented usage was quite widespread.
98. At its peak, around 1900, as many as 300,000 copies may have been sold each week. By 1904 it had some 62,000 registered subscribers and a total circulation around 100,000. See C. Segieth, 'Im Zeichen des Secessionismus' (PhD dissertation, University of Munich, 1994), p. 95.
99. 'Spring' was the theme of the first poem in *Jugend*, as well as the subject of paintings by Eckmann, Pankok, Vogeler, Ludwig von Hofmann and Ferdinand Hodler.

100. Particularly apparent in the work of Josef Hoffmann (1870–1956) and Adolf Loos (1870–1933), who were both inspired by Charles Rennie Mackintosh (1868–1928) and the Glasgow school.
101. See S. Madsen, *Sources of Art Nouveau* (New York: Wittenborn, 1956).
102. The 'wavy line' appealed to such disparate talents as the American glassware specialist Louis C. Tiffany (1858–1933); the young English illustrator Aubrey Beardsley (1872–98); and the Barcelona architect Antoni Gaudi (1852–1926). In Catalonia, Scotland, Finland and Belgium, as well as in Germany, the search for a new style in architecture was closely linked to the question of national identity.
103. J. Heskett, *Design in Germany, 1870–1918* (London: Trefoil, 1986), p. 26.
104. Quoted by Simon, *Sezessionismus*, pp. 80–1.
105. This exclusive monthly journal was founded by the Bremen dandy Alfred Walter Heymel with his cousin Rudolf Alexander Schröder, a writer and interior designer, and O. J. Bierbaum. It covered both literary and visual arts. *Die Insel* only appeared for three years, but from the journal developed a major publishing house, also called Insel (1902), which became noted for the quality of its book covers and typography.
106. Riemerschmid began as a landscape painter before contributing some early front covers to *Jugend*. His first foray into furniture design followed shortly after, and soon he was receiving commissions to design whole rooms. In 1896 he designed and furnished his own house near Munich. After 1900 Riemerschmid concentrated solely on architecture and furniture design.
107. Hamburg-born Behrens was a founder member of the Munich Secession. He provided graphic art for *Pan*, before turning to the design of books, glassware, cutlery, furniture and eventually architecture.
108. Heskett, *Design in Germany, 1870–1918*, p. 46.
109. H. Glaser, *Die Kultur der wilhelminischen Zeit* (Frankfurt: Fischer, 1984), p. 289.
110. The dispersal of the Munich group was rapid: Eckmann departed for Berlin in 1897, to be followed by Endell in 1901 and by Paul in 1907. Behrens moved to Darmstadt in 1899, and Pankok to Stuttgart in 1901.
111. Behrens directed the play. Georg Fuchs wrote most of the text and Willem de Haan the music. Fuchs had long sought to develop Wagner's ideas for national festival productions, and saw Darmstadt as offering an opportunity to celebrate the patriotic bonds that united the whole community, from the Grand Duke to the humble craftsman.
112. In Germany the term *Jugendstil* retained its negative connotations until the 1950s and 1960s, when a series of retrospective exhibitions began its rehabilitation. It was not until the late 1960s, however, that the style experienced a genuine revival, thanks to its adoption by a new generation of rebellious youth. In the historiography of modern design *Jugendstil* has been depicted as both a crucial early stepping

stone to modernism, and as the final decadent chapter in the nineteenth-century's procession of decorative styles. Ultimately, it had a foot in both centuries, and is perhaps best characterized as the product of a period of transition.

113. Quoted by R. Münster (ed.), *Jugendstil-Musik? Münchener Musikleben, 1890–1918* (Wiesbaden: Reichert, 1987), p. 7. Strauss also put the poems of Dehmel, Henckell and Hart to music.
114. The other composers most often connected to *Jugendstil* are Arnold Schönberg (1874–1951), whose *Verklärte Nacht* (1899) was based on a Dehmel poem of the same name; and Engelbert Humperdinck (1854–1921), whose operas explored the world of fairy tales and nature lyricism. See Münster, *Jugendstil-Musik?*
115. See E. Neumeister, *Thomas Manns frühe Erzählungen: Der Jugendstil als Kunstform im frühen Werk* (Bonn: Bouvier, 1977).
116. Cited by K. E. Webb, *Rainer Maria Rilke and Jugendstil* (Chapel Hill: University of Carolina Press, 1978), p. 46.
117. Webb, *Rainer Maria Rilke and Jugendstil*, p. 8.
118. Webb, *Rainer Maria Rilke and Jugendstil*, p. 87.
119. Indeed, much of the furniture was originally attributed to Behrens rather than Dehmel.
120. Simon, *Sezessionismus*, p. 105.
121. Amongst recent studies see S. Breuer, *Ästhetischer Fundamentalismus: Stefan George und der deutsche Antimodernismus* (Darmstadt: Wissenschaftliche Buchgesellschaft, 1995); and G. Heintz, *Stefan George: Studien zu seiner künstlerischer Wirkung* (Stuttgart: Hauswedell, 1986).
122. Nipperdey, *Deutsche Geschichte, 1866–1918*, vol. 1, p. 779.

Notes to Chapter 5: 'Wilhelminism' and its Discontents

1. See, for instance, R. vom Bruch's essay, 'Kaiser und Bürger. Wilhelminismus als Ausdruck kulturellen Umbruchs um 1900', in A.M. Birke and L. Kettenacker (eds), *Bürgertum, Adel und Monarchie* (Munich and London: K.G. Saur, 1989); or W.J. Mommsen, 'Kultur und Wissenschaft im kulturellen System des Wilhelminismus', in G. Hübinger, R. vom Bruch and F.W. Graf (eds), *Kultur und Kulturwissenschaften um 1900*, vol. 2 (Stuttgart: F. Steiner, 1997).
2. H.-U. Wehler, *The German Empire* (Leamington Spa: Berg, 1985), p. 64.
3. The latter two elements are cited by vom Bruch in his essay 'Kaiser und Bürger'.
4. The language of Wilhelm II and of his higher officials is parodied not only in the speech patterns of Diederich Hessling in Heinrich Mann's *Der Untertan*, but by Theobald Maske in Carl Sternheim's *Die Hose*, and in other fictional works from the Wilhelmine era.
5. N. Sombart in J. C. G. Röhl and N. Sombart (eds), *Kaiser Wilhelm II: New Interpretations* (Cambridge: Cambridge University Press), p. 287.
6. According to M. Stather, *Die Kunstpolitik Wilhelms II* (Konstanz: Hartung-Gorre, 1994), pp. 7–8, this was Wilhelm's only comment in his

memoirs (*Kaiser Wilhelm II: Ereignisse und Gestalten aus den Jahren, 1878–1918*) on the arts.

7. R. Pfefferkorn, *Die Berliner Secession* (Berlin: Haude & Spener, 1972).
8. P. Paret, *The Berlin Secession* (Cambridge MA and London: Harvard University Press, 1980); Stather, *Die Kunstpolitik Wilhelms II.*
9. G. Malkowsky, *Die Kunst im Dienste der Staatsidee: Hohenzollerische Kunstpolitik vom Grossen Kurfürsten bis auf Wilhelm II* (Berlin: Patria, 1912), p. 235. He liked to present statues as gifts, including one of Goethe to the city of Rome, and one of Frederick the Great to the United States.
10. He was particularly keen on naval scenes, and received special tuition from the maritime painter Carl Saltzmann, who also accompanied him on several North Sea cruises.
11. His best-known composition was *Sang an Aegir,* a sentimental song of Nordic heroism, which was published in 1894 to raise money for the construction of a memorial tower on the battlefield of Gravelotte. It was available in English, Italian and French translations.
12. Quoted by Stather, *Die Kunstpolitik Wilhelms II,* p. 67.
13. Quoted by Paret, *The Berlin Secession,* p. 42.
14. Quoted by Paret, *The Berlin Secession,* p. 25.
15. Malkowsky, *Die Kunst im Dienste der Staatsidee,* p. 237.
16. Malkowsky, *Die Kunst im Dienste der Staatsidee,* p. 12.
17. Speech of 18 December 1901, quoted by Paret, *The Berlin Secession,* pp. 26–7. Although the term was not actually used, it was this speech that gave birth to the notion of 'gutter-art' (*Rinnsteinkunst*), which gained widespread usage amongst those hostile to modernism.
18. See C. With, *The Prussian Landeskunstkommission, 1862–1911* (Berlin: Mann, 1986).
19. It should be remembered, however, that Wilhelm II's Berlin was by no means the only monarchical stage set built in the early twentieth century. In London, for instance, Admiralty Arch was built in 1910; the new Mall, with its plane trees, flagpoles and galleon-topped lampposts, was widened and extended to make a processional route in 1911; and Buckingham Palace itself was not finished until 1913. See E. Hobsbawm and T. Ranger (eds), *The Invention of Tradition* (Cambridge: Cambridge University Press, 1983).
20. Quoted by Paret, *The Berlin Secession,* p. 25. Wilhelm also expressed similar sentiments in speeches on 25 January and 2 November 1902.
21. D. Blackbourn, *The Fontana History of Germany,* (London: Fontana, 1997) p. 390.
22. It appeared in vol. 6, no. 30, of *Simplicissimus* in 1902.
23. See P. Jelavich, *Berlin Cabaret* (Cambridge, MA: Harvard University Press, 1993), p. 96.
24. Quoted by C. Hepp, *Avantgarde: Moderne Kunst, Kulturkritik und Reformbewegungen nach der Jahrhundertwende* (Munich: DTV, 1987), p. 52. *Der Kunstwart* was first published in 1887. Readers and writers soon considered themselves part of a '*Kunstwart* Community', but this remained very small for most of the next decade. The twice-monthly journal had less than 1000 subscribers in the early 1890s. This rose to

around 8000 in 1900 and 23,000 in 1907, by which time it was one of the Wilhelmine reformers' most important forums. See G. Kratzsch, *Kunstwart und Dürerbund* (Göttingen: Vandenhoeck & Ruprecht, 1969).

25. Quoted by Paret, *The Berlin Secession*, p. 162.
26. See H. Väth-Hinz, *Odol: Reklame-Kunst um 1900* (Lahn-Giessen: Anabas, 1985).
27. Thereafter Wilhelm refused to meet 'Odol-Lingner': the product's manufacturer Karl August Lingner.
28. Quidde, whose academic career suffered as a result of his pamphlet, won the Nobel Peace Prize in 1927. See L. Quidde, *Caligula: Schriften über Militarismus und Pazifismus* (Frankfurt: Syndikat, 1977).
29. The *Fliegende Blätter* first appeared in Munich in 1844, and once counted Carl Spitzweg and Wilhelm Busch as regular contributors. It generally avoided political issues.
30. *Der wahre Jakob* had a larger circulation – around 230,000 in 1908 – than any of the middle-class satirical journals, but even this paled against the sales of the illustrated and 'apolitical' family magazines, such as the *Berliner Illustrierte*, which claimed a circulation of 600,000 in 1914.
31. See A. T. Allen, *Satire and Society in Wilhelmine Germany* (Lexington: University Press of Kentucky, 1984),
32. Over an 18-month period Wedekind wrote 15 poems, 3 short stories, 6 fictitious interviews, and numerous joke captions for *Simplicissimus* (P. Jelavich, *Munich and Theatrical Modernism* (Cambridge: MA and London: Harvard University Press, 1985), p. 146). His plays combined elements of Naturalism, Symbolism and Expressionism, and were characterized by economy of language and powerful imagery. *Frühlings Erwachen* ('Spring Awakening') attacked all the major instruments of socialization – family, school and church – and contained scenes of masturbation and flagellation. Thus, although written in 1890–91 it was not performed even in censored form until 1906 (in Britain it could not be performed until long after World War Two). His important *Lulu* plays, which dealt with the social dangers of suppressing natural sexual drives, suffered in much the same way. *Erdgeist* ('Earth Spirit', 1895) was premiered in Leipzig in 1898 but was rarely performed in following years; while the *Büchse der Pandora* ('Pandora's Box') was banned in print form until 1918, and staged only once in the lifetime of the Empire.
33. See Allen, *Satire and Society*, p. 119.
34. P. Jelavich, *Munich and Theatrical Modernism* (Cambridge, MA, and London: Harvard University Press, 1985), p. 268.
35. Jelavich, *Berlin Cabaret*, p. 33.
36. T. Nipperdey, 'War die Wilhelminische Gesellschaft eine Untertanen-Gesellschaft?' in *Nachdenken über die deutsche Geschichte* (Munich: Beck, 1986).
37. Jelavich, *Berlin Cabaret*, p. 288.
38. The song described how Waldersee held his marshall's baton 'firmly' in his hand everywhere he went, including – as the climax related – in the lavatory. See Jelavich, *Berlin Cabaret*, p. 49.

39. Jelavich, *Berlin Cabaret*, p. 63.
40. Quoted in E. Mai, S. Waetzold, and G. Wolandt (eds), *Ideengeschichte und Kunstwissenschaft* (Berlin: Mann, 1983), p. 373.
41. T. Nipperdey, 'War die Wilhelminische Gesellschaft eine Untertanen-Gesellschaft?', p. 178.
42. The best survey is provided by D. Kerbs and J. Reulecke (eds), *Handbuch der deutschen Reformbewegungen, 1880–1933* (Wuppertal: Hammer, 1998). See also W. Krabbe, *Gesellschaftsveränderung durch Lebensreform* (Göttingen: Vandenhoeck & Ruprecht, 1974); J. Frecot, 'Die Lebensreformbewegung', in K. Vondung (ed.), *Das wilhelminische Bildungsbürgertum* (Göttingen: Vandenhoeck & Ruprecht, 1976); J. Frecot, J.F. Geist and D. Kerbs, *Fidus 1868–1948. Zur ästhethischen Praxis bürgerlicher Fluchtbewegungen* (Munich: Rogner and Bernhard, 1972); T. Rohkrämer, *Eine andere Moderne? Zivilisationskritk, Natur und Technik in Deutschland, 1880–1933* (Paderborn: Schöningh, 1999).
43. The organizations generally styled themselves as 'leagues' (*Bünde*) rather than 'clubs' or 'associations' (*Vereine*), in part to gain distance from the pedantic *Vereinsmeierei* of German associational life, with its petty functionaries and well-thumbed rule books, but sometimes also in a conscious effort to evoke the more 'healthy' and 'organic' world of the 'community' (*Gemeinschaft*) rather than 'society' (*Gesellschaft*).
44. T. Nipperdey, *Deutsche Geschichte, 1866–1918*, vol. 1 (Munich: Beck, 1990–92), p. 822.
45. Quoted in Frecot, Geist and Kerbs, *Fidus, 1868–1948*, p. 56.
46. For Eden see Hepp, *Avantgarde*; also E. Meyer-Renschhausen and H. Berger, 'Bodenreform', in Kerbs and Reulecke, *Handbuch der deutschen Reformbewegungen.*
47. A successful appeal meant they only had to serve a few days.
48. Quoted by P. Bridgwater in *Poet of Expressionist Berlin: The Life and Work of Georg Heym* (London: Libris, 1991), p. 173.
49. J. Posener, *Berlin auf dem Wege zu einer neuen Architektur: die Zeitalter Wilhelms II* (Munich: Prestel, 1979), p. 389.
50. Rudolf Steiner (1861–1925), a writer and expert on Goethe who became acquainted with Fidus in 1900s Berlin, founded the 'Anthroposophische Gesellschaft' in 1912. The following year the society established its headquarters at Dornach in Switzerland. Fidus was bitterly disappointed when Steiner did not consult him on the design of the building, which was made largely of wood and was known as the Goetheaneum. After a fire destroyed the building it was rebuilt in concrete, but once again Fidus's ideas were overlooked.
51. Quoted by R. Kauffeldt and G. Cepl-Kaufmann, *Berlin-Friedrichshagen. Literaturhauptstadt um die Jahrhundertwende* (Munich: Boer, 1994), p. 109.
52. Quoted by D. Sternberger, *Panorama* (Frankfurt: Insel, 1978), p. 206.
53. See K. Ellwanger and E. Meyer-Renschhausen, 'Kleidungsreform', in Kerbs and Reulecke, *Handbuch der deutschen Reformbewegungen*, pp. 87–102. Also B. Stamm, 'Auf dem Weg zum Reformkleid', in E. Siepmann (ed.), *Kunst und Alltag um 1900* (Lahn-Giessen: Anabas, 1978).
54. See W. Laqueur, *Young Germany: A History of the German Youth Movement*

(New York: Basic Books, 1962); and Peter Stachura, *The German Youth Movement, 1900–1945* (New York: St Martins, 1981). Also T. Koebner, R.-P. Janz and F. Trommler (eds), *Mit uns zieht die neue Zeit: Der Mythos Jugend* (Frankfurt: Suhrkamp, 1985).

55. See W. Mogge, 'Jugendbewegung', in Kerbs and Reulecke, *Handbuch der Deutschen Reformbewegungen*, p. 181.
56. Quoted by H. Glaser, *Die Kultur der wilhelminischen Zeit* (Frankfurt: Fischer, 1984), p. 63.
57. The 'Jewish question' became an issue for the *Wandervogel* movement in 1912–14; years which some suggest saw a general increase in anti-semitic activity in Germany after two decades of relative quiet. After much acrimonious discussion it was left to individual groups to decide whether to accept Jewish members or not. Some Jewish youths did become *Wandervögel*, but others opted for one of the wide range of specifically Jewish youth organizations: pro- or anti-zionist, bourgeois or Socialist. Similarly, although there were also Catholic *Wandervögel*, most young Catholics remained true to their own cultural milieu.
58. This idea was largely a consequence of the memoirs of former *Wandervogel* Hans Blüher (1888–1955). More recent historical research has found Blüher's account to be inaccurate in many respects.
59. Laqueur, *Young Germany*, p. 5.
60. Laqueur, *Young Germany*, p. vii.
61. Both quotes from Rilke in B. Küster, *Das Barkenhoff Buch* (Bremen: Worpsweder Verlag, 1989) pp. 19, 29.
62. He was a regular contributor to *Die Insel*, and illustrated works by Hoffmannsthal, Hauptmann, Ricarda Huch and Oscar Wilde, but his most celebrated collaboration was with Rilke, for whom he illustrated the 1899 collection *Mir zur Feier*.
63. In addition, Vogeler married Martha Schröder, Rilke married Clara Westhoff and Paula Becker's father died.
64. Within a year of Modersohn-Becker's death a major retrospective of her work was held in Bremen. At least a dozen studies of her life and work have appeared in recent years, including G. Perry, *Paula Modersohn-Becker: Her Life and Work* (New York and London: Harper and Row, 1979).
65. Quoted by U. Linse, *Zurück o Mensch zur Mutter Erde: Landkommunen in Deutschland, 1890–1933* (Munich: DTV, 1983), p. 73.
66. Lou Andreas-Salomé (1861–1937) was a Russian-born writer and psychoanalyst, who had relationships with Nietzsche, the politician Georg Ledebour, Rilke and Freud, but turned down Wedekind.
67. Else Lasker-Schüler (1869–1945) was a poet, dramatist and artist, whose eccentric dress – she wore sandals with bells, all manner of trinkets and a black jockey-cap – reflected her alter ego, 'Jussuf, Prince of Thebes'. She later emigrated to Palestine.
68. *Die Welträtsel* sold 250,000 copies in Germany in less than ten years and was translated into over thirty languages. It was read not only by the educated middle classes but also in working-class circles. For many socialists it helped to explain Marx's work and the SPD's Karl Kautsky was a big admirer. Haeckel's own political sympathies lay more to the

right: he was a supporter of the ultra-nationalist Pan-German League. D. Gasman's *The Scientific Origins of National Socialism: Social Darwinism in Ernst Haeckel and the German Monist League* (London: Macdonald, 1971) makes much of this, but overlooks the fact that most Monists tended to the political left.

69. Kauffeldt and Cepl-Kaufmann, *Berlin-Friedrichshagen*, p. 168.
70. Quoted by H. Scherer, *Bürgerlich-oppositionelle Literaten und sozialdemokratische Arbeiterbewegung nach 1890* (Stuttgart: Metzler, 1974), pp. 27–8.
71. M. Green, *Mountain of Truth: The Counterculture Begins. Ascona, 1900–1920* (Hanover and London: University Press of New England, 1986), p. 3.
72. See J. Michaels, *Anarchy and Eros: Otto Gross' Impact on Expressionist Writers* (Frankfurt: Lang, 1983).
73. For the *Heimat* movement in general see C. Applegate, *A Nation of Provincials: The German Idea of Heimat* (Berkeley and London: University of California Press, 1990); E. Klueting (ed.), *Antimodernismus und Reform: Zur Geschichte des deutschen Heimatbewegung* (Darmstadt: Wissenschaftliche Buchgesellschaft, 1991); W. Hartung, *Konservative Zivilisationskritik und regionale Identität am Beispiel der niedersächsischen Heimatbewegung* (Hanover: Hahn, 1991).
74. Thoma's first solo exhibition was, rather bizarrely, held in Liverpool in 1884. He was in his fifties before he gained recognition in Germany for his moody glorifications of the south German countryside.
75. Quoted in H. J. Schoeps (ed.), *Zeitgeist im Wandel* (Stuttgart, Klett, 1967), p. 144.
76. Green, *Mountain of Truth*, p. 227.
77. See M. Jefferies, 'Heimatschutz: Environmental activism in Wilhelmine Germany', in Colin Riordan (ed.), *Green Thought in German Culture* (Cardiff: University of Wales Press, 1997); W. Rollins, *A Greener Vision of Home*; A. Knaut, *Zurück zur Natur! Die Würzeln der Ökologiebewegung* (Bonn: Arbeitsgemeinschaft Naturschutz, 1993); J. Hermand, *Grüne Utopien in Deutschland: Zur Geschichte des ökologischen Bewusstseins* (Frankfurt: Fischer, 1991).
78. M. Jefferies, *Politics and Culture in Wilhelmine Germany* (Oxford and Washington, DC: Berg, 1995).
79. N. Borrmann, *Paul Schultze-Naumburg, 1869–1949* (Essen: Bacht, 1989).
80. Rollins, *A Greener Vision of Home*, p. 155.
81. Rollins, *A Greener Vision of Home*, p. 171.
82. From the writings of the American Henry George (1839–97); or J. S. Mill's 'Land Tenure Reform Association' in Britain, for instance.
83. For Damaschke see K. Repp, *Reformers, Critics and the Paths of German Modernity* (Cambridge, MA, and London: Harvard University Press, 2000).
84. Oppenheimer was even invited to speak at the youth movement's famous Hohe Meissner gathering in 1913. See E. Meyer-Renschhausen and H. Berger, 'Bodenreform', in Kerbs and Reulecke, *Handbuch der deutschen Reformbewegungen*, p. 268.
85. Oppenheimer enjoyed some limited success with the Bärenklau estate

north of Berlin in the 1920s. See Meyer-Renschhausen and Berger, 'Bodenreform', p. 272.

86. Schmidt's enterprise merged with a similar Munich undertaking in 1907 and was thereafter known as the 'Deutsche Werkstätten'.
87. At Krupp, and most other firms, workers stood to lose their company homes if they changed jobs, became involved in strike action, or joined the SPD.
88. Other pre-1914 visitors to Hellerau included the architects Mies van der Rohe and Le Corbusier; the painters Nolde and Schwitters; and the writers Zweig, Rilke, Ball, Werfel and Franz Kafka, who was a great admirer of Karl Schmidt's furniture.
89. Quoted by K. Hartmann in Kerbs and Reulecke, *Handbuch der deutschen Reformbewegungen*, p. 296.
90. Quoted in Hans Eckstein (ed.), *50 Jahre Deutscher Werkbund* (Frankfurt: Metzner, 1958), p. 19.
91. See Jefferies, *Politics and Culture in Wilhelmine Germany*; J. Campbell, *The German Werkbund: The Politics of Refom in the Applied Arts* (Princeton: Princeton University Press, 1978); F. Schwartz, *The Werkbund: Design Theory and Mass Culture before the First World War* (New Haven and London: Yale University Press, 1996).
92. T. Nipperdey, *The Rise of the Arts in Modern Society* (London: German Historical Institute, 1990), p. 20.
93. G. Hübinger, *Versammlungsort moderner Geister: der Eugen-Diederichs-Verlag* (Munich: Diederichs, 1996). See also G. Stark, *Entrepreneurs of Ideology* (Chapel Hill: University of North Carolina Press, 1981). Diederichs is probably best-known for the journal *Die Tat*, established in 1909. He also published the works of Bölsche and many other monists; Bergson and works of life-philosophy; together with translations of Tolstoy, Kierkegaard, Ruskin and the English Fabians.
94. See G. Kratzsch, '*Der Kunstwart* und die bürgerlich-soziale Bewegung', in Mai, Waetzoldt and Wolandt, *Ideengeschichte und Kunstwissenschaft*, p. 385. The Dürerbund claimed a membership in excess of 300,000, although most of these were affiliated members, from land reform, garden city, lifestyle reform and *Heimat* associations. A large proportion of its members were teachers. See Kratzsch, *Kunstwart und Dürerbund*.
95. See K. Toepfer, *Empire of Ecstasy: Nudity and Movement in German Body Culture, 1910–1935* (Berkeley and London: University of California Press, 1997).
96. Green, *Mountain of Truth*, p. 170.
97. See Jelavich, *Munich and Theatrical Modernism*, pp. 208–17.
98. M. Eksteins, 'When death was young', in R. Bullen, H. Pogge von Strandmann and A. Polonsky (eds), *Ideas into Politics* (London and Sydney: Croom Helm, 1984), p. 30.
99. It is important to remember there were various forms of Social Darwinism in Imperial Germany: racist groups never had a monopoly over biologistic social theory. See P. Weindling's *Darwinism and Social Darwinism in Imperial Germany* (Stuttgart and New York: Gustav Fischer, 1991); and A. Kelly's *The Descent of Darwin*(Chapel Hill, NC: University of North Carolina Press, 1981).

100. Hauptmann's interest in the implications of Darwin's work long predated his treatment of heredity as a theme in *Before Sunrise.* At school in Breslau Hauptmann had formed a secret society 'for the toughening of the race' with Alfred Ploetz, who was later to become one of Germany's most prominent 'racial hygienists'.
101. The Werdandibund staged its first *Werdandifest* in 1908, including an exhibition of paintings by Baluschek, Klinger, Vogeler and Fidus.
102. See G. Eley, 'German History and the Contradictions of Modernity', in Eley (ed.), *Society, Culture, and the State in Germany, 1870–1930* (Ann Arbor: University of Michigan Press, 1996); J. Herf, *Reactionary Modernism* (Cambridge: Cambridge University Press, 1984).
103. Given the Wihelmine reformers' preoccupation with personal health and social rejuvenation, it was perhaps inevitable that some would be attracted by the notion that humanity's sickness could be cured through careful planning and proper breeding. However, while eugenics and 'racial hygiene' were embraced by many modern spirits in early twentieth-century Germany, one should not forget this was the case throughout Europe, and in the United States too. Eugenics was seen as a key element of the new century's progressive thought, on the political left as well as the right. See P. Weindling, *Health, Race and German Politics* (Cambridge: Cambridge University Press, 1989).
104. Repp, *Reformers, Critics and the Paths of German Modernity,* p. 16. It is interesting to note that both Repp's study and Thomas Rohkrämer's *Eine andere Moderne?* employ the concept of an 'alternative modernity' as a means of avoiding the simplistic 'modern'/'anti-modern' schema.
105. For instance, the invention of telephones and typewriters (late 1870s), Kodak cameras (1880s), Emil Berliner's gramophone (1887), radio broadcasts (1900s).
106. In 1897 there were 3405 newspapers in the German Empire with a combined circulation of more than 12 million (40 times the figure a century earlier). Well over half the German population was regularly reading a newspaper by the end of the century. The biggest circulation, 150,000, was claimed by August Scherl's *Berliner Lokalanzeiger* founded in 1893. *Anzeiger* titles, as their name implied, were driven by advertising. In order to deliver large numbers of readers to the advertisers, such newspapers had to be non-political, or 'above party politics'. The circulations of party newspapers were generally much smaller.
107. Quoted by Jelavich, *Berlin Cabaret,* p. 16.
108. See C. Lamberty, *Reklame in Deutschland, 1890–1914* (Berlin: Duncker & Humblot, 2000).
109. D. Gross in G. Stark and B. K. Lackner (eds), *Essays on Culture and Society in Modern Germany* (Arlington: Texas University Press, 1982), p. 77.
110. G. Poggi, *Money and the Modern Mind: Georg Simmel's Philosophy of Money* (Berkeley and London: University of California Press, 1993), p. 52.
111. Poggi, *Money and the Modern Mind,* p. 53.
112. Schwartz, *The Werkbund.*
113. D. Gross in Stark and Lackner, *Essays on Culture and Society,* p. 71.

114. Stark, 'Cinema, society and the state', in Stark and Lackner, *Essays on Culture and Society*, p. 164.
115. G. Stark, 'Cinema, society and the state', p. 132.
116. Quoted by Stark, 'Cinema, society and the state', p. 153.

Notes to Chapter 6: Expressionism, Nationalism and War

1. V. Woolf, *Collected Essays* (London: Hogarth, 1966), vol. 1, p. 320.
2. Quoted by P. Bridgwater in *Poet of Expressionist Berlin: The Life and Work of Georg Heym* (London: Libris, 1991), p. x.
3. See T. Harrison, *1910: The Emancipation of Dissonance* (Berkeley and London: University of California Press, 1996), p. 51.
4. M. Biddiss, 'Intellectual and cultural revolution', in P. Hayes (ed.), *Themes in Modern European History, 1890–1945* (London: Routledge, 1992), p. 88.
5. Quoted by C. Hepp, *Avantgarde* (Munich: DTV, 1987), p. 126.
6. Quoted in Z. Felix (ed.), *Erich Heckel 1883–1970* (Munich: Prestel, 1983).
7. W. Sokel, introduction to *Anthology of German Expressionist Drama* (Garden City, NY: Doubleday, 1963), p. xiv.
8. See, for example, G. B. Pickar and K. E. Webb (eds), *Expressionism Reconsidered: Relationships and Affinities* (Munich: Fink, 1979); S. E. Bronner and D. Kellner (eds), *Passion and Rebellion: The Expressionist Heritage* (New York and London: Columbia University Press, 1985); R. Sheppard (ed.), *Expressionism in Focus* (Blairgowrie: Lochee, 1987); J. Lloyd, *German Expressionism: Primitivism and Modernity* (New Haven and London: Yale University Press, 1991); I. Rogoff (ed.), *The Divided Heritage: Themes and Problems in German Modernism* (Cambridge: Cambridge University Press, 1991); S. Behr, D. Fanning and D. Jarman (eds), *Expressionism Reassessed* (Manchester: Manchester University Press, 1993).
9. See W.-D. Dube, *The Expressionists* (London: Thames and Hudson, 1972), p. 18. The first documented use of the word 'Expressionist' in Britain was in 1910; in Germany the word *Expressionismus* first appears in the catalogue of the Berlin Secession's 22nd exhibition (April 1911), when the French artists Braque, Derain, Picasso and Dufy – normally described as Cubists or Fauves – were termed Expressionists. The first monograph on Expressionism was written by the German critic Paul Fechter and was published in Munich in 1914. Fechter took the name to mean the German counter-movement against Impressionism, parallel to Cubism in France and Futurism in Italy.
10. Quoted by Matthias Eberle, *World War One and the Weimar Artists: Dix, Grosz, Beckmann, Schlemmer* (New Haven and London: Yale University Press, 1985), p. 4.
11. In many ways, the self-portrait was the quintessential Expressionist subject. The willingness of artists like Schönberg, Kokoschka and Egon Schiele to portray themselves in less than ideal terms was shocking to many contemporaries.

12. Sokel, *Anthology of German Expressionist Drama*, p. x.
13. F. Trommler, 'The Creation of a Culture of *Sachlichkeit*', in G. Eley (ed.), *Society, Culture and the State in Germany, 1870–1930* (Ann Arbor: University of Michigan Press, 1996), p. 483.
14. It was illustrated by Kokoschka himself, and later put to music by Paul Hindemith. J. M. Ritchie, 'Introduction' to *Seven Expressionist Plays* (London: Calder, 1980), p. 8.
15. This was just one of four plays written by Kandinsky between 1909 and 1914: the others were *Green Sound, Black and White* and *Violet.*
16. See W. S. Bradley, *Emil Nolde and German Expressionism* (Ann Arbor: University of Michigan Press, 1986).
17. The line appears in his 1933 play *Schlageter.*
18. The hero of Goebbels' novel states 'We men of today are all expressionists, men who wish to mould the outer world from within. The expressionist builds a new world within himself. It is fervour which is his secret and his power'. Quoted in Behr, Fanning and Jarman, *Expressionism Reassessed*, p. 170.
19. Dube, *The Expressionists*, p. 31.
20. Here quoted by I. Rogoff in E. Kolinsky and W. van der Will (eds), *The Cambridge Companion to Modern German Culture* (Cambridge: Cambridge University Press, 1998, p. 261
21. Eberle, *World War One and the Weimar Artists*, p. 5.
22. C. Haxthausen, 'Images of Berlin in the art of the Secession and Expressionism', in K. Morris and A. Woods (eds), *Art in Berlin, 1815–1989* (Washington: University of Washington Press, 1989), p. 73.
23. Men such as Dresden light-bulb manufacturer Karl-Max Seifert, the Hamburg judge Gustav Schiefler, or the Cologne tobacco dealer Joseph Feinhals, who all became 'passive members' of the Brücke by subscribing to their portfolios of prints.
24. See Lenman's 'Painters, patronage and the art market', *Past and Present*, 123 (1989), 109–40; and Jensen's *Marketing Modernism in Fin-de-siècle Europe* (Princeton: Princeton University Press, 1994).
25. Rogoff, in Kolinsky and van der Will, *The Cambridge Companion to Modern German Culture*, p. 264.
26. Marc and Kandinsky made up the name one day at Sindelsdorf. Both artists loved the colour blue; Marc had a passion for horses and Kandinsky had often painted riders.
27. Quoted by Dube, *The Expressionists*, p. 131.
28. Quoted by Dube, *The Expressionists*, p. 111. For Kandinsky see Rose-Carol Washton Long, *Kandinsky: The Development of an Abstract Style* (Oxford: Clarendon, 1980).
29. See T. Nipperdey, *Wie das Bürgertum die Moderne fand* (Berlin: Siedler, 1988).
30. As Robin Lenman points out: 'By 1914 Imperial Germany had become the most important foreign market for French Impressionism after the United States'. R. Lenman, *Artists and Society in Germany* (Manchester: Manchester University Press, 1997), p. 171.
31. C. Hailey, 'Musical Expressionism: the search for autonomy', in Behr, Fanning and Jarman, *Expressionism Reassessed*, p. 104. See also J. C. and

D. L. Crawford, *Expressionism in Twentieth-Century Music* (Bloomington: Indiana University Press, 1993).

32. Two months later the première of Stravinsky's *The Rite of Spring* produced similar scenes in Paris.
33. Harrison, *1910. The Emancipation of Dissonance*, p. 51.
34. Quoted by E. Wellesz in *Arnold Schoenberg: The Formative Years* (London: Galliard, 1971), p. 10.
35. See P. Franklin, 'Wilde Musik: Composers, Critics and Expressionism', in Behr, Fanning and Jarman, *Expressionism Reassessed.*
36. See H. Fritz, *Literarischer Jugendstil und Expressionismus*; also D. Kasang, 'Wilhelminismus und Expressionismus: Das Frühwerk Fritz von Unruhs, 1904–21', University of Hamburg PhD dissertation, 1980.
37. The phrase was coined by Johannes R. Becher, quoted in P. Raabe (ed.), *The Era of Expressionism* (London: Calder and Boyars, 1974), p. 313. The poem was published in the weekly *Der Demokrat* in January 1911.
38. Bridgwater, *Poet of Expressionist Berlin*, p. 232.
39. Harrison, *1910: The Emancipation of Dissonance*, p. 117.
40. P. Raabe's *Die Autoren und Bücher des literarischen Expressionismus* (Stuttgart: Metzler, 1992) lists 328 male and just 19 female Expressionist writers.
41. Quoted in Raabe, *The Era of Expressionism*, p. 51.
42. Ritchie, 'Introduction' to *Seven Expressionist Plays*, p. 9. The term was particularly appropriate since Stramm was employed by the Imperial Post Office.
43. Sokel, introduction to *Anthology of German Expressionist Drama*, p. xviii.
44. Sokel, introduction, pp. xv–xvi.
45. Sokel, introduction, pp. x–xi.
46. The title *Der Sturm* was the inspiration of Walden's first wife, the poet Else Lasker-Schüler. From 1916 Walden was assisted by Lothar Schreyer, who became the journal's editor-in-chief. For further details see R. Allen, *Literary Life in German Expressionism and the Berlin Circles* (Ann Arbor: University of Michigan Press, 1983).
47. Both Walden and Pfemfert were fanatical about their publications; both were genuine in their enthusiasm for the avant-garde; and both died in exile, thousands of miles from home: the former in a Soviet camp in Siberia, the latter in Mexico.
48. As Carol Eliel points out, both Meidner and Heym depicted the very same Berlin gasometer in 1911 (Eliel, *The Apocalyptic Landscapes of Ludwig Meidner* (Munich: Prestel, 1989), p. 88).
49. Haxthausen, 'Images of Berlin', p. 68.
50. Quoted by Eliel, *The Apocalyptic Landscapes*, p. 63.
51. Quoted by Eliel, *The Apocalyptic Landscapes*, p. 77.
52. Haxthausen, 'Images of Berlin', p. 69.
53. Haxthausen, 'Images of Berlin', p. 70.
54. Eliel, *The Apocalyptic Landscapes*, p. 67.
55. Quoted by Lenman, *Artists and Society in Germany*, p. 185.
56. Bridgwater, *Poet of Expressionist Berlin*, p. 117.
57. The 'mentalities' approach – which looks at the systems of beliefs,

values and representations of a particular era – was pioneered by historians associated with the French journal *Annales: Économies, sociétés, civilisations*. See Roger Chartier, *Cultural History* (Cambridge: Polity, 1988).

58. M. Doerry, *Übergangsmenschen. Die Mentalität der Wilhelminer und die Krise des Kaiserreiches* (Weinheim and Munich: Juventa, 1986), p. 12. Doerry's thesis is based on the study of some 500 autobiographies; seven of which are examined in particular detail. The fact that he could find so many autobiographies of Germans born between 1853 and 1865 at least suggests that the Wilhelmine generation had a strong desire to reminisce.
59. Doerry, *Übergangsmenschen*, pp. 9 and 29.
60. M. Doerry, *Übergangsmenschen, p.* 177.
61. See H. Glaser, *Die Kultur der wilhelminischen Zeit.* In addition to Simmel and Freud, Glaser refers to books by W. Erb, *Über die wachsende Nervosität unserer Zeit* (1893); O. L. Binswanger, *Die Pathologie und Therapie der Neurasthenie* (1896); R. von Krafft-Ebing, *Nervosität und neurasthenische Zustände* (1895); and W. Hellpach, *Nervosität und Kultur* (1902).
62. S. Freud quoted in H. Glaser (ed.), *The German Mind of the Nineteenth Century* (New York: Continuum, 1981), p. 341.
63. Most recently, V. Ullrich's *Die nervöse Grossmacht. Aufstieg und Untergang des deutschen Kaiserreichs, 1871–1918* (Frankfurt: Fischer, 1997) and J. Radkau's *Das Zeitalter der Nervositat: Deutschland zwischen Bismarck und Hitler* (Munich: Hanser, 1998).
64. For a well-balanced discussion see P. Burke, 'Strengths and weaknesses of the history of mentalities', in his collection *Varieties of Cultural History* (Cambridge: Policy, 1997), pp. 162–82.
65. P. Fritzsche, *Germans into Nazis* (Cambridge, MA, and London: Harvard University Press, 1998), p. 27.
66. Later in 1911, the founder of the Insel publishing house, Alfred Walter Heymel, also published a collection of responses to Vinnen entitled *Im Kampf um die Kunst: Die Antwort auf den 'Protest deutscher Künstler'.*
67. M. Werenskiold in Behr, Fanning and Jarman, *Expressionism Reassessed,* p. 24.
68. F. Spotts, *Bayreuth* (New Haven and London: Yale University Press, 1994), p. 133.
69. See W. Siemann, 'Krieg und Frieden in historischen Gedenkfeiern des Jahres 1913', in D. Düding *et al.*, (eds), *Öffentliche Festkultur* (Reinbek: Rowohlt, 1988).
70. The German gymnastics movement had around 1.1 million male members in over 11,000 clubs in 1913. Siemann believes their role was important in shaping the attitudes of the generation that went to war in 1914. See Siemann, 'Krieg und Frieden in historischen Gedenkfeiern des Jahres 1913'.
71. Quotes from W. Hardtwig, *Geschichtskultur und Wissenschaft* (Munich: DTV, 1990), pp. 287–89.
72. T. Nipperdey, 'Nationalidee und Nationaldenkmal in Deutschland im 19. Jahrhundert', p. 163. See also K. Keller and H.-D. Schmid (eds),

Vom Kult zur Kulisse: das Völkerschlachtdenkmal als Gegenstand der Geschichtskultur (Leipzig: Universitätsverlag, 1995).

73. Quoted by Hepp, *Avantgarde*, p. 75.
74. See P. Stachura, *The German Youth Movement, 1900–1945* (New York: St Martin's, 1981), p. 32.
75. P. Paret, *The Berlin Secession* (Cambridge, MA, and London: Harvard University Press, 1980), pp. 229–30.
76. G. F. Keenan, *The Decline of Bismarck's European Order* (Princeton: Princeton University Press, 1979), p. 3.
77. Armin Wegner in Raabe, *The Era of Expressionism*, p. 26.
78. Harrison, *1910: The Emancipation of Dissonance*, p. 219.
79. Quoted by Bridgwater, *Poet of Expressionist Berlin*, p. 219.
80. See S. E. Aschheim, *The Nietzsche Legacy in Germany* (Berkeley: University of California Press, 1992), p. 128. Aschheim also notes that the Sarajevo assassin Gavrilo Princip was fond of reciting Nietzsche's short poem *Ecce Homo*, and particularly the line 'Insatiable as flame, I burn and consume myself'.
81. Quoted by Aschheim, *The Nietzsche Legacy in Germany*, p. 130.
82. Aschheim, *The Nietzsche Legacy in Germany*, pp. 135–7. According to Aschheim, 'About 150,000 copies of a specially durable wartime *Zarathustra* were distributed to the troops'. He concludes, however, that: 'in the field *Zarathustra* was not as popular as proponents of the Nietzschean myth claimed'.
83. M. Swales in Kolinsky and van der Will, *The Cambridge Companion to Modern German Culture*, p. 183.
84. K. Vondung, 'Deutsche Apokalypse 1914', in Vondung (ed.), *Das wilhelminische Bildungsbürgertum* (Göttingen: Vandenhoeck & Ruprecht, 1976).
85. Vondung, 'Deutsche Apokalypse 1914', p. 155.
86. Quoted by M. Eksteins, *Rites of Spring* (London: Bantam, 1976), p. 138.
87. Reprinted in Hepp, *Avantgarde*, pp. 205–8.
88. P. Buitenhuis, *The Great War of Words: Literature as Propaganda, 1914–18 and After* (London: Batsford, 1989). All except Hardy contributed propaganda pieces of one sort or another during the course of the war.
89. See K. Unruh, *Langemarck. Legende und Wirklichkeit* (Koblenz: Bernard and Graefe, 1986).
90. Stachura, *The German Youth Movement*, p. 36.
91. Eksteins, *Rites of Spring*, pp. 137–8.
92. W. J. Mommsen (ed.), *Kultur und Krieg. Die Rolle der Intellektuellen, Künstler und Schriftsteller in Ersten Weltkrieg* (Munich: Oldenbourg, 1996), p. 8.
93. The figure was estimated by Julius Bab in an article for *Das literarische Echo* in October 1914, cited by Andreas Schumann in Mommsen, *Kultur und Krieg*, p. 221.
94. Eksteins, *Rites of Spring*, p. 99.
95. For the 'Ideas of 1914' see Mommsen, *Kultur und Krieg*. Also H. Fries, *Die grosse Katharsis: Der Erste Weltkrieg in der Sicht deutscher Dichter und Gelehrter* (Konstanz: Verlag am Hockgraben, 1994); F. Ringer, *The Decline of the German Mandarins: The German Academic Community,*

1890–1933 (Cambridge, MA, and London: Harvard University Press, 1969).

96. W. Kruse, *Krieg und nationale Integration: Eine Neuinterpretation des sozialdemokratischen Burgfriedensschlusses 1914/15* (Essen: Klartext, 1993). See also J. T. Verhey, *The Spirit of 1914: Militarism, Myth and Mobilization in Germany* (Cambridge: Cambridge University Press, 2000).
97. W. Kruse, 'War Euphoria in Germany in 1914', in H. Herwig (ed.), *The Outbreak of World War One* (Boston, MA: Houghton Mifflin, 1997), p. 103.
98. V. Ullrich, *Kriegsalltag: Hamburg im Ersten Weltkrieg* (Cologne: Prometh, 1982); M. Stöcker, *Augusterlebnis 1914 in Darmstadt. Legende und Wirklichkeit* (Darmstadt: Roether, 1994); C. Geinitz, *Kriegsfurcht und Kampfbereitschaft. Das August-Erlebnis in Freiburg* (Essen: Klartext, 1998).
99. Kruse, 'War Euphoria in Germany in 1914', p. 99.
100. H. Herwig, *The First World War: Germany and Austria-Hungary, 1914–18* (London: Arnold, 1997), p. 33. Eventually some 13 million Germans were called up.
101 See R. J. Evans, *Kneipengespräche im Kaiserreich* (Reinbek: Rowohlt, 1989), p. 415.
102 In total, some 700,000 Germans would die of malnutrition. See T. Rohkrämer, *Eine andere Moderne* (Paderborn: Schöningh, 1999), p. 237.
103 Herwig, *The First World War*, p. 3.
104 G. Hübinger, 'Eugen Diederichs und eine neue Geisteskultur', in Mommsen (ed.), *Kultur und Krieg*, p. 267.
105 Detailed in Toller's *Eine Jugend in Deutschland* (Reinbek: Rowohlt, 1963, first published in 1933).
106 P. Gay, *Weimar Culture* (Harmondsworth: Penguin, 1974), p. 6
107 W. Laqueur, *Weimar: A Cultural History* (London: Weidenfeld and Nicolson, 1974), preface.
108 D. Peukert, *The Weimar Republic* (Harmondsworth: Penguin, 1991), p. 164.
109 'The Birth of Modernism' is, for instance, a chapter heading in R. Burns (ed.), *German Cultural Studies: An Introduction* (Oxford: Oxford University Press, 1995), p. 53
110 F. Trommler, 'The Creation of a Culture of *Sachlichkeit*', in Eley, *Society, Culture, and the State in Germany, 1870–1930*, p. 479.
111 J. J. Sheehan, *Museums in the German Art World* (Oxford: Oxford University Press, 2000), p. 185.
112 J. Willett, *The New Sobriety* (London and New York: Thames and Hudson, 1978), p. 10.
113 Lenman, *Artists and Society in Germany*, p. 183.
114 See G. Naylor, *The Bauhaus Reassessed: Sources and Design Theory* (London: Herbert, 1985).
115 See B. Miller Lane, *Architecture and Politics in Germany, 1918–45* (Cambridge, MA: Harvard University Press, 1985).
116 F. Schwartz, *The Werkbund* (New Haven and London: Yale University Press, 1996), p. 215.

117 Peukert, *The Weimar Republic*, p. 164.
118 Willett, *The New Sobriety*, p. 12.
119 Schwartz, *The Werkbund*, pp. 216–17.
120 The declaration appeared in Gustav Stresemann's journal *Deutsche Stimmen*, 30 (1918), 47.

Bibliography

Abrams, L., *Workers Culture in Imperial Germany: Leisure and Recreation in the Rhineland and Westphalia* (London: Routledge, 1992).

Ahlers-Hestermann, F., *Stilwende: Aufbruch der Jugend um 1900* (Berlin: Mann, 1956).

Ahlzweig, C., *Muttersprache – Vaterland. Die deutsche Nation und ihre Sprache* (Opladen: Westdeutscher Verlag, 1994).

Allen, A. T., *Satire and Society in Wilhelmine Germany: Kladderadatsch and Simplicissimus, 1890–1914* (Lexington: University Press of Kentucky, 1984).

Allen, R., *Literary Life in German Expressionism and the Berlin Circles* (Ann Arbor: University of Michigan Press, 1983).

Applegate, C., *A Nation of Provincials: The German Idea of Heimat* (Berkeley and London: University of California Press, 1990).

Arndt, M., *Die Goslarer Kaiserpfalz als Nationaldenkmal* (Hildesheim: Lax, 1976).

Aschheim, S. E., *The Nietzsche Legacy in Germany, 1890–1990* (Berkeley: University of California Press, 1992).

Bartmann, D., *Anton von Werner: zur Kunst und Kunstpolitik im deutschen Kaiserreich* (Berlin: Deutsche Verlag für Kunstwissenschaft, 1985).

Bartmann, D. (ed.), *Anton von Werner: Geschichte in Bildern* (Munich: Hirmer, 1993).

Behr, S., Fanning, D. and Jarman, D. (eds), *Expressionism Reassessed* (Manchester: Manchester University Press, 1993).

Berger, R., *Malerinnen auf dem Weg ins 20. Jahrhundert: Kunstgeschichte als Sozialgeschichte* (Cologne: Dumont, 1982).

Berghahn, V., *Imperial Germany, 1871–1914: Economy, Society, Culture, and Politics* (Providence and Oxford: Berghahn, 1994).

Bergius, B., Frecot, J. and Radicke, D. (eds), *Architektur, Stadt und Politik* (Lahn-Giessen: Anabas, 1979).

Bergmann, K., *Agrarromantik und Grossstadtfeindschaft* (Meisenheim am Glan: Hain, 1970).

Berman, R., *Cultural Studies of Modern Germany: History, Representation and Nationhood* (Madison: University of Wisconsin Press, 1993).

Blackbourn, D., *The Fontana History of Germany, 1780–1918: The Long Nineteenth Century* (London: Fontana, 1997).
Blackbourn, D. and Eley, G., *The Peculiarities of German History* (Oxford: Oxford University Press, 1984).
Blackbourn, D. and Evans, R. (eds), *The German Bourgeoisie* (London: Routledge, 1991).
Blochmann, G., *Zeitgeist und Künstlermythos: Untersuchungen zur Selbstdarstellung deutscher Maler der Gründerzeit* (Münster: Lit, 1991).
Boberg, J., Fichter, T. and Gillen, E. (eds), *Exerzierfeld der Moderne: Industriekultur in Berlin im 19: Jahrhundert* (Munich: Beck, 1984).
Boberg, J., Fichter, T. and Gillen, E. (eds), *Die Metropole: Industriekultur in Berlin im 20: Jahrhundert* (Munich: Beck, 1985) .
Borrmann, N., *Paul Schultze-Naumburg, 1869–1949* (Essen: Bacht, 1989).
Bramsted, E. K., *Aristocracy and the Middle Classes in Germany: Social Types in German Literature, 1830–1900* (Chicago and London: University of Chicago Press, 1964).
Brix, M. and Steinhauser, M. (eds), *Geschichte allein ist zeitgemäss: Historismus in Deutschland* (Lahn-Giessen: Anabas, 1978).
Bruch, R. vom, *Wissenschaft, Politik und öffentliche Meinung: Gelehrtenpolitik im Wilhelminischen Deutschland* (Husum: Matthiesen, 1980).
Bruch, R. vom, Graf, F. and Hübinger, G. (eds), *Kultur und Kulturwissenschaften um 1900*, 2 vols (Stuttgart: Steiner, 1989 and 1997).
Buddensieg, T., *Industriekultur: Peter Behrens and the AEG, 1907–1914* (Cambridge, MA, and London: MIT Press, 1984).
Burke, P., *Varieties of Cultural History* (Cambridge: Polity, 1997).
Burns, R., *German Cultural Studies: an Introduction* (Oxford: Oxford University Press, 1995).
Campbell, J., *The German Werkbund: The Politics of Reform in the Applied Arts* (Princeton, NJ: Princeton University Press, 1978).
Chapple, G. and Schulte, H. (eds), *The Turn of the Century: German Literature and Art* (Bonn: Bouvier, 1981).
Chickering, R. (ed.), *Imperial Germany: A Historiographical Companion* (Westport, CT and London: Greenwood, 1996).
Confino, A., *The Nation as a Local Metaphor: Württemberg, Imperial Germany and National Memory, 1871–1918* (Chapel Hill and London: University of North Carolina Press, 1997).
Craig, G., *Germany, 1866–1945* (Oxford: Clarendon, 1978).
Cullen, M., *Der Reichstag: Die Geschichte eines Monuments* (Berlin: Frölich & Kaufmann, 1983).
Dann, O. (ed.), *Religion – Kunst – Vaterland: Der Kölner Dom im 19: Jahrhundert* (Cologne: Bachem, 1983).
Doerry, M., *Übergangsmenschen: Die Mentalität der Wilhelminer und die Krise des Kaiserreichs* (Weinheim: Juventa, 1986).
Dolgner, D., *Historismus: Deutsche Baukunst, 1815–1900* (Leipzig: Seemann, 1993).
Dollinger, H., *Preussen: Eine Kulturgeschichte in Bildern und Dokumenten* (Munich: Süddeutscher Verlag, 1980).
Dube, W.-D., *The Expressionists* (London: Thames and Hudson, 1972).

Düding, D., Friedemann, P. and Münch, P. (eds), *Öffentliche Festkultur: Politische Feste in Deutschland von der Aufklärung bis zum Ersten Weltkrieg* (Reinbek: Rowohlt, 1988).

Eksteins, M., *Rites of Spring: The First World War and the Birth of the Modern Age* (London: Bantam, 1989).

Eley, G. (ed.), *Society, Culture and the State in Germany, 1870–1930* (Ann Arbor: University of Michigan Press, 1996).

Forderer, C., *Die Grossstadt im Roman: Berliner Grosstadtdarstellungen zwischen Naturalismus und Moderne* (Wiesbaden: DUV, 1992).

Forster-Hahn, F. (ed.), *Imagining Modern German Culture, 1889–1910* (Hanover, NH: University Press of New England, 1996).

Frecot, J., Geist, J. and Kerbs, D., *Fidus, 1868–1968: Zur ästhetischen Praxis bürgerlicher Fluchtbewegungen* (Munich: Rogner & Bernhard, 1972).

Frevert, U., *Women in German History: From Bourgeois Emancipation to Sexual Liberation* (Oxford: Berg, 1988).

Fritzsche, P., *Reading Berlin, 1900* (Cambridge, MA, and London: Harvard University Press, 1996).

Gaehtgens, T., *Anton von Werner: Die Proklamierung des Deutschen Kaiserreichs. Ein Historienbild im Wandel preussischer Politik* (Frankfurt: Fischer, 1990).

Gall, L., 'Die Germania als Symbol nationaler Identität im 19. und 20. Jahrhundert', *Nachrichten der Akademie der Wissenschaften in Göttingen: 1. Philologisch-Historische Klasse* (Göttingen: Vandenhoeck & Ruprecht, 1993).

Gasman, D., *The Scientific Origins of National Socialism: Social Darwinism in Ernst Haeckel and the German Monist League* (London: Macdonald, 1971).

Gay, P., *Weimar Culture: The Outsider as Insider* (Harmondsworth: Penguin, 1974).

Glaser, H., *Die Kultur der wilhelminischen Zeit: Topographie einer Epoche* (Frankfurt: Fischer, 1984).

Glaser, H. (ed.), *So viel Anfang war nie: Deutscher Geist im 19. Jahrhundert: Ein Lesebuch* (Frankfurt: Fischer, 1984).

Glaser, H., *Bildungsbürgertum und Nationalismus: Politik und Kultur im Wilhelminischen Deutschland* (Munich: DTV, 1993).

Gordon, D., *Expressionism: Art and Idea* (New Haven, CT, and London: Yale University Press, 1987).

Green, A., *Fatherlands: State-building and Nationhood in Nineteenth-Century Germany* (Cambridge: Cambridge University Press, 2001).

Green, M., *Mountain of Truth: The Counterculture Begins – Ascona, 1900–1920* (Hanover, NH: University Press of New England, 1986).

Grimm, R. and Hermand, J. (eds), *Deutsche Feiern* (Wiesbaden: Athenaion, 1977).

Haaff, R., *Gründerzeit: Möbel und Wohnkultur* (Westheim: Rhein-Verlag-Haaff, 1992).

Hamann, R. and Hermand, J., *Epochen deutscher Kultur von 1870 bis zur Gegenwart* (Frankfurt: Fischer, 1977): vol. 1: *Gründerzeit*; vol. 2: *Naturalismus*; vol. 3: *Impressionismus*; vol. 4: *Stilkunst um 1900*; vol. 5: *Expressionismus.*

Hammerschmidt, V., *Anspruch und Ausdruck in der Architektur des späten Historismus in Deutschland, 1860–1914* (Frankfurt: Lang, 1985).

Hansen, W., *Nationaldenkmäler und Nationalfeste im 19: Jahrhundert*

(Lüneburg: Niederdeutscher Verband für Volks- und Altertumskunde, 1976).
Hardtwig, W., *Geschichtskultur und Wissenschaft* (Munich: DTV, 1990).
Harrington, A., *Re-enchanted Science: Holism in German Culture from Wilhelm II to Hitler* (Princeton, NJ: Princeton University Press, 1996).
Harrison, T., *1910: The Emancipation of Dissonance* (Berkeley and London: University of California Press, 1996).
Hartmann, K., *Die deutsche Gartenstadtbewegung: Kulturpolitik und Gesellschafts-reform* (Munich: Moos, 1976).
Hartmann, W., *Der Historische Festzug: Seine Entstehung und Entwicklung im 19. und 20. Jahrhundert* (Munich: Prestel, 1976).
Hartung, W., *Konservative Zivilisationskritik und regionale Identität am Beispiel der niedersächsischen Heimatbewegung, 1895–1919* (Hanover: Hahn, 1990).
Haubner, B., *Nervenkitzel und Freizeitvergnügen: Automobilismus in Deutschland 1886–1914* (Göttingen: Vandenhoeck & Ruprecht, 1998).
Hein, P. U., *Transformation der Kunst: Ziele und Wirkungen der deutschen Kultur- und Kunsterziehungsbewegung* (Cologne: Böhlau, 1991).
Hepp, C., *Avantgarde: Moderne Kunst, Kulturkritik und Reformbewegungen nach der Jahrhundertwende* (Munich: DTV, 1987).
Herf, J., *Reactionary Modernism: Technology, Culture and Politics in Weimar and the Third Reich* (Cambridge: Cambridge University Press, 1984) .
Hermand, J., *Der Schein des schönen Lebens – Studien zur Jahrhundertwende* (Frankfurt: Athenaeum, 1972).
Herre, F., *Jahrhundertwende 1900: Untergangsstimmung und Fortschrittsglauben* (Stuttgart: DVA, 1998).
Herzogenrath, W. et al. (eds), *Der westdeutsche Impuls, 1900–1914: Die Deutsche Werkbund-Ausstellung Cöln 1914* (Cologne: Kölnischer Kunstverein, 1984).
Heskett, J., *Design in Germany, 1870–1918* (London: Trefoil, 1986).
Hesse-Frielinghaus, H. (ed.), *Karl Ernst Osthaus: Leben und Werk* (Recklinghausen: Bongers, 1971).
Hirschmann, G., *Kulturkampf im historischen Roman der Gründerzeit, 1859–1878* (Munich: Fink, 1978).
Hübinger, G., *Versammlungsort moderner Geister: der Eugen-Diederichs-Verlag* (München: Diederichs, 1996).
Hübinger, G. and Mommsen, W. J. (eds), *Intellektuelle im deutschen Kaiserreich* (Frankfurt: Fischer, 1993).
Hughes, H. S., *Consciousness and Society: The Reorientation of European Social Thought, 1890–1930* (New York: Knopf, 1958).
Iggers, G. G., *The German Conception of History* (Middletown, CT: Wesleyan University Press, 1968).
Jefferies, M., *Politics and Culture in Wilhelmine Germany: The Case of Industrial Architecture* (Oxford and Washington: Berg, 1995).
Jelavich, P., *Munich and Theatrical Modernism* (Cambridge, MA, and London: Havard University Press, 1985).
Jelavich, P., *Berlin Cabaret* (Cambridge, MA, and London: Harvard University Press, 1993).
Jensen, R., *Marketing Modernism in Fin-de-siècle Europe* (Princeton, NJ: Princeton University Press, 1994).

Junge, H. (ed.), *Avantgarde und Publikum: Zur Rezeption avantgardistischer Kunst in Deutschland, 1905–33* (Cologne: Böhlau, 1992).

Junghanns, K., *Der deutsche Werkbund: sein erstes Jahrzehnt* (East Berlin: Henschelverlag, 1982).

Kauffeldt, R. and Cepl-Kaufmann, G., *Berlin-Friedrichshagen: Literaturhauptstadt um die Jahrhundertwende* (Munich: Boer, 1994).

Kelly, A., *The Descent of Darwin: The Popularization of Darwinism in Germany, 1860–1914* (Chapel Hill: University of North Carolina Press, 1981).

Kerbs, D. and Reulecke, J. (eds), *Handbuch der deutschen Reformbewegungen, 1880–1933* (Wuppertal: Hammer, 1998).

Kern, S., *The Culture of Time and Space, 1880–1918* (London: Weidenfeld and Nicolson, 1983).

Kiefer, S., *Dramatik der Gründerzeit* (St Ingbert: Röhrig, 1997).

Kocka, J. (ed.), *Bürger und Bürgerlichkeit* (Göttingen: Vandenhoeck & Ruprecht, 1985).

Kocka, J. (ed.), *Bürgertum im 19. Jahrhundert* (Munich: DTV, 1988).

Kohl, P. and Fawcett, C. (eds), *Nationalism, Politics and the Practice of Archaeology* (Cambridge: Cambridge University Press, 1995).

Kolinsky, E. and van der Will, W. (eds), *The Cambridge Companion to Modern German Culture* (Cambridge: Cambridge University Press, 1998).

Koreska-Hartmann, L., *Jugendstil – Stil der 'Jugend'* (Munich: DTV, 1969).

Koszinowski, I., *Von der Poesie des Kunstwerks* (Hildesheim: Olms, 1985).

Krabbe, W., *Gesellschaftsveränderung durch Lebensreform: Strukturmerkmale einer sozialreformerischen Bewegung in Deutschland der Industrialisierungsperiode* (Göttingen: Vandenhoeck & Ruprecht, 1974).

Kramer, H., *Deutsche Kultur zwischen 1871 und 1918* (Frankfurt: Athenaion, 1971).

Kranz-Michaelis, C., *Rathäuser im deutschen Kaiserreich, 1871–1918* (Munich: Prestel, 1976).

Kratzsch, G., *Kunstwart und Dürerbund* (Göttingen: Vandenhoeck & Ruprecht, 1969).

Kuchenbuch, T., *Die Welt um 1900* (Stuttgart: Metzler, 1992).

Kulhoff, B., *Bürgerliche Selbstbehauptung im Spiegel der Kunst: Untersuchungen zur Kulturpublizistik der Rundschauzeitschriften im Kaiserreich* (Bochum: Brockmeyer, 1990).

Küster, B., *Max Liebermann: Ein Maler-Leben* (Hamburg: Ellert & Richter, 1988).

Laqueur, W., *Young Germany: A History of the German Youth Movement* (New York: Basic Books, 1962).

Laqueur, W., *Weimar: A Cultural History* (London: Weidenfeld and Nicolson, 1974).

Lenman, R., *Die Kunst, die Macht und das Geld: zur Kulturgeschichte des kaiserlichen Deutschland* (Frankfurt and New York: Campus, 1994).

Lenman, R., 'Politics and culture: the state and the *avantgarde* in Munich, 1886–1914', in R. J. Evans (ed.), *Society and Politics in Wilhelmine Germany* (London: Croom Hall, 1978).

Lenman, R., 'Painters, patronage and the art market in Germany, 1880–1914', *Past and Present* (May 1989).

Lenman, R., *Artists and Society in Germany, 1850–1914* (Manchester: Manchester University Press, 1997).
Lewis, M., *The Politics of the German Gothic Revival: August Reichensperger* (Cambridge, MA, and London: MIT, 1993).
Lidtke, V., *The Alternative Culture: Socialist Labor in Imperial Germany* (New York and Oxford: Oxford University Press, 1985).
Link, J. and Wülfing, W. (eds), *Nationale Mythen und Symbole in der zweiten Halfte des 19. Jahrhunderts* (Stuttgart: Klett-Cotta, 1991).
Linnenkamp, R., *Die Gründerzeit, 1835–1918* (Munich: Heyne, 1976).
Linse, U., *Zurück, o Mensch, zur Mutter Erde: Landkommunen in Deutschland, 1890–1933* (Munich: DTV, 1983).
Lipp, W., *Natur-Geschichte-Denkmal: zur Entstehung des Denkmalbewusstseins der bürgerlichen Gesellschaft* (Frankfurt: Campus, 1987).
Lloyd, J., *German Expressionism: Primitivism and Modernity* (New Haven, CT: Yale University Press, 1991).
Mai, E. and Waetzoldt, S. (eds), *Kunstverwaltung, Bau- und Denkmalpolitik im Kaiserreich* (Berlin: Mann, 1981).
Mai, E. and Paret, P. (eds), *Sammler, Stifter und Museen: Kunstförderung in Deutschland im 19. und 20. Jahrhundert* (Cologne: Böhlau, 1993).
Mai, E., Pohl, H. and Waetzoldt, S. (eds), *Kunstpolitik und Kunstförderung im Kaiserreich* (Berlin: Mann, 1982).
Mai, E., Paul, J. and Waetzoldt, S. (eds), *Das Rathaus im Kaiserreich* (Berlin: Mann, 1982).
Mai, E., Waetzoldt, S. and Wolandt, G. (eds), *Ideengeschichte und Kunstwissenschaft im Kaiserreich* (Berlin: Mann, 1983).
Makela, M., *The Munich Secession: Art and Artists in Turn-of-the-Century Munich* (Princeton, NJ: Princeton University Press, 1990).
Malkowsky, G., *Die Kunst im Dienste der Staats-Idee: Hohenzollerische Kunstpolitik vom Grossen Kurfursten bis auf Wilhelm II* (Berlin: Patria, 1912).
Marshall, A., *The German Naturalists and Gerhart Hauptmann: Reception and Influence* (Frankfurt: Lang, 1982) .
Masur, G., *Imperial Berlin* (London: Routledge, 1970).
Mittig, H. E. and Plagemann, V., *Denkmäler im 19. Jahrhundert* (Munich: Prestel, 1972).
Mommsen, W. J., *Bürgerliche Kultur und künstlerische Avantgarde: Kultur und Politik im deutschen Kaiserreich* (Berlin: Propyläen, 1994).
Mommsen, W. J., *Imperial Germany, 1867–1918: Politics, Culture and Society in an Authoritarian State* (London: Arnold, 1995).
Mommsen, W. J. (ed.), *Kultur und Krieg: Die Rolle der Intellektuellen, Künstler und Schriftsteller im Ersten Weltkrieg* (Munich: Oldenbourg, 1996) .
Mosse, G. L., *The Nationalization of the Masses* (New York: Fertig, 1975).
Mosse, G. L., *The Crisis of German Ideology: Intellectual Origins of the Third Reich* (London: Weidenfeld and Nicolson, 1966).
Müller, J. (ed.), *Der westdeutsche Impuls, 1900–1914: Die Folkwang-Idee des Karl Ernst Osthaus* (Cologne: Kölnischer Kunstverein, 1984).
Mundt, B., *Die deutschen Kunstgewerbemuseen im 19. Jahrhundert* (Munich: Prestel, 1974).
Nipperdey, T., 'Nationalidee und Nationaldenkmal in Deutschland im 19. Jahrhundert', *Historische Zeitschrift*, 206, (1968).

Nipperdey, T., *Wie das Bürgertum die Moderne fand* (Berlin: Siedler, 1988).
Nipperdey, T., *Deutsche Geschichte, 1866–1918*, 2 vols (Munich: Beck, 1990–2).
Nipperdey, T., *The Rise of the Arts in Modern Society* (London: German Historical Institute, 1990).
Nitschke, A., Ritter, G. A., Peukert, D. and vom Bruch, R. (eds), *Jahrhundertwende: Der Aufbruch in die Moderne*, 2 vols (Reinbek: Rowohlt, 1990).
Oettermann, S., *Das Panorama: Die Geschichte eines Massenmediums* (Frankfurt: Syndikat, 1980).
Ogger, G., *Die Gründerjahre: Als der Kapitalismus jung und verwegen war* (Munich: Knaur, 1982).
Otto, H., *Gründerzeit: Aufbruch einer Nation* (Bonn: Keil, 1984).
Pape, W. (ed.), *German Unifications and the Change of Literary Discourse* (Berlin and New York: Walter de Gruyter, 1993).
Paret, P., *The Berlin Secession: Modernism and its Enemies in Imperial Germany* (Cambridge, MA, and London: Harvard University Press, 1980).
Paret, P., *Art as History: Episodes in the Culture and Politics of Nineteenth-Century Germany* (Princeton, NJ: Princeton University Press, 1988).
Park, E.-C., *Fontanes Zeitromane: Zur Kritik der Gründerzeit* (Frankfurt: Lang, 1997).
Pascal, R., *From Naturalism to Expressionism: German Literature and Society, 1880–1918* (London: Weidenfeld and Nicolson, 1973).
Patterson, M., *The Revolution in German Theatre, 1900–33* (London: Routledge, 1981).
Petsch, J., *Architektur und Gesellschaft: Zur Geschichte der deutschen Architektur im 19. und 20. Jahrhundert* (Cologne: Böhlau, 1977).
Petsch, J., *Eigenheim und gute Stube: Zur Geschichte des bürgerlichen Wohnens* (Cologne: Dumont, 1989).
Pickar, G. B. and Webb, K. E. (eds), *Expressionism Reconsidered: Relationships and Affinities* (Munich: Fink, 1979).
Plagemann, V. (ed.), *Industriekultur in Hamburg* (Munich: Beck, 1984).
Posener, J., *Berlin auf dem Wege zu einer neuen Architektur: das Zeitalter Wilhelms II* (Munich: Prestel, 1979).
Radkau, J., *Das Zeitalter der Nervosität: Deutschland zwischen Bismarck und Hitler* (Munich: Hanser, 1998).
Repp, K., *Reformers, Critics and the Paths of German Modernity: Anti-Politics and the Search for Alternatives, 1890–1914* (Cambridge, MA, and London: Harvard University Press, 2000).
Reulecke, J. and Weber, W. (eds), *Fabrik, Familie, Feierabend: Beiträge zur Geschichte des Alltags im Industriezeitalter* (Wuppertal: Hammer, 1978).
Ringer, F., *The Decline of the German Mandarins: The German Academic Community, 1890–1933* (Cambridge, MA, and London: Harvard University Press, 1969).
Rogoff, I. (ed.), *The Divided Heritage: Themes and Problems in German Modernism* (Cambridge: Cambridge University Press, 1991).
Rohkrämer, T., *Eine andere Moderne? Zivilisationskritik, Natur und Technik in Deutschland, 1880–1933* (Paderborn: Schöningh, 1999).

Röhl, J. C. G. and Sombart, N. (eds), *Kaiser Wilhelm II: New Interpretations* (Cambridge: Cambridge University Press, 1982).
Röhl, J. C. G., *The Kaiser and his Court* (Cambridge: Cambridge University Press, 1996).
Röhl, J. C. G., *Young Wilhelm: The Kaiser's Early Life, 1859–88* (Cambridge: Cambridge University Press, 1998).
Roper, K., *German Encounters with Modernity: Novels of Imperial Berlin* (Atlantic Highlands, NJ, and London: Humanities Press, 1991).
Rose, P. L., *Wagner: Race and Revolution* (New Haven, CT, and London: Yale University Press, 1992).
Ross, R. J., *The Failure of Bismarck's Kulturkampf: Catholicism and State Power in Imperial Germany, 1871–1887* (Washington, DC: Catholic University of America Press, 1998).
Rossbacher, K., *Heimatkunstbewegung und Heimatsroman* (Stuttgart: Klett, 1975).
Russell, F. (ed.), *Art Nouveau Architecture* (London: Academy Editions, 1979).
Sarfert, H.-J., *Hellerau: Die Gartenstadt und Künstlerkolonie* (Dresden: Hellerau, 1993).
Scharf, H., *Kleine Kunstgeschichte des deutschen Denkmals* (Darmstadt: Wissenschaftliche Buchgesellschaft, 1984).
Scherer, H., *Bürgerlich-oppositionelle Literaten und sozialdemokratische Arbeiterbewegung nach 1890: Die 'Friedrichshagener' und ihr Einfluss auf die sozialdemokratische Kulturpolitik* (Stuttgart: Metzler, 1974).
Scheuer, H. (ed.), *Naturalismus: Bürgerliche Dichtung und soziales Engagement* (Stuttgart: Kohlhammer, 1974).
Schieder, T., *Das deutsche Kaiserreich von 1871 als Nationalstaat* (Göttingen: Vandenhoeck & Ruprecht, 1992).
Schieder, T. and Deuerlein, E. (eds), *Reichsgründung, 1870–71* (Stuttgart: Sewald, 1970).
Schiefler, G., *Eine Hamburgische Kulturgeschichte, 1890–1920: Beobachtungen eines Zeitgenossen* (Hamburg: Verein für Hamburgische Geschichte, 1985).
Schivelbusch, W., *Lichtblicke: Zur Geschichte der künstlichen Helligkeit im 19. Jahrhundert* (Munich: Hanser, 1983).
Schivelbusch, W., *The Railway Journey: The Industrialisation of Time and Space in the Nineteenth Century* (Leamington Spa: Berg, 1986).
Schivelbusch, W., *Das Paradies, der Geschmack und die Vernunft: Eine Geschichte der Genussmittel* (Frankfurt: Fischer, 1990).
Schlapeit-Beck, D., *Frauenarbeit in der Malerei, 1870–1900* (Berlin: Elefanten, 1985).
Schoeps, H. J. (ed.), *Zeitgeist im Wandel: Das Wilhelminische Zeitalter* (Stuttgart: Klett, 1967).
Schorske, C. E., *Fin-de-Siècle Vienna: Politics and Culture* (Cambridge: Cambridge University Press, 1981).
Schorske, C. E., *Thinking with History: Explorations in the Passage to Modernism* (Princeton, NJ: Princeton University Press, 1998).
Schüler, W., *Der Bayreuther Kreis, von seiner Entstehung bis zum Ausgang der wilhelminischen Ära* (Münster: Aschendorff, 1971).
Schutte, J. and Sprengel, P. (eds), *Die Berliner Moderne, 1885–1914* (Stuttgart: Reclam, 1987).

Schwartz, F., *The Werkbund: Design Theory and Mass Culture before the First World War* (New Haven and London: Yale University Press, 1996).
Schwarzer, M., *German Architectural Theory and the Search for Modern Identity* (Cambridge: Cambridge University Press, 1995).
Segieth, C., 'Im Zeichen des "Secessionismus" – die Anfänge der Münchener *Jugend.* Ein Beitrag zum Kunstverständnis der Jahrhundertwende in München' (University of Munich, PhD dissertation, 1994).
Seidel, P., *Der Kaiser und die Kunst* (Berlin: Reichsdruckerei, 1907).
Selle, G., *Design-Geschichte in Deutschland* (Cologne: Dumont, 1990).
Selz, P., *German Expressionist Painting* (Berkeley and London: University of California Press, 1957).
Sembach, K.-J., *Jugendstil* (Cologne: Taschen, 1990).
Sheehan, J. J., *German Liberalism in the Nineteenth Century* (Chicago and London: University of Chicago Press, 1978).
Sheehan, J. J., *Museums in the German Art World: From the End of the Old Regime to the Rise of Modernism* (Oxford: Oxford University Press, 2000).
Siepmann, E. (ed.), *Kunst und Alltag um 1900* (Lahn-Giessen: Anabas, 1978).
Simon, H.-U., *Sezessionismus: Kunstgewerbe in literarischer und bildender Kunst* (Stuttgart: Metzler, 1976).
Sperber, J., *Popular Catholicism in Nineteenth-Century Germany* (Princeton, NJ: Princeton University Press, 1984).
Sperber, J., *The Kaiser's Voters: Electors and Elections in Imperial Germany* (Cambridge: Cambridge University Press, 1997).
Spotts, F., *Bayreuth: A History of the Wagner Fesival* (New Haven, CT, and London: Yale University Press, 1994).
Stachura, P., *The German Youth Movement, 1900–1945* (New York: St Martin's, 1981).
Stark, G. D., *Entrepreneurs of Ideology: Neoconservative Publishers in Germany, 1890–1933* (Chapel Hill, NC: University of North Carolina Press, 1981).
Stark, G. D. and Lackner, B. K. (eds), *Essays on Culture and Society in Modern Germany* (Arlington: Texas University Press, 1982).
Stather, M., *Die Kunstpolitik Wilhelms II* (Konstanz: Hartung-Gorre, 1994).
Stern, F., *The Politics of Cultural Despair* (Berkeley and London: University of California Press, 1961).
Sternberger, D., *Panorama oder Ansichten vom 19. Jahrhundert* (Frankfurt: Insel, 1981).
Strieder, A., *'Die Gesellschaft' – Eine kritische Auseinandersetzung mit der Zeitschrift der frühen Naturalisten* (Frankfurt: Lang, 1985).
Suval, S., *Electoral Politics in Wilhelmine Germany* (Chapel Hill, NC, and London: University of North Carolina Press, 1985).
Syndram, K. U., *Kulturpublizistik und nationales Selbstverständnis: Untersuchungen zur Kunst- und Kulturpolitik in den Rundschauzeitschriften des Deutschen Reiches* (Berlin: Mann, 1989).
Tacke, C., *Denkmal im sozialen Raum: Nationale Symbole in Deutschland und Frankreich im 19. Jahrhundert* (Göttingen: Vandenhoeck & Ruprecht, 1995).
Taylor, R., *Berlin and its Culture: A Historical Portrait* (London: Yale University Press, 1997).
Taylor, S., *Left-Wing Nietzscheans: The Politics of German Expressionism, 1910–20* (Berlin and New York: de Gruyter, 1990).

Teeuwisse, N., *Vom Salon zur Secession: Berlin Kunstleben zwischen Tradition und Aufbruch zur Moderne* (Berlin: Deutscher Verlag für Kunstwissenschaft, 1986).

Teich, M. and Porter, R. (eds), *Fin-de-Siècle and its Legacy* (Cambridge: Cambridge University Press, 1990).

Thiekötter, A. and Siepmann, E. (eds), *Packeis und Pressglas: Von der Kunstgewerbebewegung zum Deutschen Werkbund* (Lahn-Giessen: Anabas, 1987).

Thomas, R. Hinton, *Nietzsche in German Politics and Society, 1890–1914* (Manchester: Manchester University Press, 1983).

Timms, E. and Collier, P. (eds), *Visions and Blueprints: Avant-garde Culture and Radical Politics in Early Twentieth-Century Europe* (Manchester: Manchester University Press, 1988).

Traeger, J., *Der Weg nach Walhalla: Denkmallandschaft und Bildungsreise im 19. Jahrhundert* (Regensburg: Bosse, 1991).

Traill, D., *Schliemann of Troy: Treasure and Deceit* (London: Murray, 1995).

Ullrich, V., *Die nervöse Grossmacht: Aufstieg und Untergang des deutschen Kaiserreichs, 1871–1918* (Frankfurt: Fischer, 1997).

Usai, P. (ed.), *Before Caligari: German Cinema, 1895–1921* (Pordenone: Biblioteca dell'immagine, 1990).

Väth-Hinz, H., *Odol: Reklame-Kunst um 1900* (Lahn-Giessen: Anabas, 1985).

Vondung, K. (ed.), *Das wilhelminische Bildungsbürgertum: Zur Sozialgeschichte seiner Ideen* (Göttingen: Vandenhoeck & Ruprecht, 1976).

Wagner, M., *Allegorie und Geschichte: Ausstattungsprogramme öffentlicher Gebäude des 19. Jahrhunderts in Deutschland* (Tübingen: Wasmuth, 1989).

Warnke, M. (ed.), *Politische Architektur in Europa vom Mittelalter bis heute – Repräsentation und Gemeinschaft* (Cologne: Dumont, 1984).

Warnke, M., *Politische Landschaft* (Munich: Hanser, 1992).

Wehler, H.-U., *Deutsche Gesellschaftsgeschichte*, vol. 3: *Von der 'Deutschen Doppelrevolution' bis zum Beginn des Ersten Weltkriegs, 1849–1914* (Munich: Beck, 1995).

Weindling, P. J., *Health, Race and German Politics from National Unification to Nazism* (Cambridge: Cambridge University Press, 1989).

Werner, A. von, *Erlebnisse und Eindrücke, 1870–1890* (Berlin: Mittler, 1913).

Wichmann, S., *Secession: Europäische Kunst um die Jahrhundertwende* (Munich: Haus der Kunst, 1964).

Wichmann, S., *Franz von Lenbach und seine Zeit* (Cologne: Dumont, 1973).

Wiedmann, A. K., *The German Quest for Primal Origins in Art, Culture and Politics, 1900–1933* (Lampeter: Mellen, 1995).

Willett, J., *The New Sobriety: Art and Politics in the Weimar Period* (London: Thames and Hudson, 1978).

Wimmer, R. (ed.), *Das 19. Jahrhundert: Sprachgeschichtliche Wurzeln des heutigen Deutsch* (Berlin and New York: de Gruyter, 1991).

Windsor, A., *Peter Behrens: Architect and Designer* (London: Architectural Press, 1981).

With, C., *The Prussian Landeskunstkommission, 1862–1911: A Study in State Subvention of the Arts* (Berlin: Mann, 1986).

Wittkau, A., *Historismus: Zur Geschichte des Begriffs und des Problems* (Göttingen: Vandenhoeck & Ruprecht, 1992).

Index